Black and Brown in Los Angeles

Black and Brown in Los Angeles

Beyond Conflict and Coalition

EDITED BY
Josh Kun and Laura Pulido

UNIVERSITY OF CALIFORNIA PRESS

Berkeley · Los Angeles · London

University of California Press, one of the most distinguished university presses in the United States, enriches
lives around the world by advancing scholarship in the
humanities, social sciences, and natural sciences. Its
activities are supported by the UC Press Foundation and
by philanthropic contributions from individuals and institutions. For more information, visit www.ucpress.edu.

University of California Press
Berkeley and Los Angeles, California

University of California Press, Ltd.
London, England

Chapter 9 by Erin Aubry Kaplan originally appeared
as a series of op-ed columns in the Los Angeles Times,
which are reprinted here with permission: "More
Than Just the Latinos-Next-Door: It's Hard to Shake
the Feeling That Blacks, and Black Communities,
Are under Siege" (March 17, 2007); "Piercing Black
Science on Immigration: A Panel Discussion Mulls
over the Effects of Illegal Immigration and Changing
Demographics on African-American Communities"
(January 17, 2007); "Plugging Immigration's Drain
on Black Employment: A New Hotel Workers' Union
Contract Finally Recognizes That More Immigration
Has Contributed to Fewer Jobs for African Americans"
(October 25, 2006).

Chapter 15 by Josh Kun originally appeared in American
Quarterly, 56, no. 3 (September 2004): 741-58.

Library of Congress Cataloging-in-Publication Data

   Black and Brown in Los Angeles : Beyond Conflict
and Coalition / edited by Josh Kun and Laura Pulido.
      pages   cm
   Includes bibliographical references and index.
   ISBN 978-0-520-27559-1 (cloth : alk. paper)
   ISBN 978-0-520-27560-7 (pbk. : alk. paper)
      1. African Americans—California—Los Angeles.
   2. Hispanic Americans—California—Los Angeles.
   3. Minorities—California—Los Angeles.
   4. Community development—California—Los Angeles.
   5. Community life—California—Los Angeles   6. Los
Angeles (Calif.)—Ethnic relations.   7. Los Angeles
(Calif.)—Race relations   8. Los Angeles (Calif.)—Social
conditions.   I. Kun, Josh, editor of compilation.
II. Pulido, Laura, editor of compilation.
   F869.L89A245   2013
   305.8009794'94—dc23   2013013424

Manufactured in the United States of America

23 22 21 20 19 18 17 16 15 14
10 9 8 7 6 5 4 3 2 1

Contents

Illustrations

Tables

Introduction

JOSH KUN AND LAURA PULIDO

Only when the lesson of racial estrangement is learned is
assimilation complete. . . . All immigrants fight for jobs and
space, and who is there to fight but those who have both?

—Toni Morrison, "On the Backs of Blacks"

The painful truth is that blacks and Latinos have found that
the struggle for power and recognition is long and difficult.
On some issues, they can be allies. On others, they will go
it alone. Changing demographics and the rise of Latinos to
the top minority spot in America won't make the problems
of either group disappear. Nor will blaming each other for
those problems solve them.

—Earl Ofari Hutchinson, "The Black-Latino Blame Game"

The prospects of peace in the contemporary world may
well lie in the recognition of the plurality of our affiliations
and in the use of reasoning as common inhabitants of a
wide world, rather than making us into inmates rigidly
incarcerated in little containers.

—Amartya Sen, *Identity and Violence*

In February 2009, we organized a roundtable at the University of
Southern California called "Writing Race in L.A." As part of the series
Blacks and Latinos in Conflict and Cooperation, the evening featured a
group of African American and Latina/o writers—Héctor Tobar, Erin
Aubry Kaplan, Helena María Viramontes, and Dana Johnson—who

were asked about how they approach racial identity and racial representation in their writing about Los Angeles. Tobar spoke of the importance of the Black saint Martin de Porres to his immigrant Guatemalan mother (he is remembered in Tobar's middle name), the debt all Latina/o citizens of the United States owe to the Dred Scott decision and the Black struggle for civil rights, and his experiences covering South L.A. neighborhoods in the 1980s and '90s as they underwent massive population shifts from Black to Latina/o majorities. Johnson lamented that there is little integration among literary audiences: African Americans read African Americans, Latinas/os read Latinas/os. Viramontes remembered growing up in East L.A. in a Chicana/o community "segregated by cemeteries and integrated by freeways," getting her first dictionary from a Black schoolteacher, and hearing her parents worry as the Watts Riots of 1965 unfolded on the television: "We need to leave. *They* might come over *here*."

As moderator, Aubry Kaplan urged us to move beyond vocabularies of "conflict" and "coalition" and instead learn how to talk through perhaps more challenging truths of "juxtaposition" and "coexistence." Instead of repeating the myth that Black and Brown relations can be viewed only through the lens of shared poverty so it becomes strictly "a problem of the poor," she spoke of a middle-class African American "sense of displacement" and "anxiety" and the lack of willingness among African American leaders to speak honestly about these feelings in their communities. According to Aubry Kaplan, "We've not been honest about our difference, and I think we have to start there. There is a lot of overlap of Blacks and Latinos in neighborhoods throughout L.A., but our histories are not the same, our expectations are not the same. . . . There is a left-wing analysis . . . that Blacks and Browns must get together and form a coalition over their similarities. Of course they should, but before we can do that, because coalitions are not automatic, we have to figure out where we are."[1]

But when the event was opened to questions from the audience, the tone changed from literary reflection and authorial memoir to outraged demands for a more direct, frank discussion about the social and political urgencies of Brown and Black life in L.A., about Mexican gangs killing Blacks, about streets that were trembling with fear and anger. Neighborhoods were being turned upside down, kids were dying, and here we were talking about journalistic coverage and "fictional" characters born of "real" neighborhoods. Why was no one from local communities asked to be on the panel? Where were the gang leaders? Where were the local politicians? A local African American schoolteacher spoke of feeling "the tension in the hallways" between his Latina/o and Black students, and a former African American gang member wanted to know what our panel of writers had to say about Mexicans writing "nigger killer" on the walls of once Black neighborhoods. It was, to say the least, a profound example of not just how complicated and how loaded discourse and dialogue around Brown and Black relations in L.A. have become but also of how few spaces actually exist to have those discourses and dialogues in public forums in a city that is—as we witnessed that night—boiling over with a desire to speak about the unhealed and, in some cases, still barely dressed wounds of the past and the challenges that still lie ahead in twenty-first-century L.A.

Five months later, Tobar returned to the conversations ignited by the night in his column for the *Los Angeles Times* and admitted that while the roundtable did what it was asked to—speak about writing—maybe he and his fellow writers had been naïve to think that talking about African American and Latina/o issues in Los Angeles would not spark an emotional and impassioned discussion "about the reality of a divided, angry city," where Black L.A. and Brown L.A. coexist as much as they battle and see each other in the mirror as much as they refuse to look (one quick scroll down the heavily racially charged YouTube comments on the video for the event will discourage any easy sense of Black and Latina/o harmony). As Tobar wrote, "I know that mostly our two peoples are working, living in peace and even starting families together. And yet the seeds of a deeper intolerance lie all around us, ready to sprout. More often than we care to admit, our people segregate themselves from Blacks in schools and churches." He ended the column with a story he had told back in February: After his mother prayed to St. Martin de Porres to help her in childbirth, it was her Black neighbor who drove her to the hospital when she went into labor, one Black saint producing another. He became Tobar's godfather. "Maybe in a way," wrote Tobar, "all of us in Latino L.A. have Black godparents we need to make the effort to acknowledge."[2]

Those acknowledgments of influence and inspiration are perhaps most commonly seen in the realm of culture, where Latina/o and African American artistic legacies are widely recognized—and celebrated—as being inextricably linked and where so many stories of Black-Brown exchange and conversation commonly have their source. In the late 1940s and early 1950s, Mexican American and African American musicians, dancers, and fans were central to the creation of what Anthony Macías has called "a multicultural urban civility" on the post–World War II dance floors and bandstands of East and South L.A. nightclubs and ballrooms.[3] Mexican American *pachucos* and African American hepcats and jitterbuggers had the zoot suit in common, and African American R&B artists found a loyal fan base among Mexican Americans, whether at clubs up and down Central Avenue or at Angeles Hall in Boyle Heights, where in the early 1950s Johnny Otis held R&B revues on Sunday nights for mixed Black and Brown audiences. Mexican American bassist Don Tosti turned the boogie-woogie into the "Pachuco Boogie," and African American saxophonist Chuck Higgins unleashed his own "Pachuko Hop." After T-Bone Walker left Texas for Los Angeles in the 1940s, he wrote "Plain Old Down Home Blues," a blues that begins, over a skeletal rumba beat, with an African American impersonation of a Mexican L.A. welcome—*Buenas días, Señor T-Bone*—and ends with an invitation to a night of entertainment with *cinco chiquitas* for *twenty pesos*. When Walker hears the price, the cross-cultural, bilingual communication suddenly breaks down: *Man, I didn't hear a word you said.*

When racial tensions between African American and Latina/o students began to flare up in the early '70s at Hollenbeck Junior High in Boyle Heights, Ruben Leon formed the Black and Brown Brotherhood Band as a direct response. "We wanted to prove that by working together we could make something beautiful happen," said Leon. "We wanted to show you how Black and Brown cooperation works." With funding support from the Local 47 musicians' union, Leon merged Mexican American pianist Eddie Cano's Afro Jazz Quartet with four Black soloists (among them L.A. jazz legend Buddy Collette) to create a band designed to show students that if Black and Brown can make music together, then they can get along offstage as well. "Every instrument is different," Leon told the *Los Angeles Times* in 1979 after a reunion concert. "We use them together, we live together, to do something big and beautiful. We recognize the differences but we know what we can do together."[4]

Or there is the oft-told story of a Mexican American band from San Gabriel High School who in the late '60s changed their name from the VIP's to El Chicano (at the urging of white East L.A. music manager and promoter Eddie Davis) but whose first recording was "Viva Tirado," a low-and-slow 1969 cruising instrumental that was a cover of a song originally penned by African American jazz composer Gerald Wilson. Wilson originally wrote it in 1962 in homage to the Mexican bullfighter José Ramón Tirado. The version by El Chicano—who would soon make history as the first Mexican American band to headline the legendary Apollo Theater in Harlem—became synonymous with the Chicana/o civil rights movement, the rise of the UFW, and the burst of Chicana/o political consciousness that emerged in the wake of the LAPD's violent suppression of the 1970 Chicana/o Moratorium demonstration against the Vietnam War. When East L.A. rapper Kid Frost went to record his pioneering Chicano rap anthem "La Raza," with its calls for Brown pride and Aztec warriors, he sampled El Chicano's "Viva Tirado," completing a remarkable cycle of Black-Brown cultural cross-talk: a song by a Black artist inspired by a Mexican bullfighter is covered by a Chicano band inspired by the Black civil rights movement, whose version is sampled by a Chicano MC working in hip-hop.

The song's intercultural and cross-racial genealogy, while perhaps singular in its loops of influence, tells a story of Black and Brown artistic collaboration that repeats throughout twentieth- and twenty-first-century musical history, from Chicano funk bands like Tierra to the Black band who called themselves Señor Soul, dressed in *sombreros* and *sarapes,* and later morphed into War and recorded the ultimate Chicana/o car culture anthem "Lowrider," and from African American R&B ballads becoming the official music of Mexican American lowriders to Mexican American and Mexican immigrant hip-hop artists sampling both Black and Mexican music to craft their own sound. One of those artists, the hip-hop duo Akwid, whom Josh Kun writes about in his chapter in this volume, were born in Michoacán, Mexico, but raised in African American and Latina/o neighborhoods across South L.A. in the 1980s and '90s. "The music gets all mixed up here," they've said. "When you are raised around both Black and Mexican communities, you are able to see both sides and have a wider perspective than if you were raised in just one. You don't get stuck in one or the other."[5] Those wider perspectives are not limited to music, of course, but can be found throughout the cultural history of L.A.: the Mexican and African American lowrider car clubs that Denise Sandoval writes about in her essay, the Black and Brown visual art traditions showcased in murals, street art, and in contemporary art (like that of Nery Gabriel Lemus, the son of Guatemalan immigrants, who explores Brown and Black male hair culture in his exhibition that we feature here), and the larger cultural formations (radio, the built environment) that impact what Gaye Theresa Johnson writes about here as "spatial entitlement."

Our goal with this volume is to approach the complex pasts, presents, and futures of Black and Latina/o life in L.A. by not isolating the world of the arts and culture from that of politics and "the reality of an angry, divided city." As the work of George Lipsitz, Robin D. G. Kelley, George Sánchez, George Yudice, and Daniel Widener, among many others, has shown us, expressive culture can be a rehearsal for politics, a symbolic forum for political discourse and mobilization, a "resource" for cultural policy and cultural citizenship in the age of global manufacturing and neoliberalism, and, indeed, expressive culture is often politics itself (or to paraphrase Judith Butler, there is no culture that is "merely cultural").

By visiting the social and economic worlds behind efforts to create new coalitions between Latinas/os and African Americans and by surveying the transformational connections that have been at the core of cultural exchange and borrowing between the two groups for decades, this anthology is an attempt, to paraphrase Aubry Kaplan's call, to better figure out where we are. Our goal with this volume has been to treat Black and Brown conflict and cooperation using methods from both the social sciences and the humanities, both journalism and the visual arts, both social history and contemporary policy, examining Black and Latina/o relations in Los Angeles through an interdisciplinary prism and through a methodological mix. Our interests here are compelled both by the historical import of Brown and Black relations in the social, cultural, and political life of Los Angeles and by the urgent contemporary situation that finds debates and discussion of African American and Latina/o violence and community building at the forefront of Los Angeles's urban politics and urban discourse—discourse that extends from the streets of the city to city hall, from the English- and Spanish-language press to the hallways, classrooms, and schoolyards of young Angelenos.

. . .

As we began conceiving this collection, the headlines were mounting daily. Black and Brown students clashed at Jefferson, Crenshaw, and Locke High Schools while their parents clashed over what languages would be spoken in school meetings. Latina/o residents of south L.A. cities such as Compton charged African Americans with being unwilling to share political power, as the city council remained overwhelmingly Black. Other observers, including African Americans, maintain (and some resent) that Latinas/os have displaced African American workers in key sectors. A Latino man targeted African Americans in a spree of freeway shootings, and Florencia 13, a South L.A. Latino street gang, was charged with waging a murderous campaign—two hundred killings in three years—against rival African American gangs in their Florence-Firestone neighborhood, which is now 90 percent Latina/o. According to the Los Angeles County Commission on Human Relations, the majority of hate crimes in 2006 were committed by Latinas/os against African Americans and vice versa.[6]

These stark events can be understood only in light of the major spatial and demographic changes that Los Angeles has undergone in recent decades. In Los Angeles County, which was once almost 90 percent white, Latinas/os are now poised to become the majority ethnic group. The most intense and dramatic demographic shifts that brought about this change occurred in the 1980s and '90s, when—among other factors—the 1986 Immigration Reform and Control Act provided amnesty for recently arrived undocumented immigrants, and Mexico's economic crisis and peso devaluation prompted new immigrants north. Latinas/os now account for nearly half of the county's population, and as of 2010, African Americans accounted for 8.7 percent. It is estimated that roughly 75 percent of Los Angeles Unified School District students are Latina/o. Numbers like these only add to the concerns of African American residents, who increasingly see themselves as being cast as minor characters in the dramas of the city's urban future; at the same time, Latinas/os are trying to figure out their relationship to Black Angelenos, given that the latter group has historically been more visible and powerful.[7]

The much publicized and often media-stoked profiles of Black and Brown conflict in Los Angeles support what Nicolas Vaca has described as the fallacy of "the presumed alliance" that has long been believed to exist between the two groups.[8] During the civil rights movements of the 1960s, Latinas/os and African Americans were often seen as "a kind of latter-day Rainbow Musketeers against the evil White Empire," fighting a common enemy out of mirrored histories of segregation and unequal treatment. While the notion of the presumed alliance may be productive and powerful, it also enables us to gloss over significant differences between the two groups. As Stokely Carmichael and Charles Hamilton put it in their 1967's *Black Power,* "Parties entering into a coalition have to recognize their respective self-interests. Whether Blacks were forming coalitions with Asians, Whites, or Latinos, it had to be understood that each group came to the table with different interests that are unique to its own group."[9]

In the decades following the 1960s, those different interests and respective self-interests have come to the forefront of Brown and Black relations in the form of struggles over educational resources, political power, and access to labor and employment. Sentiments are perhaps best summed up by Charles B. Johnson of the Pasadena, California, chapter of the NAACP, who spoke of "undocumented aliens . . . taking the food from Black children" and "a multitude of undocumented aliens who will take the jobs of Blacks and other minorities."[10] While these struggles have been unfolding on a national level, it is in California, and Los Angeles specifically, that they have taken on the most intense, and at times ugly, profile. David O. Sears's 2002 UCLA study of racial and ethnic conflict in Los Angeles revealed that more than half the Latinas/os surveyed said they were in conflict with Black people, and two-thirds of Black respondents said they were in conflict with Latinas/os.[11]

Yet as we see in many of the essays included here, this narrative of a presumed alliance disintegrating into a presumed conflict or presumed tension—"as if it's endemic to our DNA to have conflict," in the words of Mayor Villaraigosa—is not by any stretch universally accepted as true.[12] Media outlets prefer stories of Black and Brown conflict to stories of coalition. Leaders like Karen Bass, Mark Ridley-Thomas, and María Elena Durazo have all done important work as coalition builders, as have many community organizations such as South L.A.'s SCOPE (Strategic Concepts in Organizing and Policy Education) and the Community Coalition. Likewise, many challenge the accepted truism that Latina/o immigrants are taking Black jobs, and both city officials and researchers have refuted the idea that African Americans and Latinas/os are continually waging war against each other on the streets. Our hope is that this anthology moves us away from the simple dichotomy of either a presumed alliance or a presumed opposition and instead examines the complexities, ambivalences, and cultures of coexistence that mediate and shape Brown and Black life in contemporary Los Angeles.

BROWN AND BLACK HISTORIES OF LOS ANGELES

When writing about Black and Brown L.A., many authors begin with the fact that Los Angeles was established by a multiracial group of settlers. For example, Pilar Marrero, writing in *La Opinión,* notes, "Of the 44 original inhabitants that settled in El Pueblo de Nuestra

Señora la Reina de los Ángeles de Porciúncula . . . in 1781 . . . 26 were of African origin. And that is how Mexicans, descendents of Spaniards and Native Americans, founded Los Angeles along with descendents of Africans brought over to the continent as slaves by the Spaniards."[13] This account is typical in that it highlights the presence of Afro-Mexicans, mestizos, indigenous Mexicans, and Europeans. While there may be various reasons why writers choose to include this point, presumably they wish to stress that Los Angeles has *always* been racially diverse. While this is certainly true and an important fact, we also have to be cautious in inferring what such stories suggest about interethnic relations writ large in Los Angeles today. A particular problem with this narrative, and, indeed, the larger literature, is that while many take this as a starting place, there is rarely any kind of systematic follow-up: Exactly where does such an origin story take us? What does it imply, if anything, about how diverse peoples got along? How does it help us to understand the contemporary moment, aside from the fact that Los Angeles has always had a mix of people?[14]

The reality is that relations have changed over time between Brown and Black people, and they continue to do so today. Demographically speaking, at some times African-origin peoples have dominated; at other times, Mexicans have (more on what happened to Afro-Mexicans in a moment). There have been occasions when the two populations have worked together in unison, although usually they have developed along separate, parallel paths, and occasionally elements of each community have been explicitly antagonistic toward each other. The history of Brown and Black Los Angeles is not only the story of the two groups intersecting but also the story of many groups connecting and diverging within the context of a larger regional history—a history that African Americans and Latinas/os have also shaped.

One of the first changes that took place after this founding moment was that the African-origin population was fairly quickly subsumed within the larger Mexican community. Despite a sizable Afro-Mexican population in Mexico and the fact that a relatively large number made the trek up to Alta California, there were few African Americans at the time in Los Angeles. Consequently, the Afro-Mexican population was not replenished and became increasingly mestizo over time. Although Mexican society was characterized by deep racial inequality, along the frontier the racial hierarchy was more fluid, which is perhaps why so many Afro-Mexicans took a chance in coming north. In fact, under both the Spanish and the Mexican rule, it was the local native people, the Tongva, who were the primary targets of violence and forced labor.[15]

After the U.S. conquest of Alta California (1848), the Mexican working class experienced intense violence and continued impoverishment. In addition, it was soon joined by the more elite Californias/os, who experienced downward mobility as they lost their land and wealth. The flood of Anglo Americans and others coming into Los Angeles soon rendered the Mexicana/o population a small minority, as the language, legal system, currency, economy, and political power all shifted toward Anglos. It was during this time that Mexicans began relocating from their traditional home around the Plaza to east of downtown, as they were pushed out by whites and others who wanted their land. Even the large number of Mexicans who fled the Mexican Revolution and arrived in Los Angeles did not significantly alter the balance of power.[16] During this time the Black population was extremely small, although there were important figures, such as Biddy Mason. Mason had been brought to Los Angeles as a slave and secured her freedom in 1856. She went on to become wealthy through real-estate investment, helped to establish the First African Methodist Episcopal Church, and assisted the poor of all races.[17]

Starting in the 1920s, however, the situation began to change as African Americans began relocating to Los Angeles in significant numbers.[18] In many ways, Los Angeles was considered a land of opportunity for African Americans. Despite the existence of legal discrimination, racial hostility against African Americans was not as severe as it was in other parts of the country, and thus they were able to build communities, and some even secured middle-class occupations, such as the Pullman porters. African Americans considered the 1920s a "golden era" in Los Angeles because not only were their numbers small, thereby constituting less of a threat to whites, but also other racial groups, including native Californians, Chinese and Japanese immigrants, and Mexicans, were the primary targets of white racism. Legislation such as the Alien Land Law (1913) prohibited Asian immigrants from owning land, and during the Great Depression ethnic Mexicans, many of whom were U.S. citizens, were targeted for deportation through Repatriation, as it was believed they were swelling the welfare rolls.

Los Angeles's racial landscape changed drastically with World War II, however. One of the most important developments of that era was simply massive population growth as millions arrived in Southern California in the hopes of securing employment in the burgeoning defense economy. African Americans were a central part of this migration. Black southerners from Texas, Louisiana, Arkansas, and Oklahoma arrived in large numbers, hoping for a new life. They joined the preexisting African American population, but it was not always easy going. Many of the long-standing Black residents resented the newcomers, whom they considered to be "backward" and rural and jeopardizing the hard-won respect and acceptance that some Black Angelenos had achieved. It was at this time that race relations in Los Angeles began to look more like those in the rest of the United States, with growing hostility toward African Americans, increased residential segregation, and heightened Jim Crow practices. Indeed, African Americans had to fight a long and hard battle just to be allowed to work in the defense industry. In many ways, World War II marks the beginning of Los Angeles's contemporary Black population.[19]

For the Mexican-origin population, World War II marked the beginning of greater access to the formal economy and union jobs. Previous to this time, Mexicans were largely relegated to the informal economy, agriculture, and the most menial of labor. With the war's attendant labor shortage, however, they found themselves finally able to make some economic progress.[20] Although they were still the target of white racial wrath, as seen in the Zoot-Suit riots, there was now a path of upward mobility within the working class.

During this time and continuing into the 1950s, there were numerous points of contact between African Americans and Mexican Americans. As discussed in the previous section, not only was there cultural mixing, especially in terms of music, but there was also some spatial overlap. While most ethnic Mexicans lived somewhere in the greater East Side and most African Americans in South L.A., pockets of both groups also existed in the northeastern San Fernando Valley, such as Pacoima, and there is a long history of Mexicans living in parts of South L.A., including Watts and Compton.[21] In addition, the decades spanning the 1930s through the 1960s saw numerous civil rights organizations and initiatives arise from both communities. Gaye Johnson has begun excavating some crucial historical linkages, as seen in the life and work of such activists as Charlotta Bass and Luisa Moreno, and in particular in the Sleepy Lagoon Defense Committee, but such consciousness and collaboration appear to be more the exception.[22] While almost never hostile, the two populations only occasionally worked in conjunction, instead seeing themselves as largely separate entities. For example, the Asociación Nacional México-Americana (ANMA), a leftist civil rights

group based in Los Angeles, regularly invited other minoritized populations, including Jews and African Americans, to participate in their
cultural events in the 1950s, even though no efforts were made to forge
a larger political agenda.[23] There may be several reasons for this. First,
as previously suggested, Los Angeles was a place of extreme residential
segregation. This meant not only the separation of whites and people
of color but also the separation of various ethnicities within the larger
population of color. So, for example, while the relatively small Japanese
American population lived among Mexicans in the East Side and African Americans in South L.A., relatively few African Americans lived
on the East Side. In the 1930s and '40s some African Americans lived
in diverse communities such as Boyle Heights, but with the decline of
white-ethnic residential segregation after World War II and heightened
residential discrimination against African Americans, the area became
increasingly Mexican, and, with this, came a decline in the Black East
Side population. Second, as table I.1 suggests, until 1970, both populations were relatively comparable in size. Thus, they may not have felt
the need for support from another group. Although Bernstein argues
that the Cold War actually compelled interracial activism as a matter
of survival, the record is relatively thin between African and Mexican Americans, albeit with some important exceptions, including *Mendez v. Westminster,* the election of Edward Roybal to the Los Angeles
City Council, and the Community Service Organization.[24] This is actually a key historical question that has not been adequately investigated
by scholars: Why was there *not* greater collaboration between ethnic
Mexicans and African American Angelenos during these decades? Two
essays in this volume (those of Martinez HoSang and Felker-Kantor)
directly tackle this question, and both suggest that because of distinct
racial positions and intraclass tensions, each group experienced discrimination, whether it was inferior education or residential segregation, in unique ways, which made cooperation difficult.[25] This also
raises the larger question regarding Mexican Americans' racial subjectivity, a topic that has only recently been broached: Did they see themselves as potentially white and thus eschew the possibility of solidarity
with African Americans?[26]

It was not until the rise of radical activism in the late 1960s that both
groups began seeing each other in new ways: as potential partners,
competitors, and teachers. The politics of the late 1960s were such that
whatever ambivalence young Mexican Americans may have had about
who they were racially, such concerns dissipated as they embraced a

TABLE I.I   GROWTH IN THE BLACK AND LATINA/O POPULATIONS
OF LOS ANGELES COUNTY, 1940–2000

Year	African Americans	Percentage of Total Population	Latinos	Percentage of Total Population
1940	75,206	2.6	61,248	2
1950	214,897	5	249,173	5.7
1960	459,806	7.5	582,309	9.6
1970	755,719	10.7	1,288,716	18.3
1980	924,774	12.3	2,071,530	27.5
1990	931,449	10.46	3,359,526	38
2000	930,957	9.5	4,242,213	45
2005	883,911	9.2	4,658,878	47.1

SOURCES: Phil Ethington, "Total Population, Showing Ethnic Composition, Los Angeles County, 1940–1960," in *Segregated Diversity: Race-Ethnicity, Space and Political Fragmentation in Los Angeles County, 1940–1994*, Final Report to the John Randolph Haynes and Dora Haynes Foundation, July 2000, 12; United Way, *2003 State of the County Report* (Los Angeles: United Way of Greater Los Angeles, 2003), 32; American Community Survey, Demographic and Housing Estimates, Los Angeles County, 2005–7; U.S. Census Bureau, Geographic Comparison Table, Los Angeles County, 2000.

nonwhite identity.[27] Two events in particular mark this era of political change and activism in Los Angeles. First was the Watts Riots/uprising of 1965, and second was the Chicana/o Walkouts of 1968. In the first case Black Los Angeles exploded on a hot August day—the precipitating factor being a "routine" traffic stop. While this was largely a Black affair, at least one participant explained that he was just waiting for East L.A. to explode also—"and then what would have L.A. history looked like?"[28] But it did not. In fact, when greater resources began to flow to African Americans subsequent to Watts in 1965, mainstream Mexican Americans were concerned that Latinas/os were being "punished" for not rioting.[29] It was not until 1968 that the East Side would erupt in response to a long and painful history of inadequate education. It was through this and similar events that activists in both communities came to more fully appreciate each other. In some cases, there was collaboration, such as between the Black Panther Party and the Brown Berets, in others, there was a more distant but strategic and calculated politics of solidarity, and in still others, there was awareness that much could be learned from the others' experiences. For example, Black activists were keen to study La Raza Unida Party, a third-party electoral strategy developed in southern Texas that spread throughout the Southwest, including Los Angeles.

The 1970s witnessed the beginning of a new political and economic reality—one that we are still living with—that was ushered in by several major shifts: deindustrialization, the rise of post-Fordism, and neo-liberalism.[30] Not only did these three related processes directly affect the economic fortunes of all Angelenos, but, equally important, they also ushered in a new political climate with profound consequences for people of color. At its most basic level, deindustrialization translated into the decline/erasure of middle-class manufacturing jobs: jobs that provided a modicum of economic security to modestly educated people. This was devastating for thousands and thousands of workers, as huge industrial concentrations, such as those along the Alameda Corridor, closed shopped and headed to Orange County, Mexico, and China. African Americans were hit especially hard by these changes, as they were often the last hired in these firms and, therefore, the first let go. In place of those jobs rose a new manufacturing economy, one predicated on low-wage employment. Latinas/os have continued to be heavily attached to manufacturing and construction, while African Americans have made strides in public sector employment, yet unemployment remains stubbornly high, especially for African American youth.[31] In the wake of declining economic opportunity, there was an increase in gang activity in both Latina/o and African American communities, as well as a change in the nature of this activity. While previously gangs were largely about turf, respect, and protection, they shifted to drug dealing, bringing an unprecedented wave of violence to both Brown and Black communities.[32]

Alongside these economic shifts were political changes that began emerging in the 1970s and continue with us today. The 1970s and '80s planted the seeds of a neoliberal political order in which not only are individuals' fates increasingly left to the market, but also the political discourse and policies that accompany such shifts have drawn upon a color-blind racial ideology in conjunction with continued antipathy toward people of color, especially poor African Americans and Latina/o immigrants. In this new era there are increasing opportunities for well-heeled people of color and shrinking ones for the millions belonging to the impoverished working class. Consequently, in the 1980s we begin to see such things as the rise of the prison-industrial complex as the preferred means to deal with surplus labor and social problems; the election of Los Angeles's first Black mayor, Tom Bradley; the almost complete abandonment of the public school system by whites and the middle class of all colors; the suburbanization of both the Black and Brown middle class as people of color moved farther away from the woes of the central city and in search of affordable housing; and the emergence of Los Angeles as the capital of the working poor.[33]

Two other key developments emerged in the 1980s that are essential to understanding contemporary Brown and Black Los Angeles: immigration and grassroots community activism. As mentioned in the previous section, Latin American and Asian immigration has profoundly transformed Los Angeles. Through this process ethnic Mexicans were transformed into Latinas/os, as immigrants from all quarters of Latin America arrived, especially Central America. In turn, Latinas/os went from being one, albeit important, ethnic group to being the largest one in the county. Given the sheer size of the Latina/o population, no Angeleno can escape contact with this vast, dynamic, and diverse population, especially African Americans, given that both groups now share the space of South L.A. as well as many other parts of the region. African Americans and Latinas/os mingle on the job, on the bus, and in the neighborhood.[34] Because these two populations are largely low income, it should be no surprise that there would be such an overlap. The inevitable tensions that accompany such dramatic demographic change have drawn the attention of many scholars, and while such interest is understandable, this is only a slice of a much larger tale.

The story of immigration is especially complex and will be fleshed out by several chapters in this volume. However, it is impossible to introduce Brown and Black L.A. without first acknowledging the role of the "illegal," as this trope has become a backdrop to local (and increasingly national) race relations. While Mexican immigration has always been marked by a mix of authorized and unauthorized people and crossings, over the last several decades, and especially post-9–11, the "illegal" has become a political rallying point. Certainly there is no denying that a large unauthorized population poses many challenges to society, but opposition to unauthorized immigration goes far beyond that, as it readily morphs into anti-Latina/o and, specifically, into anti-Mexican sentiment.[35] In this era of supposedly politically correct and color-blind ideology, it may be inappropriate to demean or legally exclude Latinas/os and ethnic Mexicans, but it is perfectly acceptable to attack "illegals"—a political category, anti-immigrant activists routinely insist, rather than a racial or national one.[36] In this way, anti-Latina/o sentiment has found an important new outlet. African Americans are an increasingly important part of this discourse, given their spatial and economic proximity to Latina/o immigrants in Los Angeles and other cities. Again, while there are genuine concerns about economic competition, which, Manuel Pastor, for example, discusses in his chapter, many claims of displacement are inflated and posed in such a way as to blame Latinas/os (regardless of nativity) for the long-standing economic problems of Black Angelenos—as if Latinas/os are primarily responsible for Black poverty, rather than centuries of white supremacy. Moreover, African Americans are themselves increasingly becoming vocal players in immigration discussions. While this is to be expected and welcomed, what is unprecedented is the extent to which blackness is being used by both whites and Blacks to bolster anti-immigrant politics, leading to even greater tensions.[37]

The final major change that developed in the 1980s and '90s is the rise of a remarkable network of grassroots activists fighting for social justice. Several threads have contributed to this formation, including the legacies of the social movements of the 1960s; the rise of environmental justice activism in the 1980s, which centered on both the East Side and South Central Los Angeles; the region's extreme income inequality; and, perhaps most important, the resurgence of labor organizing beginning in the 1980s, as seen in such campaigns as the Justice for Janitors project of the Service Employees International Union (SEIU).[38] The work of unions and organized labor in general has not only sought to foster class consciousness but has also included major campaigns that have channeled thousands of low-income workers, especially Latinas/os, into the political arena. While many of these movements and initiatives are centered in either the Black or the Brown community, several have deliberately tried to create a multiracial consciousness and politics. Organizations such as the Community Coalition and the Labor/Community Strategy Center have placed the cultivation of interracial unity at the center of their political work with impressive results. Unfortunately, such stories are not well known, and they represent only one type of connection among the myriad that characterize contemporary Brown and Black Los Angeles, which is precisely one of the reasons we felt this book was necessary.

STUDYING BROWN AND BLACK RELATIONS

The scholarly literature exploring the relationships and connections between Latinas/os and African Americans is rapidly growing. While there is some work that dates back to the 1980s and before, the vast majority is of a more recent vintage, beginning in the 1990s.[39] Several factors account for the heightened interest at this particular moment in time. First, and not surprisingly, is demographic change. While this volume is centered on Los Angeles, many regions of the United States, including places in the Southeast, Midwest, and Northeast have been dramatically changed by Latina/o immigration.[40] Because of immigration, as well as natural increase, Latinas/os registered as the largest racial minority in the United States in 2000. Thus, it is hardly surprising that such demographic shifts would engender questions about not only how the two largest populations of color in the United States affect each other, and do/don't get along, but also what these numbers mean for the larger racial formation. These demographics have prompted researchers to document attitudes and experiences between the two groups. This includes survey data, such as the findings of Paula McClain as well as the research team of Mindiola, Neimann, and Rodriguez, and has been complemented by case studies that illuminate intergroup dynamics, beginning with Heather Rose Parker's study of community activism in Los Angeles and Al Camarillo's early studies of Compton.[41] Within this literature, one of the most consistent themes is the reliance on the competition-cooperation model. Drawing on long-standing sociological theories, scholars seek to ascertain to what extent, if any, groups are in conflict, as well as when and how they might cooperate. This is a powerful narrative that some literature explicitly references, whereas other work does so more implicitly. Quantitative social scientists tend to speak more directly to this paradigm, and humanities scholars also do, often in their quest to show a history of cooperation and sharing. This can be seen, in particular, in studies of activism from the 1960s and '70s, such as the scholarship of Lauren Araiza on the UFW and the Black Panther Party and Jason Feirrera's examination of San Francisco's Third World activism.[42] This latter work is incredibly important because it captures a significant part of the everyday lived experience and history that surveys simply cannot. In addition, as historians and others have shown, African Americans and Latinas/os often have little sense of the historical connections between their two communities, including a larger understanding of the kinds of cultural sharing that has taken place over the decades. Thus, this scholarship addresses a crucial void.

A distinguishing feature of this recent literature is the extent to which both scholars and activists have drawn upon it in efforts to bolster their various claims and positions. For instance, in an influential piece in *Souls,* Rochmes and Griffin have pointed to evidence of Latina/o hostility toward African Americans as a sign of Latinas/os attempting to claim whiteness by following in the path of other immi-grant groups by subordinating African Americans.[43] While not based on a full reading of the literature, their argument that Latinas/os are deeply invested in whiteness is well taken and needs to be more fully acknowledged by others. Likewise, Vaca, in *The Presumed Alliance,* reminds us of Latinas/os' many historical contributions to the develop-ment of the civil rights movement in the United States—contributions that are frequently forgotten by those who see Latinas/os as strictly newcomers. Unfortunately, however, the larger tone of the book often borders on hostility, underscoring African Americans' anxieties in response to Latinas/os' rising numerical and political clout. As can be seen, data can be used for a variety of different purposes and political projects. Indeed, it is precisely the political productivity and usefulness of research on Latinas/os and African Americans that make it some-thing of a growth industry.

A second, and related factor contributing to this burgeoning area of research is larger changes in the racial formation itself. While for decades U.S. racial politics was largely defined as black and white, such is no longer the case. Thus, not only has there been a very real racial diversification of the United States, but this has also been accompa-nied by a new set of concepts and frameworks to account for the move beyond a biracial structure. Some authors have argued, for example, that the United States is undergoing an "ever-expanding circle of white-ness" in which growing numbers of nonblack people of color will be accepted as whites, while other observers suggest that the United States may be headed for a triracial structure consisting of whites, honorary whites, and the collective black.[44]

This brings us to the third factor contributing to the current growth in this topic: the development of comparative ethnic studies as a sub-stantive field within the discipline of ethnic studies itself. Although eth-nic studies scholars used to focus on particular populations in relative isolation, it was accepted that the unspoken point of comparison was whites or Anglo Americans. Given the U.S. racial structure, this made sense, but increasingly scholars understand that racial formations are composed of a field of racial positions, as Claire Jean Kim has pointed out, and these positions inform one another and are in constant con-versation.[45] Accordingly, this relatively recent research has been incred-ibly productive and sheds new light on how white supremacy operates, the extent to which all of us may be complicit in it, and the possibilities for resistance.[46] One of the more innovative concepts to emerge from this literature is John Márquez's concept of "foundational blackness," which he uses to understand African American and Latina/o cooperation in Houston.[47] In this case, Márquez argues that Latinas/os in Houston have borrowed or absorbed a Black political consciousness, given the latter group's longer history in that particular region. Though still treating Latinas/os and African Americans as discrete, Márquez illuminates the degree to which exchange and borrowing have shaped each group, whether deliberate or not.

While we too have approached African Americans and Latinas/os as two distinct populations, this overlooks the possibility of hybrid spaces for those who identify as both Black *and* Brown, otherwise known as Black Latinas/os, Afro-Mexicans, or Blaxicans. In fact, it is precisely this mixed zone that is one of the most dynamic topics within comparative ethnic studies.[48] While it is true that conceptualizing Brown and Black communities as isolated and distinct is something of a fiction, it is also true that much of the mixing that constitutes such communities has not historically characterized Los Angeles. In this regard, Los Angeles stands in contrast to places like New York, with its Puerto Rican and Dominican populations, or Miami with its Cuban heritage. This is not to suggest that such mixing does not exist in Los Angeles. Mexico was, in fact, on the receiving end of millions of Africans, and as Martha Menchaca has shown, some of this presence can still be seen not only in the features of some Mexicans but also in aspects of that country's culture. What we have in Los Angeles, however, are millions of ethnic Mexicans who have not historically seen themselves as part of the African diaspora and are only now (re)connecting with their African roots via African Americans. Los Angeles is a place that has historically been marked by more cultural and political mixing, rather than biological—but even this is starting to charge.

THE STRUCTURE OF THE BOOK

We have divided the volume into five sections. In reality, however, many of the essays are interdisciplinary and cross-cutting and could have been placed in several possible locations. The first section, "The Economics of People and Places," contains three essays that approach economic and spatial change as well as local business itself using distinct methods. The section opens with Manuel Pastor's essay, "Keeping It Real: Demographic Change, Economic Conflict, and Interethnic Organizing for Social Justice in Los Angeles." Pastor's essay serves as a foundation, as he not only documents the demographic and economic change that has affected Los Angeles in recent years, and people of color in particular, but also problematizes the oft-heard complaint of immigrants taking jobs from African Americans and how a number of community-based organizations are approaching this issue in highly innovative ways. Not only does Pastor's work seek to measure the extent to which Latina/o immigrants may "cost" African Americans in the job market, but he also puts these figures into a larger context so that the reader can understand the multitude of forces contributing to Black unemployment and poverty. This discussion is especially important because many of the other chapters touch on this issue of job competition. Pastor's chapter is followed Abigail Rosas's study of the evolution of Broadway Federal Bank, one of the leading financial institutions in South Los Angeles formed as a specifically African American bank in the 1940s. Rosas carefully documents this history via oral interviews and explores how it has changed over time in response to demographic shifts, particularly after the civil unrest of 1992. She finds that the bank and its Black leadership are having a difficult time negotiating their identity in a community that is increasingly Latina/o—an issue that Erin Aubry Kaplan eloquently addresses in a later chapter that explores African American responses to the growing Latina/o population.

The final chapter in this section examines African American attitudes toward both Latinas/os and immigrants. Drawing on data from the Los Angeles County Social Survey (2007), Lorrie Frasure-Yokley and Stacey Greene analyze responses to survey questions and explore factors beyond traditional models of economic competition. Like Pastor, Frasure-Yokley and Greene grapple with feelings of competition and displacement in nuanced ways. Overall, their findings indicate a very mixed set of attitudes and responses on the part of African Americans toward Latinas/os, and Latina/o immigrants in particular.

The second section in the volume, titled "Urban Histories," presents a crucial subfield of the developing scholarship within Latina/o and African American relations. The three chapters it contains are marked by rigorous analyses of how Mexican Americans and African Americans struggled to overcome educational and residential discrimination. In the first chapter, "The Changing Valence of White Racial Innocence: Black-Brown Unity in the 1970s Los Angeles School Desegregation Struggles," Daniel Martinez HoSang not only takes up a little known topic within Los Angeles history—the story of 1970s school desegregation—but also traces out the distinctive responses on the part of both Mexican Americans and African Americans. He documents the kinds of hardships each group encountered in public education, the different kinds of improvements each group sought, and why they ultimately were not able to work together during the struggle. In turn, he shows how these differences primarily reflected not only the particularities of each group's position but also their differing levels of power and political clout.

Max Felker-Kantor takes a similar approach in his insightful essay "Fighting the Segregation Amendment: Black and Mexican American Responses to Proposition 14 in Los Angeles." Proposition 14 was an effort in 1964 to basically overturn California's Rumford Act and to open the door once again to residential discrimination. Activists, especially in the African American community, developed an intensive campaign to overturn the initiative. Early plans called for cooperation with Mexican Americans, but that never materialized. Felker-Kantor offers a detailed account of each community's response to the proposition and, in particular, highlights the role of class tensions within each population. He argues that ultimately African Americans were able to overcome their class divisions and close ranks in opposition to the proposition, but Mexican Americans were not and remained a split community and vote.

The final chapter in this section embodies a very different kind of history and approach. Denise Sandoval provides a cultural history of that quintessentially Los Angeles phenomenon, lowriding. In "The Politics of Low and Slow/*Bajito y Suavecito*: Black and Chicano Lowriders in Los Angeles, from the 1960s through the 1970s," Sandoval not only details the emergence of lowriding in Los Angeles (and thus, the world) but also places it within a larger social framework, so we can better understand how and why this practice developed and what it means to its adherents, both Mexican and African American. With a particular focus on the Ruelas family in the 1970s, who could be called the "first family" of lowriding, Sandoval uncovers their deep and multifaceted relationship with both African American culture and Black lowriders in particular.

The third section of the book, "Community Life and Politics," includes a diversity of approaches and perspectives. The section opens with a study by Matt Barreto, Ben Gonzalez, and Gabriel Sánchez that explores Latina/o attitudes toward African Americans in California, an important contribution, given that much of the recent attitudinal survey research has concentrated on African Americans' attitudes toward Latinas/os. But "Rainbow Coalition in the Golden State? Exposing Myths, Uncovering New Realities in Latino Attitudes toward Blacks" also is important for methodological reasons. The authors do not simply measure the extent to which Latinas/os may see themselves in competition with African Americans but consider the extent to which Latinas/os see themselves in competition with other groups as well. This is an important corrective to much of the race relations literature, which concentrates heavily on competition between two supposedly antagonistic groups. Barreto, Gonzalez, and Sánchez find that Latinas/os are actually more competitive with other Latinas/os than with African Americans.

In the subsequent chapter Ofelia Ortiz Cuevas examines issues of criminality, interethnic relations, and state violence. Starting from the place of the Los Angeles County Jail, Cuevas asks how we have collectively come to participate in a process of dehumanization, one that disproportionately affects African Americans and Latinas/os. Cuevas offers us an archaeology of human relations discourse and policy in Los Angeles, arguing that its earliest uses in the region were for the explicit purpose of maintaining wartime productivity and that the dehumanization of those categorized as criminals is part and parcel of the human relations narrative as practiced in Los Angeles (and most likely other places).

So many of the debates around Black and Brown relations in Los Angeles have been historically carried out in local and regional media, with journalists and op-ed writers taking a strong hand in shaping discourse around the subject, making galvanizing and controversial arguments and publishing pathbreaking reporting. The book's next section features two *Los Angeles Times* writers who have been particularly active in writing on Black-Brown issues: Erin Aubry Kaplan and Sam Quinones. In a series of op-ed columns republished here, Aubry Kaplan addresses African American anxiety toward Latina/o immigrants in Los Angeles in frank terms and grapples with what demographic change means for African Americans in Los Angeles. She offers us nuance and honesty as she seeks to articulate the sentiments of loss and displacement that characterize much of Black Los Angeles's response to Latinas/os. For many African Americans, Latina/o numbers are simply a sign of their growing irrelevance, and it is uncertain whether they will become relevant again. Aubry Kaplan has long argued for the need for Latinas/os and African Americans to discuss their differences honestly, because without honesty we can never move toward solving our problems and working together; these essays are her attempt to do so. Quinones puts racism and racial attitudes at the center of his detailed investigation of L.A.'s gang life and drug economy—a piece that is previously unpublished. Quinones unravels the story behind one particularly sensationalized murder, the death of Cheryl Green. He follows the trail of gang violence all the way to the prisons to document the rise of the "Latino gang hate-criminals" who were following orders to kill African Americans. Such orders, in turn, were linked to major changes in the drug economy, real estate prices, and immigration, among other factors. Given that California has the largest prison complex on the planet, it is critical to see how the prison helps shape everyday life on the outside. Indeed, Quinones's story offers a very different vantage point and perspective of the prison industrial complex from the essay by Cuevas.

The book closes with "City Cultures" and highlights the diverse forms of everyday culture—music, urban landscape, barbershops, the Raiders—that are so influential in structuring and negotiating race and class identities and social relations. Gaye Johnson's "Spatial Entitlement: Race, Displacement, and Sonic Reclamation in Postwar Los Angeles" challenges us in two ways. First, she makes a productive link between the massive urban development and displacement that affected people of color in Los Angeles in the postwar years, with their desire and need for spatial entitlement, as evidenced in such things as cruising and the spaces of popular music, including radio, dance halls, and concerts. Second, she illustrates the cultural exchange, what she calls the "diasporic overlap," between African Americans and Mexican Americans as seen in music. In addition to presenting a compelling history that provides background on such L.A. legends as Huggy Boy and Art Laboe, she suggests what such exchanges mean, without romanticizing them, "Black and Brown communities . . . have consistently envisioned futures that include each other's memories and histories, even when it wasn't always a conscious choice."

That same back-and-forth is at the heart of Josh Kun's "What Is an MC If He Can't Rap to Banda? Making Music in Nuevo L.A." By focusing on one song by the L.A. Mexican hip-hop duo Akwid, Kun traces the layers of influence and exchange heard in the song's mix of *banda sinaloense* and West Coast hip-hop that are born directly out of Akwid's experience of growing up in South Los Angeles in the

1980s. The gangsta rap of 1980s and 1990s South Los Angeles also figures in Priscilla Leiva's "'Just Win, Baby!' The Raider Nation and Second Chances for Black and Brown L.A." Leiva explores the imagined African American and Latina/o community of the Raider Nation as both a pointed construction of the franchise, its owner, its Latino coach, and its Latino and Black players, as well as attempts by Raiders fans themselves to position their team as a symbol of a Los Angeles of "second chances," where the underdogs and the invisible can bring a trophy home to their city.

The final section also includes two pieces born of visual art projects. *On Fallen Nature and the Two Cities*, from the Pasadena-based artist Nery Gabriel Lemus, takes as its point of departure the lined-up fade, a popular hairstyle among both young Brown and Black males in Los Angeles. In this sampling of the larger project he includes photos of men with the haircuts, men getting the haircut in the barbershop, collages of men with the cut, and drawings of the cut. The overall result is a powerful reflection of a contemporary cultural practice that echoes Gaye Johnson's point that, whether consciously or not, African American and Latina/o Angelenos both draw from each other's experiences. As Lemus points out in the accompanying text, he has no illusions that this study will somehow resolve long-standing tensions; rather, his intention is to encourage us to consider the origins of these divisions, by going back to something as fundamental as our bodies.

Whereas Lemus is concerned with the body in intimate spaces such as the barbershop, the photo essay by Wendy Cheng operates at a different scale: the neighborhood and the street. She turns her camera to the urban landscape of South Los Angeles, where African Americans and Latinas/os are in their closest proximity and where the changes in the landscape register viscerally with local residents. Through Cheng's lens we can see the historical evolution of neighborhoods, such as a house with distinctly Japanese American landscaping and the juxtaposition of Latina/o and African American icons, as seen in the area's many murals. We also get a glimpse of how the local state attempts to respond to the city's demographic change through its banner campaign that supposedly "celebrates" the identity of local neighborhoods as well as the city's racial and cultural diversity (all Angeleno readers will immediately recognize the banners). As geographers have shown, landscapes are not inconsequential. Rather, they are deeply held and become part of our identities, and just as the proliferation of Latina/o-oriented streetscapes may be a welcome sign to some, their presence can also signify loss to others. We hope that these photographs are emblematic of what all the essays in this collection allow us to do: to see the transformations, coalitions, and struggles of Los Angeles with a new kind of vision.

NOTES

1. Full video of the event is available at www.youtube.com/watch?v= O5w2 Sk_fhqo.

2. Héctor Tobar, "A Call for Unity, Not Hate," *Los Angeles Times,* June 16, 2009, A2.

3. Anthony Macías, "Bringing Music to the People: Race, Urban Culture, and Municipal Politics in Postwar Los Angeles," *American Quarterly* 56, no. 3 (September 2004): 693–717.

4. Ursula Vils, "Hot Mixed Band Cools Racial Tensions," *Los Angeles Times* November 8, 1979. Also see "Latins and Blacks Say It with Music," *Los Angeles Sentinel,* April 26, 1973. We thank Adam Bush for tipping us to the Black and Brown Brotherhood Band.

5. Josh Kun, "Hecho en El Lay," *Los Angeles* magazine, September 2010.

6. Earl Ofari Hutchinson, "The Black-Latino Blame Game: Finger-Pointing between the Two Minorities Is Not Going to Help Either Group," *Los Angeles Times,* November 25, 2007, M1.

7. See, for example, L. Aubry, "Honesty Is Key to Improving Black-Latino Relations," *Los Angeles Sentinel,* February 5, 2010, A7.

8. Nicolas C. Vaca, *The Presumed Alliance: The Unspoken Conflict between Latinos and Blacks and What It Means for America* (New York: HarperCollins, 2004).

9. Stokely Carmichael and Charles Hamilton, *Black Power: The Politics of Liberation* (New York: Vintage, 1967), 75.

10. Quoted in Vaca, *The Presumed Alliance,* 5.

11. See also Mark Sawyer, "Politics in Los Angeles," in *Just Neighbors? Research on African American and Latino Relations in the United States,* ed. E. Telles, M. Sawyer, and G. Rivera-Salgado (New York: Russell Sage Foundation, 2011), 187.

12. Phil Willon, "Villaraigosa Says Racial Tensions Due to Poverty: In Speech, L.A. Mayor States Blacks, Latinos Must Address Strains," *Los Angeles Times,* October 7, 2008, B4.

13. Pilar Marrero, "Blacks and Latinos: Parallel Histories" *La Opinión,* November 2, 2006.

14. For an important exception to the pattern of not following up on this origin story, see Paul Robinson, "Race, Space, and the Evolution of Black Los Angeles," in *Black Los Angeles: American Dreams and Racial Realities,* ed. Darnell Hunt and Ana-Christina Ramón (New York: New York University Press, 2010), 21–59.

15. This is actually an important point in Black-Brown relations. In other parts of the United States there is significant mixing, and the terms *Black* and

Latina/o are not mutually exclusive. Given the size and diversity of Los Angeles's population, it has relatively few Black Latinas/os. For instance, the 2000 census found that only 3.17 percent of all Latinas/os in Los Angeles identified as Black. (Los Angeles Almanac, "Racial/Ethnic Composition, Los Angeles County, 2000 Census," www.laalmanac.com/population/po13.htm, accessed September 16, 2010). For more on Mexico's colonial racial formation, see María Elena Martínez, *Genealogical Fictions: Limpieza de Sangre, Religion, and Gender in Colonial Mexico* (Stanford, CA: Stanford University Press, 2008). On the fluidity of border racial hierarchies, see Pablo Mitchell, *Coyote Nation: Sexuality, Race, and Conquest in Modernizing New Mexico, 1880–1920* (Chicago: University of Chicago Press, 2006) See Michael González, *This Small City Will Be a Mexican Paradise: Exploring the Origins of Mexican Culture in Los Angeles, 1821–1846* (Albuquerque: University of New Mexico, 2005), on unfree labor, captivity, and violence.

16. On the decline of the Californios/as, see Leonard Pitt, *Decline of the Californios: A Social History of the Spanish-Speaking Californias, 1846–1890* (Berkeley: University of California Press, 2006); Douglas Monroy, *Thrown among Strangers: The Making of Mexican Culture in Frontier California* (Berkeley: University of California, 1993); and Bill Deverall, *Whitewashed Adobe: The Rise of Los Angeles and the Remaking of Its Mexican Past* (Berkeley: University of California, 2005). On Mexican immigration during the Mexican Revolution, see Douglas Monroy, *Rebirth: Mexican Los Angeles from the Great Migration to the Great Depression* (Berkeley: University of California Press, 1999). See Ken Gonzalez-Day's, *Lynching in the West: 1850–1935* (Durham, NC: Duke University Press, 2006), on violence against Mexicans.

17. The 1850 census counted fifteen African Americans in Los Angeles. For more on Biddy Mason, see Dolores Hayden, *The Power of Place: Urban Landscapes as Public History* (Cambridge, MA: MIT Press, 1997).

18. On early Black Los Angeles, see J. Max Bond, "The Negro in Los Angeles," PhD dissertation, University of Southern California, 1936; Lawrence B. de Graaf, "The City of Black Angels: Emergence of the Los Angeles Ghetto, 1890–1930," *Pacific Historical Review* 39, no. 3 (1970): 323–52; and Douglas Flamming, *Bound for Freedom: Black Los Angeles in Jim Crow America* (Berkeley: University of California Press, 2005). Overall, the historiography of Black Los Angeles is underdeveloped in comparison to Chicana/o history. On Black historiography, see Scott Kurashige, "Rethinking Black History in Multiethnic Los Angeles" *Social History* 33, no. 1 (2008): 1–11.

19. For a detailed account of the Double-V campaign, see Scott Kurashige, *The Shifting Grounds of Race: Black and Japanese Americans in the Making of Multiethnic Los Angeles* (Princeton, NJ: Princeton University Press, 2007), ch. 6. On the formation of Los Angeles's Black community more generally, see Josh Sides, *L.A. City Limits: African American Los Angeles from the Great Depression to the Present* (Berkeley: University of California Press, 2003); R.J. Smith, *The Great Black Way: L.A. in the 1940s and the Lost African-American Renaissance* (New York: Public Affairs, 2006); and Robinson, "Race, Space, and the Evolution of Black Los Angeles."

20. Ricardo Romo, *East Los Angeles: History of a Barrio* (Austin: Univer-

sity of Texas Press, 1983), ch. 6; George Sánchez, *Becoming Mexican American* (New York: Oxford University Press), ch. 9.

21. Alberto M. Camarillo, "Chicano Urban History: A Study of Compton's Barrio, 1936–1970," *Aztlán* 2 (Spring 1970): 79–106; see also James Allen and Eugene Turner, *The Ethnic Quilt: Population Diversity in Southern California* (Northridge: California State University Center for Geographical Studies, 1997).

22. Gaye Johnson, "Constellations of Struggle: Luisa Moreno, Charlotta Bass, and the Legacy for Ethnic Studies" *Aztlán* 33 (Spring 2008): 155–72.

23. Laura Pulido, "Checkered Choices, Political Assertions: The Unarticulated Racial Identity of the Asociación Nacional México-Americana," in *Critical Ethnic Studies Anthology,* ed. D. Rodriguez, J. Kim, D. Hernandez, S. Redmond, A. Smith, and D. Spade (forthcoming); Shana Bernstein's, *Bridges of Reform: Interracial Civil Rights Activism in Twentieth-Century Los Angeles,* offers an in-depth look at interethnic activism in Los Angeles at this time (New York: Oxford University Press, 2011).

24. Bernstein, *Bridges of Reform,* chs. 5 and 6; see also Philippa Strum, *Mendez v. Westminster: School Desegregation and Mexican American Rights* (Lawrence: University of Kansas Press), especially ch. 9.

25. For a similar argument, see Brian Behnken, *Fighting Their Own Battles: Mexican Americans, African Americans, and the Struggle for Civil Rights in Texas* (Chapel Hill: University of North Carolina Press, 2011); and Neil Foley, *Quest for Equality: The Failed Promise of Black-Brown Solidarity* (Cambridge, MA: Harvard University Press, 2010).

26. This literature has grown rapidly in recent years. See Carlos Blanton, "George I. Sánchez, Ideology and Whiteness in the Making of the Mexican American Civil Rights Movement, 1930–1960," *Journal of Southern History* 72 (August 2006): 569–604; Thomas Guglielmo, "Fighting for Caucasian Rights: Mexicans, Mexican Americans, and the Transnational Struggle for Civil Rights in World War II Texas," *Journal of American History* (March 2006): 1212–37; John Logan, *How Race Counts for Hispanic Americans,* Lewis Mumford Center for Comparative Urban and Regional Research, State University New York at Albany, 2003; Joseph Michael and Jeffrey Timberlake, "Are Latinos Becoming White? Determinants of Racial Self-Identification in the U.S.," in *Racism in Post-Race America: New Theories, New Directions,* ed. C. Gallagher (Chapel Hill: Social Forces, 2008), 107–22; and Clara Rodríguez, *Changing Race: Latinos, the Census, and the History of Ethnicity in the United States* (New York: New York University Press, 2000).

27. Ian Haney-López, *Racism on Trial: The Chicano Fight for Justice* (Cambridge, MA: Harvard University Press, 2003). For examples of political collaboration in Los Angeles and beyond, see Lauren Araiza, "In Common Struggle against a Common Oppression: The United Farm Workers and the Black Panther Party, 1968–73," *Journal of African American History* 94 (Spring 2009): 200–223; Jason Ferreira, "All Power to the People: A Comparative History of Third World Radicalism in San Francisco, 1968–1974," PhD dissertation, University of California, Berkeley, 2003; and Laura Pulido, *Black, Brown, Yellow and Left: Radical Activism in Los Angeles* (Berkeley: University of California Press, 2006), ch. 5.

28. Interview with Kumasi Aguilar, conducted by Laura Pulido, July 15, 2000, Los Angeles. For the definitive work on the Watts uprising, see Gerald Horne, *Fire This Time: The Watts Uprising and the 1960s* (Charlottesville: University of Virginia, 1995). On the East L.A. walkouts, see Dolores Bernal, "Grassroots Leadership Reconceptualized: Chicana Oral Histories and the 1968 East Los Angeles School Blowouts," *Frontiers* 19 (1998): 113–42.

29. Pulido, *Black, Brown, Yellow, and Left*, 72–73.

30. On how deindustrialization and post-Fordism affected the region, see Ed Soja, *Postmodern Geographies* (New York: Verso, 1989), chs. 8 and 9; Victor Valle and Rodolfo Torres, *Latino Metropolis* (Minneapolis: University of Minnesota Press, 2000), ch. 1; and Mike Davis, *City of Quartz* (New York: Verso, 1990), ch. 4.

31. African Americans' concentration in public employment, has, in fact, been a source of conflict between Latinas/os and African Americans. See Vaca, *The Presumed Alliance*, 51–60; Paula McClain, "The Changing Dynamics of Urban Politics: Black and Hispanic Municipal Employment—Is There Competition?" *Journal of Politics* 55, no. 2 (May 1993): 399–414; and Jerry Yaffe, "Discrimination against Hispanics in the Public Sector Work Force: Past, Present, and Future," *Journal of Intergroup Relations* 20 (Spring 1993): 39–50.

32. See Mike Davis, *City of Quartz*, ch. 5. On the more general decline of South Los Angeles, see João Costa Vargas, *Catching Hell in the City of Angels: Life and Meanings of Blackness in South Central Los Angeles* (Minneapolis: University of Minnesota, 2006); Josh Sides, "Straight into Compton: American Dreams, Urban Nightmares, and the Metamorphosis of a Black Suburb," *American Quarterly* 56 (2004): 583–605; and Albert Camarillo, "Black and Brown in Compton: Demographic Change, Suburban Decline, and Inter-group Relations in a South Central Los Angeles Community, 1950–2000," in *Not Just Black and White: Immigration, Race, and Ethnicity, Then and Now,* ed. George Frederickson and Nancy Foner (Los Angeles: Russell Sage Foundation, 2004), 358.

33. On the rise of the prison-industrial complex in Los Angeles and throughout California, see Ruth Wilson Gilmore, *Golden Gulag: Prisons, Surplus, Crisis, and Opposition in Globalizing California* (Berkeley: University of California, 2007); on the Bradley election and regime, see Raphael Sonenshein, *Politics in Black and White* (Princeton, NJ: Princeton University Press, 1994); on the abandonment of the Los Angeles Unified School District, see Dan Martinez HoSang, "The Changing Valence of White Racial Innocence: The Los Angeles School Desegregation Struggles of the 1970s," in this volume; and Valerie Ledwith and William Clark, "The Effect of the Residential Mosaic and 'White Flight' on Public School Composition: Evidence from Los Angeles County," *Urban Geography* 28 (2007): 160–80; for a discussion of Los Angeles's working poor and emergent Latina/o middle class, see Los Angeles Alternatives for a New Economy (LAANE), *The Other Los Angeles: The Working Poor in the City of the 21st Century* (Los Angeles: LAANE, 2000); and Jody Agius Vallejo, *From Barrios to Burbs: The Making of the Mexican American Middle Class* (Stanford, CA: Stanford University Press, 2012).

34. For a detailed analysis of contact between African Americans and Latina/o immigrants, see Manuel Pastor, Juan de Lara, and Justin Scoggins,

All Together Now? African Americans, Immigration and the Future of California, Center for the Study of Immigration, Integration, University of Southern California, 2011.

35. One need only look at events in Arizona in 2010 and 2011 to see how this happens. In April 2010 Arizona passed SB 1070, which makes it a crime for immigrants not to carry immigration documents at all times and gives the police broad authority to detain anyone suspected of being in the United States illegally. In 2011 the state superintendent of education banned Tucson's Mexican American studies program. Otto Santa Ana and Celeste González de Bustamante, *Arizona Firestorm: Global Immigration Realities, National Media, and Provincial Politics* (Lanham, MD: Rowman and Littlefield, 2012).

36. Of course, this overlooks the extent to which *illegal* has become a racialized term. Mae Ngai, *Impossible Subjects: Illegal Aliens and the Making of Modern America* (Princeton, NJ: Princeton University Press, 2004).

37. Manning Marable, *How Capitalism Underdeveloped Black America: Problems in Race, Political Economy, and Society,* rev. ed. (Cambridge, MA: South End Press, 1999); Chrisshonna Grant Nieva, "This Is My Country: The Use of Blackness in Discourses of Racial Nativism Towards Latino Immigrants," PhD dissertation, University of Southern California, 2011.

38. Andy Merrifield, "The Urbanization of Labor: Living Wage Activism in the American City," *Social Text* 18 (2000): 31–54; Mary Pardo, *Mexican American Women Activists* (Philadelphia: Temple University Press, 1998); Laura Pulido, "Multiracial Organizing among Environmental Justice Activists in Los Angeles," in *Rethinking Los Angeles,* ed. Michael Dear, Greg Hise, and Eric Schockman (Newbury Park, CA: Sage Publications, 1996), 171–89; Gilmore, *Golden Gulag,* ch. 5; Robert Gottlieb, Regina Freer, Mark Vallianatos, and Peter Dreier, *The Next Los Angeles: The Struggle for a Livable City* (Berkeley: University of California Press, 2006); Ruth Milkman, Joshua Bloom, and Victor Narro, *Working for Justice: The L.A. Model of Organizing and Advocacy* (Ithaca, NY: ILR Press, 2010); Manuel Pastor: "Common Ground at Ground Zero? The New Economy and New Organizing at Ground Zero," *Antipode* 33 (2001): 260–89; Monica Varsanyi, "The Paradox of Contemporary Immigrant Political Mobilization: Organized Labor, Undocumented Migrants, and Electoral Participation in Los Angeles," *Antipode* 37 (2005): 775–95.

39. One example of early work is Melvin Oliver and James Johnson, "Interethnic Conflict in an Urban Ghetto: The Case of Blacks and Hispanics in Los Angeles," *Research in Social Movements, Conflict and Change* 6 (1984): 57–94.

40. Víctor Zúñiga and Rubén Hernández-León, *New Destinations: Mexican Immigration in the United States* (New York: Russell Sage Foundation, 2006).

41. Heather Rose Parker, "The Elusive Coalition: African American and Chicano Political Organizing in Los Angeles," PhD dissertation, University of California, Los Angeles, 1996; Camarillo, "Black and Brown in Compton."

42. Jason Ferreira, "All Power to the People: A Comparative History of Third World Radicalism in San Francisco, 1968–74," PhD dissertation, University of California, Berkeley, 2003; Lauren Araiza, "In Common Struggle

against a Common Oppression: The United Farm Workers and the Black Panther Party, 1968–73," *Journal of African American History* 94 (2009): 200–223. For an excellent overview, see Luis Alvarez and Danny Widener, "A History of Black and Brown: Chicana/o-African American Cultural and Political Relations," *Aztlán* 33 (Spring 2008): 143–54.

43. Daniel Rochmes and G. A. Elmer Griffin, "The Cactus That Must Not Be Mistaken for a Pillow: White Racial Formation among Latinos," *Souls* 8, no. 2 (2006): 77–91. See also Mary Waters, *Black Identities: West Indian Immigrant Dreams and American Realities* (Cambridge, MA: Harvard University Press, 1999).

44. Jonathan Warren and France Winddance Twine, "White Americans, the New Minority? Non-Blacks and the Ever-Expanding Boundaries of Whiteness," *Journal of Black Studies* 28, no. 2 (1997): 200–218; George Yancey, *Who Is White? Latinos, Asians, and the New Black/Nonblack Divide* (Boulder, CO: Lynne Rienner, 2003); Eduardo Bonilla-Silva, "From Bi-racial to Tri-racial: Towards a New System of Racial Stratification in the USA," *Ethnic and Racial Studies* 27, no. 6 (2004): 931–50.

45. Claire Jean Kim, "The Racial Triangulation of Asian Americans," *Politics & Society* 27, no. 1 (1999): 105–38.

46. Behnken, *Fighting Their Own Battles;* José Luis Benavides, "'Californios! Whom Do You Support?' *El Clamor Público's* Contradictory Role in the Racial Formation Process in Early California," *California History* 84, no. 2 (2006): 54–73; Neil Foley, *The White Scourge: Mexicans, Blacks, and Poor Whites in Texas Cotton Culture* (Berkeley: University of California Press, 1997) and *Quest for Equality;* Scott Kurashige, *The Shifting Grounds of Race: Black and Japanese Americans in the Making of Multiethnic Los Angeles* (Princeton, NJ: Princeton University Press, 2007); Tiya Miles, *Ties That Bind: The Story of an Afro-Cherokee Family in Slavery and Freedom* (Berkeley: University of California Press, 2005); Natalia Molina, *Fit to Be Citizens? Public Health and Race in Los Angeles, 1879–1939* (Berkeley: University of California Press, 2006); Pulido, *Black, Brown, Yellow and Left;* Edward Telles, Mark Sawyer, and Gaspar Rivera Salgado, *Just Neighbors? Research on African Americans and Latinos in the United States* (New York: Russell Sage Foundation, 2011). For analyses of how people of color may be complicit in white supremacist projects, see Andrea Smith, "Indigeneity/Settler Colonialism/White Supremacy," in *Racial Formation in the Twenty-First Century,* ed. D. HoSang, O. LaBennet, and L. Pulido (Berkeley: University of California Press, 2012), ch. 4; Chrisshonna Grant Nieva, Laura Pulido, and Nate Sessoms, "Beyond Conflict and Competition: How Color-Blind Ideology Affects Blacks' and Latinos' Understanding of Their Relationships," *Kalfou: A Journal of Ethnic Studies* (in press).

47. John Márquez, *Black-Brown Solidarity: Racial Politics in the Gulf South* (Austin: University of Texas Press, 2013).

48. Anani Dzidzinyo and Suzanne Oboler, *Neither Enemies nor Friends: Latinas/os, Blacks, and Afro-Latinos* (New York: Palgrave Macmillan, 2005); Miriam Jiménez Román and Juan Flores, *The Afro-Latin@ Reader: History and Culture in the United States* (Durham, NC: Duke University Press, 2010); Rebecca Romo, "Between Black and Brown: Blaxican (Black-Mexican) Multiracial Identity in California," *Journal of Black Studies* 42 (2011): 402–26.

PART ONE

The Economics
of People and Places

1

Keeping It Real

Demographic Change, Economic Conflict,
and Interethnic Organizing for Social Justice
in Los Angeles

MANUEL PASTOR

INTRODUCTION

In June 2011, federal authorities indicted fifty-one members of a Latino gang that had engaged in racially motivated attacks on black residents in a struggling suburb named Azusa, California, near Los Angeles. The tally of crime was high: between 1996 and 2001, at least eight families saw their houses firebombed, and in 2000, a young black nurse named Ge'Juan Salle was gunned down as he strolled out of an auto parts store with his cousin (Sewell 2011).

Over the last decade, a flurry of media stories has tended to focus on exactly these sorts of conflicts, creating the appearance of steadily increasing and worsening tensions between African Americans and Latinos (especially Mexicans) in Southern California. Aside from the fascination with gang activity, reporters have often focused on local politics and youth demographics, weaving together tales of troubled ethnic successions in cities like Compton and student conflagrations in the high schools of Los Angeles. The often unstated subtext: an underlying economic dynamic drives most of the conflict, with the basic storyline suggesting that Latinos, particularly immigrants, "take" jobs and impair black economic fortunes.

Both the local conflicts and the economic concerns are real—but often exaggerated or just one part of the story. For example, while the events in Azusa caused some African Americans to leave, others stayed as the city formed a hate crime task force that eventually became the

Human Relations Commission, which now hosts an annual youth conference to address issues of race and difference; one of the former gang members has said, "We were all brainwashed. . . . Maybe the cycle will be broken now and future generations will not see color" (Sewell 2011). The failure to tell the whole tale goes beyond just one Southern California suburb or just one wave of hate incidents; in general, the media tends to overreport crime by minorities, between races, and in the inner city (Dorfman and Schiraldi 2001). This focus on the negative is endemic to journalism—it stems, in part, from news organizations' disproportionate interest in conflict. But the media's particular fixation on black-Latino conflict also seems to be related to an attempt to portray all groups, and not just whites, as having to overcome prejudice. This reportorial sleight of hand, intentional or not, takes the focus from racist structures to racist attitudes (Nieva 2009). It not only misses the daily accommodations and negotiations within neighborhoods; it also has its own ripple effect of distancing groups—and given the pressing needs of inner-city communities, there is just not much room for that.

This is not to dispute the reality of economic and other concerns: tensions do exist, and there is some evidence of job displacement by Latino immigrants, particularly in key areas of the local economy. Since this is happening to blacks, who have historically been excluded from job markets, the Latino influx can be conveniently considered as the contemporary cause of an ongoing problem. Yet, as it turns out, research suggests that the effects on black employment are overstated, and those suffering the most harm from immigrant labor market competition may actually be U.S.-born Latinos, who are crowded into market niches very similar to those of blacks. Moreover, the positive impacts of Latinos on local labor markets, particularly the newfound ability to unionize, are rarely lifted up in the popular storyline. Nuances like these—as well as examples of groups working together—should serve to relax the overwrought and unchallenged narrative of black-Latino conflict.

In fact, African Americans and Latinos have more than enough reasons to get past the dominant paradigm of competition. These two groups not only share fences in areas like South L.A.; they also share critical social needs: healthy neighborhoods, good schools, decent public transportation, well-paying work, and neighborhood safety. Forward-looking coalitions have been trying to forge ties over these issues. Laura Pulido (2006), Jaime Regalado (1994), and others have well documented the generations of these coalitions in Los Angeles. However, in this era, the sheer size of the Latino population and its increasingly immigrant character, the relative and continuing decline of black-based political power, and the changing nature of the Los Angeles economy and the stresses that this has placed on both ethnic groups constitute new dynamics, challenges, and possibilities.

Indeed, the current era is also marked by an extraordinary opening for municipal influence that has been created by community-based groups in Los Angeles, many of whom have gone well beyond the neighborhood in their organizing and have explicitly focused on building black-brown alliances. To do so, they have had to go beyond the traditional—and easier—common-issue politics; they have instead lifted up differences and divisions and worked through them to create an uncommon but inspiring movement for social justice. Thus, I argue against the pessimism that has marked many accounts of demographic transformation in contemporary L.A. and instead stress the realities and possibilities of interethnic organizing in the years to come.

I begin by reviewing the demographic change that has brought African Americans and Latinos into close geographic, and ultimately political, proximity in Los Angeles. I then turn to the economics of the situation, pointing to some of the reasons why tensions have developed and telling a new and—I hope—more accurate story of the nature of black-Latino competition *and* complementarity. I then consider the coalitional possibilities, highlighting the efforts of some groups to develop leadership, including that of youth, and to take racial equity into account as they focus on addressing the underlying economic and educational challenges. I argue that these efforts are well-poised to create a new set of regional and national possibilities for progressive and multiracial politics.

A quick caveat about my use of "Latinos" as a category (and even "brown" as a shortcut). Latinos are certainly not monolithic, including in skin tone. In Los Angeles County, for example, those marking themselves with the ethnic categorization "Hispanic or Latino" are more than 75 percent Mexican, but nearly 15 percent are Central American (mostly Guatemalan and Salvadoran), and about 2.5 percent are South American.[1] Moreover, some Latinos are black; in Los Angeles, 0.5 percent of Latinos mark their race as "black." And because the U.S. Census asks all Latinos to choose a "race," another 43 percent of L.A.'s Latinos mark themselves as "white," 53 percent as "other," and 0.5 percent as indigenous (or Native American). This is a different mix from those in other parts of the nation; on the East Coast, Puerto Ricans and Cubans make up much larger shares of the Latino population, and more Latinos choose black as their racial identification. All these distinctions matter—in Los Angeles, the country-of-origin distinctions for the immigrant portion of the Latino population often correlate with particular sending periods and receiving neighborhoods—but with the overall focus in this essay on the broad topic of black-Latino relations, I leave those important details for other authors and future essays.

DEMOGRAPHY AND GEOGRAPHY IN L.A.

Los Angeles has always been the canvas to demographic flux. Boyle Heights was once home to Jewish immigrants; it is now a key center of Latino L.A. Little Tokyo was the heart of the prewar Japanese immigrant population; with World War II and the internment, it became Bronzetown, a new home for incoming black workers, only to morph into a sort of tourist trap and now artist colony. Hollywood was the suave center of entertainment; it was transformed into a shabby set of boulevards with drugs and prostitution before its current incarnation as a regional nightlife hub and the home of Little Armenia. The city and its places, in short, have always been the objects of repopulation and reinvention, and the current era is no exception.

To understand the present, however, requires that we understand the past: onto what racial landscape are we etching yet another set of groups and dynamics? The broad trends are shown in figure 1.1, in which the steady decline in the percentage of whites in Los Angeles County can be seen over the period 1940–2007. As dramatic as the percentage shifts may be, perhaps more startling is looking at the raw numbers (figure 1.2): the number of whites in Los Angeles County actually peaked in 1960 and has been declining since; the number of African Americans has been falling since 1990, and population growth has been driven by Latinos and Asians.[2]

But a look at the data does not tell the whole and much longer story. From World War II until the late 1960s, five million African Americans left the South, fleeing rampant racism and joblessness as part of the second "Great Migration." Blacks from Texas and Louisiana, in particular, moved to Los Angeles where the World War II defense industry created a constant demand for laborers in ship, plane, and steel production. Both male and female African Americans found upward mobility

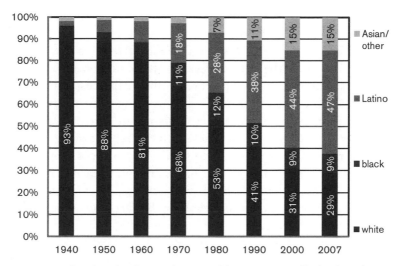

FIGURE 1.1. Los Angeles County demographics, 1940–2007. Native Americans are not included. Sources: Vaca 2004: 53 and PERE analysis of U.S. Census and American Community Survey data.

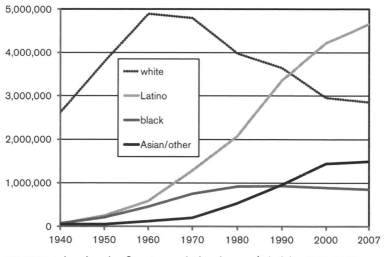

FIGURE 1.2. Los Angeles County population, by race/ethnicity, 1940–2007.

in employment from World War II through the 1960s; unemployment figures dropped and skills rose.

While this healed some historical wounds, new ones were soon inflicted: as early as the 1960s access to the hard-won jobs in L.A.'s industrial sectors began to slip. For one thing, the best manufacturing jobs were held by whites in the farther-flung parts of the region, which inner-city blacks could not as easily reach. Moreover, employer preferences shifted away from blacks as new populations grew; Josh Sides interprets data from the U.S. Equal Employment Opportunity Commission that show that by the 1960s "the preference of industrial employers for Mexican over black workers—especially in the metal and food industries—had become thoroughly entrenched, further eroding opportunity for black workers in blue-collar occupation" (Sides 2003: 94). This set the stage for what would be further deterioration in black economic fortunes when a wave of deindustrialization (and later immigration) struck Los Angeles and the nation in the 1970s and 1980s, a topic I explore in the next section.

Focusing on the geography of L.A.'s demography, I start with black Los Angeles and its identified heart: South Central. Until 1953, African Americans were boxed into specific neighborhoods within South Central by racially restrictive housing covenants.[3] When covenants lost their power, whites fled the industrial neighborhoods of South L.A. and its adjoining suburbs (such as Compton) and took flight for the beaches and the San Fernando Valley. Black families soon stretched into new areas of South L.A.; spurred by the 1965 unrest, prosperous blacks moved from the central city to the ethnically mixed neighborhoods near Crenshaw Boulevard (Sides 2006: 121). In the 1980s, South Central remained more than 50 percent black, but many upwardly mobile families moved to Inglewood, Hawthorne, Downey, Paramount, and Long Beach, leaving behind a more impoverished and disadvantaged African American community. By 1990, another trend surfaced: the natural rate of increase in the black community was being offset by out-migration from Los Angeles County (Morrison and Lowry 1994: 28–29).

Latinos have been members of the Los Angeles landscape longer than African Americans. Despite the long-standing history of Latinos in Los Angeles, however—Mexicans retained an influence here after the United States annexed this part of Mexico in the nineteenth century—Latino immigration has always been a tenuous matter. For example, L.A. was the site of mass deportations in the Depression (Garcia 2001: 108), but it was also a main focus for the Bracero Program during

World War II. Garcia (2001) describes how white Angelenos went to war, leaving the citrus industry—a regional economic driver—without workers. During this time, the U.S. government contracted Mexican nationals, undercutting U.S.-born Latino wages. Even though the program ended, the desire for cheap labor remained, in part setting up the illegal and unstable nature of immigrant labor that we see today.

This history helped embed Los Angeles as a gateway city for immigrants, a status resulting—surprisingly—from the civil rights movement. President Lyndon B. Johnson's enactment of the Great Society gave legs to the hopes of many protestors seeking humane treatment of all people. A natural corollary was to end discrimination against soon-to-be Americans, an issue addressed in the Immigration Act of 1965, which opened American borders and reshaped the L.A. landscape (Briggs 2004: 12). Migration then builds on migration; as Enrico Marcelli (2004) notes, more than other factors, established immigrant communities are attractive to new migrants, because long-time migrants can help the newcomer transition into the new society. Thus, East Los Angeles has become a hub for immigrant Latinos. Similarly, Pico-Union hosts new El Salvadorans, just as it was once the entry point for their refugee predecessors (Morrison and Lowry 1994: 29).

Through the 1980s, the 1990s, and the early part of this century, black and Latino concentrations have loosened and shifted (see figure 1.3). In 1980, African Americans were distinctly in South Los Angeles, Altadena, and Pacoima. Latinos were concentrated in East Los Angeles and the Gateway Cities, and to the east. But in the following decades, the sheer numbers of Latinos increased, crossing older territorial boundaries, while the black population shifted its center west to Crenshaw Boulevard and shrank. One way to see this is through the "isolation index," a measure that indicates the percentage of the same-group population in the census tract where the average member of that racial/ethnic group lives. Figure 1.4 reports that over the past few decades, blacks have become less residentially isolated (so have whites but they remain much more highly segregated than blacks). While some African Americans have moved to nonblack neighborhoods, the more reasonable explanation is that many Latinos have moved into historically black neighborhoods. The dashed line shows that the exposure index—the probability of black Angelenos having Latino neighbors—has risen from 4 percent in 1940 to 41 percent in 2000.

Figure 1.4 also tells us that the change is not symmetric: in fact, Latinos are more isolated than ever. This is possible because they have

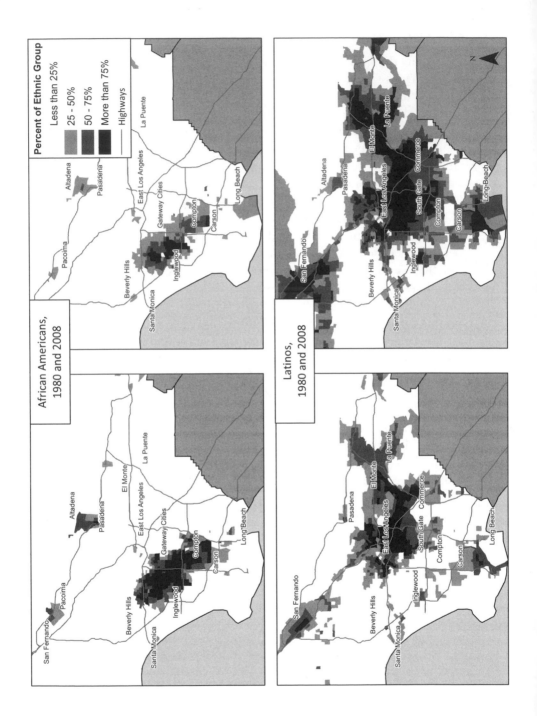

Percent of Ethnic Group

Less than 25%
25 - 50%
50 - 75%
More than 75%
Highways

African Americans, 1980 and 2008

Latinos, 1980 and 2008

become even more concentrated in certain locations, including the inner-ring suburbs of Huntington Park, Bell, Cudahy, South Gate, and elsewhere down the Alameda Corridor. This can lead to a county-level lack of awareness on the part of Latinos regarding the dramatic shifts in exposure that have occurred for blacks; some Latinos are dealing with this issue but most are not. In general, Latinos need to be aware of how blacks may be somewhat defensive of their territory, but many are not in a situation in which they have to confront this issue on a regular basis (Zhou 2001: 221).

One place where the demographic sea change has been most dramatic is in South Los Angeles high schools. Pastor and Ortiz (2009) show how in the early 1980s, African Americans constituted well over half of all the student bodies of Crenshaw, Dorsey, Fremont, Jefferson, Jordan, Locke, Manual Arts, and Washington Prep High (see figure 1.5).[4] While the disproportionate representation does reflect segregation, the schools were also some of the only majority black public institutions in the region and hence were anchors of the community. In the 2008–9 school years, however, only Crenshaw, Dorsey, and Washington Prep were majority African American, with Latinos having the majority in all other South L.A. schools (see figure 1.6).

Some scholars have argued that the Latino "invasion" of black communities was the underlying tension for the 1992 unrest (Morrison and Lowry 1994: 32). Our own research (Pastor 1995), including a multivariate analysis of the factors that drove the pattern of physical damage, suggests that economic distress was more the factor than was black-brown tension. Still, there were significant struggles that emerged in the wake of the unrest, particularly over the allocation of jobs in construction and other sectors that were promised as part of the rebuilding process.

Among changing demographics, one thing has stayed the same: the disinvestment of the common turf that low-income Latinos and African Americans call home. South L.A. is denser, dirtier, and in more disarray than other parts of L.A. Figure 1.7 shows that blacks and Latinos generally live in neighborhoods that are denser than those of whites or Asians in L.A., although this is strongest for Latinos. The figure shows L.A. County census tracts by density, where tracts in the 1st decile are the least dense, and those in the 10th are the most dense.[5] Asians and

FIGURE 1.3 *(opposite)*. Los Angeles County demographic change. Source: 2008 numbers from Geolytics/PERE Analysis, 1980 U.S. Census data.

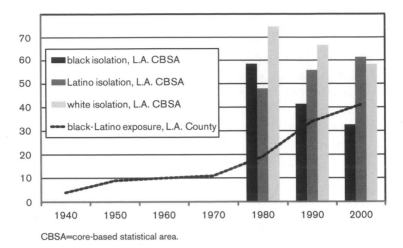

CBSA=core-based statistical area.

FIGURE 1.4. Residential segregation, by race/ethnicity. High values indicate high concentration/isolation. Sources: Isolation index data from the Building Resilient Regions database, CBSA includes Los Angeles and Orange counties. Exposure Index data from Ethington, Frey, and Meyers 2001: 16.

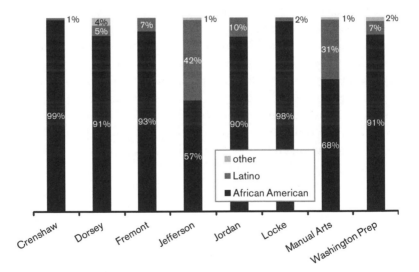

FIGURE 1.5. South Central high school demographics, 1981–82 school year.

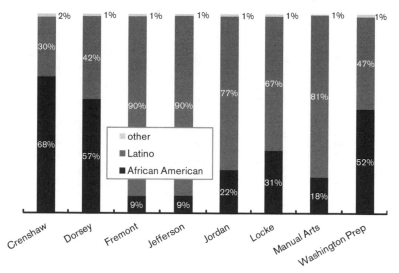

FIGURE 1.6. South Central high school demographics, 2008–9 school year.

Pacific Islanders (API) and blacks have little variation by decile (that is, across the bars in figure 1.7); at fairly consistent rates, they tend to live in neighborhoods across the density spectrum. Whites and Latinos on the other hand have the greatest variation, virtually trading off with each other. Latinos make up the majority of residents in the 7th, 8th, and 9th densest sets of tracts in the region.[6] South Los Angeles itself is not the densest in terms of its physical infrastructure, in part because it has a solid stock of single-family homes, but many of these homes have been converted into multiple dwellings or have large, extended families or several families, living under one roof. Such conditions put an added amount of strain on the day-to-day lives of inner-city Angelenos.

Just like crowded roommates who may or may not like each other, Latinos and blacks living in close quarters are bound for an occasional fight. Tensions do exist: in the county, blacks and Latinos are "the most frequent victims of hate crimes and the majority of black victims were targeted by Latino suspects and vice versa" (Los Angeles County Commission on Human Relations 2008: 10).[7] However, surveying a broader slice of regional hate crimes by the victim's national origin and ethnicity, Pastor and Ortiz (2009) note that when looking from 1991 to 2006 there appears to be a stronger correlation between hate crimes and economic and social stressors than between hate crimes and demo-

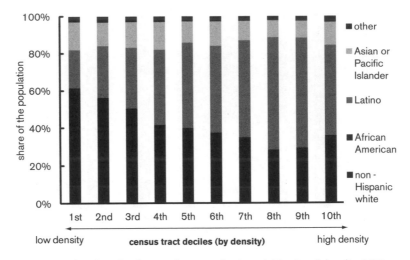

FIGURE 1.7. Los Angeles County demography, by neighborhood density, 2000.

graphic changes. For example, it seems more likely that the deep recession and the racialized immigration debates of the early twenty-first century have caused more violence than have Latino-black interactions in South Los Angeles (21).

And while the neighborhood may produce tension, it also produces a commonality of problems, including higher levels of environmental hazards. Blacks and Latinos have cooperated on issues of "environmental justice," with one of the earliest examples being the solidarity and support between Concerned Citizens of South Central Los Angeles and the Mothers of East LA to resist the placement of a "waste to energy" incinerator in the area bordering their two neighborhoods in the mid-1980s. But serious problems remain: Morello-Frosch, Pastor, and Sadd (2001), for example, have studied the cumulative health risks due to air pollution of Southern California, finding that across each and every income band, blacks and Latinos (and Asians) suffer a greater risk of cancer from air pollution from all sources, both stationary and mobile, than do whites (see figure 1.8). One mobile source receiving attention of late is the diesel truck traffic wending its way through South L.A. and the adjoining inner-ring suburbs and, in the process, pumping exhaust and carcinogenic particulate matter into the lungs of residents. As for stationary sources, the industrial history of South L.A. has left contaminated sites called "brownfields" with toxins in the soil.

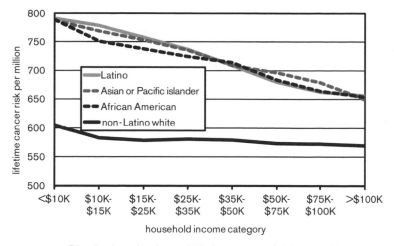

FIGURE 1.8. Distribution of estimated lifetime cancer risk from ambient hazardous air pollutant exposures, by race/ethnicity and income, Southern California, 1999–2000. Sources: PERE analysis of demographic data from U.S. Census 2000, pollutant data from 1999.

And South L.A. is not known particularly well for its lush greenery, either, which is a concern in and of itself, especially as we head toward a warmer global climate. As temperatures increase, places like South L.A. will warm at a faster rate because of the "heat-island" effect, wherein a lack of greenery and an abundance of dark materials like asphalt absorb heat and raise neighborhood temperatures (Morello-Frosch et al. 2009: 8; Oke 1973). Morello-Frosch and Jesdale (2008) found that in Los Angeles, the poorest and most nonwhite communities have the smallest tree canopies and the most impervious surfaces.[8] Further, research by the USC Center for Sustainable Cities (Sister et al. 2007) finds that the South L.A. subregion has the fewest parks per capita in Los Angeles. While this has implications for physical health related to exercise, it also means that as the climate warms, South L.A. residents are highly susceptible to heat-related illness and death (Morello-Frosch et al., 2009).

DEMOGRAPHY AND ECONOMY IN LOS ANGELES

While I have concentrated above on the changing spatial patterns of blacks and Latinos in Los Angeles, the economic dimension is equally important. In general, this story has often been told with an emphasis on competition and with few voices challenging the dominant narrative. Getting the story right is a worthy cause, because, as it turns out, the economic competition, although present, pales in comparison to the range of potential common interests. But getting to commonality is not simple: it requires understanding where tensions and differences are real so that these can then be addressed and defused. I'll get to that challenge soon, but first we should review the history of the Los Angeles economy and the ways in which it has impacted African Americans and Latinos.

Los Angeles's economic history seems to be a sort of national story writ large. In the post–World War II era, Los Angeles bloomed because of federal defense contracts and federally subsidized suburbanization. Good jobs in auto, aerospace, and steel industries grew the middle class of all colors, and in 1964, believing that blacks were rising buoyantly with this tide, the Urban League proclaimed Los Angeles as the best among sixty-eight cities for African Americans (Soja 1998: 434). Strikingly, this was right on the eve of the Watts unrest, a revolt catalyzed by police action but deeply rooted in unemployment and poverty.

If manufacturing was key to black economic progress, its decline similarly led to challenges. Manufacturing employment in Los Angeles peaked in 1979 and has been slipping ever since. The fall in Los Angeles was cushioned by military spending during the Reagan years and the birth of what might be termed "reindustrialized" sectors, including light manufacturing, garments, and other industries reliant on a combination of immigrant labor and a highly responsive and cost-efficient logistics industry. This new manufacturing meant lower-quality and lower-paying jobs, as unionization in manufacturing fell from 34 percent in 1971 to 19 percent in 1987 (Wolff 1992: 16). And it was this weakened structure onto which an avalanche of job loss took place over the 1990s.

From 1990 to 2005, the county lost 41.4 percent of its manufacturing jobs—more than the nation (19.6 percent) or the rest of the state (7.7 percent, partly because high-tech assembly persisted in the Silicon Valley). Of the manufacturing jobs remaining, the share in durable manufacturing dropped 10 percentage points (from 65.6 to 55.9), and the share in lower-paying, nondurable manufacturing jobs rose 10 percentage points (from 34.4 to 44.1); we're talking toys and food processing instead of cars. Lower-wage service sector jobs took over, with a growth rate of 7.8 percent, more than twice that of the rest of the state. Los Angeles, in short, has been bleeding good jobs: it was in the center of the deindustrialization bust of the 1980s and 1990s *and* on the periphery of the tech boom of the latter part of the 1990s (California Budget Project 2006).

Amid this poor economic outlook, there is a sense that Latinos are not only taking space but also taking jobs and lowering income. Data from 2005 to 2007 show that Latino wages are actually well below those of African Americans, on average: $11.50/hour and $17.51/hour, respectively. But looking at workers in poor households only, the gap is smaller: $7.05/hour for Latinos and $7.65/hour for blacks. However, Latino workers in poor households have significantly higher total earnings; they earn $12,074/year while poor black workers earn only $7,546/year, on average.[9] In essence, Latinos are working more hours, something that illustrates that a major driver for African American poverty in Los Angeles is joblessness, while for Latinos the problem may be low wages. Of course, both groups are doing worse than non-Hispanic whites: in 2005–7 the median household income for whites in Los Angeles County was $65,402, a premium of 75 percent over black households and 61 percent over Latino households.[10]

A review of the size of the labor force shows that in 1970 there were 428,100 working-age Latinos (ages 25–64), a number that grew consistently to 2.3 million during 2005–7 and one that likely underestimated undocumented workers. For working-age African Americans, those numbers increased from 319,600 to 444,494 over the same time span.[11] The sheer size of the Latino population in the labor market, as well as the long hours they work (mentioned above), creates the sense that Latinos, particularly immigrants (see figure 1.9), are flooding the labor market and seemingly "leapfrogging" over lower-income African Americans. The bypass can feel particularly galling because it is the civil rights struggle of blacks that first opened up jobs to ethnic minorities and, as I have stressed above, played a key role in the 1965 immigration reform that led to increased immigration from Latin America.

But, what is the reality with regard to the negative effects of immigrants on black wages and employment? At the national level, it is pretty much a wash. Economists generally agree that immigrants provide both labor complements and substitutes and that the complementary effect—enhancing the U.S.-born labor market and keeping industries alive in the United States—dominates, yielding employment and income gains for the native-born. But we must also look at the effect on native subgroups: many prominent economists argue that immigrant labor has had "marked adverse impacts" on high school drop-outs (Borjas,

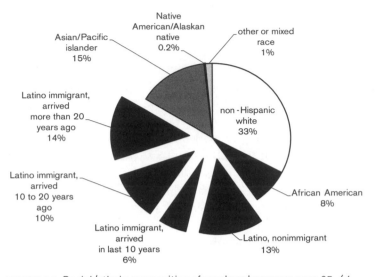

FIGURE 1.9. Racial/ethnic composition of employed persons ages 25–64, Los Angeles, 2005–7.

Freeman, et al. 1997: 3). Borjas and his colleagues estimate a 5 percent decline in real wages for natives without high school diplomas over a twenty-year period (1980—2000), attributable to immigrant workers (Borjas et al. 2010). While this decline applies equally to all those without high school diplomas, it hits African Americans especially hard, because they have a higher percentage of people without diplomas.

However, their analysis focuses entirely on the substitution effect; Borjas acknowledges that taking into account the impact on productivity and the mix of capital and labor, "the negative wage effect declines to 2.4 percent relative to the college-educated (who actually saw their wages rise) over that twenty year period" (Pastor and Carter 2009: 148, utilizing data from Borjas et al. 2010: 34). Giovanni Peri (2006) suggests an even lower impact, on the order of 1 percent, while David Card (2005) believes the overall impact on less-skilled workers is nonexistent when regional or metropolitan effects are taken into account. Assume that 3 percent is a reasonable figure, particularly since it leans disproportionately in the direction of those most worried about immigration. Using that standard, a joint effort by blacks and Latinos to raise the nation's minimum wage by, say, one dollar, would overcome about a century's worth of immigration-induced wage decline. Coalition, not competition, would therefore make the most sense.

Of course, all those data hold at the national level, but no one really lives there, and it's the local effects that are felt the most strongly. In an older but still relevant study on the Los Angeles region, Ong and Valenzuela (1996) found that recent Latino immigrants with low levels of education do increase African Americans job loss, but those African Americans who remained employed actually enjoy slight wage increases as a result of the complementary labor effect (175). In particular, African Americans indirectly have more opportunities as increases in immigration put more demand on public services, a sector wherein blacks are particularly concentrated (175). Ong and Valenzuela, however, pointedly argue that if the market weren't racially biased in the first place (that is, if we were to live in a country where racial inequality in, say, education, did not put blacks behind whites in work readiness), then competition between African Americans and Latinos wouldn't be an issue in the first place (166, 175).

It is quite possible, however, that the localized displacement impacts may have increased in recent years. Utilizing a novel procedure to calculate the share of undocumented Latino immigrants by industry, Pastor and Marcelli (2004) found that in California, wages and the number of positions did drop for black laborers in occupations that now have a large number of unauthorized immigrant employees. However, wages and employment in all other occupational groupings rose, echoing the complementary impact found earlier by Ong and Valenzuela. Pastor and Marcelli speculate that if individual characteristics—education, for example—are accounted for, then those blacks left behind in this phenomenon might be those with the least human capital (118) and suggest that policy attention should be focused on education rather than immigration.

Another area for attention may be labor market discrimination. Consider, for example, the median earnings of various ethnic groups at different levels of education in Los Angeles County. Note that African Americans who did not go to high school or dropped out fare worse than whites and Latinos. With either a high school diploma or some college, blacks regain their edge over Latinos throughout the remaining educational categories, something that suggests why the labor market competition may feel less pressing to African American professionals. Still, both groups experience a persistent gap with whites at all levels of education. Other evidence of employer preferences suggests that discrimination is a big issue for lower-skilled African Americans (Moss and Tilly 2001), something that seems apparent in the large

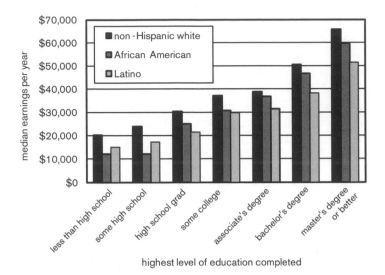

FIGURE 1.10. Median earnings, by race and educational category, 2005–7, Los Angeles County.

wage gap for blacks with less than a high school diploma, as shown in figure 1.10.[12]

Of course, another part of the picture is immigration status: L.A.'s Latino workforce includes a significant number of undocumented migrants, and so part of the lower returns on education reflect the advantage that employers take of those who are less secure workers. On the other hand, many employers prefer immigrant labor, not simply because of low wages, but also because immigrants often refer other immigrants into employment, something that lowers the cost of job searches for both the immigrant and the employer. William Julius Wilson (2009), who has recently tried to weave together structural and cultural reasons for poverty, argues that the "chronic poverty and exploitation in poor black neighborhoods tends to feed inclinations to distrust," and, therefore, black workers may also be less willing to recommend members of their neighborhood networks to employers, further limiting the "bridging" function associated with social capital (94). As economist Michael Stoll (2006) notes, these patterns lead black men to jobs for which applicants do not need a network to be hired, including public sector jobs that often rely on straightforward testing by civil service standards.

What does this mean for the composition of employment for African

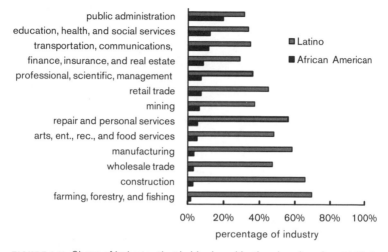

FIGURE 1.11. Share of industry that is black and Latino, Los Angeles, 2005–7.

Americans and Latinos? In figure 1.11, I look at the relative shares of blacks and Latinos in industrial sectors in Los Angeles. As can be seen, the highest Latino presence—apart from the very high percentage in the very small agricultural sector in the few parts of Los Angeles County that remain rural—is in construction; manufacturing; and repair and personal services. Arts, entertainment, recreation, and food services; wholesale trade; and retail trade are not far behind. While not shown in the graph, a more detailed breakdown reveals that the presence of specifically immigrant Latinos is disproportionately large in the same exact industries, showing that immigrants may actually crowd U.S-born Latinos more than they do African Americans. Blacks have an extraordinarily small footprint in construction, wholesale trade, and manufacturing; their largest shares are in public administration and education, health, and social services, as well as in transportation, communications, and utilities, again reflecting a drive to participate in industries that may rely on more formal procedures, like civil service exams, bus driving tests, and other objective tests that were precisely intended to avoid bias, discrimination, and favoritism inherent to hiring through networks.

The important role of public employment to black workers has led to some tension. Latinos have sometimes argued that their share of public employment should reflect population parity. While that makes some sense, a better measure might be the share of native-born Latinos who

TABLE 1.1   PERCENTAGE OF PUBLIC (VS. PRIVATE) EMPLOYMENT
AS A SHARE OF ETHNICITY

		White	Black	Latino, Not Immigrant	Black-Latino Gap
1990	L.A.	12.7	28.2	18.5	9.7
	U.S.	16.6	26.9	22.2	4.7
2000	L.A.	13.5	27.9	19.1	8.8
	U.S.	15.9	23.9	20.2	3.7
2005–7	L.A.	13.5	26.4	18.1	8.3
	U.S.	16.0	22.6	19.1	3.5

SOURCES: PERE analysis of 2005–7 ACS; and 1990 and 2000 U.S. Census data.

hold public sector jobs. Table 1.1 suggests a disparity between Latinos and blacks, although it is shrinking (see last column). Both African Americans and U.S.-born Latinos are more reliant on public employment than whites are, but a much larger share of the African American workforce is in the public sector; over time, the gap between the two has shrunk nearer to parity nationally, but the progress in reducing the gap in Los Angeles County has been slow. Still, it is notable that the share of whites holding public employment in Los Angeles actually rose slightly between 1990 and 2005–7, while it fell by nearly two percentage points for blacks and about half a percentage point for U.S.-born Latinos. As with immigration, competition in this arena *between* blacks and Latinos is misplaced; both groups have actually lost shares relative to whites.

Of course, it's not just jobs at stake: given the close proximity of the two populations in urban areas, many Latinos have been suggesting that some traditionally African American public institutions, including places like the downsized Martin Luther King Jr./Drew medical center in South L.A.,[13] should become more sensitive to the needs of a burgeoning Latino and immigrant population *and* diversify their workforces. However, it is no small thing to ask African Americans to relinquish the exact jobs they fought for years ago and, instead, enter sectors with less formal hiring structures that enable discrimination.

Another obfuscated issue is the degree of work effort and labor market disconnection as it relates to poverty. Analysts of urban poverty tend to suggest that African American poverty results mainly from joblessness, while Latino poverty is driven by low wages at steady jobs. In other work, we have shown that this is a bit of a mischaracterization

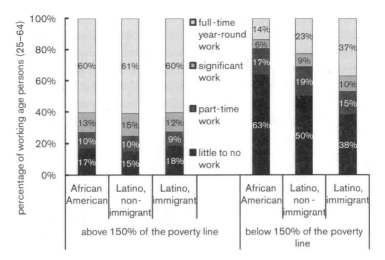

FIGURE 1.12. Black and Latino work efforts, by poverty status, Los Angeles, 2005–7. Work definitions are based on hours/week and weeks/year worked: (1) little or no work: less than 10 hours, less than 10 weeks; (2) part-time: at least 10 hours, at least 10 weeks; (3) significant work: more than 25 hours, more than 35 weeks; (4) full-time: at least 35 hours, at least 50 weeks.

at the national level once we account for nativity: African Americans and U.S.-born Latinos living below the poverty line have similar rates of full-time year-round work and other workforce attachment similarities (Pastor and Carter 2009). Figure 1.12 shows that the situation is dramatically different in Los Angeles, however, where a breakdown of work effort for blacks, U.S.-born Latinos, and immigrant Latinos shows very different patterns, particularly for those falling below the poverty line.

On the policy side, the challenge is that these two different routes to poverty—working and not working—call for very different strategies for improvement. Disconnection calls for job training and job placement, with the underlying model being one in which workers are provided long-term programming as they build a bridge back to the labor market; working poverty, on the other hand, calls for living wage strategies, rapid unionization, and training programs that occur in small doses, such as adult education either on the job or at night to accommodate work schedules.

One of the most significant issues of disconnection is incarceration and its aftermath. Nationally, black men are incarcerated a rate 6.7

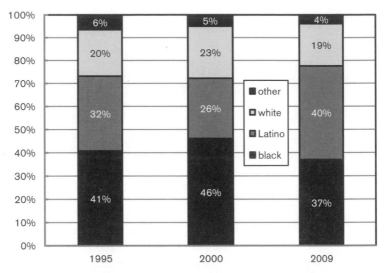

FIGURE 1.13. California State Prison, Los Angeles County, inmate population (men only). Source: State of California Department of Corrections, as analyzed by the Data Analysis Unit, Offender Information Services Branch. These data were requested by and e-mailed to PERE on June 11 and October 6, 2009.

times that of whites and 2.7 that of Latinos.[14] In Los Angeles in 2009, 37 percent of state prison inmates (men only) identified as African American, 40 percent as Hispanic, and 19 percent as white (see figure 1.13). Nationally, African Americans also compose the largest share of incarcerated people in all age categories (West and Sabol 2008), but in L.A., black men are the plurality (49 percent) only from ages 40 to 59; Latinos compose the majority (52 percent) of men aged 18–39. Across all ethnicities, the largest group of incarcerated men is in the age bracket 25–29 years, with 55 percent of them Latinos and 28 percent blacks.[15] This share of the population is squarely at the beginning of prime working age—and they will encounter persistent discrimination and disadvantage once they leave the system and try to make their way into communities and labor markets.

DEMOGRAPHY AND COALITIONS IN LOS ANGELES

Rather than suggesting that Latinos and blacks are squarely at odds with one another, the analysis above suggests Latinos and African Americans alike need better and more work. But building real coalitions also requires recognizing difference. Labor market disconnection is important for everyone, but it is particularly important for African Americans, especially those returning to the economy after prison. Major investments in adult education are important for everyone but particularly for immigrant Latinos, and key to this is a vast expansion of English classes, given that improving language skills can lead to significant increases in wages as well as enhanced mobility. Immigration does bring competition between groups, but that competition is overstated, as is the conflict around the higher shares of blacks in public sector employment, particularly when we understand how it is that public jobs have helped blacks move past discriminatory barriers and how both U.S.-born Latinos and blacks have seen their share of public employment slip. Popular rhetoric is correct in that there are some tensions, but those tensions are workable, and the benefits of working together should dominate.

Indeed, both groups share the key elements needed in a workforce agenda: a better performing education system at all levels, a broad commitment to new employment that can replace the role of manufacturing, and the sort of public transit system that will connect blacks and Latinos to jobs. But getting there will involve getting past the obvious agreements to what we have termed "uncommon common ground"—the places where conversations are tougher exactly because there are differences, trade-offs, and hopefully agreements about how to move forward together (Blackwell et al. 2010). This is the stuff of coalition building, and it has been preoccupying the attention of progressive organizers in Los Angeles for decades (Pastor and Pritchard 2012).

Indeed, black-brown coalitions have a long pedigree in Los Angeles (Pulido 2006), and in the words of one long-time Latino activist in Watts, Arturo Ybarra, "Day to day, we all get along" (Ciria-Cruz 2007). Part of this day-to-day living together is also the result of the heroic efforts of numerous community groups that have tried to go beyond a simple notion of "same struggle, same fight" and instead have forged a common strategy based on an honest discussion of differences. They have understood the nuances and realities of demographic change and workforce issues within the black Latino dynamic and used scalpels, not axes, to produce both better politics and better policy. They have helped inform others about respective histories of organizing for justice, including the civil rights struggle, the Chicano movement, and the leadership of immigrants in the revitalized labor movement. But they have also taken seriously the sense of economic and social displacement felt by African Americans as immigrants make use of the hard-won language of civil rights.[16]

These efforts to unite black and brown in Los Angeles are too many to name and analyze, ranging from the geographically focused Watts/Century Latino Organization, which Arturo Ybarra heads, to the regionwide Bus Riders Union, a highly successful effort to organize the mostly black and Latino users of mass transit in L.A. For reasons of space, I highlight here three efforts focused on workforce issues: the attempt by unions to enhance their black membership, the youth workforce development of the Community Coalition in South L.A., and the broader economic strategies pursued by Strategic Concepts in Organizing and Policy Education (SCOPE) and the Los Angeles Alliance for a New Economy (LAANE).

The union effort represents a 180-degree turn from L.A.'s history as the viciously anti-labor "wicked city" of the early twentieth century (Milkman 2006). The revitalization has occurred because of the mobilization of a largely immigrant workforce in service industries, such as hotels and cleaning. Indeed, one of the hallmark moments of the new labor movement was the Justice for Janitors campaign, which eventually led to a strike and the June 1990 demonstration in Century City, which drew an attack by police. The public and political backlash was significant enough to produce union contracts in nearly all Century City buildings, "the largest private sector organizing success among Latino immigrants since the United Farm Workers' victories nearly two decades earlier" (Waldinger et al. 1996: 1).

The 1990s brought a wave of service sector organizing, cresting when the janitors fought for a new contract in April 2000. Strikingly, their march and demonstration, again in Century City, was led by elected city officials and cheered on by bystanders, and it resulted in a 25 percent increase in wages over a three-year period, more than had been won in any other janitorial contract in the previous twenty years (Cleeland 2005). The union movement had also gained ground in terms of public policy, with the passage of a citywide living wage ordinance in 1997 and the winning of a community benefits agreement in 2001 that guaranteed that a majority of the jobs generated from the expansion of the Staples Center would be either living-wage or union. In order to ensure that African Americans would not be left behind and to shore up a black-Latino alliance, special efforts were undertaken. The Service Employees International Union (SEIU), the union that had led the janitorial campaign, launched the Five Days for Freedom campaign to sign up thousands of licensed security guards—a sector that is 70 percent African American in the region. Explicit in their campaign was the desire to bring economic benefits to black Angelenos: "If L.A.'s multibillion-dollar-a-year real estate industry paid security officers the same wages and benefits it has agreed to pay janitors, it would bring an estimated $100 million more a year into South Los Angeles, where most of the security officers live."[17] In November 2006, more than five thousand guards won the right to unionize.[18]

In the same vein, UNITE-HERE! Local 11 is using collective bargaining to ensure that African American workers are hired by the hotel industry. Starting in 2005 with the Beverly Hilton, UNITE-HERE! Local 11 began securing contracts with diversity clauses that require hotels to hire African American workers, among others—clauses now ubiquitous in UNITE-HERE! contract negotiations. However, managers have struggled to fulfill their obligation, because, they say, many African American applicants are not work ready. In October 2009, UNITE-HERE! held its first week-long Hospitality Diversity "Bootcamp" in collaboration with hotel managers and LAANE, mainly intended for out-of-work African Americans. UNITE-HERE! is working on both the supply and demand, making sure that hotels are hiring the right people and that those people are ready.[19]

The organizers at the Community Coalition of South Los Angeles focus on youth and workforce readiness. While CoCo (the organization's nickname) started with ousting liquor stores from street corners, mostly because of concerns that the stores were crime magnets making life difficult for nearby residents, the organization now has a focus on bringing together black and Latino youth to agitate for better education and better job possibilities. In 2005, the mostly black and Latino students led the Equal Access to College Prep Classes campaign, an effort to ensure that schools in South L.A. and elsewhere in the region would provide the same platform for university entrance, and they won in a 6–1 vote by the Los Angeles Unified School District.[20] Amid cheers of "the students united will never be defeated," then CoCo organizer, Alberto Retana, said that this "woke up a whole new generation of activists."

Interestingly, that generation, as well as their parents and other community members, turned to a whole new fight: the creation of the Architecture, Construction, and Engineering (ACE) Academy. CoCo members and allied organizations, specifically the building trades, strategized about how to prepare students straight out of high school for construction jobs and, simultaneously, for college, where they would have a leg up in becoming engineers or architects. With the hopes of moving toward greater parity in the building trades, a sector that provides quality jobs and has seen some inroads by Latinos, especially in the lower-end laborers category, CoCo originally tried to house the ACE Academy at Dorsey High School, an institution with a relatively high percentage of black students (recall figures 1.5 and 1.6). But because there was more receptivity at Locke High School, the academy opened there in the fall of 2009 with the hopes of equipping its students with an applied, rigorous education and options after graduation—ensuring that the next generation of black and Latino workers will have more opportunities than the last.[21]

Finally, two community-based organizations have been especially regional in their strategies for restoring lower-income neighborhoods. When the City of Los Angeles awarded a public subsidy to DreamWorks for its entertainment center development, a condition of that award was a program to train residents from lower-income areas. That condition was granted only because of the pressure applied by Strategic Concepts in Organizing and Policy Education. SCOPE has also helped create a health care training program and has now launched a "green jobs" campaign, mobilizing its mostly black and Latino membership along the way. The Los Angeles Alliance for a New Economy is a labor-affiliated think tank that has worked with black and Latino residents of Inglewood to stop a low-wage Wal-Mart from setting up in the area and also led a recent effort to clean up the port trucking industry while securing better working conditions for its mostly immigrant Latino drivers.

Profiled extensively in Pastor et al. 2009, these groups have built coalitions by broadening their sights beyond their South L.A. sites to the wider region; as the founder of SCOPE, Anthony Thigpenn says, "If you want to help South L.A. you can't talk about South L.A. apart from the region" (121). Scaling up from the neighborhood to the region helps put black-Latino neighborhood issues in perspective. The regional level helps the organizations discover more resources to be tapped, more sectors with whom to forge alliances, and a larger low-income and minority constituency for their broad social justice agenda.[22]

While their scope may be regional, particularly concerning jobs, the organizing has been decidedly local, personal, and nuanced. LAANE and the unions have paid attention to the inclusion of African

Americans, even though the labor movement has been revitalized mostly by Latino immigrant constituencies. CoCo has consistently groomed a youth leadership capable of bridging the black-Latino divide in an area of the region, South L.A., where the most day-to-day contact is. SCOPE (see below) has hosted black-Latino dialogues for their members, creating a space to stop and reflect amidst their busy work.

In his landmark study of the Industrial Areas Foundation, an interfaith and interethnic network, Mark Warren (2001) notes that these conversations about race are like those of marriages: it's not a question of whether conflict will come up; it's how you deal with it (155). Covering an earlier period, Regalado (1994) argued that without open and honest dialogue, "healing" moments don't happen, and multiracial coalitions stay stuck in symbolism. That describes the Bradley era; the delight about a black mayor was matched by the lack of neighborhood progress for low-income communities, fueling the cognitive dissonance that produced the L.A. civil unrest. The newest efforts are focused on the heart of the matter—neighborhood crowding, institutional change, and workforce competition—and the hard conversations necessary to defray tension, build trust, and keep the focus on developing solutions.

THE LOS ANGELES AHEAD

In October 2007, shortly after I had moved back to Los Angeles to take a job at USC, I was asked by organizers at SCOPE to help lead a conversation to launch a new "green jobs" initiative. One would have thought that the initial discussion would have been mostly about environment constraints, climate change, and workforce development, but no: I was asked, along with Karen Bass (the founder of CoCo and the first African American female to be speaker of a state assembly) to lead a group of constituents through a discussion of black-brown tensions.

With a crowd of 150 eager to engage, Bass and I did a tag team presentation about South L.A.'s past and present, then opened it up to the audience. The questions and statements were heartfelt and sometimes just a bit rude. One young man related, "I used to like Mexicans, but I just don't like these new Mexicans." An older man suggested that "Latinos are taking jobs because these young black guys don't want to work." It was clearly not the polite chit-chat of an ethnic studies colloquium, but it was definitely real.

And it produced something else in the end that was very real: starting with the differences and working through the tensions, SCOPE was able to organize a broad coalition that eventually won a city ordinance in April 2009 for the "green" retrofitting of city buildings, including a priority on those buildings in inner-city communities and policies that included local hiring, creating career pathways, and promoting unionization through project labor agreements.[23] In terms of dealing with economic revival and social justice, more remains to be accomplished, to be sure, but getting there will involve the sort of honest, frank, and forthright discussion that SCOPE has modeled, all in the service of fortifying the black-Latino alliance that is an important part of the rebirth of progressive politics in Los Angeles.

Despite the doom and gloom many observers offer—something about L.A. just screams for *noir*—the region has come a long way. The city has just experienced eight years of a Latino mayor with deep roots in the progressive community and a long history of commitments to civil rights issues. City officials are responding to economic justice movements with a range of innovative new policies to promote job creation, extend financial services, and improve education. All of this is taking place on a landscape scarred by decades of deindustrialization and now battered by the economic collapse that started in 2008. But we are a far cry from the pessimism—about both the economy and race relations—that the region felt after the 1992 civil unrest.

Multiracial and transformative organizing has been essential to restoring that sense of hope. As for the Los Angeles ahead, the way won't be easy. It will require tough conversation as well as clear policy to overcome historical and current racial and ethnic tension. But one of the ways that analysts in the academy can help activists on the ground is to provide the facts and frameworks that directly challenge the dominant narrative of competition. Competition, after all, may be part of the truth, but making it the whole story serves to divide and disempower, perhaps explaining exactly why it has become the dominant and singular portrayal of black-brown relations in L.A.

Competition isn't the whole story at all. Groups like LAANE, SCOPE, and CoCo are seeking both to reshape power structures and to build relationships among their members along the way. Staffing them is a generation of community organizers that seems attuned to the concept of interwoven destiny, and being organized by them is a generation of black and Latino youth that have been raised in adjacent homes in Los Angeles, unlike their parents. Their relationship is much more "we" than it is "us" and "them," and this is exactly the model that Los Angeles will have to embrace if the hype about black-Latino conflict is to be set aside in favor of an alliance that can transform this region and, one hopes, the rest of metropolitan America.

Acknowledgments: Thanks to Josh Kun and Laura Pulido for their encouragement of this essay, to the two of them and to two anonymous reviewers for their comments on early drafts, to Vanessa Carter for her able research assistance, and to the Evelyn and Walter Haas Jr. Fund for supporting the research underlying this work.

NOTES

1. 2005–7 American Community Survey data, calculated by the Program for Environmental and Regional Equity (PERE) using American FactFinder.

2. 1940–90 data from Ethington 2000: 7, chart 2.2. 2000 and 2005–7 are PERE calculations of U.S. Census and American Community Survey data.

3. The Supreme Court decisions *Shelley v. Kraemer* (1948) and *Barrows v. Jackson* (1953) ended racially restrictive housing covenants (Sides 2003: 95). However, African Americans in Los Angeles had been challenging such restrictions since 1919 (Sides 2006: 120).

4. There figures have been modified from Pastor and Ortiz 2009. They now include Dorsey High School and use 2008–9 school data, instead of 2004–5 data.

5. Population density was calculated by dividing the 2000 total population estimate for each census tract by residential land area. Residential land area was generated by taking the product of total tract area from the 2000 census and the percentage of residential land area for each tract, derived by using information from the 2001 U.S. Geologic Survey Land Cover Characterization Program. All census tracts were then ranked by population density into "deciles" (ten sets of census tracts divided into even groupings by density), and the 2000 racial/ethnic composition was calculated for all tracts within each decile.

6. The highest-density tracts do include a strong share of whites, but these are places like Westwood, Santa Monica, and the land-scarce beach areas, where density is largely related to gentrification.

7. The report also notes that most gang violence of these two groups is actually Latino on Latino and black on black hate crimes. In 2007, "Latino gang members were responsible for 34% of Latino on Black crimes. In contrast, gang members were responsible for 42% of Black on Latino crimes" (Los Angeles County Commission on Human Relations 2008: 10).

8. This is consistent with a large body of other research that has found significant disparities in environmental amenities by race and income in Los Angeles; for a summary, see Pastor et al. 2005.

9. The wage and income data analysis is by PERE, using the 2005–7 Integrated Public Use Microdata Series and U.S. Census Bureau data. These aver-

ages are median figures based on wage and salary income. Poverty is defined as being in a household where the total income is below 150 percent of the federally defined poverty line, an adjustment to account for the high cost of living in Los Angeles.

10. Latinos may have lower wages, but their households generally are larger and include more workers who work longer hours, so family and household incomes are higher than those for African Americans.

11. All analysis in this paragraph is by PERE, using 1970, 1980, 1990, 2000, 2005–7 IPUMS and U.S. Census Bureau data.

12. Acs and Loprest (2009: 7) also found that even when adjusting for individual, work, and employer characteristics, blacks suffer wage discrimination in low-income work, but Latinos, compared to whites with similar characteristics, do not.

13. After a prolonged debate and against community wishes, the Los Angeles County Board of Supervisors voted to downsize MLK/Drew medical center from a full-service hospital to a "multi-service ambulatory care center." Efforts are currently underway to restore it to a full-service hospital.

14. Based on the percentage of each racial/ethnic group imprisoned, the data reflect the ratio of average imprisonment from 2000 to 2008. Original data taken from the U.S. Department of Justice, Bureau of Justice Statistics, "Prison and Jail Inmates at Midyear," for 1999 through 2008, available at www.ojp.usdoj.gov/bjs/prisons.htm. Data include persons under age eighteen. Based on calculations provided in Pastor and Carter 2009.

15. Data source: the State of California Department of Corrections, as analyzed by the Data Analysis Unit, Offender Information Services Branch. These data are for the California State Prison, Los Angeles County only, in June 2009. They do not include city or county institutions, jails, or female offenders, nor is there any assurance that these inmates came from Los Angeles County as opposed to other parts of the state. These data were requested by and e-mailed to PERE on June 11 and October 6, 2009.

16. For a practical suggestions about these conversations, see the Opportunity Agenda's "African Americans and Immigrants: Moving Forward Together," available at http://opportunityagenda.org/files/field_file/African%20Americans%20and%20Immigrants.pdf.

17. "Security Officers, Black Clergy, Community Groups from South LA to Launch Intensive One-Week Worker Outreach Drive to Fight Poverty Conditions in Private Security Industry," Los Angeles, PRNewswire, June 26, 2006, http://finance.jsonline.com/jsonline/news/read/124369/security_officers. For more on the SEIU's nationwide movement to unionize security guards, see www.StandForSecurity.org.

18. See www.standforsecurity.org/, or previously, www.standforsecurity coalition.com/news/0611220urweekly.html, accessed March 20, 2009.

19. Phone conversation with union organizer Donald Wilson of UNITE-HERE! Local 11 on September 30, 2009.

20. For a video recap of the campaign: www.youtube.com/watch?v = sb GPP-gnVIM&feature = player_embedded.

21. Phone conversation with Alberto Retana, of the Community Coalition, on September 29, 2009.

22. See chapter 4 of Pastor et al. 2009 for the analysis of "going regional" in Los Angeles.

23. For more, see the Los Angeles Apollo Alliance's press release from April 7, 2009, "Los Angeles Adopts Landmark Green Jobs Ordinance," at www .scopela.org/article.php?list = type&type = 35.

REFERENCES

Acs, G., and P. Loprest. 2009. "Working for Cents on the Dollar: Race and Ethnic Wage Gaps in the Noncollege Labor Market." Low-Income Working Families, Paper 13. Washington DC: Urban Institute.

Blackwell, A., S. Kwoh, and M. Pastor. 2010. *Uncommon Common Ground: Race and America's Future.* New York: W.W. Norton.

Borjas, G., R. Freeman, L. Katz, J. DiNardo, and J. Abowd. 1997. "How Much Do Immigration and Trade Affect Labor Market Outcomes?" *Brookings Papers on Economic Activity* 1: 1–90.

Borjas, G., J. Grogger, and F. Hanson. 2010. "Immigration and the Economic Status of African-American Men." *Economica* 77 (306): 255–82.

Briggs, V. 2004. "The Economic Well-Being of Black Americans." In *The Impact of Immigration on African Americans,* ed. S. Shulman, 1–26. New Brunswick, NJ: Transaction Publishers.

California Budget Project. 2006. *Left Behind: California Workers and Their Families in Changing Los Angeles.* Special Report.

Card, D. 2005. "Is the New Immigration Really So Bad?" *Economic Journal* 115, no. 506 (October): 300–323.

Ciria-Cruz, R.P. 2007. "To Live and Let Live in South Los Angeles." *NACLA Report on the Americas* 40, no. 3 (May–June): 37(5).

Cleeland, N. 2005. "L.A. Janitors OK Contract." *Los Angeles Times*, April 25.

Dorfman, L., and V. Schiraldi. 2001. "Off Balance: Youth, Race and Crime in the News." Building Blocks for Youth. www.buildingblocksforyouth.org/media/media.pdf.

Ethington, P.J. 2000. *Segregated Diversity: Race-Ethnicity, Space, and Political Fragmentation in Los Angeles County, 1940–1994.* Los Angeles: University of Southern California.

Ethington, P.J., W.H. Frey, and D. Myers. 2001. *The Racial Resegregation of Los Angeles County.* University of Southern California Race Contours Project, Public Research Report 2001–04.

Garcia, M. 2001. *A World of Its Own: Race, Labor, and Citrus in the Making of Greater Los Angeles, 1900–1970.* Chapel Hill: University of North Carolina Press.

Los Angeles County Commission on Human Relations. 2008. *2007 Hate Crime Report.* http://humanrelations.co.la.ca.us/hatecrime/hatecrimereport .htm, accessed March 20, 2009.

Marcelli, E. 2004. "From the Barrio to the 'Burbs? Immigration and the Dynamics of Suburbanization." In *Up against the Sprawl*, ed. J. Wolch, M. Pastor, and P. Dreier. Minneapolis: University of Minnesota Press, 123–150.

Milkman, R. 2006. *L.A. Story: Immigrant Workers and the Future of the U.S. Labor Movement*. New York: Russell Sage Foundation.

Morello-Frosch, R., and B. Jesdale. 2008. Unpublished impervious surface and tree cover data. Data for this analysis were derived from U.S. Geological Survey's National Land Cover Dataset 2001, www.mrlc.gov/nlcd.php, accessed on June 20, 2007; and from ESRI's ArcMap census boundary files, www.census.gov/geo/www/cob/bdy_files.html, accessed June 6, 2008.

Morello-Frosch, R., M. Pastor Jr., and J. Sadd. 2001. "Environmental Justice and Southern California's 'Riskscape': The Distribution of Air Toxics Exposures and Health Risks among Diverse Communities." *Urban Affairs Review* 36 (4): 551–78.

Morello-Frosch, R., M. Pastor Jr., J. Sadd, and S.B. Shonkoff. 2009. The Climate Gap: Inequalities in How Climate Change Hurts Americans and How to Close the Gap. Report. USC Program for Environmental and Regional Equity, Los Angeles. http://dornsife.usc.edu/pere/documents/FacingThe ClimateGap_web.pdf.

Morrison, P., and I. Lowry. 1994. "A Riot of Color: The Demographic Setting." In *The Los Angeles Riots: Lessons for the Urban Future*, ed. M. Baldassare, ch. 2. Boulder, CO: Westview Press.

Moss, P., and C. Tilly. 2001. *Stories Employers Tell: Race, Skill, and Hiring in America*. Pp. 165–92. New York: Russell Sage Foundation.

Nieva, Chrisshonna Grant. 2009. "Racialized Representations in the *Los Angeles Times*." Unpublished manuscript, University of Southern California, Los Angeles.

Oke, T. 1973. "City Size and the Urban Heat Island." *Atmospheric Environment* 7: 769–79.

Ong, P., and A. Valenzuela. 1996. "The Labor Market: Immigrant Effects and Racial Disparities." In *Ethnic Los Angeles*, ed. R. Waldinger and M. Bozorgmehr. New York: Russell Sage Foundation.

Pastor, M. 1995 "Economic Inequality, Latino Poverty, and the Civil Unrest in Los Angeles." *Economic Development Quarterly* 9 (3): 238–58.

Pastor, M., C. Benner, and M. Matsuoka. 2009. *This Could Be the Start of Something Big: How Social Movements for Regional Equity are Reshaping Metropolitan America*. Ithaca, NY: Cornell University Press.

Pastor, M., and V. Carter. 2009. "Conflict, Consensus, and Coalition: Economic and Workforce Development Strategies for African Americans and Latinos." *Race and Social Problems* 1 (3).

Pastor, M., and E. Marcelli. 2004. "Somewhere over the Rainbow? African Americans, Unauthorized Mexican Immigration, and Coalition Building." In *The Impact of Immigration on African Americans*, ed. S. Shulman, 107–36. New Brunswick, NJ: Transaction Publishers.

Pastor, M., and R. Ortiz. 2009. "Immigrant Integration in Los Angeles: Strategic Directions for Funders." Program for Environmental and Regional

Equity. Available at http://college.usc.edu/geography/ESPE/documents/immigrant_integration.pdf.

Pastor, M., and M. Pritchard. 2012. "L.A. Rising: The 1992 Civil Unrest, the Arc of Social Justice Organizing, and the Lessons for Today's Movement Building." Report, Program for Environmental and Regional Equity, Los Angeles. http://dornsife.usc.edu/pere/publications/LA_Rising.cfm.

Pastor, M., J. Sadd, and R. Morello-Frosch. 2005. "Environmental Inequity in Metropolitan Los Angeles." In *The Quest for Environmental Justice: Human Rights and the Politics of Pollution*, ed. R. Bullard, 108–24. San Francisco: Sierra Club Books.

Peri, G. 2006. "Rethinking the Effects of Immigration on Wages: New Data and Analysis from 1990–2004." *Immigration Policy in Focus* 5 (8). www.immigrationpolicy.org/images/File/infocus/IPC%20Rethinking%20Wages,%2011–2006.pdf.

Pulido, L. 2006. *Black, Brown, Yellow, and Left: Radical Activism in Los Angeles*. Berkeley: University of California Press.

Regalado, J. 1994. "Community Coalition-Building." In *The Los Angeles Riots: Lessons for the Urban Future*, ed. M. Baldassare, ch. 9. Boulder, CO: Westview Press.

Sewell, A. 2011. "Hate-Crime Arrests Bring Up Memories." *Los Angeles Times*, June 19.

Sides, J. 2003. *L.A. City Limits: African American Los Angeles from the Great Depression to the Present*. Berkeley: University of California Press.

———. 2006. "A Simple Quest for Dignity: African American Los Angeles since World War II." In *City of Promise: Race and Historical Change in Los Angeles*, ed. M. Schiesl and M.M. Dodge, 109–36. Claremont, CA: Regina Books.

Sister, C., J. Wolch, J. Wilson, A. Linder, M. Seymour, J. Byrne, and J. Swift. 2007. *The Green Visions Plan for 21st Century Southern California*. 14. Park and Open Space Resources in the Green Visions Plan Area, University of Southern California GIS Research Laboratory and Center for Sustainable Cities, Los Angeles, California.

Soja, E. 1998. "Los Angeles, 1965–1992: From Crisis-Generated Restructuring-Generated Crisis." In *The City: Los Angeles and Urban Theory at the End of the Twentieth Century*, eds. A.J. Scott and E. Soja, chp. 14. Berkeley: University of California Press.

Stoll, M. 2006. "Workforce Development in Minority Communities." In *Jobs and Economic Development in Minority Communities*, ed. P. Ong and A. Loukaitou-Sideris, ch. 4. Philadelphia: Temple University Press.

Vaca, N. 2004. *The Presumed Alliance: The Unspoken Conflict between Latinos and Blacks and What It Means for America*. New York: Rayo/Harper Collins Publishers.

Waldinger, R., C. Erickson, R. Milkman, D.J.B. Mitchell, A. Valenzuela, K. Wong, and M. Zeitlin. 1996. *Helots No More: A Case Study of the Justice for Janitors Campaign in Los Angeles*. Los Angeles: Lewis Center for Regional Policy Studies, School of Public Policy and Social Research, UCLA.

Warren, M. 2001. *Dry Bones Rattling: Community Building to Revitalize American Democracy.* Princeton, NJ: Princeton University Press.

West, H.C., and W.J. Sabol. 2008 *Prison Inmates at Midyear 2008.* NCJ 225619, U.S. Bureau of Justice Statistics, Washington DC.

Wilson, W.J. 2009. *More Than Just Race: Being Black and Poor in the Inner City.* New York: W.W. Norton.

Wolff, G. 1992. "The Making of a Third World City? Latino Labor and the Restructuring of the L.A. Economy." Paper for the Seventeenth International Congress of the Latino American Studies Association, Los Angeles California, September.

Zhou, M. 2001. "Contemporary Immigration and the Dynamics of Race and Ethnicity." In *America Becoming: Racial Trends and Their Consequences,* vol. 1, ed. N. Smelser, W.J. Wilson, and F. Mitchell, 200–42. National Research Council Commission on Behavioral and Social Sciences and Education. Washington DC: National Academy Press.

2

Banking on the Community

Mexican Immigrants' Experiences in
a Historically African American Bank in
South Central Los Angeles, 1970–2007

ABIGAIL ROSAS

The 1992 Los Angeles uprisings caused massive destruction throughout the South Central Los Angeles region. Businesses, homes, and lives were lost all in outrage to yet another instance of state-sanctioned violence inflicted on African American and Latino bodies as the white police officers who brutally beat Rodney King a year prior went unpunished. African Americans and Latinos alike took to the streets as their economic, political, and social livelihoods were severely limited as a result of poverty, disinvestment, and injustice. The acquittal of the police officers was the last straw in years of shattered dreams and opportunities. One business lost in those tumultuous three days in April was Broadway Federal Bank, one of the few long-standing economic institutions in the community. The chairman of Broadway Federal at the time, Paul Hudson, expressed his commitment to rebuild the bank. He explained that his obligation was to the community, as he promised to continue to serve the people most affected by the uprising in South Central Los Angeles.[1] In the months that followed, the bank opened its doors in a temporary modular building across the street from the original building to continue serving the needs of committed and long-term patrons of the bank's original location.

On December 5, 1999, the bank moved from this temporary location at the corner of Forty-Fifth Street and Broadway to its new location at the intersection of Martin Luther King Boulevard and Figueroa Street to create a more visible profile. To residents in the community it looks like a typical small local bank; however, embedded within its walls is a long history of struggle and pride that was transferred from the old building to this new building. In the main corridor, Richard Wyatt's vibrant *Sunrise on Central Avenue* mural celebrates the achievements of architect Paul Williams, gospel singer Mahalia Jackson, jazz musicians Buddy Collette and Duke Ellington, labor activist César Chávez, and the bank's founder, H. Claude Hudson. It also features quotes that speak to African American history that not only illustrate a history of struggle but also point to this bank's management's commitment to honoring and nurturing its African American patrons' sense of community and history within its walls. By 1992, and most especially by the unveiling of the new building in 1999, the bank not only served the needs of long-term African American patrons but also Latino patrons. The presence of César Chávez on the mural is a symbolic move to acknowledge the growing presence of Latino patronage of the bank.

Reflecting on what happened in April 1992, Paul Hudson speculated that knowing the history of the bank and its commitment to serving the needs of South Central Los Angeles residents in general, and African Americans in particular, might have spared the original bank from being burned down during the uprising:

> We didn't think it was going to happen. I mean this had happened before . . . in Watts, and we didn't have any problems in 1965. I didn't think we were going to have any problems in 1992. But we probably wouldn't have, but it went on for so long, and people were very drunk, very drunk, and the demographic change affected us because the Hispanic population didn't really get the history of the bank. I think they saw us as a federal institution, not a part of the frustration everyone felt, as part the federal government. So instead of seeing us as a community bank they saw us as a federal bank.[2]

Hudson suggests that the fact that the Latino community was unaware of the bank's commitment to all South Central Los Angeles residents, along with high levels of intoxication and discontent toward the government, led to the demise of the original building. However, it is not clear that Hudson had made a concerted effort to inform Latinos of what a "community bank" really represents. At this point, one cannot know definitively who burned the bank in those three days of civil unrest, as to this day no arrests have been made. It could very well have been African American and Latino residents who were not bank patrons. Nonetheless, what is evident is that the bank's hiring of Latino employees starting in the late 1980s to cater to its growing Latino clientele was not enough to inspire Latino patrons to consider Broadway Federal as more than just a place to bank or worth being protected.

Understanding Paul Hudson's conceptualization of the on-the-ground transformation and inner workings of Broadway Federal and its place in South Central Los Angeles and *his* relationship to this bank's history offers a unique opportunity to investigate how institutions having a long presence and commitment to a geographic and racial community confront and deal with racial demographic change. Paul Hudson's framing of the bank's goals through its mission statement provides an opportunity to interrogate the emergence and growth of this bank and its relationship to African American progress. The mission statement speaks to the bank's commitment to serve the needs of underserved communities. As it aims to "serve the real estate, business and financial needs of customers in underserved urban communities with a commitment to excellent service, profitability, and sustained growth."[3] The bank's goals are to serve the needs of communities who in the past have not been seen as profitable clients, irrespective of race. However, in an interview with Paul Hudson he explains his relationship to the community,

> A community bank is that which is known in the community, is familiar with the leadership in the community, active in social and political activities, and in this case there is a defined community. In this case, it is the African American community of South Los Angeles. And this has been pretty much throughout the generations. This has been because we have consistently been active on city and county commissions, active in political campaigns, active on nonprofit boards. And this is true from 1946 until today. And will continue to be so.[4]

Three generations of Hudsons have served as chairmen over the course of the bank's trajectory.[5] This family's commitment to serving the needs of its African American patrons illustrates an attitude that at times takes hold in this region's politics as leaders, entrepreneurs, and institutions fail to fully understand and grapple with the ways they must adapt and reconceptualize their relationship to the community in the wake of demographic change. As chairman, Hudson expresses the goal of a "community bank" in terms of "the African American community of South Los Angeles," as well as more generally in terms of a broad racial and class category of "underserved community." Thus, he employs language and discourse that obscure how Latinos have played an active role in the bank's trajectory and growth (most especially in the last few decades). His use of language can be understood as illustrating the complexity of how leaders in a racial community must deploy a discourse that is attuned to historical legacy and emergent change. In an effort to simultaneously honor their legacy and generate profits, the Hudson family has made retaining longtime African American patronage a priority by emphasizing their historical commitment to South Central Los Angeles's African American community. The visual cues on the bank's walls and racial discourse by Paul Hudson attempt to minimize African American patrons' sense of alienation as well as minimize the reality that Latinos are a growing majority in the residential community and in the bank's patronage.

Hudson's reflection on the loss of the bank during the uprisings is intimately tied to the ways he understands and envisions the bank as much more than an economic center—as also a cultural, political, and social community center for South Central Los Angeles residents that should be protected. The scholarly literature on minority-owned banks has largely focused on the economic longevity of African American banks and the growth of Asian American banks. This scholarship has centered on discussing the importance of race as the organizing principle and success of minority-owned banks.[6] An investigation into Broadway Federal aims not only to build on the literature on minority-owned banks but also to document how an institution that imagines itself as much more than an economic institution responds to demographic change. These elements have yet to be addressed within this literature. Also, Broadway Federal serves as a prime location to investigate how a bank has thrived in a community for over sixty years when other banks have historically shied away from this community because of the limited economic and business opportunities and high levels of poverty. Through historicizing the Hudson's family's relationship to Broadway Federal Bank's emergence and management, I argue that a deep-seated commitment to African American patrons' sense of community and progress has contributed to Paul Hudson's complex and often times contradictory discourse and understanding of community and change. Latino and African American patrons of Broadway Federal and residents of South Central Los Angeles are also making sense of not only changes in the city streets but also their relationship and banking practices within a bank whose longevity has depended on the African American community and whose commitment has been to that community. By discussing the banking practices of community leaders, entrepreneurs, and patrons in relationship to one another, one begins to understand the difficulty of letting go of a race-based politics for a broader community-based politics. Such considerations open a space to understand how Latino settlement into South Central Los Angeles has not only transformed its streets but also ushered in new economic, political, and social realities.

THE NEED FOR A BANK IN SOUTH CENTRAL LOS ANGELES

In the 1920s and 1930s, African American community leaders spearheaded a host of different causes and businesses. They began by establishing a series of financial institutions that would cater to the African American community. In the late 1920s and 1930s, Liberty Savings and Loan, Golden State Mutual Life Insurance Company, Morris Plan Loan Company, and Unity Finance Company opened storefronts throughout Los Angeles for the growing number of African American migrants in Los Angeles. The most successful of these organizations was Golden State, as it was at the forefront of providing millions of dollars in loans to a growing middle-class African American community in South Central. This organization stood apart from other "mom and pop" shops that opened throughout South Central Los Angeles, and provided the model and impetus behind the support for opening a "race enterprise" that would "take care of your own."[7]

Broadway Federal Bank emerged in the post–World War II period to specially serve the needs of African Americans when banks throughout Los Angeles refused service to them. African American families' applications for home loans and general banking services were routinely denied. This was especially important, as the African American community grew exponentially in the West during the post–World War II decades. The African American population in the West grew from 1 percent to 8 percent. From 1940 to 1970, the African American community in Los Angeles grew faster than in other metropolitan cities in the country, as its population increased from 63,744 to almost 763,000.[8] Also in the twenty years following the war, African Americans made their greatest economic advances as they joined the industrial, manufacturing, and aviation workforce and acquired union jobs throughout Los Angeles's booming economy.

Real estate broker H. J. Howard realized that the largest impediment for many African Americans to becoming homeowners was that major lending institutions considered them to be character and financial risks. In the fall of 1946, middle-class, professional, and prominent African American men and women living in South Central Los

Angeles, like H. J. Howard (real estate broker), H. Claude Hudson (dentist and president of the Los Angeles NAACP branch), Paul Williams (architect), Earl Grant (businessman), Thomas Griffith Jr. (city judge), Helen Douglas, and Ellen Taylor aggressively pursued and secured the first federal charter for Broadway Federal Savings and Loan. They envisioned and committed themselves to Broadway Federal's satisfaction of African American South Central Los Angeles residents' banking needs. Through exhaustive community organizing and church fundraisers they financed the federal charter and acquisition of property on 4325 South Broadway Street in South Central Los Angeles (hence the name Broadway Federal).[9] Finally, on January 11, 1947, these men and women's dreams became a reality when Broadway Federal Savings and Loan opened its doors and welcomed the general public with a grand inaugural celebration that celebrated the "foresight and initiative taken by the Negro organizers of Broadway Federal."[10] As H. J. Howard, chairman of Broadway Federal, explained days prior to the opening, "We recognize that numerous persons, principally Negroes, have been long sufferers from rank discriminatory policies employed by many home loan establishments. This has served only to place these people at the mercy of clever loan 'sharks' and similar fly-by-night setups. Our organization has declared war on these unfair policies and seeks instead to inject into the picture fair treatment and lower rates of interest to our customers."[11]

Broadway Federal was the first Black-owned financial institution in Los Angeles and the second in the nation, secured and supervised by the federal government. It had the financial capital and resources to cater to the growing African American community. Bank founders considered Broadway Federal the core financial institution by and for the African American community. Their struggle and commitment to transform banking into a fair and accessible process for African Americans framed their mission in the late 1940s and have had a direct bearing on the continued mission of the bank. The founders continually reassured the African American community that their bank was different from other banks in the region, as it, in fact, was much more than a financial institution; it was a cultural enterprise designed to serve African Americans' particular needs.

H. Claude Hudson's tenure as chairman of Broadway Federal was from 1949 to 1973. As chairman, he set the groundwork for Broadway Federal to be seen as an economic necessity for the African American community of South Central Los Angeles. His commitment to helping the community was intimately tied to his experience of growing up in the U.S. South and moving to California in search of a better opportunity for his family. He was born in Alexandria, Louisiana, in 1896. In 1929, he arrived in Los Angeles and established his dental practice in a building designed by Paul Williams across the street from important African American locations, like the Dunbar Hotel and Golden State Mutual Life Insurance Company in the heart of Central Avenue.[12] His presence at the heart of the commercial and cultural district in African American Los Angeles and his work for the National Association for the Advancement of Colored People catapulted him, and his family, to the center of African American Los Angeles. He was active in his local NAACP branch in Louisiana, and his migration west did not change his unwavering commitment to the organization. In the late 1920s, he was instrumental in reviving the NAACP's branch in Los Angeles.[13] Hudson's activism within the NAACP was that of a commitment to attaining equality for African Americans. This was a source of joy and dedication. His commitment to building an equal political and social world also included the African American community's economic prosperity. His visible public persona within the African American community and the NAACP rendered his work in Broadway Federal an extension of his mission for social, political, and economic African American equality.

Hudson's activism within the NAACP did not waver as he worked arduously to further the bank's significance in the community. Part of his initiative within the bank was to actively recruit and train African American bank employees. He considered this part of a larger political project to educate and train future African American professionals. In 1947, one would rarely find African American men and women working as employees in commercial banks throughout the region. In an oral history Hudson stated that when the board of directors considered the workforce behind the bank, they agreed that it had to be representative of the community. As such, in the first few years of the bank its workforce was biracial, both African American and white employees.[14]

By the late 1950s, Hudson had accomplished his mission of hiring and training the next generation of the bank's accountants and tellers. Boasting that Broadway Federal was one of the fastest growing associations in South Central Los Angeles, Joan Penn Lockett stated that it was "just like a big, happy family," and "the community as a whole should be proud of Broadway Federal because it is modern in every way and completely equipped in handling customers' business efficiently."[15]

The positive appraisals of pride, honor, and a family-like employment environment serve to render Broadway Federal as not only a financial entity tied to the local community but also one that is intimately tied to the politics and economic growth of the African American community. The postwar era was a period of immense economic gains for African American Los Angeles, a period in which Broadway Federal experienced its largest growth. The *Los Angeles Sentinel*, the largest and longest-running African American newspaper in Los Angeles, ran a series of articles promoting Broadway Federal as a vital force helping African American families realize their homeownership dreams and open savings accounts, as well as providing employment to the educated and brightest African Americans in the community.[16]

The *Los Angeles Sentinel*'s coverage and photos of Broadway Federal showcased Black employees serving Black patrons. These photos inspired community patronage and enabled African Americans to see themselves as part of the success of the bank. The effect of the photos, which now adorn the walls of various Broadway Federal branches, is to place the bank squarely in the history of Black Los Angeles. The bank's history is encapsulated through visual images of three generations of Hudson leadership and African American bank employees serving the African American community. The *Sentinel*'s articles, through their rhetoric and visual representation, affirm that the bank is a "race enterprise." However, the Hudson legacy did not end when Claude retired, as he passed down the project of African American economic advancement to his son, Elbert, and his grandson, Paul.[17]

The relationship of Claude Hudson and his son, Elbert, to the African American community was shaped by their civil rights activism within the NAACP, their commitment to Black progress and education, and their leadership in Broadway Federal. By 1976, Claude Hudson became known as "the man they call 'Mr. Civil Rights'" or the "father of Civil Rights." His identity, and by extension that of his family, was intricately tied to his activism for and within the African American community.[18] Elbert Hudson followed in his father's footsteps by becoming president of the Los Angeles branch of the NAACP in the early 1970s. He was a veteran of World War II, where he served as a fighter pilot. Through the GI Bill, he attended UCLA as an undergraduate and later Loyola Law School. He practiced law for seventeen years and served on various county and local commissions. In 1973, he became chairman of Broadway Federal.[19] His activism, alongside his wife, Marilyn Hudson, ensured that Paul Hudson's commitment to the plight of minority communities, and the African American community in particular, was nurtured. She always supported Paul Hudson's activism in college, law school, and the NAACP, for which he served as president during the early 1980s.[20] Paul Hudson practiced corporate law for a few years before deciding to follow the path laid out by his father and grandfather, namely, helping the African American community through service that could best support it.

Before Paul took over as chairman of Broadway Federal in 1992, Paul, Elbert, and Claude Hudson were making history as three generations serving on L.A. county commissions. In 1978, three generations served simultaneously on various commissions for the first time in the county's history. Paul became a member of the County Hospital Commission, his father, Elbert, was part of the Human Relations Commission, while his grandfather Claude served for his eighteenth term (at the age of ninety-two) on the Real Estate Management Commission.[21] Kenneth Hanh was extremely proud of his accomplishment of placing three generations of Hudsons as leaders of various projects throughout Los Angeles. The news reports of the Hudsons' accomplishments always referenced their leadership and its centrality in and for the African American community. They were indeed three generations of race men at the helm of a "race enterprise" in Los Angeles.

BANKING IN THE COMMUNITY

The 1992 uprising was a pivotal moment for the leadership of Broadway Federal, as it had to reflect on the role the bank would play in the community. Many other enterprises left the community in the aftermath of the uprising. Broadway Federal's place within South Central Los Angeles is of critical importance. A study by the City of Los Angeles Human Relations Commission revealed that in 1990 South Central Los Angeles only had nineteen bank branches, whereas nonminority areas of equal size to South Central Los Angeles had two hundred bank branches operating within the city limits. Unsurprisingly, check cashing centers take the place of bank branches in South Central Los Angeles, which is home to 133 such centers.[22] But Broadway Federal renewed its commitment to serving the needs of the community of South Central when it opened a trailer across the street from where the original building stood.

The racial demographic shift, along with the rebuilding effort of the bank and South Central Los Angeles at large, was on the minds of not only Paul Hudson (who had just become chairman of the bank) but also African American and Latino residents. Patrons of Broadway Federal and long-term residents of South Central Los Angeles reflected that they would continue to bank at Broadway Federal, like seventy-eight-year-old African American Sang Brown, who said the bank was one of the few institutions that allowed him to borrow sixty-five hundred dollars to purchase his two-bedroom house in the neighborhood. For Sang, his commitment to Broadway Federal never wavered: "After the riots and their building was burned down, they stayed. . . . Since they didn't abandon us, I wasn't going to abandon them."[23] Sang also recalls, "I used to see the old man [Claude Hudson] who started the bank right here," which was indicative of the ways that the Hudsons had become a staple in the community across the generations. But more important, their commitment also prompted Brown's commitment. Samuel Martinez reflects that working-class people have very few outlets for attaining loans. As working-class people, he said "we get caught in a trap," and "you can't get credit unless you have it. They [Broadway Federal] were willing to take a chance with me."[24] The lack of banking options and Broadway Federal's willingness to serve the needs of South Central Los Angeles residents made Sang, Samuel, and other Latinos loyal patrons of the bank, because, as Hudson states, it has "always been a bank of last resort for people."

Institutions and their leadership must confront the ways that demographic change impacts a business's philosophy and ideology. From 1970 to 1990 the Latino population in Los Angeles County increased to more than 2.2 million people. This was an increase of 238 percent.[25] Latinos settled all over the Los Angeles basin and increasingly outside traditional destinations, like East Los Angeles barrios. The decade of the 1980s was pivotal in the racial transformation of South Central Los Angeles.[26] The 1970 and 1980 censuses reported that the African American population of South Central Los Angeles was 93 and 83 percent of the community, respectively. But by 1990, the African American population dramatically decreased to 55 percent. Vacant homes were being occupied by Mexican and Central American immigrants, who in 1980 accounted for 14 percent of the total population and by 1990 grew to 45 percent.[27] By 2000, South Central Los Angeles's Latino population had increased to 60 percent, of which 40 percent were foreign born. These demographic changes led Paul Hudson to assert, "There are a lot of folks who still believe that there is a Black market, and you can make it only in a Black market," yet to be a thriving and growing economic institution you have to have "crossover appeal."[28]

This demographic shift meant that by the mid- to late 1980s, the bank began a new way of doing business when it hired bilingual employees to help cater to its growing Latino patronage. Similar to the initial recruitment efforts of hiring African American residents from the community, Hudson looked to the community for its pool of Latino employees. His first Latino employees were friends of his or bank patrons themselves. This choice was in part due to convenience but also an extension of the mission of being a community bank that provides employment opportunities for community residents. Hiring Latinos from the community proved one of the easiest ways to attract more Mexican immigrant clients, as their options for cashing weekly paychecks were at licensed retail stores, like liquor markets or *loncheras* (lunch trucks), and formal check cashing locales.[29] These avenues, however, provided limited options, as they were one-time transactions with a fee and without an outlet to open a savings account. Hudson understood that the need for a bank was not only for African American South Central Los Angeles residents but also for recently arrived Latinos. The conscious choice to hire bilingual employees and seek out new customers is representative of the ways that Hudson and Broadway Federal had to evolve to survive in the backdrop of multiracial Los Angeles.

As Broadway Federal's workforce was slowly transitioning and becoming more representative of the community, Paul Hudson worked as a clerk assisting patrons with cashing their checks, opening bank accounts, and arranging home loans. He wanted to be treated like a normal employee and, in turn, learn the business from the bottom up. He remembers his attempts at speaking Spanish to Latino patrons: "Yes, I was trying to talk to the Hispanic patrons. I had enough words to negotiate transactions."[30] He expressed this with pride, as he considered this gesture an attempt to include and acknowledge Latino patrons. Paul Hudson's presence in the bank did not go unnoticed, as Antonio Sanchez expressed, "The owner's son was working at the bank. Well that's what they would say. I did not talk to him. . . . If anything it was for basic transactions like to cash my check. . . . But he would work there like a regular employee . . . but everyone would say that he and his father were involved in helping Blacks."[31] Despite Mexican immigrants' inability to have conversations with African

American employees (because of their limited English-speaking skills), information about Paul Hudson and his family's involvement in the African American community circulated among Mexican immigrant patrons. This was always in the form of "rumors," or at least that is how it was described. Mexican immigrants heard these "rumors" from the few Latinos who spoke English and the Latino employees of the bank. Not only were Latino employees important in satisfying banking needs, but they also expanded and sustained information networks concerning the bank owner's identity and incentives.

The pivotal moment when Mexican immigrant men felt as though they were important patrons of the bank was when they were given free prizes and rewards for being loyal patrons. Juan Rodriguez states, "I remember that in those days they would give us free tickets to go see a Dodger game—to see Fernando Valenzuela. There was a Latino manager, he was really nice and friendly. He would help us."[32] The employment of Latinos and the genuine effort of the bank owner to speak Spanish in serving Latino patrons' needs were sources of comfort for those patrons, as they felt someone had their best interests at heart, including the gift of free baseball tickets, which swept them into the fervor of Valenzuela's tenure with the Dodgers. Mexican immigrants remember getting free gifts when Latino employees began working at the bank. It is uncertain if gifts coincided with the hiring of Latino employees or if gifts had always been part of this bank's practices, but, for these Mexican immigrant patrons, the presence of Latino employees introduced a positive atmosphere of banking at Broadway Federal.

However, the employment of Latinos was not positively perceived by African American employees and patrons. By 1998, the mix of employees at Broadway Federal had dramatically changed. The branch manager of the oldest office was from the Dominican Republic, a woman from Belize was in charge of opening new accounts, and increasingly Mexican, Salvadorian, and Guatemalan immigrants worked alongside African Americans as tellers and loan officers. This demographic shift meant that Latinos made up about a quarter of Broadway Federal's fifty-six employees and managed three of the bank's five branches.[33] Latoya Raines said that part of the appeal of the bank was that she saw people from the community working there, and for her this made the bank stand out. While she understood the economic motivation behind hiring Latino employees, she also was disgruntled that African American employees were losing their jobs to make room for Latino employees. Latoya discussed how the bank actually was one more institution among many that was responding to the massive influx of Latino immigrants. Latoya believed that African Americans were becoming antagonistic toward Latinos because of what all these changes would mean for the achievements made by the African American community in South Central Los Angeles. She stated, "We fought hard for the strides we made . . . to have them cut short by Mexicans." She further elaborated, "I know how hard it is to keep something like a bank around . . . one that cares about Black people . . . who actually gives us loans . . . so to see them hire Mexicans and Mexicans bank here is threatening 'cuz I didn't know what that would mean for us."[34] Latoya motioned to the difficulty of patrons to understand what all this change, both on her block and in the bank, would mean for African American progress. Francisco Rosas, a long-term patron of Broadway Federal, discussed why African American apprehension of how Latino settlement in South Central Los Angeles transformed employment opportunities within the bank and elsewhere is warranted. In his perspective, Latinos did take jobs away from African Americans: "I saw the change. We didn't take all the jobs, because you still see Black people working in the bank, but you see a lot more Mexicans there too. . . . I honestly didn't think it would happen, to see Mexicans outnumber Blacks. Especially because when I came here everything was Black. So I understand if they feel threatened. But they should be used to it by now; it's all Mexican now anyway."[35] Francisco understood the anxiety of Latoya and other African American patrons and residents concerning how demographic change has impacted the lives of African Americans, most especially because African Americans had such a stronghold in the community.

Despite the multiracial character of Broadway Federal, the level of interaction between African American and Latino patrons is very minimal. They stand in line to cash checks and open savings and checking accounts without really speaking to one another. There might be a casual hello and good-bye, but for the most part, Latinos described talking to other Latino patrons and employees. In part, this seems to be a function of the limited English-speaking skills of Latino patrons, thus, communicating with African American patrons has proven to be difficult. Both Latinos and African Americans seek particular bank employees, as even on the busiest days they wait to be assisted by an employee of their racial background. Cultural preferences define this practice, as Latino employees are fluent in Spanish, and Mexican immigrant men have grown familiar with them, and over the course of their patronage at Broadway Federal have had conversations with tellers that extended beyond business transactions. In a similar fashion, African American patrons have also had particular tellers they frequent. This familiarity means that both Latino and African American patrons have developed friendships with bank employees as they learn a considerable amount about each other's lives. Latoya elaborates, "I didn't talk to the Mexicans. . . . I couldn't even if I wanted to. . . . I didn't understand them and they didn't understand me. . . . I mean what were we to talk about?"[36] Francisco expressed that there was some comfort in not communicating with African American patrons, as in that period, the mid- to late 1980s, the racial tension in the city streets was evident, as African Americans would verbally and physically attack some of his friends.[37] The bank in many ways sheltered Latinos from any harassment, as it was respected as a professional institution; hence, the interaction between Latinos and African Americans there was muted. Latoya and Francisco both illustrate how they were beginning to make sense of living in a multiracial and multiethnic space.

For Hudson, inclusion of Latinos in the politics and everyday practices of the bank meant hiring bilingual employees and, more recently, allowing Mexican immigrants to use a matricula consular for opening a bank account and incorporating a Spanish-language section into the bank's website. The online Spanish translation of its services provides details on how to apply for a home loan and how to open a bank account and directions to its various locales. This information is different from that provided to its English-speaking audience/patrons. Sections accessible to English-speaking audiences expand on the logistics of opening an account or applying for a home loan, but the "our community" segment of the website provides a section on the history of the bank and its struggle in opening as a minority-owned bank to serve the African American community, as well as suggestions for places of interest in Los Angeles. These places of interests are all historical landmarks in the Black community.[38] Incorporating a section on the website that speaks to the bank's history and places of interest is indicative of Paul Hudson and the board of directors' conceptualization of community—African Americans. The website's failure to translate this feature suggests the bank management's unwillingness to envision and treat Latino patrons as engaged patrons and members of the South Central "community."

Paul Hudson has not made concerted efforts to inform Latino patrons about the bank and South Central Los Angeles's history. He said, "The history is not a history of the Hispanic immigrant; it's not that type of a history," yet I would argue that despite it not being the history of the Latino immigrant there is something that could be learned by Latinos if they are made aware of the difficulties and challenges faced by the African American community. While I am not suggesting that learning the history of the bank would eradicate Latino immigrants' tensions and prejudices concerning African Americans (and vice versa), it might transform how Latinos understand banking at Broadway Federal and inform their attitude toward interacting in racially and ethnically diverse venues. Informing Latinos about the political logic of the bank could transform their attitude toward banking at Broadway Federal as not just a choice made of convenience but rather one reflective of a politics.

As Mexican immigrants reflected on their initial experiences at Broadway Federal, they began to question what has made this bank unique and set it apart from other banks in the area. On the one hand, the bank is part of a capitalist venture that aims to make a profit. On the other, it sees itself as an important cultural, social, political, and economic entity in the community of South Central Los Angeles in general and for African Americans in particular. At the end of my interviews, I shared the bank's history, commitment, and politics with Latino patrons. This intrigued them. They realized that this bank truly differs from others in the area. Upon discussing this history, they were quick to respond, "It's good to know . . . things make sense now."[39] Exposing Latino patrons to this rich history may lay the foundations for interaction truly consistent with creating and nurturing an informed sense of community. They were far more receptive to reflecting on the potential significance of the oil paintings of African American men that graced the bank's original building (the old building had pictures of H. Claude Hudson and Elbert Hudson). Similarly, not all African American patrons are aware of the history and politics behind Broadway Federal. The oil paintings, murals, and quotes are visual markers meant to do some of the cultural work that the bank imagines itself doing. South Central resident Chris Campbell stated that these visual markers make them feel welcomed in a way that they do not necessarily feel at Bank of America or a check cashing center. As a long-term patron Chris stated that he has always found a sense of warmth and history being articulated through these images. Thus, Paul Hudson's attempt to transform building walls into spaces in which to express cultural pride and belonging works for some African American patrons.

Latino and African American patrons and Hudson are equally receptive to the potential that art has in playing a symbolic role for the creation of a politics behind banking at Broadway Federal. By making reference to the symbolic function of these images, I do not aim to render the bank's rich African American history as unimportant or irrelevant to the culture and practices of the bank and its patrons; however, if Latino patrons are confined to seeing mainly African American representations of history and progress, they are not allowed the possibility of imagining Broadway Federal as their bank. Latino patrons feel a certain level of comfort because Latino employees are there to assist them, yet they still discuss and understand the bank as a business exclusively dedicated to serving the needs of the African American community. Latino patrons like Juan Rodriguez to this day believe, "the bank is for Blacks, we know that."[40] In the initial years of Latinos banking at Broadway Federal, the bank fit in line with how other institutions served the needs of South Central Los Angeles residents, namely, by catering to the needs of African Americans. This first generation of Latinos settling into South Central Los Angeles had to learn then how to navigate all institutions that worked under this logic, not just Broadway Federal. Latino patrons' persistent belief that Broadway Federal caters to African Americans is not surprising, even though it's not reflective of Broadway Federal's actual reality. Latino patrons continue to understand the role of the bank as that of serving the needs of African Americans primarily and Latinos secondarily. Thus, despite Paul Hudson's attempts to include Latinos as important patrons by hiring bilingual employees, the visual and cultural cues and racial discourse make Latinos feel that Broadway Federal is still primarily a bank by and for African Americans.

The expansion of the bank through the opening of different branches provides a glimpse into the bank's mission. Throughout the 1990s, Broadway Federal opened branches in Inglewood and Wilshire to serve diverse communities. However, it plans to open a branch in Leimert Park and also looks to expand in Carson, San Bernardino, and Riverside.[41] These communities are among the few locations in Los Angeles that still boast sizable African American populations.[42] The bank's leadership continues to envision its future as dependent on following and serving the African American community and not investing in features and services that are important to Latino immigrant communities, like offering money transfers to nations of origin. In the last few decades the growth of business of wire and money transfers from the United States to Latin American countries has grown exponentially, as sending countries and towns are dependent on the remittances of family members in the United States. In 2004, remittances between the United States and Latin American were recorded at $30 billion, with California residents alone sending roughly $10 billion. In that same year, Mexican immigrants in California sent around $4.5 billion to Mexico. This meant that money-transferring businesses throughout the state of California earned $338 million in transaction fees.[43] Businesses like Western Union, check cashing centers, and larger banks (like Bank of America and Wells Fargo) have proven to be an important resource for Latino residents of South Central Los Angeles. Broadway Federal's failure to implement a money transfer option for its patrons not only forecloses the possibility of generating meaningful profits but also fails to understand how Latino immigrants' needs may require much more than deposit, checking, and loan options.

Paul Hudson's perspective on the role that Latinos play in his bank is often contradictory and endemic in the difficult position and situation confronted by individuals who envision themselves as race leaders in general and African American leaders in particular. He is trying to understand what this demographic change means for his practices, perspective, and attitude. It is possible that acknowledging this change would erase the important strides made by previous generations of African American struggle rather than illuminate new trajectories and realities of complexity and interaction.[44] Hudson discussed the ways that Broadway Federal has made a conscious effort to market itself to Latino patrons, yet upon closer inspection one learns that he still imagines and conceptualizes Broadway Federal as bank for African Americans. At the very moment in which Paul Hudson became the spokesperson of the bank, the backdrop of the work that his father and grandfather had labored under dramatically changed. Thus, Paul Hudson's stated rationale behind his management and expansion of Broadway Federal can be understood as guarded rhetoric or his process of making sense of demographic change. He believes that the inclusion of Latinos in the discourse could mean a backlash among long-term African American patrons anxious about the Latino immigrant population's growing majority. His largest fear is that this could influence African American patrons to abandon Broadway Federal, as they would misinterpret the inclusion of Latinos as a challenge to the bank's long-standing commitment and tradition of helping the African American community.

Currently, a shared sense that the time and banking of both African American and Latino patrons are priceless makes it possible for Broadway Federal to profit from its most faithful patrons, long-term African American and Latino patrons. African American and Latino patrons alike reserve chairs lining this bank's waiting area for the elderly irrespective of race or gender and do not object to a disabled or elderly client cutting in line. Chris Campbell explains, "There isn't much in South Central. . . . the least we can do is help one another take care of business. Black . . . Latino, it is up to us to conduct business with respect, if we want this bank to make business and stick around."[45] Rosario Cruz's rationale behind her banking practices echoes Campbell's assessment of their situation: "Everyone—Latinos, Blacks, the old, youth—we have to do our part. There is very little around here, it is like an obligation to get along well so that this, the bank, stays here."[46]

Chris and Rosario believe that the continued success of the bank, and of South Central Los Angeles more broadly, lies in the continued interaction between and among African Americans and Latinos. But Broadway Federal has failed to educate many of its Latino clientele on the political and economic importance of a thriving financial institution in an impoverished community like South Central Los Angeles. To put it another way, if one reads this bank's "success" and growth as going against the grain of perceptions of how minority businesses fail to thrive over generations in an impoverished community (most especially, an economic business like a bank as opposed to a check cashing center), then there is a way in which Latinos can and should be placed in the context of how the bank's "success" is dependent not only on its rich African American history, commitment, and struggle but also in the last few decades has depended on the support of Latinos. Such considerations illustrate the ways Black and Latino people can occupy similar spaces and push forward a new vision and mission.

NOTES

1. In the months that followed the uprising, African American leaders in South Central were placing pressure on national banking institutions to help rebuild the community through not only short-term relief but also long-term economic investment and programs that would best service the community through business development programs and establishing of bank branches. See James Bates, "Large Banks Pressed to Hasten Rebuilding with Flow of Credit Money: Riots Renew a Dispute between Bankers and Community

Activists Who Accuse the Institutions of Not Doing Enough for South Los Angeles," *Los Angeles Times,* May 5, 1992, 3.

2. Oral history with Paul Hudson, conducted by author, October 16, 2007.

3. Broadway Federal Bank, "Mission Statement," www.broadwayfederal bank.com.

4. Oral history with Paul Hudson.

5. H. Claude Hudson (Paul's grandfather) was one of the original founders of the bank in 1949. He served as chairman until 1973, when his son Elbert Hudson (Paul's father) began serving as chairman until 1992. In 1992, Paul Hudson took over as chairman.

6. In the case of Los Angeles, the last three decades has seen a growth and proliferation of Asian American banks throughout Southern California. This growth parallels the mass immigration and settlement of Asian immigrants across the region. Unlike their Asian immigrant counterparts—in particular Korean and Chinese immigrants—African American banks do not have the same commercial growth or financial backing. African American–owned banking institutions must rely on the federal government for support, but the financial support of Asian American banks is intimately tied to capital back in their sending countries. The presence of these banks has proven extremely important to the growth of community business and institutions in Asian American suburbs and neighborhoods across Los Angeles. The link between the Pacific Rim and global commerce has set apart Asian American banks from the business opportunities and ventures of Broadway Federal. See Lila Ammons, "The Evolution of Black-Owned Banks in the United States Between the 1880s and 1990s," *Journal of Black Studies* 26, no. 4 (March 1996): 467–89; and Wei Li, Gary Dymski, Yu Zhou, Maria Chee, and Carolyn Aldana, "Chinese-American Banking and Community Development in Los Angeles County," *Annals of the Association of American Geographers* 92, no. 4 (December 2002): 777–96.

7. Oral History with H. Claude Hudson, November 26, 1966, Oral History Collection, African American Oral Histories, Pollack Library, California State University, Fullerton; Golden State Mutual Life Insurance Co. Records, 1866–1985, Special Collections, Charles E. Young Research Library, University of California, Los Angeles; Douglas Flamming, *Bound for Freedom: Black Los Angeles in Jim Crow America* (Berkeley: University of California Press, 2005), 258, 117.

8. Josh Sides, *L.A. City Limits: African American Los Angeles from the Great Depression to the Present* (Berkeley: University of California Press, 2003), 38, 4.

9. Oral History with H. Claude Hudson.

10. "Loan Bank Praised as Opening Set Saturday," *Los Angeles Sentinel,* January 9, 1947, 9.

11. Ibid.

12. Oral History with H. Claude Hudson; Douglas Flamming, *Bound for Freedom,* 291.

13. Douglas Flamming, *Bound for Freedom,* 271. In the early 1920s, membership was at its highest level, but by the end of 1925 membership had dra-

matically declined to 274 members. New members, such as Beatrice Thompson, felt they were not listened to by the "old guard." They also believed that the branch was operating undemocratically and not allowing new members to have much input. Thompson encouraged Hudson to become involved in the local NAACP to bridge the gap between these two factions. Hudson became involved in the local branch because he felt that the local branch was "a dead thing as it had not taken on any meaningful civil rights campaigns in years. He therefore had voiced support for those who were calling for new and aggressive leadership." He became president of the NAACP, and he believed that "most of the petty bickering had disappeared" under his leadership. Hudson was also integral to promoting the NAACP's involvement in the "beach wars" for African Americans to gain access to Los Angeles beaches. The "beach wars" consist of a group of five or six African American men and women who wanted to challenge beach segregation in Los Angeles. They went to Manhattan Beach, a racially segregated beach, and were arrested and put in jail because they violated the law. The case was eventually thrown out, and African Americans were allowed to go to the beach in Los Angeles. Also, during this period the Los Angeles chapter of the NAACP was also engaged in organizing a Budweiser boycott, which discouraged Blacks from buying beer because of Budweiser's failure to employ Blacks. They protested, "no job, no bud" as well as encouraged participation in campaigns against the Los Angeles Fire Department's discriminatory practices. See Flamming, *Bound for Freedom,* 212–14, 270.

14. Oral history with H. Claude Hudson.

15. "Broadway Federal 'Like a Big Happy Family,'" *Los Angeles Sentinel,* April 23, 1959, B13.

16. For a detailed discussion of the growth of African American employees in the banking industry throughout the United States, see R. D. Corwin, *Racial Minorities in Banking: New Workers in the Banking Industry* (New Haven, CT: New College & University Press, 1971).

17. Oral history with Paul Hudson.

18. In 1976, the *Los Angeles Sentinel* printed a roster of awards and honors bestowed on Claude Hudson. He was named Distinguished Alumnus of Howard University for his service, given the Distinguished Citizens Award from the County Conference on Community Relations, served as a member of the Los Angeles County Real Estate Advisory Committee, was a trustee of the Martin Luther King Memorial Hospital, received the Humanitarian of the Year Award by United Givers, and received a USC honorary degree because he had "devoted himself in vital labors on behalf of humanity, earning the abiding love and admiration of his fellow citizens." See "Father of Civil Rights Gets Sentinel Title," *Los Angeles Sentinel,* June 15, 1978, A1; and "The Man They Call 'Mr. Civil Rights,'" *Los Angeles Sentinel,* April 1, 1976, A1.

19. "NAACP Head Quits Police Post to Avoid Conflicts," *Los Angeles Sentinel,* January 21, 1971, A1.

20. Marilyn Hudson has always been politically active through various community organizations as well. See "A Woman Whose Work Is Never Down," *Los Angeles Times,* March 27, 1980, C1.

21. "Like Father, Like Son: The Hudsons Are Civil Rights Fighters," *Los Angeles Sentinel,* May 20, 1971, 8; "Three Hudsons Serve County," *Los Angeles Sentinel,* September 28, 1978, A3; "Three Generations of Hudson Men Make Mark in Los Angeles," *Los Angeles Sentinel,* June 29, 1978, A3.

22. "Bank Branches in South Central Are Rare and Extend Few Services," in "South Central Los Angeles: An Annotated Bibliography with Accompanying Statistics on Inner City Underdevelopment and Minority Business," compiled by the City of Los Angeles Human Relations Commission, South Central Los Angeles Documentation Collection, box 22, folder 2, Southern California Library for Social Science and Research, Los Angeles; Jube Shiver, "South L.A. Patrons Pay a Hefty Price as Bankers Leave Consumers," *Los Angeles Times,* November 26, 1991, 1. By 2005, 40 percent of all check cashing centers in Los Angeles County could be found in low-income areas. See Roberto Barragan and Leticia Rodriguez, "A Report on Check Cashing Establishments in Los Angeles," Valley Economic Development Center, Van Nuys, CA, December 2005.

23. Mitchell, John, "Tilting the Balance of Black Bank: Broadway Federal Courts South Central's Growing Latino, Asian Populations. Many Praise Institution's Expansion, but Others Fear a Loss of Identity," *Los Angeles Times,* July 3, 1998, A1.

24. Ibid.

25. David M. Grant, "A Demographic Portrait of Los Angeles County, 1970 to 1990," in *Prismatic Metropolis,* ed. Lawrence D. Bobo, Melvin L. Oliver, James H. Johnson Jr., and Abel Valenzuela Jr. (New York: Russell Sage Foundation, 2000), 52.

26. South Central's geographic parameters are: I-10, La Cienega Boulevard, I-105 (Century Freeway), and Alameda Street.

27. Héctor Tobar, "Latinos Transform South L.A.: A Massive Shift in Population Has Altered the Area's Urban Landscape, with the New Residents Bringing Their Own Mix of Culture and Traditions," *Los Angeles Times,* February 16, 1992, 1.

28. Mitchell, "Tilting the Balance of Black Bank."

29. I conducted oral histories in Spanish with six Mexican immigrant men who have been patrons of Broadway Federal since the early 1980s. I focused on long-term Latino patrons of the bank because I wanted to capture how Broadway Federal initially dealt with Latino patrons. Also through their experiences during twenty or more years banking at Broadway Federal, I aimed to track how the bank has changed (or failed to). At the end of the oral history, I openly discussed why I was interested in the bank. In doing so, I informed my interviewees of the history of the bank. This was done only after they had fully discussed their experience at the bank.

30. Oral history with Paul Hudson.

31. Oral history with Antonio Sanchez, conducted by author, October 23, 2007.

32. Oral history with Juan Rodriguez, conducted by author, September 14, 2007.

33. Mitchell, "Tilting the Balance of Black Bank."

34. Oral history with Latoya Raines, conducted by author, September 19, 2008.

35. Oral history with Francisco Rosas, conducted by author, November 1, 2007.

36. Oral history with Latoya Raines.

37. The interactions between African American and Latinos were not always negative. Francisco cites multiple instances in which he had friendly and muted interaction with African Americans. However, there were instances, the most vivid in his memory, of how his settlement in South Central Los Angeles was negative, dangerous, and uncertain (oral history with Francisco Rosas). Josh Sides, in *L.A. City Limits,* does not focus on malicious attacks between African Americans and Latinos, but he does present how long-time African American South Central Los Angeles residents have resented Latino sentiment. Sides documents how Leroy Shepared reacted to the increased presence of Mexican immigrants: "Sometimes we get mad at those doggone Mexicans." And he also quotes Sylvia McLymont: "All of a sudden, it seemed like we were invaded." See Josh Sides, *L.A. City Limits,* 204. Joao H. Costa Vargas, in his investigation on blackness in South Central Los Angeles, recalls a particular instance between African American and Latino residents, when one of his respondents negatively reacted to the prospect of a Latino potentially renting an apartment in her housing complex. Costa Vargas writes, "I noticed that Shannon [African American resident] was visibly upset. She first started with muted words that quickly became full shouts. 'I don't want to see no Latinos in this building, do you hear, you motherfuckers? No Latinos? No Sir! I don't want my kids playing with no white kids, do you hear?'" While Shannon did not violently react to her potential Latino neighbors, her sentiments do express her anxiety about and dislike of such a prospect. See João H. Costa Vargas, *Catching Hell in the City of Angeles: Life and Meanings of Blackness in South Central Los Angeles* (Minneapolis: University of Minnesota Press, 2006), 94.

38. These places are the California African American Museum, the African American Firefighter Museum, the William Grant Still Art Center, and Lady Effie's Tea Parlor. Broadway Federal Bank, "Places to Visit," www.broadway-fed.com/places.htm.

39. Also, they were satisfied to learn that what they thought was a rumor of the boss's son working as a bank employee was true. As they stated, "*Nos rosamos con el mero-mero!* [We rubbed shoulders with the boss!]"

40. Oral history with Juan Rodriguez.

41. Oral history with Paul Hudson.

42. The 2000 "census revealed that almost a one-quarter of the Black population of South Central left during the 1990s, while the Black population of Orange, Venture, Riverside, and San Bernardino, and Imperial Counties continued to grow." Josh Sides, *L.A. City Limits,* 201.

43. Jeronimo Cortina, Rodolfo de la Garza, Sandra Bejerano, and Andrew Weiner, "The Economic Impact of the Mexico-California Relationship," *Tomás Rivera Policy Institute* (September 2005).

44. Similarly to Broadway Federal, community organizations throughout South Central Los Angeles faced the challenge of learning to service and cater

to the community's growing Latino majority. One such institution is the Concerned Citizens of South Central Los Angeles, a historically African American community resource. This organization has been the most "aggressive" in reaching out to the Latino community. Concerned Citizens organized African American and Latino block clubs that would allow them to work collaboratively, as well as worked on a series of environmental issues, like building local parks for the community. Juanita Tate, as director of Concerned Citizens, actively pursued projects that would bring African American and Latino residents of South Central Los Angeles together. Tate discusses that it was not the easiest process; yet, she was steadfast in her commitment to ensuring that the needs of Latino and African American were simultaneously considered. See Alexander Von Hoffman, *House by House, Block by Block: The Rebirth of American's Urban Neighborhoods* (Oxford: Oxford University Press, 2003), 222–24.

45. Informal conversation with African American patron Chris Campbell on one of my site visits.

46. Oral history with Rosario Cruz, conducted by author, August 1, 2007.

3

Black Views toward Proposed Undocumented Immigration Policies

The Role of Racial Stereotypes
and Economic Competition

LORRIE FRASURE-YOKLEY AND STACEY GREENE

INTRODUCTION

Leimert Park, a traditionally Black neighborhood in South Los Angeles became an unlikely meeting ground for a group of anti–illegal immigration protesters in the months following the widely publicized 2006 May Day demonstrations for immigrant rights. May 3 of that year kicked off a series of demonstrations in the community, when a predominately White anti–illegal immigration group called the Minutemen Civil Defense Corp was joined by a Black anti–illegal immigration group called Choose Black America (CBA).[1] During an interview with National Public Radio, Ted Hayes, leader of Choose Black America stated, "What the Minutemen are doing today is wonderful. By guarding our borders is [sic] wonderful, particularly for us Black people—us American Black people. The illegal invaders, they are using our hard-won civil rights as a key to justify their illegal incursion across our border. If we allow for them to continue to invade our country, we are betraying Dr. Martin Luther King and the whole civil rights movement" (National Public Radio 2006).

Though the crowd of anti–illegal immigration supporters was quite modest compared to the pro-immigration supporters at subsequent demonstrations in South Los Angeles, the Minutemen's venture into Leimert Park, often called "the heart of Black Los Angeles," to expand their campaign against undocumented immigration raises several questions concerning race relations, attitudes toward out-groups, public opinion, and prospects for modern-day coalition formation in metropolitan areas. Despite vast media reports on the purported "Black-Latino" divide in Los Angeles and the lack of Black public support, particularly among Black leaders during the immigration reform debacle of 2006, there remains little systematic research on Black views toward undocumented immigration to the United States. While such views may be widely discussed in the privacy of some traditional Black spaces, such as the barbershop or beauty salon, public opinion among Blacks regarding undocumented immigration is largely unknown (but see Diamond 1998 and Morris 2000, as well as the more general empirical studies of undocumented immigration by Espenshade and Calhoun [1993]; Espenshade [1995]; and Wilson [2001]).

Immigration policy is a persistently contentious and divisive issue in the United States. Past research suggests that Blacks have been relatively positive toward immigration when compared to other racial groups (Citrin et al. 1997). However, other research shows that Blacks often view immigrants (especially undocumented immigrants) as an economic threat (Burns and Gimpel 2000). Though immigration policies are purportedly race neutral, there is evidence to suggest that many Americans associate undocumented immigration with Latinos—particularly national origin groups from Mexico and Central and South America—rendering these policies racialized. Moreover, Blacks may recognize the racial overtones of the debate and take them into consideration when developing their opinions. Some literature on intergroup attitudes suggests that this racialization may trigger feelings of group solidarity between Blacks and Latinos (Pastor and Marcelli 2003).

In this chapter, we use data from the 2007 Los Angeles County Social Survey to examine how some racial stereotypes and SES/demographic factors influence Blacks' policy preferences toward undocumented immigration. We find that attitudes toward undocumented immigration policies are often conditioned by factors beyond economic competition. Blacks with lower levels of income are more likely to reject punitive policies such as deportation, while Blacks who hold negative racial stereotypes about Latinos are more likely to favor more punitive policies toward undocumented immigrants. However, we also find that attitudes about racial identity and perceived commonality with Latinos are important influences on Blacks' views favoring more lenient policies toward undocumented immigrants.

BLACKS AND LATINOS IN LOS ANGELES

The study of American racial attitudes and the influence of such attitudes on public opinion formation have traditionally focused on Whites' attitudes toward Blacks (Key 1949; Allport 1954, Blumer 1958; Blalock 1967; Bobo and Hutchings 1996; Campbell et al. 2006). However, shifting racial/ethnic demographics in American metropolitan areas such as Los Angeles lend support to broadening the scope in order to gain a better understanding of the formation and implications of racial attitudes beyond a Black/White dichotomy. Some scholars have focused their attention on Black attitudes toward Latinos (Cummings and Lambert 1997; Gay 2006; McClain et al. 2006), particularly given the rise of the Latino population in southern states such as North Carolina.

However, numerous questions remain unanswered concerning the racial attitudes of racial/ethnic minority groups and the influence of these attitudes on public opinion formation. This area of research is particularly important given the demographic shifts taking place in historically Black locales such as South Los Angeles. Ethington and collaborators find that despite the growth of Los Angeles since 1940, Whites were only slightly more numerous in 2000 than they were before World War II. The authors note, "The growth of Los Angeles County since 1960 is almost entirely the work of non-White and non-Black groups" (Ethington et al. 2001: 10). These changing demographics make contact between Blacks and Latinos more likely than ever before. A commonly used segregation measure called the exposure index gives the probability that an individual will have a member of a certain racial/ethnic group as his or her neighbor in a given census tract. While there were increases from 1950 to 1970 in the likelihood that Blacks would meet Hispanics in their Los Angeles census tract, this trend increased dramatically beginning in the 1980s. In 1980, the probability was .19, in 1990 it was .34 and in 2000 it was .41. As a comparison, the probability that Blacks would meet Whites in their L.A. census tract steadily decreased from .45 in 1940 to .17 in 2000 (Ethington et al. 2001).

By 2006 the mix of racial/ethnic groups in South L.A. was 62 percent Latino, 31 percent Black, 3 percent White, and 2 percent Asian/Pacific Islander (U.S. Census, American Community Fact Finder). In their 2008 report "The State of South LA," Ong and collaborators examine the demographic shifts in South L.A., moving from predominantly White to Black in the early twentieth century, to predominantly Latino by the end of the twentieth century (4). Today Latinos outnumber Blacks two to one in the South L.A. (Ong et al. 2008). While Blacks are no longer the largest share of the population in South L.A., they still account for the "most highly overrepresented racial/ethnic group with about three times more Blacks living in South LA than in the County overall" (Ong et al. 2008: 5).

The racial and economically segregated nature of Los Angeles's geography has historically allowed many non-Hispanic White communities to flourish while perpetuating persistent residential isolation, marginalized economic opportunity, and diffused political power for other racial/ethnic groups (Robinson 2010; Sides 2003; Camarillo 2007; García Bedolla 2005). Beginning during World War II, Los Angeles experienced dramatic demographic shifts. There was unprecedented expansion in military and aerospace industries, which offered employment opportunities previously unavailable to non-Whites. The most rapid growth occurred in the aircraft and aerospace industry spurred by military demand from World War II, the Korean War, and the Vietnam War. At its peak, in 1957, the aircraft industry employed almost one-third of the manufacturing workforce in Southern California (Sides 2003). Yet, just as Blacks and Latinos gained footholds in these industries, the manufacturing sector in Los Angeles began to shrink, and many jobs were either eliminated or were moved to its suburbs.

The fair housing laws of the 1960s and 1970s enabled Blacks and Latinos to increase their residential mobility and begin to move beyond the traditional neighborhoods where they were once concentrated. However, the combination of deindustrialization coupled with White flight often left these cities in dire financial need. Though Blacks have suburbanized at a lower rate in Los Angeles than other minority groups, Blacks and Latinos still face similar issues.[2] Camarillo notes, "Blacks and Latinos, in particular, had the dubious distinction of inheriting communities increasingly inhabited by poor, working class people and spiraling in downward directions, characterized by diminished tax bases, weakened institutional infrastructures, mounting crime rates, and violence" (Camarillo 2007: 15).

Los Angeles is also the West's leading destination for immigrants (Allen 2005). More recent immigrants, many from Asia and Latin America, often find themselves living in cities with sizable numbers of racial minorities. Camarillo (2007) states, "In these new cities of color, inter-group relations are playing themselves out in ways reminiscent of earlier eras when native-born Americans encountered new immigrants and racial minorities as they settled in cities in large numbers"

(16). Increased residentially mobility, coupled with racial/ethnic transformation in neighborhoods, creates prospects for increased understanding but also opportunities for increased conflict over political representation and resource allocation. In addition, for many Blacks, a history of isolation has also led to "an unshakable sense of proprietorship over the community long after the disappearance of de jure housing segregation and long after many of their Black neighbors have left" (Sides 2003: 203). This sense of ownership poses potential concerns as Latinos—both immigrant and native born—move into historically Black neighborhoods.

In the next section we briefly review some existing literature on Black-Latino intergroup relations including: the role of racial stereotypes and attitudes, as well as theories of conflict or competition between racial/ethnic groups.

RETHINKING THEORIES OF RACIAL STEREOTYPES, ATTITUDES, AND COMPETITION

The Role of Racial Attitudes and Stereotypes

According to Bobo and Massagli (2001), "Racial stereotyping involves assumptions and expectations about the likely characteristics, capacities, and behaviors of members of a particular racial or ethnic category" (96). These authors contend that commonly held beliefs about members of different racial and ethnic groups "are a critical ingredient in the reproduction of patterns of racial and ethnic labor market inequality, segregation of housing, and general intergroup tension and misunderstanding" (93). In short, general attitudes about out-groups often influence life conditions and chances.

McClain et al. (2006) find that Blacks view Latinos much more favorably than Latinos view Blacks. For example, the authors find a high prevalence of negative stereotypes of Black Americans among the Latino immigrant community. Moreover, Latinos' hold a greater number of negative views of Blacks than White stereotypes of Blacks. They show that the majority of Latino immigrant respondents felt they had the most in common with Whites (78.3 percent) and the least in common with Blacks (52.8 percent). On the other hand, Blacks reported feeling they had the most in common with Latinos (49.6 percent). These feelings of commonality play an important role regarding prospects for alliances on policy issues. For example, Pastor and Marcelli (2003) argue that Proposition 187 presented an opportunity for strengthening Black-Latino alliances around immigration policy because it served as a precursor, for some Blacks, of future racialized, restrictionist policies. By the time Proposition 187 came to a vote, "the measure was seen not as a dispassionate approach to stemming the local costs of immigration but rather a broader and racialized attack on Latinos" (139). They argue that Blacks are aware that "restrictionist legislation could fuel other forms of prejudice, much as Proposition 187 in California became a precursor for Proposition 209, which banned Affirmative Action. . . . whatever gains might be made now through restriction may be undone later by anti-Black backlash (perhaps by Latinos and perhaps by Whites) on issues of central importance" (149).

Racial attitudes (including negative stereotypes) have been shown to influence policy attitudes (Hurwitz and Peffley 1997; Gilens 1996). These racial attitudes are often couched in terms of conservative ideology and "American values." We expect that respondents who may hold negative stereotypical views about Latinos will be more likely to support more punitive government policies toward undocumented immigrants, such as criminalization or deportation.

The Role of Conflict and Economic Competition

The potential for coalitions (and their stability) often depends on a set of perceived shared interests. Depending on the issue, it is debatable whether Blacks and Latinos in Los Angeles perceive more commonality or more conflict with each other. Both groups have a shared history of discrimination in the education, housing, and job markets. As compared to Whites, both Blacks and Latinos lag on measures such as educational attainment, income, and wealth. These commonalities are often cited as reasons for close ties and prospects for coalitions between the two groups. Yet these considerations are also coupled with potential competition over resources, which can potentially cause tensions and conflict.

Conflict theory traditionally focuses on Whites' response to an increasing number of Blacks in their proximity. The "power-threat" hypothesis, for example, is one of the most commonly used theories to explain racial attitudes toward out-groups (Key 1949; Blumer 1958; Blalock 1967; Bobo and Hutchings 1996). Conflict theory suggests that a "superordinate group (e.g. Whites) becomes more racially hostile as the size of a proximate subordinate group increases, which putatively threatens the former's economic and social privilege" (Oliver and Wong 2003: 568).

To further understand the role of conflict, Henry and Sears (2002) examined interracial attitudes and conflict in Los Angeles. Whites, Blacks, Asians, and Latinos were interviewed to find out their opinions on interracial conflict. Respondents were asked which group was in most conflict with their own group. Whites overwhelmingly responded that they were in the most conflict with Blacks. Latinos also responded that they were in the greatest conflict with Blacks. Blacks felt that Latinos were the group with whom they had the most conflicts. Next, the respondents were asked which issues were most likely to contribute to these conflicts. Sears found that street crime, especially gang violence, was a major source of racial conflict. "Jobs and income" and "access to higher education" were also important considerations. In contrast to Henry and Sears's results, Bobo and Hutchings (1996) found that both Blacks and Latinos seem to feel more of a threat from Asians than from each other.

The idea of a "zero-sum" game is especially prevalent in the discussion of low-wage and public sector jobs. A labor competition model predicts that those with higher education and income will be more receptive to immigrants, because they do not foresee competing with them. On the other hand, those with less education and lower incomes might be more opposed to immigration, because immigrants are seen as taking away jobs from native workers, purportedly depressing wages. Espenshade and Calhoun (1993) find only weak support for a "labor market competition" hypothesis. While they find that respondents with higher levels of educational attainment have more favorable attitudes toward undocumented immigrants, they also find cultural affinity—that is, cultural and ethnic ties to immigrants—to be an important predictor of attitudes toward immigration.

In Los Angeles, municipal jobs have been an important stepping stone for Blacks into the middle class. Recent studies suggest that as Blacks continue to hold higher numbers of public sector positions, Latinos are encountering resistance as they try to enter these jobs (Vaca 2004; McClain 1993). While McClain (1993) finds that Black and Latino municipal employment successes actually come at the expense of Whites, she also finds that "as the proportion of the Black work force increases, Hispanics suffer in their ability to gain municipal employment" (407). On the other hand, the percentage of Latinos in the workforce does not seem to have the same negative effect on Black municipal employment. Yet, McClain also cautions that there were few majority minority cities in the sample, and it is unclear how the analysis might change in cities with larger minority populations.

These studies suggest that there are multiple reasons for intergroup conflict. These reasons are often contextual and dynamic. We believe that many incidents of contention or cooperation are issue specific and are not natural or inevitable. These incidents underscore the need to examine conflict theory in multiracial settings, specifically in areas that have rapidly shifted from one minority group to another minority group. This is especially important because we know little about how Black public opinion toward undocumented immigration is influenced by one's socioeconomic status. Several individual-level factors have been shown to influence policy attitudes toward immigration, including demographic characteristics such as age (Citrin et al. 1997; Espenshade and Calhoun 1993);sex (Hood and Morris 1997); income and education (Federico 2004; Glaser 2001); and race (Hood and Irwin 1997; Ilias et al. 2008). Educational attainment is among the most consistently used predictors of both racial and policy attitudes—though the influence of education is not always intuitive. Well-educated Whites tend to be more racially liberal, in that they support egalitarian ideals more so than the less educated (Federico 2004). However, this racial liberalism does not always extend to policies that would produce equal outcomes. Oliver and Mendelberg (2000) find significant differences in the levels of acceptance of negative stereotypes between those in zip codes with high levels of educational attainment and those in zip codes with lower levels. This holds even when controlling for the individual's own education level. Therefore, we expect increased levels of education might lead to more progressive policy views toward undocumented immigration.

According to the competition hypothesis, we expect that respondents having high incomes will hold less punitive policy perspectives toward undocumented immigration, because they are not in direct economic competition. Higher-income residents are less likely to live in the same areas as the undocumented—who tend to have lower incomes—further reducing the likelihood of feeling threatened. Conversely, we expect that respondents with lower incomes will be less likely to support "open-door" policies that would allow undocumented workers to remain in the United States.

Existing literature also shows support for the role of political orientations in shaping attitudes toward undocumented immigration. Barkan (2003) finds that women, Republicans, and older persons are groups most concerned about undocumented immigration. Fenelly and Federico (2008) find that conservative ideology, more so than party identification, is a predictor of attitudes toward immigration. However, there is no uniform ideological stance with regard to specific aspects of immigration reform, such as guest worker programs. Conservatives might support them for business interests or oppose guest worker programs because they are seen as rewarding those who broke the law. Liberals and Democrats might also have conflicting views. Liberal proponents of guest worker programs might support increased levels of immigration, which create a more diverse environment. Yet, liberals might also oppose guest worker programs because of potential worker exploitation and the absence of a path to citizenship (Ilias et al. 2008).

In this study, we used data from the 2007 Los Angeles County Social Survey (LACSS), an annual random-digit-dial telephone survey of the adult population of Los Angeles, to examine the extent to which racial stereotypes and attitudes as well as socioeconomic status (SES) and demographics shape Black views toward several proposed government policy responses to undocumented immigration.[3] This dataset is ideal for our study, because it includes a number of measures on racial attitudes, stereotypes, and views toward public policy concerns, as well as a host of SES and demographic measures. Specifically, we seek to examine which factors influence Black public opinion of four proposed policy options toward undocumented immigration.

> *Government Policy Responses to Illegal Immigrants:* Which of the following comes closest to your view about what government policy should be toward illegal immigrants currently residing in the United States? Should the government: A) Make all illegal immigrants felons and send them back; B) Have a guest worker program that allows immigrants to remain in the United States; C) Allow illegal immigrants to remain in the United States; D) Grant amnesty to all illegal immigrants in the country.

Please see the appendix for the descriptions of dependent and independent variables as well as for the methods used in this chapter.

FINDINGS AND DISCUSSION

Overview of LACSS Sample

Table 3.1 reports select summary statistics regarding stereotypes and attitudes, views toward proposed government policies targeting the undocumented, and SES/demographic factors for LACSS respondents.

First we examine the average responses to views regarding proposed government policies toward undocumented immigration, by racial and ethnic group. The most favored response was allowing undocumented immigrants to remain in the United States, with over 40 percent of each racial/ethnic group selecting this option. Of the four possible policy options, Blacks in the sample favored providing a guest worker program the least (at 8 percent). Blacks in the sample, on average, were the most likely to choose a more punitive policy option (deportation) at 21 percent as compared to Whites at 14 percent, Asians at 12 percent, and Latinos at 3 percent. Asians in the sample were the most likely, on average, to favor amnesty for undocumented immigrants at 28 percent, while Latinos were the least likely group to favor amnesty at 6 percent and were the most likely group to favor a guest worker program at 47 percent.

Second, we examine some negative stereotypes and attitudes often associated with views toward undocumented immigration. In this study, we do not imply that Hispanic-origin groups are the only groups from which some of their members may arrive or remain in the United States undocumented (for example, arriving without legal documentation or overstaying their visas). In Los Angeles, however, the media coverage concerning immigration reform has largely centered on groups of Latin American descent, mainly from Mexico, reaching a boiling point during the immigrant rights marches in the spring of 2006, just months prior to the 2007 LACSS.[4] A majority of Blacks and Asians as well as half of White respondents believed that most Mexican immigrants are in the country illegally. Sixty-four percent of Blacks shared this view, as compared to 59 percent of Asians, 50 percent of Whites, and only 41 percent of Latinos. On average, Blacks in our sample were also the most likely to believe that undocumented immigration hurts the economy, at 66 percent, as compared to Asians at 39 percent, Whites at 47 percent, and Latinos at 15 percent. On average, Asians in our sample were the most likely to believe that most Latinos prefer welfare benefits, at 61 percent, as compared to Blacks at 30 percent, and both Latinos and Whites at 23 percent. Interestingly Blacks, on average, were the most likely to believe that Mexicans are like Blacks, at 46 percent, as compared to both Asians and Latinos at 21 percent and Whites at 12 percent. When asked if their race is important to their identity, Blacks were most likely to agree, at 79 percent, as compared to Latinos at 76 percent, Asians at 66 percent, and Whites at 49 percent.

Next we examine some SES and demographic characteristics for the

TABLE 3.1 SELECT SUMMARY STATISTICS FOR RESPONDENTS IN LACSS SAMPLE,
BY RACIAL/ETHNIC GROUP

	Black	Latino	Asian	White
Proposed Undocumented Immigration Policies				
Grant amnesty	.178	.061	.275	.196
Allow to stay in U.S.	.429	.436	.467	.480
Provide guest worker program	.083	.465	.108	.123
Make felon and send to home country	.207	.032	.115	.138
Stereotypes and Views				
Believe most Mexicans are here illegally	.641	.411	.585	.500
Believe illegal immigration hurts economy	.657	.146	.392	.473
Believe most Latinos prefer welfare	.302	.232	.613	.226
Believe Mexicans are more like blacks	.463	.208	.210	.123
Believe race is important to identity	.787	.762	.660	.488
Socioeconomic Status and Demographics				
High school diploma or less	.236	.560	.275	.126
Some college	.749	.403	.688	.853
Bachelor's degree or more	.320	.167	.550	.538
Income >30K	.349	.396	.289	.153
Income <30K and >60k	.269	.200	.260	.230
Income <60K and >90K	.130	.083	.126	.188
Income <90K	.112	.080	.134	.269
Age 18–24	.073	.205	.051	.031
Age 25–34	.102	.212	.094	.085
Age 35–44	.143	.208	.171	.168
Age 45–54	.209	.168	.277	.234
Age 55–64	.172	.124	.182	.234
Over 65	.297	.080	.222	.246
Female	.629	.596	.550	.534
Citizen	.981	.603	.658	.968
Political Ideology				
Liberal	.258	.316	.264	.303
Moderate	.465	.360	.427	.384
Conservative	.163	.258	.221	.234
Observations	275	275	276	260

SOURCE: Los Angeles County Social Survey (Sawyer et al. 2007).

NOTES: Table entries represent the means of a given variable and should be interpreted as percentages. The data used in this study are weighted by race and national origin.

sample, by racial and ethnic group. Latinos were the most likely, on average, to report having attained a high school diploma or less education, at 56 percent, as compared to Asians at 28 percent, Blacks at 24 percent, and Whites at 13 percent. Asians, on average, reached the highest level of educational attainment, with over half of the sample (55 percent) having attained a bachelor's degree or more, followed by Whites at 54 percent, Blacks at 32 percent, and Latinos at 17 percent. Latinos were more likely on average to report incomes of less than $30,000 (at 40 percent), followed by Blacks at 35 percent. Whites were the least likely, on average, to report incomes below $30,000, at 15 percent, and were the most likely to report incomes exceeding $90,000, at 27 percent, followed by Asians at 13 percent, Blacks at 11 percent, and Latinos at 8 percent.

Finally, we examined the reported political ideologies of respondents in the sample. All racial/ethnic groups were most likely to report holding a moderate political ideology, with Blacks at 47 percent, Asians at 43 percent, Whites at 38 percent, and Latinos at 36 percent. Blacks in the sample were the least likely to report holding a conservative political ideology, at 16 percent, while Latinos were the most likely to, at 26 percent.

These descriptive statistics underscore persistent differences and disparities between racial/ethnic groups in Los Angeles. However, they tell us little about how a combination of these factors might influence one's views toward contentious, often racialized issues such as undocumented immigration. Given the emphasis of this volume, we focus on Black respondents' views in this chapter. Moving beyond the average summary statistics for the LACSS sample discussed above, the next section examines the extent to which racial stereotypes and SES/demographics influence Blacks' views regarding proposed government policies toward undocumented immigration.

The Role of Stereotypes and Racial Attitudes on Views toward Undocumented Immigration

Stereotypes and beliefs about other racial or ethnic groups are often important factors in determining policy preferences. In this study, we find that negative stereotypes matter, and they influence Blacks' views regarding proposed policies toward undocumented immigration. Our hypothesis was confirmed that Blacks who hold negative attitudes

TABLE 3.2   INFLUENCE OF INDIVIDUAL LEVEL MEASURES ON BLACKS' VIEWS
OF PROPOSED UNDOCUMENTED IMMIGRATION POLICIES

	Criminalization and Deportation	Guest Worker	Stay in U.S.	Amnesty
Stereotypes and Views				
Most Mexicans are in U.S. illegally	0.14**	−0.07	−0.02	−0.05
Illegal immigration hurts economy	0.03	0.06	0.05	−0.13**
Most Latinos prefer welfare	0.09	0.09	−0.20**	0.02
Mexicans are more like blacks	−0.16**	−0.08	0.26***	−0.02
Race is important to identity	−0.23**	0.09	0.14	0.01
Socioeconomic Status				
Some college[1]	−0.03	0.17***	−0.04	−0.10
Bachelor's degree or more	−0.06	−0.03	0.05	0.04
Income >30K[2]	−0.25***	−0.02	0.27**	−0.00
Income <30K and >60K	−0.18***	0.00	0.20*	−0.03
Income <60K and >90K	−0.19***	−0.01	0.22*	−0.02
Other Control Variables				
Age	0.01	0.01	−0.02	−0.01
Female	0.10*	−0.07	−0.04	0.01
Liberal[3]	0.03	0.02	−0.03	−0.01
Moderate	−0.04	0.07	0.03	−0.05*
Observations	199	199	199	199

SOURCE: Los Angeles County Social Survey (Sawyer et al. 2007).

NOTES: The data used in this study are weighted by race and national origin. Each column represents the results of the marginal effects after the multinomial logistic regression analysis. Unlike logistic regression, the marginal effects are easier to interpret and help us to understand the impact of each independent variable on the dependent measure, from its minimum to maximum value, holding all others variables at their means. An asterisk indicates that the variable is statistically significant (***p < 0.01, **p < 0.05, *p < 0.10). We provide all of the variables for comparison here. However, several of the corresponding logistic regression coefficients are not statistically significant, and the marginal effects would not typically be calculated. The multinomial logistic regression table with coefficients and standard errors are available from the authors upon request.

[1]Reference category = high school diploma or less.

[2]Reference category = income <90K.

[3]Reference category = Republican.

about Latinos will favor more punitive government policies toward undocumented immigrants. First, as reported in table 3.2, we found that Blacks who believe that "more Mexicans in the U.S. tend to be undocumented than legal" were 14 percent more likely to favor deporting undocumented immigrants than Blacks who do not believe this negative view.

Second, recall the descriptive statistics from table 3.1 that showed that allowing the undocumented to remain in the United States was the most favored option among Black respondents. Forty-three percent of Black respondents chose this option. Our findings also echo those from a 2006 Pew Center report that found 47 percent of Blacks felt that undocumented immigrants should be able to stay in the United States (Doherty 2006). We recognize that "stay in the United States" is the most ambiguous of the policy options. Deportation, guest worker programs, and amnesty each have corresponding legal and practical realities. However, we found that Black respondents who held the negative perception that most Latinos prefer welfare benefits were 20 percent less likely to prefer the policy option of allowing Latinos to remain in the United States.

Third, amnesty typically refers to providing undocumented immigrants already in the country with a way to obtain legal status. In 1986 with the passage of the Immigration Reform and Control Act, amnesty referred to granting undocumented immigrants legal permanent residence after meeting residency requirements, background checks, and other criteria. Recall that in table 3.1, only 18 percent of Blacks in the sample favored granting amnesty to undocumented immigrants. Accounting for all other factors, we find that Black respondents who believe that undocumented immigration hurts the economy were 13 percent less likely to support amnesty over the other options.

Given the persistent racialization of immigration policy, particularly relating to Latinos residing in the United States, it is unsurprising that negative beliefs about Latinos, but specifically Mexicans, are related to Black views about proposed policies toward undocumented immigration. These findings are important because they shed light on the importance of the public discourse concerning immigration. The messages people receive about immigrants—that they tend to be here legally or illegally, that they hurt or help the economy—may influence their views toward immigration policies. However, this is only part of the story. In addition to examining negative stereotypes, we also examined the influence of feelings of commonality between Blacks and Latinos. Respondents that perceived a shared commonality—who believed that Mexicans are more like Blacks—were 16 percent *less* likely to favor deportation and 26 percent *more* likely to support a policy that would allow undocumented immigrants to remain the United States. In addition, Black respondents who reported that race is important to their identity were 23 percent less likely to favor deportation. We specu-

TABLE 3.3 VARIABLE DESCRIPTIONS, LACSS 2007

	Question Wording	Description
Stereotypes and Attitudinal Measures		
Most Mexicans are in U.S. illegally	Where would you rate Mexican immigrants in general on this scale, where 1 means "tend to be here legally," and 7 means "tend to be here illegally"?	Collapsed and rescaled into a dummy variable using negative perceptions coding strategy[1] Dummy: 1 = here illegally 0 = here legally
Illegal immigration hurts the economy	Some people say undocumented or illegal immigrants help the economy by providing low cost labor; others say they hurt the economy by driving wages down. Which is closer to your views?	Dummy: 1 = hurt economy 0 = help economy
Most Latinos prefer welfare	Where would you rate Latinos in general on this scale, where 1 means "prefer to be self-supporting" and 7 means "prefer to be on welfare"?	Collapsed and rescaled into a dummy variable using negative perceptions coding strategy[1] Dummy: 1 = welfare 0 = other
Mexicans are more like blacks	Next I want to know how you would categorize Mexican Americans. Do you feel that Mexicans are more like African Americans or more like Irish or Italian-Americans?	Dummy: 1 = like blacks 0 = not like blacks
Racial identity is important	Is your race/ethnicity important to your identity?	Dummy: 1 = yes 2 = no

Primary SES and Demographics Measures

Education — What is the highest grade of school or year of college you have completed?
Dummy: 1 = HS or less
Dummy: 1 = some college
Dummy: 1 = BA or more (reference category)

Income — Which of the following income groups includes your total family income in 2006 before taxes?
Dummy: 1 = <$30,000
Dummy: 1 = $30,000–59,000
Dummy: 1 = $60,000–89,000
Dummy: 1 = $90,000 and up (reference category)

Other Control Measures

Age — Which of the following categories represents your age group?
Ordinal: 18–24
25–34
35–44
45–54
55–64
65 and older

Sex — Gender of respondent
Dummy: 1 = female
0 = male

Political ideology — When it comes to politics, do you usually think of yourself as a liberal, a conservative, or a moderate?
Dummy: 1 = liberal
Dummy: 1 = moderate
Dummy: 1 = conservative (reference category)

SOURCE: Los Angeles County Social Survey (Sawyer et al. 2007).

[1]Each 7-point scale was coded so that positive and neutral perceptions were counted as 0 and any negative perceptions as 1 (see Oliver and Wong 2003: fn. 4 for a similar negative-perceptions coding strategy).

lated earlier that those feelings of solidarity might make Blacks unwilling to support deportation measures. The positive relationship we find between racial identity and disfavoring punitive immigration policies may be influenced by a feeling of group solidarity between Blacks and Latinos rather than a feeling of conflict (Pastor and Marcelli 2003), particularly given the racial overtones of the immigration debate taking place during the time of the survey.

The Role of Socioeconomic Status on Views toward Undocumented Immigration

The economic competition or conflict theories we discussed earlier in the chapter point to several potential outcomes in terms Black views on undocumented immigration policies. In table 3.2, we report the findings for socioeconomic status using two variables often used to test economic competition between groups: family income and educational attainment. These two variables also help to explain the role that conflict plays in attitudes regarding undocumented immigration policies. Conflict theories often rely on the assumption that when resources and material goods are scarce (or threatened), out-group hostilities will develop. Controlling for all other factors, educational attainment poses little influence on Blacks' views toward undocumented immigration, with the exception of Black respondents who have completed some college. That group is 17 percent more likely to support a guest worker program compared with those who have a high school diploma or less. Moreover, contrary to these expectations, we found that those with fewer resources (lower levels of family income) were the least like to support the most punitive policy toward undocumented immigrants—deportation.

Each of the income categories in table 3.2 is compared to respondents who make $90,000 or more per year. Respondents in each of the three income categories making less than $90,000 are less likely to support deportation than those making over that amount. In fact, respondents in the lowest category (those making less $30,000) are 25 percent *less* likely to favor criminalizing undocumented immigrants. Those in the lowest income categories are also 27 percent *more* likely to favor a government policy that would allow undocumented immigrants to remain in the United States. These findings are contrary to theories that suggest greater economic competition between low-income Blacks and Latinos.

CONCLUSION

The protest in Leimert Park that began this chapter was newsworthy, in part, because it was surprising that these two groups would come together—especially in South L.A. The politics of race and the politics of immigration are inevitably linked, particularly as they play out in Los Angeles, because the face of immigration (especially undocumented immigration) is often associated with Latino immigrants. This link suggests that both racial attitudes and economic insecurities among Blacks may influence their views of policies regarding undocumented immigration. However, as our analysis shows, there are multiple and often conflicting considerations. Blacks with lower levels of income are more likely to reject punitive policies such as deportation, while Blacks who hold negative racial stereotypes about Latinos are more likely to favor more punitive policies toward undocumented immigrants. However, we also find that attitudes about racial identity and perceived commonality with Latinos are important influences on Blacks' views favoring more lenient policies toward undocumented immigrants.

Understanding what factors shape minority attitudes toward outgroups and the influence of such attitudes concerning hot-button, often racialized policy issues, such as undocumented immigration, is important to providing insight into the prospects for multiracial coalition formation and sustainability. One the one hand, a shared history of marginalization might bring Blacks and Latinos together on common issues, especially if policies are seen as racially targeted. On the other hand, the perpetuation of persistent stereotypes could derail these efforts. It is important to continue to follow the social, economic, and political dynamics of Los Angeles neighborhoods in transition, particularly those communities for which Latinos are now the majority population but for which Blacks remain the majority of the electorate and continue to hold the largest number of elected and appointed positions at the local level, such as the city councils, school boards, and other elected or appointed offices.

APPENDIX

Variable Descriptions and Methods

Dependent Variable

The outcome measure in this analysis is views toward proposed undocumented immigration policies. In this analysis, we examined one dependent measure having four possible options using the following survey question:

> *Government Policy Responses to Illegal Immigrants:* Which of the following comes closest to your view about what government policy should be toward illegal immigrants currently residing in the United States? Should the government: A) Make all illegal immigrants felons and send them back; B) Have a guest worker program that allows immigrants to remain in the United States; C) Allow illegal immigrants to remain in the United States; D) Grant amnesty to all illegal immigrants in the country.

When selecting the most appropriate regression methodology, we decided not to treat the outcome variable as ordinal, because to do so assumes a natural ordering within the variable (from option A, "make felon," to option D, "grant amnesty"). However, while there are clearer distinctions between options A and D, we are less convinced of the "ordinal nature" of options B, "guest worker," and C, "remain in the United States." Instead we used multinomial logistic regression. However, interpreting the results of multinomial logistic regression analyses can be difficult, and thus we use the postestimation command "mfx2" in STATA to generate the marginal effects for each of the four possible outcomes in order to make the interpretations of our analysis clearer. The marginal effect is the change in the dependent variable as a function of a change in a certain dependent variable while all the other covariates are kept constant. In this case, they represent the probability of selecting one of the four policy choices when holding all other variables in the model at their means.

Independent Variables

In this analysis, we examined the influence of various sets of independent factors, including stereotypes and SES/demographic factors, on policy positions related to undocumented immigration. Table 3.3 describes each independent measure used in the study and its coding.

NOTES

1. CBA is a project affiliate of the Federation for American Immigration Reform (FAIR). http://web.archive.org/web/20070821044914/http://www .chooseblackamerica.org/

2. For example, in 2009, the Orange County Human Relations Commission reported an increase in the number of hate crimes targeted against racial minorities (Esquivel 2009). According to the report, Blacks have consistently

been the most frequent targets of hate crimes in Orange County—even though they make up less than 2 percent of the population. Latinos were the next most frequent target, with fifteen hate crimes reported against them in 2008, up from twelve the year before.

3. The 2007 LACSS was conducted in May through June of that year (Sawyer et al. 2007). The survey (N = 1,102) included 275 Blacks, 276 Asian Americans, 16 Native Americans/American Indians, 275 Latinos, and 260 Whites. Blacks, Spanish-speaking Latinos, and Asian Americans in Los Angeles County were oversampled. Adults of eighteen years and older were interviewed in English, Spanish, Mandarin, Cantonese, or Korean. The sample also included 216 respondents identifying as more than one race. Multirace and Native American respondents were not analyzed in this study. Latinos are defined as respondents who selected "Latino" as a first racial classification. The LACSS provides a more comprehensive accounting of racial identity (including Indio, Moreno, Mestizo, Negro, Blanco, Mulatto, and Trigueño) as well point assignments for multiracial identities.

4. The survey asked respondents if they participated in the immigration marches in 2006. Very few respondents reported participating, so this measure was not included in this analysis.

REFERENCES

Allen, James P. 2005. "Ethnic Geography Dynamics: Clues from Los Angeles." *Yearbook of the Association of Pacific Coast Geographers* 67: 97–116.

Allport, Gordon. 1954. *The Nature of Prejudice.* Cambridge, MA: Addison-Wesley Publishing Company.

Barkan, Elliott R. 2003. "Return of the Nativists? California Public Opinion and Immigration in the 1980s and 1990s." *Social Science History* 27 (2): 229–83.

Blalock, Hubert M. 1967. *Toward a Theory of Minority-Group Relations.* New York: Wiley.

Blumer, Herbert. 1958. "Race Prejudice as a Sense of Group Position." *Pacific Sociological Review* (1): 3–7.

Bobo, Lawrence, and Vincent L. Hutchings. 1996. "Perceptions of Racial Group Competition: Extending Blumer's Theory of Group Position to a Multiracial Social Context." American Sociological Review 61 (6): 951–72.

Bobo, Lawrence, and Michael Massagli. 2001. "Stereotyping and Urban Inequality." In *Urban Inequality: Evidence from Four Cities,* ed. Alice O'Connor, Chris Tilly, and Lawrence Bobo, 89–162. New York: Russell Sage Foundation.

Burns, Peter, and James G. Gimpel. 2000. "Economic Insecurity, Prejudicial Stereotypes, and Public Opinion on Immigration Policy." *Political Science Quarterly* 155 (2): 201–25.

Camarillo, Albert M. 2004. "Black and Brown in Compton: Demographic Change, Suburban Decline, and Intergroup Relations in a South Central Los Angeles Community, 1950 to 2000." In *Not Just Black and White,* ed.

Nancy Foner and George Fredrickson, 358–76. New York: Russell Sage Foundation.

———. 2007. "Cities of Color: The New Racial Frontier in California's Minority-Majority Cities." *Pacific Historical Review* 76 (1): 1–28.

Campbell, Andrea Louise, Cara Wong, and Jack Citrin. 2006. "'Racial Threat,' Partisan Climate, and Direct Democracy: Contextual Effects in Three California Initiatives." *Political Behavior* 28 (2): 129–50.

Citrin, Jack, Donald P. Green, Christopher Muste, and Cara Wong. 1997. "Public Opinion toward Immigration Reform: The Role of Economic Motivations." *Journal of Politics* 59 (3): 858–81.

Cummings, Scott, and Thomas Lambert. 1997. "Anti-Hispanic and Anti-Asian Sentiments among African Americans." *Social Science Quarterly* 78 (2): 338–53.

Diamond, Jeff. 1998. "African-American Attitudes towards United States Immigration Policy." *International Migration Review* 32 (2): 451–70.

Doherty, Carroll. 2006. *Attitudes toward Immigration: In Black and White.* Washington DC: Pew Research Center for the People and the Press.

Espenshade, Thomas J. 1995. "Unauthorized Immigration to the United States." *Annual Review of Sociology* 21: 195–216.

Espenshade, Thomas J., and Charles A. Calhoun. 1993. "An Analysis of Public Opinion toward Undocumented Immigration." *Population Research and Policy Review* 12 (3): 189–224.

Esquivel, Paloma. 2009. "Hate Crimes Decrease Again in Orange County." *Los Angeles Times,* May 29.

Ethington, Philip J., William H. Frey, and Dowell Myers. 2001. "The Racial Resegregation of Los Angeles County, 1940–2000." In *Race Contours 2000 Study,* ed. Philip J. Ethington, William H. Frey, and Dowell Myers. Public Research Report 2001-5. www-bcf.usc.edu/~philipje/Segregation/Haynes_Reports/Contours_PRR_2001–04e.pdf.

Federico, Christopher M. 2004. "When Do Welfare Attitudes Become Racialized? The Paradoxical Effects of Education." *American Journal of Political Science* 48 (2): 374–91.

Fennelly, Katherine, and Christopher Federico. 2008. "Rural Residence as a Determinant of Attitudes toward US Immigration Policy." *International Migration* 46 (1): 151–90.

García Bedolla, Lisa. 2005. *Fluid Borders: Latino Power, Identity, and Politics in Los Angeles.* Berkeley: University of California Press.

Gay, Claudine. 2006. "Seeing Difference: The Effect of Economic Disparity on Black Attitudes toward Latinos." *American Journal of Political Science* 50 (4): 982–97.

Gilens, Martin. 1996. "'Race Coding' and White Opposition to Welfare." *American Political Science Review* 90 (3): 593–604.

Glaser, James M. 2001. "The Preference Puzzle: Educational Differences in Racial-Political Attitudes." *Political Behavior* 23 (4): 313–34

Henry, P. J., and David O. Sears. 2002. "The Symbolic Racism 2000 Scale." *Political Psychology* 23 (2): 253–83.

Hood, M. V., and Irwin L. Morris. 1997. "¿Amigo o Enemigo? Context, Attitudes, and Anglo Public Opinion toward Immigration." *Social Science Quarterly* 78: 309–23.

Hurwitz, Jon, and Mark Peffley. 1997. "Public Perceptions of Race and Crime: The Role of Racial Stereotypes." *American Journal of Political Science* 41 (2): 375–401.

Ilias, Shayerah, Katherine Fennelly, and Christopher M. Federico. 2008. "American Attitudes toward Guest Worker Policies." *International Migration Review* 42 (4): 741–66.

Key, V.O. 1949. *Southern Politics in State and Nation.* 1st ed. New York: A.A. Knopf.

McClain, Paula D. 1993. "The Changing Dynamics of Urban Politics: Black and Hispanic Municipal Employment—Is There Competition?" *Journal of Politics* 55 (2): 399–414.

McClain, Paula D., Niambi M. Carter, Victoria M. DeFrancesco Soto, Monique L. Lyle, Jeffrey D. Grynaviski, Shayla C. Nunnally, Thomas J. Scotto, J. Alan Kendrick, Gerald F. Lackey, and Kendra Davenport Cotton. 2006. "Racial Distancing in a Southern City: Latino Immigrants' Views of Black Americans." *Journal of Politics* 68 (3): 571–84.

Morris, Irwin L. 2000. "African American Voting on Proposition 187: Rethinking the Prevalence of Interminority Conflict." *Political Research Quarterly* 53 (1): 77–98.

National Public Radio. 2006. "Minuteman Rallies Garner African-American Support." May 4. www.npr.org/templates/story/story.php?storyId=5382074.

Oliver, J. Eric, and Tali Mendelberg. 2000. "Reconsidering the Environmental Determinants of White Racial Attitudes." *American Journal of Political Science* 44 (3): 574–89.

Oliver, J. Eric, and Janelle Wong. 2003. "Intergroup Prejudice in Multiethnic Settings." *American Journal of Political Science* 47 (4): 567–82.

Ong, Paul, Theresa Firestine, Deirdre Pfeiffer, Oiyan Poon, and Linda Tran. 2008. "The State of South LA." UCLA School of Public Affairs, Los Angeles. www.academia.edu/220952/The_State_of_South_LA.

Pastor, Manuel, and Enrico Marcelli. 2003. "Somewhere over the Rainbow? African Americans, Unauthorized Mexican Immigration, and Coalition Building." *Review of Black Political Economy* 31 (1): 125–55.

Robinson, Paul. 2010. "Race, Space and the Evolution of Black Los Angeles." In *Black Los Angeles: American Dreams and Racial Realities,* ed. Darnell Hunt and Ana-Christina Ramon. New York: New York University Press.

Sawyer, Mark, Taeku Lee, Janelle Wong, and Jim Sidanius. 2007. Los Angeles County Social Survey.

Sides, Josh. 2003. *L.A. City Limits: African American Los Angeles from the Great Depression to the Present.* Berkeley: University of California Press.

Vaca, Nick Corona. 2004. *The Presumed Alliance: The Unspoken Conflict between Latinos and Blacks and What It Means for America.* 1st ed. New York: Rayo.

Wilson, Thomas C. 2001. "Americans' Views on Immigration Policy: Testing the Role of Threatened Group Interests." *Sociological Perspectives* 44 (4): 485–501.

PART TWO

Urban Histories

4

The Changing Valence
of White Racial Innocence

Black-Brown Unity in the 1970s Los Angeles
School Desegregation Struggles

DANIEL MARTINEZ HOSANG

On September 10, 1978, the buses finally rolled. After a fifteen-year legal battle, the Los Angeles Unified School District (LAUSD) initiated one of the largest mandatory desegregation programs in the nation's history, involving nearly forty thousand students in fourth through eighth grades.[1] Supported by large majorities of Black parents, political leaders, and civil rights organizations and championed by predominantly white liberal groups like the American Civil Liberties Union (ACLU), the plan embraced the notion that educational opportunities for Black students in particular would be maximized when they were no longer relegated to inferior, stigmatized, and segregated schools. A federal study at the time described the district as being "among the most segregated in the entire country."[2] Given the entrenched patterns of housing segregation and the vast geographic expanse of the LAUSD—encompassing 171 square miles and nearly six hundred thousand students—such desegregation required a large amount of student reassignment and busing.

At the same time, many Mexican American political leaders, educators, and parents pursued an agenda seemingly at odds with a mandatory desegregation program. By 1978, nearly half of the district's 238,000 Mexican American students were assessed as limited English speaking or non-English speaking and thus eligible for bilingual education programs that were beginning to gain a foothold in schools populated by large numbers of Mexican American students. Under a mandatory desegregation program, many of these students would be reassigned to other school sites that lacked the personnel and capacity to implement such programs. Bilingual education, which required some concentration of LES and NES students and a linguistically and culturally tailored curriculum, seemed inherently at odds with desegregation remedies that relied on geographically dispersing students and standardizing the curriculum.

The conflict came to a head only a year after the mandatory desegregation program began. In November 1979, California voters went to the polls to decide the fate of Proposition 1, a statewide ballot measure that sought to end the district's mandatory desegregation program and many others like it in the state. The ballot measure effectively required the state courts to follow stricter federal legal standards, stipulating that desegregation orders could be issued only if intentional or de jure segregation could be demonstrated. Though Proposition 1 originated from a powerful movement rooted in the white suburban enclaves of the San Fernando Valley, it was eventually embraced by a significant number of Mexican American political leaders, who reasoned that mandatory desegregation orders could spell the death of hard-fought bilingual education programs.

Proposition 1 passed in a landslide, approved statewide by nearly seven in ten voters. With nearly every Black elected official in the region opposed to the measure, African American voters in South Los Angeles voted two-to-one against Proposition 1. By contrast, most leading Mexican American officials supported Proposition 1, as did voters in predominantly Mexican American districts. After two years of continued legal battles, the U.S. Supreme Court upheld Proposition 1, and Los Angeles became the first district in the nation to reassign students from integrated classrooms back to segregated ones.

On first blush, the Proposition 1 conflict seems to fit the now familiar story of failed coalition politics, an early chapter in the ongoing struggle between Black and Brown communities for control and influence of the second largest public school system in the country. According to this framework, as the group-based interests of African American and Mexican American communities diverged, and "conflicting avenues of redress" seemed to develop, the prospects for a shared platform for realizing racial justice were diminished.[3] Within the interest-group model that dominates the study of racial politics in Los Angeles and many urban communities, these conflicts seem to represent the triumph of divergent agendas over common causes.[4] White desegregation opponents argued to Mexican American parents and voters that the greatest threat to the well-being of Mexican American students was the allegedly overreaching Black demands for educational equity and justice, rather than historical and institutional structures of white racial power and privilege.

This essay examines the debates over desegregation and bilingual education in Los Angeles in the 1970s and the larger narrative of Black-Brown conflict from a different perspective. While various forms of interracial and indeed intraracial disagreement certainly shaped these debates, I argue that these dynamics are best analyzed within transformations taking place across the broader landscape of racial politics at the time. In the aftermath of World War II, expanding movements for social and racial justice, new social science scholarship on prejudice reduction, and growing pressures in the international arena made explicit forms of segregation and racial hierarchy increasingly difficult to justify. More and more, political and legal claims had to at least acknowledge norms of equal rights and opportunity and reject assertions of innate, group-based inferiority.

These developments required political actors to demonstrate their fealty to *racial innocence,* disavowing any interest or investment in racial inequality. Only by incorporating the tenets of race neutrality and the norms of liberal anti-racism could opposition to school desegregation be legitimated politically and legally.

As claims of racial innocence applied to schools, they held that because white parents and students did not intentionally create the second-class schools to which most racial minorities were consigned nor explicitly support segregated schools as a matter of principle, they could not be compelled to participate in the schools' improvement. During the 1970s, federal jurisprudence on school segregation issues required plaintiffs to demonstrate intentional patterns and practice on the part of a school district in order for a desegregation order to be issued, thus providing legal criteria and incentives for districts to demonstrate their institutional innocence. On an individual level, assertions of racial innocence implied that one could be in favor of providing equal education opportunities to all students while preserving a system that continued to reproduce racial hierarchies and disparities.

This essay explores the ways in which struggles over desegregation and bilingual education in the late 1970s became narrated to buttress claims of white racial innocence while occluding criticisms of white racial power, a dynamic that continues to shape interpretations of Black-Brown conflict today.

HISTORICAL PATTERNS OF SCHOOL SEGREGATION IN LOS ANGELES

In the early 1960s, the white, working-class city of South Gate, a few miles south of Los Angeles, became a flashpoint for initial efforts to desegregate the LAUSD, which included schools in South Gate and twenty-one other cities adjacent to Los Angeles. Groups such as the National Association for the Advancement of Colored People (NAACP), the Congress on Racial Equality (CORE), and the umbrella United Civil Rights Committee seized on South Gate High School as a particularly egregious example of the school board's racial gerry-mandering of attendance boundaries: The attendance areas for South Gate High and nearby Jordan High School, in Watts, were regularly adjusted as Black families in Watts moved closer to the South Gate border. South Gate High remained nearly 100 percent white and was kept in far better condition than Jordan High, which was almost entirely Black and badly in need of repair. The major thoroughfare dividing the two neighborhoods, Alameda Boulevard, was dubbed by civil rights activists the "Wall of Hate," a rigidly enforced boundary of segregation and exclusion.[5]

The school board maintained that patterns of racial imbalance between schools were unintentional and that the district operated in a "color-blind" fashion. Indeed, the formal segregation of African American students was effectively outlawed by the Supreme Court of California in 1890.[6] The segregation of Mexican American students— which was widespread in most parts of Southern California well into World War II—succumbed to a legal challenge by a group of parents in Orange County. The year after the *Mendez v. Westminster* (1947) verdict was delivered, Governor Earl Warren repealed all legislative provisions allowing for the segregation of racial minorities in public schools.[7] Thus, when first confronted with evidence of racial imbalance and segregation in South Gate, the majority of the Los Angeles school board simply recited the official prevailing position: color-blind innocence. In response to NAACP charges that racially gerrymandered attendance areas sustained segregated schools, school board member Georgina Hardy insisted that the school staff "counts noses, not color."[8]

To civil rights activists, these responses were not convincing. When the school board voted to rebuild and expand Jordon High as a segregated campus rather than integrate students with nearby South Gate High, it provoked this wry retort from NAACP leader Marnesba Tackett: "You are accidentally spending over a million dollars to accidentally rebuild Jordon in its same location. Hence it will accidentally remain a segregated school. You have accidentally bought two new school sites in areas that are rapidly becoming solidly Negro. In accidental anticipation of this ethnic change you have accidentally named one of these proposed schools after a noted Negro author."[9]

Tackett's testimony demonstrates how the distinction between de facto versus de jure segregation provided little purchase toward understanding the causes of segregation in Los Angeles.[10] The boundaries of attendance zones, the location of new school sites, and the organization of feeder patterns among elementary, middle, and high schools were often based on maintaining and enforcing patterns of racial segregation. And Black students who attempted to enroll in predominantly white schools in nearby attendance areas were unilaterally rebuffed.[11] As the civil rights attorney Loren Miller explained in a 1960 public address, "There was a time in Los Angeles when I could have traced the growth of Negro residence in my city if I had known nothing else than the manner in which the boundary lines of one of our high schools expanded." He continued, "As Negroes moved south that boundary line moved south; when they moved west it moved west; when they moved east it moved east." Miller called on the school board to be "color-conscious rather than color blind" and deliberately shape attendance boundaries to create integrated schools. The board, he insisted, had "no business blundering into a situation which will produce a segregated school."[12]

Funding formulas for campus maintenance were also based on the square footage of school facilities, systematically favoring the sprawling, newly constructed campuses in the San Fernando Valley over the aging, more compact buildings in older parts of the city. The school board did not make these decisions unilaterally; parents often lobbied the board to ensure they adopted policies that would use race to assign students and allocate resources. Thus, the highly segregated school systems that developed in the region in the postwar era were driven in large part by a self-reinforcing dynamic that treated racially determined attendance and assignment patterns as "natural" and funneled disproportionate amounts of resources to schools serving white students, thus creating more opportunities in them.[13] Decades of invest-ments in residential segregation, enforced by a combination of realtors, discriminatory government-lending policies, suburban tract develop-ers, and rental apartment owners meant that seemingly neutral com-mitments to "neighborhood schools" inevitably reinforced and ampli-fied past and current practices of segregation.

Among their other demands for political representation and addi-tional resources, Tackett and the civil rights groups insisted that atten-dance boundaries be redrawn to desegregate both South Gate and Jordon High Schools, a policy that would have required minimal dis-trict-provided busing, since the schools were less than a mile apart.[14] The ACLU also filed a lawsuit to compel this change. *Crawford v. Los Angeles School Board* (1963) was eventually expanded to include the entire Los Angeles school district and all Black and Mexican American students in segregated schools; it would be nearly two decades before the case was resolved.

State courts seemed to be a particularly promising venue to advance desegregation policies. In 1963 the Supreme Court of California ruled in *Jackson v. Pasadena City School District* that where residential seg-regation existed, it was "not enough for a school board to refrain from affirmative discriminatory conduct. The harmful influence on the chil-dren will be reflected and intensified in the classroom if school atten-dance is determined on a geographic basis without corrective mea-sures." The court offered an expansive interpretation of the state Equal Protection Clause in determining that "right to an equal opportunity for education and the harmful consequences of segregation require that school boards take steps, insofar as reasonably feasible, to allevi-ate racial imbalance in schools regardless of its cause."[15] The decision essentially made the distinction between de jure and de facto discrim-ination irrelevant, foregrounding the principle of equal educational opportunity and giving local desegregation advocates a potent tool in their negotiations with school boards. The ruling placed a clear man-date on local school districts to address both racial imbalance and edu-cational inadequacy.

In the mid-1960s, more than 80 percent of Black students in the dis-trict attended schools that were predominantly Black and were often overcrowded and poorly funded facilities. School sessions had to be shortened in response to overenrollment. At the same time, some 50 percent of Mexican America students were also enrolled in segregated Mexican American schools, facing the same conditions of overcrowding.[16] The large majority of white students, by contrast, attended white majority schools in the San Fernando Valley, West Los Angeles, and San Pedro. Especially in the Valley, where residential segregation was rigidly enforced through the early 1970s, the newly built public schools often were not filled to capacity.[17]

School boards throughout the region slowly began responding to the mandate to desegregate. In Orange County, both within larger districts such as Santa Ana and Anaheim and within smaller districts such as Garden Grove, Placentia, and Orange, school boards made at least modest efforts to alleviate patterns of racial imbalance by redrawing attendance boundaries or locating new schools to ensure existing imbalances were not perpetuated. As many of these districts were relatively small and already relied on some use of busing, the remedies seemed palatable to most parents.[18]

To be sure, most of these efforts were uneven and partial rather than comprehensive and resolute. In cities such as Richmond and Pasadena, the opposition of some parents and district officials plagued desegregation efforts from the start; in other cases, the reticence of local leadership to act decisively only contributed to the perception that desegregation was unworkable and excessively burdensome. But the transformations afoot during the 1960s should not be underestimated. California schools had become segregated over the course of many decades through a complex set of forces and relationships, and it was logical that the remedies would have to be locally tailored and implemented.[19]

In addition, all white parents and students did not uniformly oppose or flee mandatory desegregation. Their actions and assessments were often contradictory, and we must seriously consider the pro-segregationist expressions of many white parents without treating them as historically inevitable. On the one hand, because local school districts often funneled the most resources—the newest buildings, the most experienced teachers, and the most comprehensive curricular offerings—to the schools serving white students, it is unsurprising that many parents would infer that maintaining a white-dominant student body and teaching staff was critical to "protecting" the quality of their schools. In many cases, they eagerly pursued and embraced the relative opportunities and privileges afforded to them by segregated school systems.

On the other hand, the doomsday admonitions that white parents would never tolerate desegregated schools also proved spurious.

Following the 1946 *Mendez* decision, most schools in Orange County desegregated without incident. When the Berkeley and Riverside School Districts voluntarily inaugurated a districtwide busing program in the late 1960s and when districts such as San Francisco, Pasadena, and Santa Barbara instituted court-ordered programs in the 1970s, the highly vocal opposition they faced typically gave way to rapid adjustment and acceptance among the majority of parents and students. Attempts to organize anti-busing boycotts failed consistently. Nor were desegregation opponents ever able to conclusively establish that mandatory desegregation programs singularly drove patterns of "white flight" into private or parochial schools and other school districts. While the debate over the causes of declines in white enrollment was complicated, most of the evidence suggests that an objection to busing and desegregation was only one among several factors contributing to the exodus of white students from urban public school systems, a trend that had been underway for many years prior to busing proposals.[20]

THE EAST LOS ANGELES BLOWOUTS

If the desegregation plans had a significant liability, it was that by focusing almost exclusively on rectifying rigidly determined racial imbalances, they often left other questions of equity involving teacher and personnel hiring, "ability tracking," allocation of resources, parental involvement, curriculum, and language policy unaddressed. Many of these issues animated the largest student-led protest in the history of California public education—the Chicano student "Blowouts" involving twenty-two thousand students centered in East Los Angeles in the spring of 1968. The students' complaints—a curriculum that ignored Mexican American history and steered Chicano students away from college and toward vocational training, the paucity of Mexican American teachers, the continued use of corporal punishment, overcrowded campuses—reflected many of the same desires for justice and opportunity pursued by desegregation advocates. But the Chicano students made little mention of desegregation as a political imperative; their priority was the immediate improvement of conditions in East Los Angeles schools.[21] The desegregation remedies proposed in Los Angeles made few commitments to address these issues or the forms of cultural domination that fueled the walkouts, reasoning that student reassignment would lead to other school improvements.

Desegregation was not a principal demand or aspiration of the walkouts, but this did not necessarily signal divergent interests between African American or Mexican American communities. Indeed, most of the organizers who played central roles in the walkouts and in the growing organizing taking place in East Los Angeles and other Chicano communities in the late 1960s were profoundly influenced by the ascendant Black Power movement. The radical and expansive assertions of Black power and self-determination that flourished during this period provided Chicano activists with a political and analytic vocabulary to analyze many of the particular conditions facing Mexican Americans in Los Angeles and in the Southwest more generally. Critiques of land appropriation, cultural domination, and the imperative of community control, refracted through a broader prism of resistance to racial subordination and Third World liberation, animated both the Black and Brown power movements. Activists and leaders from Third World left formations, including the Black Panthers, Brown Berets, the Chicano Moratorium, and other groups, regularly encountered one another while organizing in Los Angeles in the late 1960s and early 1970s.[22]

In addition, while the student walkouts in 1968 were centered in East Los Angeles and led by Chicano students, thousands of Black students in South Los Angeles also participated.[23] Indeed, the Blowouts erupted at the same time that Black parents and students at Manual Arts High School in South Los Angeles were in the midst of a year-long effort to oust the school's white principal over grievances that were almost identical to those motivating the Blowouts: the alleged use of "physical threats or coercion" against students, a refusal to take parent and student complaints seriously, disciplinary and behavioral assessment policies that too frequently removed students from regular classrooms, and a broadly authoritarian style of school management. These dynamics characterized schools in both segregated Black and Mexican American communities. At least three dozen schools in these areas experienced similar parent-and-student-led protests in the late 1960s, which created conflicts that sometimes forced the temporary closure of schools and frequently spilled over into Los Angeles Board of Education meetings. Both Black and Brown students and parents challenged the "legitimacy of an educational bureaucracy that maintained inherently unequal schools, and were challenging the hegemony of the white middle class that controlled those schools." Indeed, in 1968, as the district's student population was just over 50 percent white, 84 percent of teachers and 95 percent of principals in secondary schools were white.[24]

Black and Mexican American students and parents were also often included together as plaintiffs in litigation related to educational adequacy and reform. The plaintiff class in the *Crawford* case, seeking to desegregate Los Angeles public schools, was expanded in 1966 to include all African American and Mexican American students in segregated schools.[25] A 1970 lawsuit initiated by the U.S. Commission on Civil Rights included both Black and Chicano students as plaintiffs against the San Diego public schools over the disproportionate placement of such students within "Educable Mentally Retarded" classes.[26] And districtwide desegregation lawsuits in both Oxnard (located seventy-five miles north of Los Angeles) and San Diego included both Chicano and Black students, positing that segregation posed harm to students in both groups.[27]

Thus, well into the early 1970s, a shared criticism of white racial power shaped the demands of both Black and Mexican American education reform advocacy and organizing efforts. To be sure, no uniform consensus existed within either community about the most effective remedy to improve educational opportunities. Some embraced more confrontational strategies that would result in local control of segregated neighborhood schools, reasoning that community autonomy was central to transforming public schools. Others embraced solutions rooted in student reassignment and desegregation, asserting that integrated schools were most likely to acquire adequate resources and to reduce the legacies of group stigma and inferiority that prospered within segregated settings.

SHIFTS IN THE 1970S

Beginning in the early 1970s, two developments helped shape a growing perception that Black and Brown interests were no longer aligned when it came to education justice and school reform struggles. First, after years of litigation and political advocacy, the courts and federal and state legislators finally recognized and affirmed the rights of students from a linguistic or a national origin minority to bilingual education programs. Both the U.S. Supreme Court's 1974 decision in *Lau v. Nichols* and California's Bilingual-Bicultural Education Act of 1976 stipulated that every student designated as limited English speaking (LES) or non-English speaking (NES) be given access to some sort of bilingual instructional program.[28] The LAUSD, which had the largest number of LES/NES students of any district in the nation, soon faced challenges in meeting these requirements. In 1977, the district was denied a twenty-four-million-dollar federal grant because of inadequacies in its bilingual education programs. Only a quarter of the roughly hundred thousand LES/NES Mexican American students were enrolled in adequate bilingual programs.[29] A major obstacle to the implementation of these programs was the shortage of qualified bilingual teachers and teaching assistants. This barrier was in turn related to a large gap in the hiring of Mexican American teachers, who made up less than 6 percent of the district's full-time teaching staff, even though Mexican American students constituted 35 percent of the district's total population. Thus, much of the attention of Mexican American political leaders, parents, and activists focused on implementing and improving bilingual education programs, addressing gaps in hiring, and making the curriculum more culturally relevant to Mexican American students.

Some advocates of bilingual education, including the Mexican American Legal Defense and Education Fund and other Latino civil rights organizations, contended that quality bilingual education programs could be implemented within integrated settings and that bilingual education and desegregation were compatible if desegregation remedies paid careful attention to the needs of LES/NES students. In particular, this would require hiring many more qualified bilingual teachers, coordinating curricular planning among participating schools, and including ample numbers of white students in bilingual classes (similar to two-way language immersion programs found in some schools today) so that an adequate number of students would fill bilingual classes. In addition, Mexican American groups argued that desegregation efforts must be coupled with broader reforms that addressed discrimination in teacher hiring, curricular offerings, student "ability" tracking, discipline policy, and other issues that made schools inhospitable to many Mexican American students.[30]

As the *Crawford* desegregation lawsuit progressed, however, the courts largely ignored these concerns. The first California Superior Court ruling in Crawford in 1970 determined that the LAUSD had intentionally segregated Black and Chicano students into inferior schools and that such segregation caused serious harm. But the court's desegregation order made no mention of bilingual or bicultural education and made no distinctions among the needs of Black, Chicano, or Asian American students.[31] In 1976, following five years of appeals by the school board, the Supreme Court of California affirmed this ruling, again treating Black and Mexican American students as essentially interchangeable with regards to desegregation. It was not until another

procedural ruling in mid-July 1977 that the court began to acknowledge the district's obligations to LES/NES students and the challenges
that a student reassignment plan might pose to the implementation of
bilingual education programs.

At the same time, most desegregation advocates and political leaders mirrored the court's indifference to bilingual education programs.
Following the 1976 ruling, the LAUSD authorized the formation of
the 114-member Citizens Advisory Committee on School Integration
(CACSI) to advise the school board on the implementation of a desegregation plan. While the citywide committee included participants both
favoring and opposing mandatory desegregation, it counted only eight
Mexican Americans members. Chicano leaders fought for months to
raise particular issues before CACSI, and only toward the end of the
process was the Chicano Advisory Committee formed and authorized
to articulate these concerns. As CACSI made public its final recommendations, which included a far-reaching mandatory reassignment
plan, a group of prominent Mexican American politicians publicly criticized the process and the plan, contending that it failed to incorporate
their central concerns. One CACSI member told a community hearing in East Los Angeles that during the process, the Chicano members
"constantly had to remind [the committee], 'Hey—we're here! We're
the largest minority in this district. How many times do we have to
say that?'" Another parent declared: "I'm a pro-integrationist, but I'm
pro-integration only with guarantees for the largest student population
in Los Angeles." An East Los Angeles parent activist complained that
when she tried to explain bilingual education issues to ACLU officials
handling the *Crawford* litigation, she was rebuffed. "They didn't know
what we were talking about."[32]

Indeed, many proponents of the Los Angeles desegregation plan,
such as ACLU leader and UCLA professor John Caughey, spoke openly
of identifying "unassimilated" Mexican Americans who would be pri-
oritized in reassignment plans and distinguishing them from those who
could effectively be considered "white." (At one point, a judge in the
case announced his intention to retain a University of California, Irvine,
sociologist to assist the court in this identification and sorting process.)
Such comments resonated uneasily among Mexican Americans who had
been targeted by a long history of "Americanization" programs that
were rooted in assumptions of Mexican "cultural" pathology.[33] An editorial in the pages of the leftist *Sin Fronteras* community newspaper
commented: "Of all the struggles of the Chicano Movement, perhaps

TABLE 4.1   COMPARISON OF LAUSD STUDENT POPULATION RACE
AND ETHNICITY, 1968 AND 1978

	1968		1978	
Group	# of Students	Percentage	# of Students	Percentage
Mexican American	129,591	20.0	214,034	38.5
Black	146,686	22.6	137,363	24.7
Asian	23,141	3.6	35,610	6.4
American Indian	1,192	.2	3,387	.6
White	347,967	53.6	165,361	29.8
Total	648,577		555,755	

none was so clear as . . . defining ourselves on our own terms. We cannot now forget those struggles and passively allow racists to determine who we are."[34] The Chicano Integration Coalition within CACSI similarly announced its opposition to "an integration policy that is totally assimilationist in nature—one that does not respect the rights and needs of the culturally different." They argued repeatedly that student reassignment and desegregation were necessary but not sufficient: they demanded parity in resources, culturally relevant instruction and curricula, and attention to racial discrimination in teacher staffing and hiring.[35]

While ACLU and NAACP attorneys litigating the *Crawford* case publicly supported the principle of bilingual education and other specific issues raised by Chicano parents and advocates, the overwhelming focus of their attention was on winning a desegregation order. In Los Angeles as in most of the nation, desegregation was popularly identified and associated with Black students; the experiences of Chicano students in Southern California and the Southwest garnered much less attention. Los Angeles desegregation advocates presumed that racially isolated minority students, or "RIMs" as the district called them, would respond to and benefit equally from a mandatory desegregation order. Chicano advocates increasingly expressed their frustration with the limitations of this position. It was a division that political forces committed to preserving the racial status quo within the district would soon begin to exploit.

THE RISE OF RACIAL INNOCENCE IN THE SAN FERNANDO VALLEY

As desegregation and bilingual education advocates pressed their various claims before the courts, news media, and elected officials, their divisions would be exploited by a powerful movement rooted in the white suburbs of the San Fernando Valley that began to take shape. In 1976, a group of activists with roots in the parent teacher associations of the city of Encino formed the organization BUSTOP in anticipation of a districtwide desegregation plan that could include their schools. In 1977, BUSTOP leader Bobbi Fiedler attracted enormous attention for her insurgent and successful school board candidacy and her uncompromising stand against mandatory desegregation and busing. Fiedler had grown up in an integrated Santa Monica neighborhood and emphasized her opposition to the "deliberate segregation" that characterized the South. But Fiedler asserted that Los Angeles schools were free of such intentional actions and that desegregation plans must be limited to voluntary programs that preserved the rights of parents to keep their children in their current schools, however racially imbalanced they might be. As the school board appeared close to exhausting its legal challenges in the thirteen-year-old *Crawford* suit, Fiedler recited apocalyptic scenarios of a mammoth busing order that would destroy neighborhood schools, arousing enormous support from anxious Valley parents. By attacking desegregation remedies, rather than the principle of "forced integration," as an earlier generation of desegregation opponents had done, Fiedler and BUSTOP effectively recast the defense of segregated schools through the language of racial innocence.[36]

BUSTOP soon found a legislative champion in the Democratic state senator Alan Robbins. Robbins fashioned himself as a leading booster of Democratic causes: he spoke alongside Jane Fonda in support of the ERA and supported the United Farm Workers.[37] But he also anticipated the tremendous political capital that could be gained from opposition to mandatory desegregation programs.

Following a failed bid to unseat Mayor Tom Bradley in 1976, Robbins devoted much of his attention to the passage of an amendment to the California Constitution that would restrict the authority of state courts to issue desegregation orders. The constitutional amendment Robbins eventually authored modified the state's nearly hundred-year-old Equal Protection Clause by inserting an exception that required state courts to follow federal jurisprudence in matters of student reassignment and school desegregation; the U.S. Supreme Court had recently determined that de facto patterns of segregation alone were not sufficient grounds to issue desegregation orders. A graduate of the UCLA School of Law with a keen understanding of the state constitution gained through previous experience as a legislative aide, Robbins was aware that the courts would scrutinize any effort to restrict desegregation to determine if it was passed with discriminatory intent in violation of the Fourteenth Amendment.

Indeed, the courts overturned a 1972 ballot measure (Proposition 21) that banned all student reassignment efforts for the purpose of achieving racial balance precisely on these grounds. That measure's sponsor, conservative South Gate Republican assemblyman Floyd Wakefield, was an unapologetic John Birch Society supporter who remained adamantly opposed to all forms of desegregation. He referred to a modest Republican-backed state law to require schools to set their own voluntary plans to address racial segregation as the "forced integration law," declaring, "Courts have said we are not going to tolerate segregated (by law) schools. Now we're turning around and saying we're not going to tolerate integrating them by law either."[38] The brief ballot argument and rebuttal he wrote in favor of Proposition 21 used the phrase "forced integration" nine times, making Wakefield's politics clear: Segregation was natural and a matter of choice, while integration was artificial and required coercion.[39] The imperative of Robbins and his supporters, by contrast, was to demonstrate that opposition to mandatory desegregation was a racially neutral (or innocent) position, untainted by discriminatory intent.

Robbins quickly seized on the growing ambivalence expressed by Mexican American political leaders and activists toward prevailing desegregation remedies to make this case. He recruited state senator Alex Garcia, a prominent East Los Angeles Democrat, to be the principal cosponsor of his legislation. Though Garcia had opposed Proposition 21 five years earlier, he now contended that mandatory busing and student reassignment would undermine the tenuous status of newly established bilingual education programs. At Robbins's request, Garcia circulated a letter to colleagues urging support of the bill: "Compulsory busing in most California cities would mean the virtual end of bilingual education as we know it today. Where will you find sufficient bilingual instructors if you spread the Chicano students all over the school district? . . . Please don't force us to try it 'for our own good': Thank you, but no thanks."[40]

Garcia and Robbins also collaborated with an ad hoc group that called itself Chicanos against Mandatory Busing. In a statement supporting the Robbins's amendment, the group deployed the same rhetoric of community control and self-determination that had animated the 1968 Blowouts to oppose mandatory desegregation: "We, the Chicano, have fought long and hard for the right to be heard, to be equal, to have the right to pick and choose, and now this right is to be taken away from us by not allowing us to plan the future of *our children,* not the state's, *ours.*" The statement concluded, "It will be the children that will suffer. Give us a better and an EQUAL EDUCATION, NOT DESEGREGATION." Robbins helped to ensure that petitions and literature promoting his bill were printed in Spanish and distributed to Mexican American parents in East Los Angeles.[41]

Similar arguments for community self-determination were sounded by another leading Chicano figure recruited by Robbins, the East Los Angeles social worker and parent activist John Serrano. Serrano served as the lead plaintiff in a groundbreaking lawsuit seeking to equalize school funding between low- and high-income districts supported by the ACLU and the Western Center on Law and Poverty. Serrano became one of the leading backers of the Robbins amendment over the next two years, and coauthored the ballot argument for Proposition 1.[42]

While Serrano and Garcia claimed to be representing a uniform position among Chicanos toward busing and desegregation, their comments reflected a contentious debate rather than a fully formed consensus.[43] Some established Mexican American civil rights organizations did mobilize to oppose the Robbins amendment, holding that support for bilingual education did not require opposition to desegregation. In testifying against the Robbins bill at a Sacramento hearing in January 1978, a representative of the League of United Latin American Citizens (LULAC), the Mexican American Political Association (MAPA), the Mexican American Legal Defense and Education Fund (MALDEF), National La Raza Lawyers, and the Association of Mexican American Educators asserted, "The concept that bilingual education and desegregation are incompatible precedes from the false premise that desegregation cannot be sensitive to the unique educational needs of those children integrated."[44] Vahac Mardirosian, the director of the Hispanic Urban Education Center, argued that Mexican and Mexican American parents had to be made aware of the underlying reasons for school desegregation. He noted, "If parents are convinced that sending their children twenty-five to thirty miles will result in exactly the same education that child had when he was in the school next door, logically there really isn't a good reason for that parent to want to cooperate with a desegregation program." But he added, "If parents understand that this process of desegregation ultimately will result in a better future for their children . . . most . . . would be willing to live with the additional anxiety."[45]

The inclusion of prominent Chicano leaders, however, along with a small number of African American activists (but no prominent Black political leaders), performed important ideological labor. It leant legitimacy to Robbins's claims that his effort to oppose mandatory desegregation was indeed racially innocent and that an embrace of desegregation programs was actually racially offensive to some Chicano communities.[46] Garcia's endorsement of Robbins's bill did reveal a deep ambivalence about nominal desegregation efforts that seemed unable to deliver significant changes in opportunity or equity. Garcia's comments reflected the growing demands for "community control" of schools sounded by both Chicano and even some Black political leaders who had grown apprehensive of a desegregation debate that rarely seemed to include their participation or perspective.

Robbins's own anti-racist claims must be viewed with more suspicion. While he carefully developed his ties to visible Chicano leaders, he was unafraid of addressing and cultivating the reactionary populist sensibilities of white voters. These actions are brought into sharp relief in a strategy memo for a direct mail effort to raise money for the anti-busing campaign in the summer of 1978, developed by consultants hired by Robbins. The memo suggested targeting particular middle-class white communities across the state in fundraising appeals by referencing the nearby "undesirable areas" to which their children might be bused. Thirteen predominantly Black or Chicano neighborhoods across the state were listed, next to an adjoining white neighborhood or city whose residents could be targeted for an anti-busing direct mail appeal. "South Central Los Angeles" and "East Los Angeles" were identified as the "undesirable areas" within Los Angeles County.

Evidence such as this suggests the tenuous basis on which anti-busing campaigns sought to include Chicano spokespersons. While their participation was made possible by a deep-seated apprehension toward prevailing desegregation proposals, their inclusion was mainly sought to legitimate assertions of white racial innocence. Fiedler later said that in preparing BUSTOP's legal challenge to the desegregation order, the group "focus[ed] heavily on minority children, because we knew that the charge of racism would be made in the minute that we started trying to go to court."[47] Indeed, even as Fiedler was also voicing concern for the future of bilingual education programs in the wake of a large desegregation order, she warned BUSTOP supporters in a 1979 fund-raising letter of the "shocking recommendations" within the desegregation plan under consideration by the court, including a requirement "that at least one *bilingual* course be taught for *all* students, *whether they need it or not*."[48]

In personal fundraising appeals to his Valley supporters, Robbins continued to associate busing and desegregation with the dangers that lurked beyond the familiar environs of their subdivisions; busing outside one's own neighborhood would inevitably lead to tragedy. He explained: "Children in strange, unfamiliar neighborhoods are much more prone to violence than they would be in their own neighborhood, close to the safety of their own home, family and friends. And there's always the danger of a child missing the bus, becoming terrified and getting lost—which again multiples the opportunity for some sick person to make your child a victim of violence."[49]

Yet Robbins's putative incorporation of anti-racist themes and tactics proved to be effective. Previous calls among busing opponents for the protection of "majority rights" quickly waned in favor of arguments that represented the interests of "all children." The *Los Angeles Herald Examiner* explained that the anti-busing movement "is not (and should not be) racist in either intent or effect. The goal of the movement is not to deny minority students a quality education, but to deny the state the power to wreck neighborhoods and lives."[50] Robbins affirmatively embraced "integration carried out in an orderly fashion" as a desirable goal, but asserted, "Compulsory busing, where it has been mandated by the courts against the will of local residents, has caused not only racial tension, but actual racial strife, an unfortunate ingredient that we ought not to weave into the social fabric of our society."[51] Robbins's claim that the remedy—mandatory school desegregation—was the cause of rather than the solution to "racial strife" recited a theme that was familiar in postwar debates about anti-racism. Yet when sounded with populist, pluralist accents, it seemed more like a pragmatic assessment than a racist disavowal. Robbins adopted the slogan "We Love All Kids" to promote his anti-desegregation ballot measure.

PROPOSITION 1 AND ITS AFTERMATH

Robbins failed twice to qualify his amendment by direct petition in 1977 and 1978; he could not muster the organizational resources and capacity necessary to collect the hundreds of thousands of signatures required. But as the mandatory desegregation program in Los Angeles took effect, an increasing number of Democrats in the California State Legislature concluded that opposition to busing among the electorate was growing too powerful to overcome. In March 1979, the Legislature agreed to place the Robbins amendment (Proposition 1) on the ballot and called for a rare special election that November. As the election approached, a coalition of civil rights groups, faith-based organizations, and labor unions scrambled to defeat the measure. But the campaign against Proposition 1 made few inroads in winning endorsements among Asian American and Latino political leaders or organizations. Virna Canson, of the NAACP, a fierce critic of school segregation who shrewdly understood the implications of Robbins's appeal to Latino voters in particular made the case for a multiracial, interdependent defense of education rights: "Chinese, Japanese, Chicanos, Filipinos have all been discriminated against in their pursuit of public education in California. . . . Our history is filled with the struggles of these groups to throw off the yoke of segregated schools. All of these groups know that history. This time the educational opportunities of Blacks is the target, the next time the target will be employment opportunities, the next attack will be on bi-lingualism, the next attack on rights of women, the next on abortion and so on down the line."[52]

But Canson's pleas fell on deaf ears. Most of the desegregation proposals under consideration by the court offered only vague support for bilingual education and other compensatory programs. Robbins, by contrast, promised that once mandatory busing was ended, money would be freed up to directly fund such programs. Particularly after the passage of Proposition 13 in June 1978, which dramatically reduced funding for public schools, this contention was especially devastating to desegregation advocates. Other than the Los Angeles–based Hispanic Urban Education Center, which had taken an active role in the *Crawford* case, the anti–Proposition 1 effort secured little formal support from Latino organizations or elected officials and none from Asian American organizations. Moreover, three of the most powerful Mexican American elected officials—Senators Alex Garcia, Ruben Ayala, and Joseph Montoya—endorsed the Robbins measure, reasoning that bilingual education and other compensatory programs would not weather a large-scale desegregation plan. The ad hoc Black-Chicano School Integration Task Force met briefly in late 1979 to discuss common issues and strategy in relation to the *Crawford* desegregation case but made no attempt to engage or mobilize community members.[53]

Proposition 1 triumphed in a landslide, winning 69 percent of the ballot statewide. Los Angeles County passed the measure by 74 percent. The west San Fernando Valley communities that formed the nucleus of the anti-busing movement voted nine to one in favor of Proposition 1, with a 43 percent turnout rate. In the three South Los Angeles city council districts represented by African Americans, the measure was defeated by a two to one margin, but turnout lagged at 25 percent. It passed by almost 70 percent in the generally liberal West Side and was approved by significant margins in the heavily Latino East Side district.[54]

As Latino voters constituted only a small proportion of the overall electorate, they did not play a decisive role in passing the measure. But the incorporation of their criticism against the desegregation plan helped to allow Robbins and others to raise the flag of racial innocence even as they attacked a plan to address widespread patterns of segregation and inequality in the city's public schools.

Robbins's legal strategy to end mandatory desegregation in Los Angeles was completely vindicated. In its December 1980 decision upholding the constitutionality of the measure, the California Court of Appeal, Second Appellate District, determined that the electorate had not acted with discriminatory intent in adopting the measure, calling the charge "pure speculation." The three-judge panel also rejected the ACLU's assertion that the markedly inferior conditions in predominantly Black and Latino schools demonstrated a pattern of intentional discrimination. The court held, "The two problems (unequal facilities and discrimination) frequently parallel one another but they are distinct and different problems."[55]

When the Supreme Court of California refused to review the appellate decision in March 1981, it opened the door for the anti-busing faction controlling the L.A. school board to immediately end its mandatory desegregation program. The court's decision not to review the case surprised both sides and led superior court judge Paul Egly to remove himself from the *Crawford* case after four years, charging that the school board had "failed to even meet the [separate but equal] standard of Plessy v. Ferguson." In the three years it had been in effect, the LAUSD desegregation program had grown to include 153 schools and about fifty-eight thousand students in grades one through nine. Critics noted it was the first time in U.S. history that a court ruling resulted in the reassignment of minority students from desegregated schools to segregated ones.[56]

The ACLU and NAACP were granted one last opportunity to present their arguments when the U.S. Supreme Court agreed to hear the case in 1982. Many of the amicus briefs submitted in the case supporting the ballot measure also raised the banner of racial innocence. Bobbie Fiedler, by then a member of Congress, averred, "Proposition 1 is racially neutral," adding that "Californians of every race and ethnic background" had determined that "the experiment" of mandatory desegregation was not working. Robbins's brief drew from his own biography to establish the innocence of the measure: "The author of Proposition 1 is a Democrat, a 20-year supporter of Rev. Martin Luther King, the elected representative of a district where half of the school children are members of minority groups, and a strong committed advocate of achieving integration through open housing in the community" and various voluntary means.[57]

In Los Angeles, Robbins and other anti-busing activists vowed after their court victory to make full use of "voluntary measures" to achieve desegregation, including magnet schools and voluntary busing programs that provided students transportation to attend schools outside their neighborhood. In reality most of these voluntary efforts were "one-way" programs, requiring students of color from Central, East, and South Los Angeles to be bused from their neighborhood schools to attend better-resourced schools in West Los Angeles and in the San Fernando Valley. By 1985, the district was busing fifty-seven thousand students each day—more than at the height of the mandatory desegregation program—for voluntary programs and to relieve overcrowding.[58] Ironically, some students in South Gate High School, which by the early 1980s was predominantly Latino, were forced to ride a bus thirty-five miles each way to the Valley community of Tujunga in order to relieve overcrowding.[59] The end of mandatory desegregation meant that the burden of busing had fallen almost exclusively on students of color. One East Los Angeles high school teacher demanded, "Where is Bustop now? Where are all the anti-busing activists who assured us that the issue was not racism or integration but busing itself? If busing was wrong for children from the San Fernando Valley, then it follows that busing should be wrong for children from the inner city."[60]

Nor did Robbins offer much support to those politicians and activists he had recruited to join the Proposition 1 campaign in the name of preserving bilingual education programs. The attacks on bilingual education and language rights began almost immediately after the busing debate subsided. In 1984 an emerging group of immigration-restriction activists successfully passed ballot measures putting the state on record against the mandatory provision of bilingual voting materials. In 1986, the same group passed a measure to declare English the official language of the state. By the mid-1990s, when ballot initiatives were launched seeking to bar undocumented immigrants from public schools and to ban bilingual education entirely, Robbins was already out of politics. In November 1991, he pled guilty to federal racketeering charges after accepting bribes from insurance companies while serving as chair of the Senate Insurance Committee. He served two years in prison.

CONTEMPORARY LEGACIES

During the debates over mandatory desegregation in the late 1970s, as the courts increasingly legitimated long-standing charges that Los Angeles schools were marked by rampant racial segregation and inequality, opponents of desegregation seized upon the precarious state of bilingual education programs to buttress their own claims of racial innocence. They premised their appeals to Mexican American parents and advocates on the assumption that the unjustified and overreaching efforts of African Americans posed a greater threat to their well-being than any historical or institutional investments in white racial power.

By the 1990s, the valence of claims of white racial innocence had shifted. Immigration restrictionists now charged that expansive immigration policy and Latino immigrants' claims to rights implicitly disenfranchised Black communities. Again, these charges seized upon particular political dynamics and ambivalences within Black communities: the steady erosion of living-wage jobs, the decline of public schools and the social safety net, and the growing frustration with elected officials and political leaders to solve entrenched social problems. Here, the terms were reversed. According to immigration restrictionists, Black progress and empowerment had become limited because of growing claims on limited public resources by newcomers rather than because of decades of racist policies, structures, and abandonment.

These arguments reached particular intensity in April 2005, as dozens of local and national reporters descended on Jefferson High School in South Los Angeles to report on allegations of "racial brawls" erupting between Black and Latino students. Jefferson High, like most schools in the southern, central, and eastern parts of the LAUSD, experienced continued abandonment in the wake of the end of court-ordered desegregation.[61] Indeed, a 2004 report suggested that patterns of racial segregation in Los Angeles schools were at historically high rates and that white students in the district had one of the lowest "exposure rates" to Black students in the nation.[62] But as the coverage on NPR, MSNBC, and the *Los Angeles Times* had it, it was marauding Latino students who threatened to overrun their Black classmates.[63] An (entirely unattributed) incident recounted in nearly every story had some Latino students yelling "Go Back to Africa" as they hurled trash and racial invective. A December 2005 cover story, "Black vs. Brown: Diversity in the New L.A.," in the *American Conservative* (authored by a white conservative raised in segregated South Gate) began: "Jesse Jackson's Rainbow Coalition has a ways to go in Los Angeles, where Mexicans and blacks are killing each other at record rates." It depicted a racial dystopia in which rampaging and lawless youth terrorized one another and their neighbors, utterly justifying their broader social abandonment. The regime of white racial innocence continues.[64]

NOTES

1. "Busing Becomes a One Issue Dispute," *Los Angeles Times*, September 24, 1978.

2. David Ettinger, "The Quest to Desegregate Los Angeles Schools," *Los Angeles Lawyer* (March 2003): 254. The lawsuit was *Crawford v. Board of Education of the City of Los Angeles*, 17 Cal. 3d 280, 287 n. 2 (1976).

3. One generative articulation of this thesis can be found in Mark Brilliant, *The Color of America Has Changed: How Racial Diversity Shaped Civil Rights Reform in California, 1941–1978* (Oxford: Oxford University Press, 2010).

4. Raphael Sonenshein, *Politics in Black and White: Race and Power in Los Angeles* (Princeton, NJ: Princeton University Press, 1993).

5. Becky M. Nicolaides, *My Blue Heaven: Life and Politics in the Working-Class Suburbs of Los Angeles, 1920–1965* (Chicago: University of Chicago Press, 2002), 288.

6. *Wysinger v. Crookshank*, 82 Cal. 588, 720 (1890).

7. *Mendez v. Westminster School District of Orange County*, 64 F. Supp. 544 (D.C. Cal. 1946). On this case see Vicki Ruiz, "South by Southwest: Mexican Americans and Segregated Schooling, 1900–1950," *OAH Magazine of History* 15, no. 2 (2001); and Gilbert Gonzalez, "Segregation of Mexican Children in a Southern California City: The Legacy of Expansionism and the American Southwest," *Western Historical Quarterly* 16, no. 1 (1985). On an earlier anti-segregation case near San Diego, see Roberto Alvarez, "The Lemon Grove Incident: The Nation's First Successful Desegregation Court Case," *Journal of San Diego History* 32, no. 2 (1986).

8. "Who Is Becoming Color Blind?" *Los Angeles Times*, September 13, 1962, A4.

9. "'Gerrymandering in the Los Angeles City School Districts,' Presented by NAACP and UCRC June 27, 1963, by Marnesba Tackett," box 5, folder 3, Dorothy Doyle Collection , Southern California Library for Social Studies and Research, Los Angeles (hereafter DD).

10. See Matthew Lassiter, "De Jure/De Facto Segregation: The Long Shadow of a National Myth," in *The End of Southern Exceptionalism*, ed. Matthew Lassiter and Joseph Crespino (Oxford: Oxford University Press, 2009).

11. For one such example, see "NAACP Meets Rebuff on School Enrollment," *Los Angeles Times*, September 24, 1962, 24.

12. Loren Miller, speech "For Free Men: Freedom," box 44, folder 2, Loren Miller Papers, Huntington Library, San Marino, CA.

13. On the history of African American segregation in California schools, see Charles Wollenberg, *All Deliberate Speed: Segregation and Exclusion in California Schools, 1855–1975* (Berkeley: University of California Press, 1976); Irving Hendrick, *The Education of Non-Whites in California, 1849–1970* (San Francisco: R&E Research Associates, 1977); and John Caughey and LaRee Caughey, *School Segregation on Our Doorstep: The Los Angeles Story* (Los Angeles: Quail Books, 1966), 4. Other accounts of the Crawford case include Fred Okrand, oral history interview, conducted 1982 by Michael Balter, UCLA Oral History Program, http://content.cdlib.org/xtf/view?docId = ft258003n2&brand = calisphere, accessed October 29, 2006; Jeanne Thiel Landis, "The Crawford Desegregation Suit in Los Angeles 1977–1981," PhD dissertation, University of California Los Angeles, 1984; Jess Carrillo, "The Process of School Desegregation: The Case of the Los Angeles Unified School District," PhD dissertation, University of California Los Angeles, 1978; and Carlos Manuel Haro, *Mexicano/Chicano Concerns and School Desegregation in Los Angeles* (Los Angeles: Chicano Studies Center Publications, University of California Los Angeles, 1977).

14. On the early protests before the LAUSD, see Caughey and Caughey, *School Segregation on Our Doorstep*.

15. *Jackson v. Pasadena City School District,* 59 Cal. 2d 876 (1963).

16. Judith Kafka, "'Sitting on a Tinder Box': Racial Conflict, Teacher Discretion, and the Centralization of Disciplinary Authority," *American Journal of Education* 114 (2008): 250.

17. *Diaz v. San Jose Unified School District,* 412 F. Supp. 310 (N.D. Cal. 1976); *Soria v. Oxnard School District,* 328 F. Supp. 155 (C.D. Cal. 1971).

18. "'Mason-Dixon Line' Must Go, Duarte Vows," *Los Angeles Times*, May 19, 1968, SG_B1; "Ethnic, Racial Housing Patterns Affect Schools," *Los Angeles Times*, October 20, 1968, OC1.

19. Case studies of desegregation and busing struggles in these cities include Doris Fine, *When Leadership Fails: Desegregation and Demoralization in the San Francisco Schools* (New York: Transaction Books, 1986); and Lillian Rubin, *Busing and Backlash: White against White in a California School District* (Berkeley: University of California Press, 1972).

20. The University of Chicago sociologist James Coleman became the lead-

ing advocate of the theory that mandatory desegregation programs resulted in increased (re)segregation, because such plans drove white students out of large districts. Coleman's 1975 report was answered by critics such as Gary Orfield and Thomas Pettigrew, who challenged several methodological issues in his study. They generally contended that at most, mandatory desegregation accelerated "white flight" only in the first year or two of the programs and generally not by large proportions. For a summary of this debate, see Dianne Ravitch, "The 'White Flight' Controversy," in *Busing U.S.A.*, ed. Nicolaus Mills (New York: Teachers College Press, 1979). The relevant issue for my purposes is why parents understood desegregation and busing as harmful or beneficial to their children's education.

21. For an excellent account of the student walkouts, see Ian Haney Lopez, *Racism on Trial: The Chicano Fight for Justice* (Cambridge, MA: Belknap Press, 2003).

22. Ibid., 162. See also Laura Pulido, *Black, Brown, Yellow, and Left: Radical Activism in Los Angeles* (Berkeley: University of California Press, 2006).

23. Kafka, "'Sitting on a Tinder Box,'" 250.

24. Ibid., 254.

25. San Diego's desegregation lawsuit, *People v. San Diego Unified School District* (96 Cal. Rptr. 658, 19 Cal. App. 3d 252 California Court of Appeals, 1971) was also filed on behalf of all Chicano, Black, Asian American, and American Indian students in the district.

26. *Covarrubias v. San Diego Unified School District*, Civ. Act. No. 70–394 T (S.D. Cal., filed Dec. 1970).

27. Ibid.; and *Soria v. Oxnard School District*, 328 F. Supp. 155 (C.D. Cal. 1971).

28. *Lau v. Nichols*, 414 U.S. 563 n. 1974, was filed in 1970 by Chinese American families in San Francisco; it charged that the school district failed to provide an adequate education to non-English-speaking students and established a legal framework for requiring districts to provide bilingual education programs.

29. "LA Schools Denied $24 Million Grant," *Los Angeles Times*, October 24, 1977; Frank Del Olmo, "Chicano Leaders Hit Desegregation Plan," *Los Angeles Times*, January 18, 1978; letter from Thomas Minter, U.S. Department of Health, Education, and Welfare, to LAUSD William Johnston, February 28, 1980, box 7A, Carlos Haro School Desegregation Collection, Chicano Studies Research Center, UCLA.

30. See generally Beatriz Arias, "Mexican American Student Segregation and Desegregation in California," in *Critical Perspectives on Bilingual Education*, ed. Raymond Padilla and Alfredo Benavides (Tempe, AZ: Bilingual Press/ Editorial Bilingue, 1992).

31. *Crawford v. Board of Education of the City of Los Angeles*, Cal. S. Ct., Los Angeles, No. 822 854 (1970).

32. "Latins Hit School Integration Planning," *Los Angeles Times*, February 10, 1977.

33. George Sánchez, *Becoming Mexican American: Ethnicity, Culture and Identity in Chicano Los Angeles, 1900–1945* (Oxford: Oxford University Press, 1995).

34. "What Is a Mexican? The Arrogance of Fear," *Sin Fronteras,* June 1977, 8.

35. Haro, *Mexicano/Chicano Concerns and School Desegregation in Los Angeles.*

36. This shift in strategies used to discredit court-ordered school desegregation was occurring in other cities as well. See, for example, Matthew Lassiter, *The Silent Majority: Suburban Politics in the Sunbelt South* (Princeton, NJ: Princeton University Press, 2005).

37. *Los Angeles Times,* May 26, 1976.

38. "2 Groups Promise Court Challenge to Busing Proposition," *Los Angeles Times,* November 9, 1972, A20.

39. California Secretary of State, *California Ballot Pamphlet, General Election, November 7, 1992,* Sacramento, 1972.

40. Alex Garcia letter, November 30, 1977, "Busing" folder, series 1, box 2, Alan Robbins Collection, California State University Northridge (hereafter AR).

41. Statement of "Concerned Parents in Support of SCA 48," January 4, 1978, AR, box 3, "SCA 48-MISC Legislative re Busing" folder.

42. *Serrano v. Priest,* 5 Cal. 3d 584 (1971) *(Serrano I); Serrano v. Priest,* 18 Cal. 3d 728 (1976) *(Serrano II); Serrano v. Priest,* 20 Cal. 3d 25 (1977) *(Serrano III);* California Secretary of State, Ballot Arguments for 1977 Special Election, Sacramento; "Serrano Still Waits for Change," *Bulletin-News,* April 1, 1978.

43. For a discussion of the "conflicting avenues of redress" pursued by advocates of desegregation and bilingual education, see Mark Brilliant, "Color Lines: Civil Rights Struggles on America's Racial Frontier, 1945–75," PhD dissertation, Stanford University, 2003, ch. 9.The court ruling affirming the right to bilingual education was *Lau v. Nichols,* 414 U.S. 563 (1974). The federal Bilingual Education Act, which established a legislative mandate and funding for these programs, was passed in 1968 and amended in 1974. See James Crawford, *At War with Diversity: US Language Policy in an Age of Anxiety* (Tonawada, NY: Multilingual Matters, 2000).

44. Statement by Peter Roos in opposition to Senate Constitutional Amendment 48, January 19 1978, "Committee Testimony" folder, box 5, series 1, AR; "A Summary of the Position and Policy Statement of the Chicano Subcommittee of the Citizens' Advisory Committee on Student Integration," folder 10, box 5, DD.

45. Mardirosian quoted in Haro, *Mexicano/Chicano Concerns and School Desegregation in Los Angeles,* 38.

46. Other than at a few committee hearings, Robbins placed less emphasis on demonstrating Asian American opposition to mandatory busing, though when it did happen, similar themes were emphasized. Tony Trias, a former president of an Asian education advisory group in Los Angeles, testified before the California Assembly on behalf of the Robbins bill: "Asian Americans are

concerned about the idea of dividing the family. We came here for freedom of choice and equality of opportunity. We want to keep our children close. We're not concerned about integration. We are concerned about being bused out of our neighborhoods." Press release, January 4, 1978, "Busing Press Releases" folder, box 2, series 1, AR.

47. Interview with Bobbi Fiedler, by Richard McMillian, transcribed by Farah Ortega, November 17, 1988, California State University Northridge, Department of History and Urban Archives Library.

48. "Dear Friend and Concerned Taxpayer" letter, box 5, "Busing Dear Friends Letters" folder, AR.

49. Alan Robbins, "Dear Opponent of Forced Busing" letter, n.d., box 38, folder 9, Records of the National Association for the Advancement of Colored People (NAACP), Region I, Bancroft Library, University of California Berkeley.

50. "Quarrels with the Courts," *Los Angeles Herald Examiner,* January 12, 1979.

51. Alan Robbins, guest editorial, *Los Angeles Times,* October 28, 1977, 14.

52. CAP 1 press release, August 3, 1978, box 38, folder 9, NAACP, Bancroft Library.

53. From "Black-Chicano School Integration Task Force, September 5, 1979, Working Agenda for Taskforce," folder 233, box 7B, Carlos Haro Desegregation Collection, Chicano Studies Research Center, UCLA. The task force met a few times in late 1979 and 1980.

54. "Most of L.A. Voted Heavily for Prop. 1," *Los Angeles Times,* November 9, 1979; "Prop 1 May Face Early Court Test," *Los Angeles Times,* November 8, 1979, B3; "Vote on Proposition One by Assembly District," "Busing Voting Records" box 6, "Californians Against Forced Busing" folder, AR.

55. *Crawford v. Los Angeles Board of Education,* 113 Cal. App. 3d 633, 170 Cal. Rptr. 495 (1981); "Prop 1, Upheld: Bars L.A. Busing," *Los Angeles Times,* December 20, 1980, A1; "Foes of Busing Hail Los Angeles Victory," *New York Times,* March 13, 1981; Ettinger, "The Quest to Desegregate Los Angeles Schools."

56. "Prop 1 Upheld," *Los Angeles Times,* December 20, 1980, A1.

57. Supreme Court A/C Brief of Alan Robbins in *Crawford v. Los Angeles Board of Education,* No. 81-38, January 29, 1982, 2–3.

58. "For L.A. Schools, Double Jeopardy: Segregation, Overcrowding," *Los Angeles Times,* October 27, 1985, OC_A7.

59. "School Busing Furor Erupts in South Gate," *Los Angeles Times,* June 28, 1981, SE1.

60. "School Busing Takes a U-Turn," *Los Angeles Times,* December, 13, 1981, H5.

61. On Jefferson, see also "Two Students, Two Schools—20 Miles and a World Apart," *Los Angeles Times,* June 22, 2009, which reports that only 27 percent of Jefferson students are able to graduate in four years and only 16 percent take a college prep curriculum.

62. Gary Orfield and Chungmei Lee, "Brown at 50: King's Dream or Plessy's Nightmare?" Harvard Civil Rights Project, Cambridge, MA, 2004.

63. Sandy Banks and Nicholas Shields, "Searching for Lessons in Jefferson High Melee," *Los Angeles Times,* July 6, 2005; Lee Baca, "In L.A., Race Kills," *Los Angeles Times,* June 12, 2008.

64. Roger D. McGrath, "End of the Rainbow: South Central Los Angeles Ushers in a New Era of Racial Tension—This Time between Blacks and Hispanics," *American Conservative,* December 19, 2005.

5

Fighting the Segregation Amendment

Black and Mexican American Responses to Proposition 14 in Los Angeles

MAX FELKER-KANTOR

On June 20, 1964, the United Civil Rights Committee (UCRC), a predominantly African American civil rights organization, began a voter registration drive in Los Angeles's black and Mexican American neighborhoods in hopes of defeating Proposition 14 in the November election. The goal of the drive, according to the city's weekly African American newspaper, the *Los Angeles Sentinel,* was to "register 200,000 non-voting Negro and Mexican Americans in the local community in a massive all out effort to defeat Proposition 14—the anti-fair housing initiative." The UCRC believed that increasing the number of black and Mexican American voters would bolster the campaign against Proposition 14, a proposed amendment to California's constitution that allowed the state's homeowners and landlords to sell or rent—or refuse to sell or rent—their property to anyone they wished. Walter Hyman, UCRC's voter registration chairman, organized weekly drives in Central, South, and East Los Angeles. "We must," Hyman demanded, "get out the vote to defeat Proposition 14, the real estate segregation amendment."[1]

Despite the UCRC's intention of mobilizing Mexican American voters, the registration drive concentrated in African American neighborhoods and did not increase voting rolls among Mexican Americans. Although the UCRC was an interracial organization, the predominantly African American group did little to openly cooperate with Mexican American leaders to defeat Proposition 14. When the Mexican

Chamber of Commerce came out in favor of Proposition 14, however, African American activists and community members felt betrayed by the Mexican American community. The African American newspaper the *California Eagle* ran a headline that read, "Snakes in the Grass: Mexican American 'Stab' in the Back." Even if Mexican Americans did not openly unite with blacks in struggle, some blacks felt that Mexican Americans should at least express solidarity with blacks in the struggle against Proposition 14. The Mexican chamber changed its stance to neutral as a result of pressure from Mexican American activists who saw Proposition 14 as a threat to their community. Some segments of the African American and Mexican American communities, it seemed, had common responses to the dangers posed by Proposition 14.[2]

Although campaigns against Proposition 14 existed in both the Mexican American and the black communities, the two did not develop an interracial coalition, nor did they respond to the proposition in the same way. As this essay demonstrates, both interracial cooperation and tension marked the battle against Proposition 14 in Los Angeles. The Proposition 14 fight mobilized black residents to a greater degree than Mexican Americans. Black residents needed little prodding to come out against the initiative. While the black community exhibited class-based tensions, organizers forged cross-class solidarity by stressing the initiative's threat to all blacks. In contrast, many Mexican American residents knew little about the proposition or believed that it was a black-white issue leading to lukewarm opposition. Mexican American activists worked to convince their community that the struggle against Proposition 14 was their fight too. The Mexican American response also pointed to persistent fissures in the community. Despite the threat Proposition 14 posed to Mexican Americans, for example, some members of the middle class openly supported the initiative. Blacks and Mexican Americans perceived Proposition 14 in different ways because of their uneven awareness of the issue, their positions in Los Angeles's racial hierarchy, and their historical experience with housing segregation and homeownership.[3]

Focusing on black and Mexican American struggles to uphold the Rumford Fair Housing Act reframes the history of Proposition 14 in terms other than one centered on homeowner rights, white backlash, and the failure of racial liberalism that has dominated historical scholarship. A number of works have focused on white resistance to fair housing embodied by the California Real Estate Association and its state-level opposition, the Californians Against Proposition 14 (CAP

14), a group organized by liberal white activists and the Democratic Party.[4] While members of CAP 14 opposed Proposition 14, their campaign avoided an open defense of the Rumford Fair Housing Act and attempted to assuage white fears that fair housing threatened property rights. They upheld an ideology of citizenship based in civic nationalism that explained white privilege and inequality through a nonracial discourse of homeowner identity.[5] Although nominally allied with CAP 14, this essay demonstrates that blacks and Mexican Americans engaged in their own struggles and, to different degrees, took a stand against Proposition 14. Black and Mexican American leaders defended the Rumford Act and stressed that Proposition 14 was a deliberate race-based attack on the progress made in the field of housing and in civil rights more generally.[6]

By exploring African American and Mexican American activism, this essay demonstrates how the impact of residential segregation and fissures within each community shaped their different responses to Proposition 14. This essay argues that Proposition 14, instead of being an issue of homeowner rights or white backlash, was part of racially and ethnically distinct struggles for equality, fair housing, and first-class citizenship in Los Angeles. California's approval of Proposition 14, moreover, left blacks and Mexican Americans with the bitter taste of persistent white racism that fed frustrations, contributing to the 1965 urban uprising in Watts and the Chicano movement of the late 1960s. Through an examination of black and Mexican American activism this essay shows how each group thought about equal rights, mobilized its community, and struggled against housing segregation and Los Angeles's unequal racial geography. Finally, this essay explores both the possibilities and the limitations of intra- and interracial cooperation in post–World War II Los Angeles.[7]

RESIDENTIAL SEGREGATION AND THE BLACK AND MEXICAN AMERICAN COMMUNITIES

In March 1963, the Los Angeles County Commission on Human Relations reported that between 1950 and 1960 the African American population of the county had grown from 217,881 to 461,546, while the Spanish-surname population had expanded from 287,614 to 576,716.[8] While the Spanish-surname population had outpaced African Americans in the county at large, within the city of Los Angeles the black community had outnumbered the Spanish-surname population by 74,527, as they had grown to 334,916 and 260,389, respectively. The rapid growth in the black and Mexican American populations combined with restricted housing opportunities led to increased concentrations of blacks and Mexican Americans within segregated sections of both the city and the county by the late 1950s. Through the use of restrictive covenants, zoning ordinances, discriminatory real estate practices, and Federal Housing Administration lending policies, realtors and suburban residents constructed a "Wall of Hate" in Los Angeles.[9]

The degree of housing discrimination and segregation differed for blacks and Mexican Americans over that decade, however. Blacks experienced greater levels of residential concentration than Mexican Americans did in the city of Los Angeles. By 1960 a larger percentage of African Americans than those of Spanish surnames lived within the city limits in Los Angeles County (72 percent and 45 percent, respectively).[10] As the California Fair Employment Practices Commission reported in 1965, by 1960 only one-fifth of the Spanish-surname population was concentrated in three neighborhoods of East Los Angeles, while more than half of all blacks in the county lived in seven neighborhoods in South Los Angeles.[11] Indeed, African Americans experienced the most acute forms of residential exclusion of any nonwhite group in Los Angeles. Of the 461,546 African Americans in the county in 1960, 68 percent, or 313,866, lived in the city's central district, an area consisting of thirty neighborhoods. Nearly 87 percent of those in the district, however, lived in just nine of those communities. African Americans, moreover, made little headway in Los Angeles suburbs, and when they did it was on a segregated basis. In fact, nearly 83 percent of blacks in the county lived in areas where nonwhites made up from 65 to 100 percent of the population.[12]

Mexican Americans did not experience the same level of residential concentration or discrimination. "The Spanish surname population," the L.A. County Commission on Human Relations reported in 1963, "is more dispersed than either the Negro or other non-white populations." This dispersal occurred largely along segregated lines, however. While only 30.5 percent, or 175,898 of the 576,716 of the county's Spanish-surnamed residents, lived in East Los Angeles, they constituted 51.5 percent of the residents in the area. Although many Mexican Americans lived in East Los Angeles neighborhoods, others resided in smaller, segregated barrios or moved into segregated neighborhoods in suburbs such as El Monte and Pico Rivera.[13] "Even as East Los Angeles witnessed a growing concentration of Mexican and Chicano poverty during the postwar period," historian Eric Avila argues, "the barrio did not encompass the experience of Los Angeles' Mexican American community to the same extent that the ghetto characterized the postwar experiences of African Americans." The different experiences with housing segregation and discrimination shaped perceptions and reactions of blacks and Mexican Americans to Proposition 14.[14]

Patterns of homeownership also varied. Within the predominantly African American area of South Central Los Angeles, an area encompassing Watts, Central, Avalon, Florence, Green Meadows, Exposition, and Willowbrook, the rate of owner-occupied housing was 38 percent in 1965. In the Mexican American neighborhoods of Boyle Heights, City Terrace, and East L.A., homeownership rates were slightly lower, at 35 percent.[15] Within Los Angeles County as a whole, however, 41 percent of nonwhites and 47 percent of the Spanish-surname population lived in owner-occupied housing.[16] Although more research on homeownership is needed, this cursory evidence suggests that while homeownership rates within the segregated areas of South and East Los Angeles were relatively similar, Mexican Americans had higher rates of homeownership countywide because of their opportunity to purchase homes in some suburbs. The ability to access suburban housing suggests two reasons why some Mexican Americans were more willing to support Proposition 14 than their African American counterparts were: defense of property rights and a belief that housing discrimination was a thing of the past.

PROPOSITION 14: THE STATEWIDE CAMPAIGNS

In 1963, the California state assemblyman Byron Rumford, one of the state's African American legislators, introduced legislation to make discrimination in the sale or rental of housing illegal in California. The Rumford bill built on the 1959 Fair Employment Practices law and was part of the proliferation of state fair housing laws passed after World War II.[17] After much debate, the California State Assembly passed a weak version of Rumford's housing bill on June 21, 1963. As Daniel HoSang notes, the Rumford Act by one estimate "covered only about twenty-five percent of the nearly 3.8 million single family homes in the state and less than five percent of the 857,000 duplexes, triplexes, and fourplexes."[18] Yet, blacks and Mexican Americans across California viewed the Rumford Act as a step toward their goal of equal opportunity and a blow to segregation, racial subordination, and white supremacy.[19]

The limited coverage of the Rumford Act notwithstanding, the California Real Estate Association (CREA) denounced the fair housing law as the "Forced Housing Act."[20] During the fall of 1963 and early 1964, white real estate interests organized a movement to repeal the Rumford Act and to prevent future fair housing legislation by sponsoring an amendment to California's constitution. That initiative became Proposition 14 and appeared as a ballot referendum in the November 1964 statewide election. CREA, under the banner of the Committee for Home Protection, used color-blind language of the defense of property rights to frame its argument against the Rumford Act and to mobilize white voters across California. The color-blind rhetoric of property rights allowed white voters to absolve themselves of the charges of racism and to uphold a civic creed of racial progress.[21]

In response to CREA, California Democrats and Governor Pat Brown organized Californians Against Proposition 14, which led a massive effort to convince California voters to oppose the initiative. Made up of a coalition of Democratic Party members, liberal politicians, and interest groups, CAP 14 argued that the proposition was a threat to racial progress and hoped to assuage the fears of white residents that fair housing would hurt property values or the rights of homeowners. "CAP 14," HoSang argues, "declined to endorse or defend the original purpose of the Rumford Act in any meaningful way. Liberal activists rarely mentioned the housing crisis which drove black communities and civil rights organizations to demand the passage of the legislation in the first place, or referenced the overwhelming levels of discrimination many home buyers and renters still faced."[22] The Democratic Party and CAP 14, moreover, discouraged mass demonstration and direct action by civil rights groups, because its supporters believed public protest would hurt the campaign's appeal to moderate white voters.[23]

Leaders of African American and Mexican American civil rights organizations framed Proposition 14 in the terms that CAP 14 avoided. Loren Miller, a longtime NAACP lawyer, housing activist, and editor of the weekly black newspaper the *California Eagle*, reminded the black community that Proposition 14 would not only repeal the Rumford Act but also, by codifying discrimination in the California Constitution, reeked of state action to maintain racial and ethnic subordination more generally. "Nothing would please them [CREA] more," Miller concluded, "than to find a way to turn the clock back to the good old days when they were protected by the state in their discriminatory practices."[24] Black leaders pushed their argument beyond the defense of property and individual uplift. They lauded the Rumford Act and framed the issue in the broad language of fair housing and equal rights. Mexican American activists, such as the realtor Sal Montenegro, also defended the Rumford Act. "My concern is for the future of my children. For I hope and pray that the Rumford bill is never defeated." Montenegro, moreover, revealed the persistent housing discrimination faced by members of his community. "Mexican-Americans have waited for over 100 years in order to purchase a home without the fear of discrimination," he argued. "I have asked do they want us to wait an additional 100 years?"[25] Black and Mexican American leaders moved beyond CAP 14's arguments to an outright defense of the Rumford Act and revealed the continued presence of housing discrimination In Los Angeles.

Blacks and Mexican Americans not only attacked CREA's ballot referendum but also the historical structure of whiteness, property rights, and state-sponsored housing discrimination. They understood the ways that space, race, and power worked together to produce urban inequality more generally. Residential segregation was especially harmful because it produced a hierarchical racial geography that buttressed white advantage and racial subordination more generally. In other words, residential segregation served as the basis for the invidious and structural nature of racial inequality that has relegated blacks and Mexican Americans to underserved urban neighborhoods and denied their children the opportunity to attend good schools and to gain access to high-paying jobs.[26] Black and Mexican American activists recognized that the walls of residential segregation would not fall easily. Dismantling the connections between opportunity, race, and geography necessitated a "total war" against Proposition 14.[27]

OPPOSITION TO THE ANTI–FAIR HOUSING INITIATIVE IN THE LOS ANGELES BLACK COMMUNITY

After the passage of the Rumford Act, black leaders hoped that the California real estate industry would support the law. On September 22, 1963, the NAACP and the United Civil Rights Committee (UCRC) organized a demonstration at CREA's annual convention at the Biltmore Hotel in Los Angeles.[28] The NAACP-UCRC wanted to expose the "evils of segregation and discrimination in housing," announcing, "We no longer will tolerate segregated housing as a way of life, and demand that housing in California be made available immediately without discrimination because of race, color or religion."[29] CREA had no intention of supporting the Rumford Act and initiated a campaign to repeal it through a ballot initiative. News of CREA's ballot referendum alarmed black activists in Los Angeles. The NAACP worked to raise awareness of the threat the initiative posed to fair housing. In a program of counteraction, the NAACP took legal steps against the initiative, engaged in boycotts and selective buying campaigns of realtors that supported the initiative, and planned a voter registration drive that targeted voters specifically concerned with human relations.[30]

The NAACP and other African American organizations framed their argument against Proposition 14 in terms of equal rights and fair housing. The NAACP along with the Urban League, CORE, and the UCRC defended the Rumford Act and its benefits to the black community by stressing that repeal of the fair housing law would reinforce barriers to black equality.[31] "Beware of the Realtor's Initiative," read a Los Angeles NAACP flier, "HOLD OPEN THE DOORS OF FAIR HOUSING!" The NAACP elaborated on the reasons for the black community to defend the Rumford Act: "The whole future of human rights is at stake—here, in California! If passed by a majority in the November election, this initiative would freeze housing segregation into the State Constitution. It would revise the Constitution to bar all future laws and court action for ending discrimination in the sale or rental of homes based on race, color, ancestry or religion. It would permanently shut minority group persons away from the opportunity for free and equal choice of homes."[32]

The NAACP defined the debate over Proposition 14 as one of protecting their hard-won civil rights gains over the previous two decades. The CREA initiative threatened to set back civil rights in California and the nation more generally. Finally, the NAACP encouraged community involvement in the campaign against Proposition 14.[33]

Throughout the campaign, black organizations stressed how residential segregation structured unequal educational and employment opportunities for the black community. They viewed Proposition 14 and the threat to equal housing opportunities as the basis for unequal access to public services, jobs, and quality education for black Angelenos. "The evils of segregation and discrimination in housing," stated the NAACP-UCRC, "[cause] segregated schools, segregated jobs, segregated churches and a segregated society."[34] Housing segregation functioned to shape the boundaries of inequality more broadly, making the defeat of Proposition 14 crucial for the black community.

MOBILIZING VOTERS AND CLASS DIVISIONS IN
THE BLACK COMMUNITY

Once Proposition 14 was placed on the November ballot, the UCRC focused on defeating the initiative at the voting booth. Between June and October, the UCRC organized volunteers to go into black and Mexican American neighborhoods and wage a door-to-door voter registration campaign, hoping to register two hundred thousand unregistered black and Mexican American voters in Los Angeles with the aid of CAP 14, the Urban League, CORE, and the NAACP. H.H. Brookins, chairman of the UCRC, emphasized the importance of the UCRC voter registration campaign for ensuring equal opportunity and fair housing. "The job is as serious here," Brookins argued, "as it is in Mississippi." California—Los Angeles in particular—was the front line in the battle against the forces of hate in the West.[35] Volunteer registrars passed out leaflets that emphasized opposition to Proposition 14 as an attack on the equal rights of minority citizens, because it threatened to dismantle one of the tools—fair housing laws—that enabled middle-class blacks to obtain housing in the suburbs.[36] "Protect YOUR Right to Buy, YOUR Right to Rent," stated a flier, "Register Today so you can Vote NO!! on the Realtors' Jim Crow Housing Proposition."[37]

Despite the UCRC's stated desire to register Mexican Americans, however, the drive focused on the black community. Furthermore, black activists and the community they claimed to represent were not as united as they seemed. Class tensions were never far from the surface. Indeed, the black middle class promoted fair housing because they saw open access as a step toward anti-discrimination in housing and an escape from segregated neighborhoods. Proposition 14, according to the *California Eagle*, was a symbol of the forced nature of residential segregation and an obstacle to middle-class access to white neighborhoods; similarly the cartoon depicted in figure 5.1 also suggests that Proposition 14 would prevent blacks from escaping the ghetto. However, for working-class blacks, segregation was largely unavoidable anyway, because they could not afford to live in more expensive white neighborhoods. As James O'Toole argued in his study of the black community in preriot Watts, "The poor people of Watts tended

This It Why We Must Vote NO on Prop. 14

FIGURE 5.1. This editorial cartoon, from the *California Eagle* on September 10, 1964, depicts the threat of Proposition 14 to the black community by blocking escape from the inner city.

to feel that their leaders were working for status ends, such as integrating white neighborhoods for middle-class blacks, instead of welfare ends for their constituents."[38] Working-class blacks, then, may have felt that equality required improvement of their neighborhood rather than the ability to move next to whites.[39]

Class divisions had the potential to fracture black opposition. Shortly after journalist Louis Lomax joined the fight against Proposition 14 in early September, he demanded that middle-class blacks and organizations such as the NAACP coordinate with working-class blacks in the struggle. "Old line Californians," Lomax said, "are showing the same type of thinking as bigoted whites. Those of us living on top of the hills who cannot communicate with our people down on Central, Normandie and Manchester, will someday find themselves trampled, along with their neighbors, by their own people."[40] In addition, the nationalist Afro-American Citizens Council, one of the few black organizations that supported Proposition 14, stated, "It is inconsistent for us to back a law [Rumford] which encourages the more affluent and educated Negroes to shirk their community responsibilities." Repealing the law, council spokesman Ernie Smith believed, "would force these people to stay." While Lomax encouraged native black Californians to raise awareness of housing rights and opportunities with their brethren in the central district, the council promoted Proposition 14 in order to maintain the black community and promote self-awareness and community empowerment.[41]

Taken together, the statements made by the *California Eagle,* Lomax, and the Afro-American Citizens Council suggest that civil rights organizations and their middle-class membership perceived Proposition 14 as an obstacle to an escape from segregated neighborhoods. Lomax, however, urged the black middle class to recognize that Proposition 14 threatened all blacks. He argued that the referendum was part of a general attack on the opportunity for blacks to live in decent housing wherever it was located. Even though class divisions were present within the black community, the actions of the NAACP, the Urban League, the UCRC, and CORE reflected a desire to unite black residents against the proposition, albeit for more pragmatic purposes than those of Lomax. Indeed, during the fall campaign blacks were able to transcend class lines, as nearly all segments of the black population rallied to the cause of defeating Proposition 14 and volunteered their time and labor to do so. Even if working-class blacks could not avail themselves of the opportunity to live anywhere they wished because of financial limitations, they viewed Proposition 14 as an attack on equality more generally and worked with the middle-class-led organizations to wage an all-out fight against the referendum.[42]

Leaders predicted racial tension and potential violence in Los Angeles if the measure passed. If voters supported Proposition 14, NAACP chairman Christopher Taylor explained, disillusionment among blacks would be unavoidable. Black Los Angeles, Taylor believed, would erupt in protest if Californians shut the door on the legal, albeit largely symbolic, route to equal housing opportunities. Taylor did not see any reason to discourage potential protest. "I would have no moral duty to do so," Taylor stated. "If I got in their way, I would be run over too. I am not going to get white overnight, so I will be with them. A few Uncle Toms will try to get in the middle, but they will have to go along eventually." Although the bulk of the opposition to Proposition 14 may have rested with middle-class blacks, Taylor showed that as a fundamental issue of equality, the initiative held great import for most of the black community.[43]

When voter registration ended on September 10, 1964, the UCRC claimed an initial triumph. The UCRC registered over forty thousand new black voters in just under three months. Voter registration in Watts alone rose by 11.5 percent in 1964.[44] Although the UCRC fell far short of its lofty goal of one hundred thousand to two hundred thousand new voters, the committee lauded the efforts of the volunteers and the response of the black community. "The United Civil Rights Committee, as headquarters of the largest registration mobilization in the United States exceeding in manpower the Mississippi Summer Project," stated Chairman H.H. Brookins, "concluded the most successful registration drive ever attempted in Los Angeles and the State of California this week." During the final weeks before the election, the UCRC and other civil rights organizations encouraged all registered blacks to vote no on Proposition 14. While the black community did not disappoint, the larger effort to defeat the initiative failed miserably.[45]

Proposition 14 passed by a two to one margin in California. According to Josh Sides, "65 percent of state voters and 70 percent of Los Angeles County voters supported Proposition 14." In contrast, out of the ninety-three precincts in the NAACP Headquarters's organizing area, the no vote on the proposition outnumbered the yes vote by 17,490 to 2,649. In other words, nearly 86.6 percent of the community within the NAACP-organizing area voted against Proposition 14. As Philip Ethington has shown, a statistical analysis of voting returns in Los Angeles County revealed widespread opposition to the initiative within majority-black census tracts.[46]

The passage of Proposition 14 discouraged many in the black community who had high expectations for racial progress. "The single fact that emerges with crystal clarity," stated the *California Eagle,* "is that, by and large, white Americans—for a complex of reasons including that of race prejudices—do not want to live next door to Negroes. No amount of rationalizing can submerge this truth."[47] An editorial cartoon in the *Eagle* portrayed a fictional white character, representing Proposition 14, stating to two black homebuyers, "I don't mind Negroes overcoming, as long as they don't come over." Blacks in Los Angeles saw their faith in racial progress and equality run aground on the shoals of the fair housing battle.[48]

FIGURE 5.2. An editorial response by the *California Eagle*, on November 19, 1964, to the passage of Proposition 14 highlighted the contradiction between California's supposedly liberal racial politics and the vote to overturn the Rumford Act, which stated, "I don't mind Negroes overcoming, as long as they don't come over."

Black civil rights organizations mobilized their community across class lines, and the majority of black voters cast their ballots against the initiative. Even if some working-class blacks felt that fair housing primarily benefited middle-class blacks with the economic standing to leave segregated neighborhoods, they recognized that Proposition 14 and the hierarchical racial geography produced by housing discrimination posed a fundamental attack on equal rights and opportunities for all blacks. Despite apparent black unity, however, class divisions did not entirely disappear during the anti–Proposition 14 campaign. The 2,649 votes in favor of the proposition in the NAACP organiz-

ing district, the Afro-American Citizens Council, and Lomax's anec-
dotal comments, for example, suggest underlying intrablack tensions.
Working-class black residents may have felt that opposing Proposition
14 would allow those in the black middle class to shirk their responsibility to the community and would lead to neighborhood deterioration, poor schools, lack of employment opportunities, and enhanced
inequality. In August 1965 the black community's frustrations erupted
in violence during the Watts uprising. While class divisions remained
submerged during the Proposition 14 struggle, Watts revealed a sense
of working-class disillusionment with and rejection of middle-class
leadership and civil rights strategies. The defeat of fair housing demonstrated that California was hardly a place of racial progress. If white
Californians did not respond to efforts to maintain equality through
state-sanctioned elections, then the black community would take measures into its own hands.[49]

THE MEXICAN AMERICAN COMMUNITY AND PROPOSITION 14

Black organizers were not the only activists in Los Angeles to defend
the Rumford Act. Mexican Americans also opposed the CREA initiative. Organizers worked diligently to convince their community that
Proposition 14 threatened Mexican American rights and to mobilize residents to vote against the initiative. The response revealed that
Mexican Americans either knew little about the proposition or believed
it to be primarily a black-white issue. The community was also more
divided on Proposition 14 than African Americans were as a result
of different historical experiences with housing discrimination, class
divisions, and a nascent homeowner identity among some Mexican
Americans who had gained access to growing suburbs. Black-brown
solidarity, in other words, was not guaranteed, and Proposition 14 created different meanings and tensions within each community.[50]

The Los Angeles chapter of the Mexican American Political Association (MAPA) and the Council of Mexican American Affairs (CMAA)
strongly opposed Proposition 14. Attorney Frank Muñoz, of MAPA,
argued that Proposition 14 implicated the Mexican American community and its struggle for equality. "Recent events indicate that many
Mexican Americans do not understand the threat that passage on Prop.
14 would pose to vital interests of our Community. . . . The bigots have
misled some of our people into believing that Prop. 14 is aimed solely
at repealing the Rumford Act, which, they claim, helps only Negroes,"

Muñoz stated, adding, "Nothing could be further from the truth." While Mexican American organizing was not as extensive as that of the African American community, in the view of some Mexican Americans Proposition 14 represented a similar threat to their rights and opportunities.[51]

Divisions in the Mexican American community based on geography and class arose in a CMAA-sponsored debate on March 19, 1964, titled "The Effects of the Rumford Housing Act Initiative on the Mexican American Community." Joseph Vargas, the mayor of suburban South El Monte, spoke in favor of Proposition 14, while East Los Angeles realtor Salvador Montenegro opposed the measure. Vargas was part of a burgeoning group of Mexican Americans who moved to suburban enclaves in Los Angeles County. Mexican Americans would achieve racial progress, Vargas argued, by conforming to American standards of property ownership and individual uplift, ideals he believed Proposition 14 protected.[52]

Sal Montenegro, in contrast, argued that Proposition 14 threatened racial progress, explaining why Mexican American should oppose the measure. The initiative, he argued, marked a threshold upon which the future of Mexican Americans' fight for equality and first-class citizenship would be decided. Montenegro attacked the real estate industry and recounted the history of housing discrimination faced by Mexican Americans. "The Mexican American community has faced discrimination in the field of housing," Montenegro explained, "for after the Second World War, we saw the middle-class migrate to the eastside of Atlantic Blvd in the County of Los Angeles. Immediately the bigots erected barriers to keep the Mexican Americans from buying in their neighborhoods." Montenegro did not deny that some Mexican Americans had made progress in the field of housing. Mexican Americans, for example, had gained access to housing in Monterey Park, Montebello, Pico Rivera, Alhambra, and the City of Commerce. Montenegro was careful not to overly laud the extent of racial progress, however, and presented three cases of discrimination against Mexican American home seekers during 1964. Although Mexican Americans made gains in the field of housing, as Montenegro suggested, the county's racial geography continued to produce unequal opportunities for Mexican Americans.[53]

Montenegro also called out the Mexican American community for a lack of activism and demanded it take a stand against Proposition 14. "Today we find that the Mexican Americans have become complacent because they have been able to purchase homes," Montenegro stated. "They feel that the Rumford bill is only to protect Negroes."[54] Montenegro suggested that this outlook within the Mexican American community was the reason for its weak opposition to Proposition 14. Perhaps Mexican Americans, who faced less residential segregation than blacks, only halfheartedly opposed Proposition 14 because they did not perceive housing discrimination as a major impediment to Mexican American progress. He indicated that alternatively, Mexican Americans such as Joseph Vargas and other suburban residents may have believed that the route to equality required adopting white middle-class notions of property ownership and color blindness. Montenegro's displeasure with the attitude of Mexican American realtors and home-owners supports such an assertion. As Montenegro's evidence of three middle-class home seekers' experiences with discrimination revealed, middle-class Mexican Americans continued to confront residential discrimination. Montenegro believed that many Mexican Americans were naïve to the reality of housing discrimination.[55]

Although Mexican Americans were more ambivalent toward Proposition 14 than the majority of African Americans, there were instances of solidarity between the two communities. At the state and local level, MAPA supported the campaign against Proposition 14. A fledgling political coalition emerged after a number of black leaders attended MAPA's state conference on June 14, 1964. Blacks asked the Mexican Americans to help them "defeat the initiative to repeal the Rumford Housing Act," and Mexican Americans responded, "Yes, if you help us elect a Mexican American to the State Assembly from Imperial Valley."[56] Political expediency notwithstanding, the convention called for united action against Proposition 14 and Public Law 78, which related to bracero workers:

> WHEREAS, the anti–fair housing initiative if enacted will affect adversely all Californians, but will operate most oppressively against minority groups such as the Mexican-American and Negro peoples . . . WHEREAS, it is important and imperative that the California body politic be given constant evidence of the unity and solidarity of the Mexican-American and Negro minorities in their determined resistance to discrimination and oppression in any and all of its forms . . . be it resolved . . . [MAPA] hereby calls for joint action with representatives of the Negro community to defeat the anti-fair housing initiative and to defeat Public Law 78.[57]

MAPA called upon its local chapters to work within black organizations. The Los Angeles chapter supported the resolution to defeat

Proposition 14 and, along with black leaders, made a rhetorical commitment of cooperation. Yet, a coalition based on joint activism remained elusive.[58]

Two weeks after MAPA's convention almost one hundred black and Mexican American community leaders met in Los Angeles to discuss the possibility of united action. Black and Mexican American leaders, stated the *California Eagle,* "pledged . . . to join in efforts to win the election of a Mexican-American to the Assembly from Imperial County and to fight the CREA-sponsored initiative against the Rumford Housing Act." The meeting, however, did not provide a substantive plan for joint organizing. Within Los Angeles those involved in the struggle against Proposition 14 remained separated by race, ethnicity, and geography.[59]

In August the relationship between blacks and Mexican Americans on Proposition 14 captured public attention. Just as the "the campaign against Proposition 14 . . . is beginning to gather momentum in the Mexican American community," stated *Carta Editorial,* the Los Angeles Mexican Chamber of Commerce decided to support Proposition 14 in a vote in which only sixty out of three hundred chamber members participated. Moreover, according to *Carta Editorial,* a Cuban doctor engineered the chamber's promotion of Proposition 14. While the chamber's vote revealed potential middle-class Mexican American support for Proposition 14, many Mexican American organizers in Los Angeles were upset that the chamber's position on the proposition was based on the vote of a minority of its members led by a non–Mexican American.[60]

The chamber received harsh scrutiny from MAPA as well as from members of the black community. The *California Eagle* ran a headline that read, "Snakes in the Grass: Mexican American 'Stab' in the Back." Billy G. Mills, a black city councilman, felt that the chamber's decision forced the black community to take on the "the burden of initiating, of winning and preserving legislation" that was just as important to the Mexican American community as it was to the black community.[61] Los Angeles councilman Gilbert Lindsay similarly called the decision "disgraceful, shameful and a disregard for the well-being of the Mexican people," adding, "I regret very much that the Mexican Chamber of Commerce members allowed some supposed leaders to betray them by voting against the best interests of the Mexican community and indicating to the Mexican people that this is a Negro fight."[62] Although black leaders felt betrayed, their support of organizing in the Mexican American community had been rhetorical at best.

Mexican American leaders took a strong stand against the L.A. Mexican Chamber of Commerce. Realtor Salvador Montenegro and unionist J.J. Rodriguez released a statement arguing that Mexican Americans continued to face discrimination in housing and that the chamber had "voted to bring bigotry back to California, but those few people do not represent the one and a half million Mexican Americans in Southern California." They stressed that nearly every Mexican American political and community organization in California opposed Proposition 14.[63] As a result of the outcry, the chamber changed its stance on Proposition 14 from yes to neutral. A neutral resolution, as the historian Jerry Gonzalez notes, was not a strong statement of opposition and allowed the chamber to avoid further humiliation by stating that political statements were contrary to the organization's bylaws. A past president and member of the CMAA, attorney Manuel Sanz, however, recognized the chamber's hypocrisy, given Mexican American experience with past discrimination. "My contention is that it was immoral for us to endorse something like that," Sanz stated, "especially since Mexican Americans have been discriminated against for so many years. I can say for sure that the majority of Mexican Americans will support the movement to kill Prop. 14."[64] Community leaders used the chamber debacle to raise awareness of the consequences of Proposition 14 for Mexican Americans.

Mexican American knowledge of Proposition 14 was marginal in comparison to that of the black community. In September 1964, two UCLA graduate students conducted a study of the Mexican American residents in East Los Angeles and Monterey Park. They revealed that 76 and 53 percent of working- and middle-class residents, respectively, knew almost nothing about the initiative. In Monterey Park, 52 percent of the Mexican American residents did not know if the Rumford Act benefited Mexican Americans. When told what Proposition 14 intended to accomplish, however, many respondents reacted negatively, which, according to an issue of *Carta Editorial,* pointed to the potential opposition to Proposition 14 among Mexican Americans.[65]

To increase Mexican American opposition, activists allied with CAP 14 to form Mexican American Californians Against Proposition 14 (MACAP). Chaired by J.J. Rodriguez, MACAP received support from the CMAA, the Community Service Organization, the GI Forum, the League of United Latin American Citizens, MAPA, and the Mexican American Lawyers Club. The purpose of MACAP was to "reach the Mexican-American voters in as many towns and hamlets of the southland in an attempt to activate, help coordinate, and/or orientate them against Proposition 14." MACAP's efforts coincided with those of black activists but the two groups did not coordinate joint action. Although MACAP was associated with the CAP campaign, as was the UCRC, they focused their efforts on mobilizing Mexican Americans.[66]

Unlike the black community, MACAP had to persuade Mexican Americans that housing discrimination was a relevant issue for their community. MACAP warned Mexican Americans that Proposition 14 would lead to greater housing segregation. A double-sided flier presented MACAP's argument in Spanish as well as English. On the Spanish side, it read in part: "¡Esta Lucha Tambien es Suya! Derrote la Proposicion 14" On the English side: "It's YOUR fight, too! Vote 'NO' on 14." The flier openly connected the threat of Proposition 14 with higher rents, school segregation, and unemployment. It reminded Mexican Americans that they "continue to suffer from discrimination and oppression. Don't put a stop to the progress we have made toward equal opportunity for us all."[67] MACAP organized an anti–Proposition 14 rally on September 6 in East Los Angeles to raise community interest and to distribute voter registration materials. They also sponsored the "No on 14" float in the September 16 Mexican Independence Day parade to "dramatically illustrate [the Mexican American] people's united stand against the housing discrimination that Proposition 14 seeks to unleash on [the] community."[68]

Just as black leaders framed their opposition to Proposition 14 within the context of how residential segregation preserved white advantage in schooling and employment, Mexican American organizers linked their argument against housing discrimination to unequal education and employment opportunities. As the East Side Realtors, an interest group initiated to oppose Proposition 14 led by Salvador Montenegro, explained, "Where a family lives determines also where the children of that family will go to school. And that determines in large measure the extent of opportunities in life for those children. Where a man lives also can seriously affect his job possibilities." Residential segregation was the base upon which the twin pillars of white supremacy and racial subordination rested. The East Side Realtors recognized this link and believed Proposition 14 was a central piece to the structure of white supremacy that used seemingly nonracial geographic advantages to perpetuate Mexican American inequality.[69]

The Mexican American community remained divided over Proposition 14, however. While the East Side Realtors and MACAP opposed

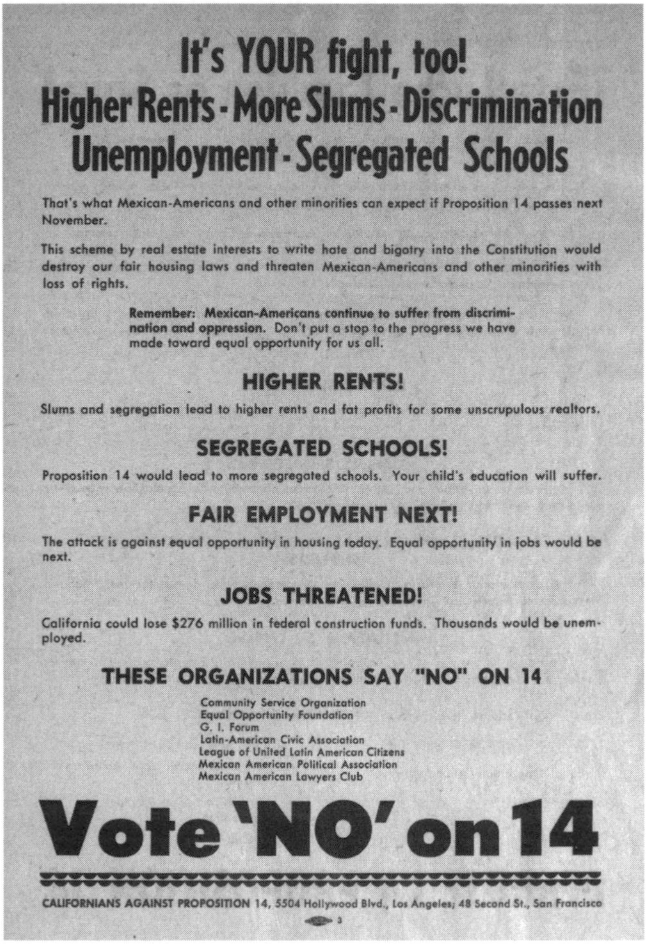

It's YOUR fight, too!
Higher Rents - More Slums - Discrimination
Unemployment - Segregated Schools

That's what Mexican-Americans and other minorities can expect if Proposition 14 passes next November.

This scheme by real estate interests to write hate and bigotry into the Constitution would destroy our fair housing laws and threaten Mexican-Americans and other minorities with loss of rights.

Remember: Mexican-Americans continue to suffer from discrimination and oppression. Don't put a stop to the progress we have made toward equal opportunity for us all.

HIGHER RENTS!

Slums and segregation lead to higher rents and fat profits for some unscrupulous realtors.

SEGREGATED SCHOOLS!

Proposition 14 would lead to more segregated schools. Your child's education will suffer.

FAIR EMPLOYMENT NEXT!

The attack is against equal opportunity in housing today. Equal opportunity in jobs would be next.

JOBS THREATENED!

California could lose $276 million in federal construction funds. Thousands would be unemployed.

THESE ORGANIZATIONS SAY "NO" ON 14

Community Service Organization
Equal Opportunity Foundation
G. I. Forum
Latin-American Civic Association
League of United Latin American Citizens
Mexican American Political Association
Mexican American Lawyers Club

Vote 'NO' on 14

CALIFORNIANS AGAINST PROPOSITION 14, 5504 Hollywood Blvd., Los Angeles; 48 Second St., San Francisco

FIGURES 5.3 AND 5.4. These two images are from a "Mexican American Californians against Proposition 14" two-sided flyer outlining the argument against Proposition 14 for the Mexican American community. The flyer was developed in conjunction with the Californians against Proposition 14.

Proposition 14, some Mexican Americans agreed with CREA that Proposition 14 safeguarded their property rights and the freedom to sell or rent their homes to anyone they wished. The Montebello District Board of Realtors and South El Monte mayor Joseph Vargas, for example, strongly supported Proposition 14. Suburban Mexican Americans negotiated a dual identity as homeowners and as a racialized minority, what Jerry Gonzalez refers to as an ambivalent whiteness, making their

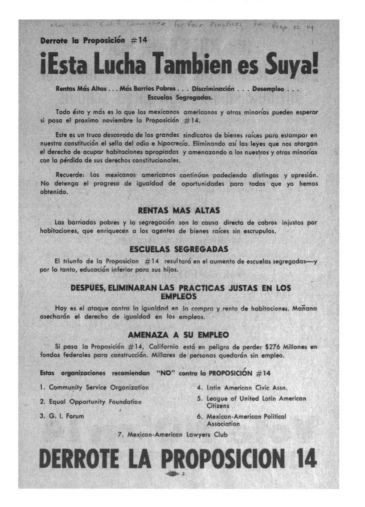

stance against Proposition 14 more ambiguous than that of working-class Mexican Americans and blacks.[70]

Opposition to Proposition 14 was not as strong among Mexican Americans as it was among blacks. As Phil Ethington's analysis of voting returns shows, the strongest opposition to Proposition 14 coincided with black neighborhoods and Mexican American East Los Angeles. Outlying suburban areas with growing Mexican American populations, such as South El Monte, Pico Rivera, Norwalk, Monterey Park, and Montebello, expressed support for the proposition. The voting returns suggested divisions within the Mexican American community by class and residence. While many working-class Mexican Americans may have been unaware of the effects of Proposition 14 or believed it to be a black-white issue, some among the middle class, especially in the suburbs, may have supported the proposition because they did not perceive housing discrimination as an impediment to their ability to live where they wished. Such evidence suggests that class, residence, and their relationship to whiteness influenced Mexican Americans in their support of or opposition to Proposition 14. Yet, Mexican American organizing also showed that opposition to Proposition 14, as an issue of fair housing and equality, resonated with many Mexican Americans regardless of class standing or residential location.[71]

. . .

The Supreme Court of California overturned Proposition 14 in 1966.[72] The success of Proposition 14, however, contributed to disillusionment on the part of both black and Mexican American communities for the hope of racial progress. The struggles of blacks and Mexican Americans underscored their respective awareness that more was at stake than equal access to housing in the ballot referendum. Both communities recognized—to varying degrees—that Proposition 14 symbolized the ways in which white supremacy rested on a hierarchical racial geography that worked to distribute resources and opportunities in a profoundly unequal way. Blacks and Mexican Americans both understood the success of Proposition 14 as part of the structural nature of racism that produced and reinforced racial and ethnic subordination more generally under the guise of seemingly race-neutral housing policies. That the Blacks and Brown Power movements emerged following the campaign against Proposition 14 was no coincidence. The Proposition 14 struggle marked a threshold for both blacks and Mexican Americans. Its passage contributed to a sense of bitterness that in turn contributed to the outbreak of the 1965 Watts uprising in the black community and the Chicano movement's 1968 school blowouts.[73]

Class dynamics within the black and Mexican American communities likely played a part in their support or opposition to Proposition 14. Louis Lomax criticized the middle-class black community for ignoring the experience of working-class blacks. Proposition 14 was an issue of equal housing opportunities that, as the middle-class organizations such as the NAACP and UCRC demonstrated, threatened the ability of blacks to buy or rent a house or an apartment anywhere they wished. Proposition 14 also reinforced the structural nature of inequality faced by the Los Angeles black population more generally. It revealed the concerns of working-class blacks as it underscored the dashed expectation for progress, equality, and freedom rather than solely a desire to live next to whites in California's ever-expanding suburbs. When Watts erupted in violence a year after the vote on Proposition 14, the black working class expressed its rage at the false promises of moderate civil rights strategies, progress, and racial equality.

Class divisions within the Mexican American community are similarly difficult to uncover. As the Mexican Chamber of Commerce, the South El Monte mayor, Mexican American homeownership rates, and the suburban voting record seem to indicate, there were likely some middle- and upper-class Mexican Americans who maintained an investment in a white identity and did not see the repeal of fair housing as an obstacle to their success. As Jerry Gonzalez suggests, Mexican American suburbanites developed an ambivalent whiteness out of the combination of homeownership and continued discrimination. This ambivalent whiteness, this essay suggests, may have made them more willing to support Proposition 14 than those who lived in East Los Angeles were. As Sal Montenegro's appeals highlighted, however, there was a nascent sense of a Mexican American identity among some middle-class members of the population who came out strongly against Proposition 14. In part, class and spatial dynamics within the black and Mexican American communities reflected the different nature of their responses to Proposition 14.

The role that black and Mexican American organizations and their leaders played in Los Angeles demands attention. Blacks and Mexican Americans demonstrated a wide range of activities and responses to Proposition 14 that have been distorted by arguments focused on state-level Democratic politics, homeowners, and white backlash. Their efforts show that multiracial organizing was hard work and that the meaning of rights and equality differed for each community. While there were moments of potential multiracial organizing, black and Mexican American leaders voiced different concerns about the impact that Proposition 14 would have in their communities. Much of the evidence suggests that a multiracial coalition remained elusive because of differing perceptions of the impact of housing discrimination on blacks and Mexican Americans. The lack of unity foreshadowed the contested nature of the War on Poverty between Black Power and Chicano activists in Los Angeles, as Robert Bauman has pointed out.[74]

Proposition 14 was not simply a referendum on property rights or the limits of liberalism. From the perspective of black and Mexican American activism and the conflict surrounding it, Proposition 14 is better viewed as part of struggles for equal rights and opportunities. For both blacks and Mexican Americans, Proposition 14 reinforced the invidious nature of residential segregation and raised questions about the ability to make change from within the political system. In their respective ways, the campaigns against Proposition 14 were part of the larger struggles for equality waged by black and Mexican American communities in Los Angeles.

NOTES

1. *Los Angeles Sentinel,* July 9, 1964.

2. *California Eagle,* August 20, 1964; *Carta Editorial,* August 20, 1964, box 54, folder 8, Manuel Ruiz Papers, Stanford Library Special Collections (hereafter MRP). Jerry Gonzalez provided me with sources from the Stanford Library. I am grateful to him for his willingness to share his materials and part of his unpublished work.

3. This is not to say that blacks and Mexican Americans never cooperated. As Laura Pulido has shown, organizations involved with the Third World Left in the late 1960s and the 1970s exhibited a willingness to work with one another; Pulido, *Black, Brown, Yellow, and Left: Radical Activism in Los Angeles* (Berkeley: University of California Press, 2006), 2–8, 25–27, 34–58. See also Kevin Allen Leonard, "'Brothers under the Skin'? African Americans, Mexican Americans, and World War II in California," in *The Way We Really Were: The Golden State in the Second Great War,* ed. Roger W. Lotchin (Urbana: University of Illinois Press, 2000).

4. The common historiographic analysis is to place Proposition 14 within the framework of the decline of New Deal liberalism. Robert Self argues that homeowner politics, taxation, and Black Power were intertwined throughout the postwar period within the metropolitan network of cities and suburbs that make up what he calls growth liberalism. See Self, *American Babylon: Race and the Struggle for Postwar Oakland* (Princeton, NJ: Princeton University Press, 2003). See also Mark Brilliant, *The Color of America Has Changed: How Racial Diversity Shaped Civil Rights Reform in California, 1941–1978* (New York: Oxford University Press, 2010); and Daniel HoSang, *Racial Propositions: Ballot Initiatives and the Making of Postwar California* (Berkeley: University of California Press, 2010).

5. The Californians for Fair Housing, the precursor to CAP 14, stated, "Defense of the Rumford Law and fair housing will be a subordinate but essential part of the campaign." They focused more heavily on targeting the real

estate interest and other "bigots" in California. Californians for Fair Housing, *Californians for Fair Housing Campaign Manual*, 1964, box 4, folder 20, Max Mont Papers. See also HoSang, *Racial Propositions*, 53–90. On civic nationalism, see Gary Gerstle, *American Crucible: Race and Nation in the Twentieth Century* (Princeton, NJ: Princeton University Press, 2001).

6. Blacks and Mexican Americans did ally with the CAP 14 coalition against Proposition 14. However, I contend that blacks and Mexican Americans in Los Angeles County organized their own campaigns against Proposition 14, which centered on arguments and language about equality and rights fundamentally different from those of CAP 14. Japanese American organizations strongly opposed Proposition 14. See Scott Kurashige, *The Shifting Grounds of Race: Black and Japanese Americans in the Making of Multiethnic Los Angeles* (Princeton, NJ: Princeton University Press, 2008), 264–65. The story of Japanese Americans regarding Proposition 14 is an important part of the history of multiracial Los Angeles, but their role is outside the scope of this study. I realize that neglecting Asian Americans in this essay reduces the study of multiracial organizing in Los Angeles and is a future path of research.

7. Jeanne Theoharis and Komozi Woodard, *Freedom North: Black Freedom Struggles Outside the South, 1940–1980* (New York: Palgrave Macmillan, 2003), 1–15. Theoharis and Woodard call for rethinking northern and western black freedom struggles to highlight the role of black organizing and grassroots mobilization rather than viewing those struggles through a framework of white backlash and resistance.

8. Los Angeles County Commission on Human Relations, "Population and Housing in Los Angeles County," March 1963, series I, box 19, "Housing" folder, Edward Roybal Papers, UCLA Chicano Studies Research Center (hereafter ER); Los Angeles County Commission on Human Relations, *The Urban Reality*, 42. The index of dissimilarity between Spanish and Anglo surnames in Los Angeles was 57.4; for blacks and Anglos it was 87.6. See Leo Grebler et al., *The Mexican-American People: The Nation's Second Largest Minority* (New York: Free Press, 1970), 275. Note also the distinction between the city of Los Angeles and Los Angeles County.

9. Daniel HoSang, "Racial Propositions: 'Genteel Apartheid' in Postwar California," Ph.D. dissertation, University of Southern California, 2007, 134–37. HoSang adds an important element to the history of housing segregation and discrimination that was particular to California. He calls the specific development of homeownership and a possessive investment in whiteness the "Race Property Nexus." HoSang contributes to studies of white housing discrimination by arguing that all white homeowners in California shared an underlying assumption of property rights and whiteness. However, we should not think that neighborhood segregation developed so neatly. As Sánchez says, segregated neighborhoods in Los Angeles before the 1950s were places of multiethnic and multiracial interaction. George Sánchez, "'What's Good for Boyle Heights Is Good for the Jews': Creating Multiracialism on the Eastside during the 1950s," *American Quarterly* 56, no. 3 (September 2004): 635. Historian Philip Ethington poignantly captures residential segregation in Los Angeles as one of "segregated diversity." Phil Ethington, "Segregated Diversity: Race-Ethnicity, Space,

and Political Fragmentation in Los Angeles County, 1940–1994," Final Report to the John Randolph Haynes and Dora Haynes Foundation (Los Angeles, 2000). See also Mark Henry Wild, *Street Meeting: Multiethnic Neighborhoods in Early Twentieth-Century Los Angeles* (Berkeley: University of California Press, 2005); and Mike Davis, *City of Quartz: Excavating the Future in Los Angeles* (New York: Vintage Books, 1992), 160–70, on the history of home-owner politics and residential exclusion in Los Angeles.

10. "Population and Housing in Los Angeles County," Los Angeles County Commission on Human Relations, March 1963, series I, box 19, "Housing" folder, ER.

11. California Department of Industrial Relations, Division of Labor Statistics and Research and California, *Negroes and Mexican Americans in South and East Los Angeles: Changes between 1960 and 1965 in Population, Employment, Income, and Family Status: An Analysis of a U.S. Census Survey of November 1965* (San Francisco: State of California, Division of Fair Employment Practices, 1966).

12. "Population and Housing in Los Angeles County," Los Angeles County Commission on Human Relations, March 1963, series I, box 19, "Housing" folder, ER. This is by no means to argue that blacks in Los Angeles were a unified group. As with Mexican Americans, class stratification governed opportunities to move out of segregated neighborhoods. See Josh Sides, *L.A. City Limits: African American Los Angeles from the Great Depression to the Present* (Berkeley: University of California Press, 2006); George J. Sánchez, *Becoming Mexican American: Ethnicity, Culture, and Identity in Chicano Los Angeles, 1900–1945* (New York: Oxford University Press, 1993); and Albert Camarillo, "black and Brown in Compton," in *Not Just Black and White: Historical and Contemporary Perspectives on Immigration, Race, and Ethnicity in the United States*, ed. Nancy Foner and George Fredrickson (New York: Russell Sage Foundation, 2004), 363.

13. "Population and Housing in Los Angeles County," Los Angeles County Commission on Human Relations, March 1963, series I, box 19, "Housing" folder, ER. Jerry Gonzalez discusses the suburbanization of Mexican Americans in Los Angeles County and notes that the initial suburban *colonias* were segregated from white housing in places such as Pico Rivera and El Monte. Jerry Gonzalez, "'A Place in the Sun': Mexican Americans, Race, and the Suburbanization of Los Angeles, 1940–1980," PhD dissertation, University of Southern California, 2009.

14. Eric Avila, *Popular Culture in the Age of White Flight Fear and Fantasy in Suburban Los Angeles* (Berkeley: University of California Press, 2004), 52. On the relationship between space and politicization in Los Angeles, see Pulido, *Black, Brown, Yellow, and Left,* 34–59; and Grebler et al., *The Mexican-American People,* 286.

15. California Department of Industrial Relations, *Negroes and Mexican Americans in South and East Los Angeles,* 17.

16. The nonwhite population in Los Angeles was largely African American but also consisted of other groups, such as Japanese Americans, Chinese Americans, and Filipinos. Because of the aggregated form of these data, a

more accurate percentage of African American homeownership rates is difficult to determine. Los Angeles County Commission on Human Relations, *The Urban Reality: A Comparative Study of the Socio-Economic Situation of Mexican Americans, Negroes, and Anglo-Caucasians in Los Angeles County* (Los Angeles: County of Los Angeles Commission on Human Relations, 1965).

17. Thomas W. Casstevens, *Politics, Housing, and Race Relations: California's Rumford Act and Proposition 14* (Berkeley: Institute of Governmental Studies, University of California, 1967), 8–17; Mark Robert Brilliant, "Color Lines: Civil Rights Struggles on America's 'Racial Frontier,' 1945–1975," PhD dissertation, Stanford University, 2002; James M. Galbraith, "The Unconstitutionality of Proposition 14: An Extension of Prohibited 'State Action,'" *Stanford Law Review* 19, no. 1 (November 1966): 233–40; Kurashige, *The Shifting Grounds of Race;* Self, *American Babylon.* On the national level see Stephen Grant Meier, *As Long as They Don't Move Next Door;* and David M. P. Freund, *Colored Property: State Policy and White Racial Politics in Suburban America* (Chicago: University of Chicago Press, 2007).

18. Casstevens, *Politics, Housing, and Race Relations,* 30–37; HoSang, "Racial Propositions," 163. However, HoSang also notes that the Rumford Act gave the state FEPC jurisdiction over housing grievances and covered nearly 99 percent of the 738,000 apartment buildings of five or more units, 162–63.

19. Sides, *L.A. City Limits,* 130–68; Gonzalez, "'A Place in the Sun,'" 129–54.

20. HoSang, *Racial Propositions,* 71; Casstevens, *Politics, Housing, and Race Relations,* 49

21. Casstevens, *Politics, Housing, and Race Relations,* 48–69; HoSang, *Racial Propositions,* 53–90. The exact wording of Proposition 14 read: "Initiative measure to be submitted directly to the electors. Sales and rentals of residential real property. Initiative constitutional amendment. Prohibits State, subdivision, or agency thereof from denying, limiting, or abridging right of any person to decline to sell, lease, or rent residential real property to any person as he chooses. Prohibition not applicable to property owned by State or its subdivisions; property acquired by eminent domain; or transient lodging accommodations by hotels, motels, and similar public places." Box 115, "CAP 14" folder, ACLU Papers, University of California, Los Angeles, Special Collections (hereafter ACLU).

22. HoSang, "Racial Propositions," 162, 171. HoSang acknowledges that the black community's rhetoric was categorically different from that of the official CAP 14 campaign. However, his study focuses on the construction of whiteness and the development of property ownership as a political identity rather than on the black or Mexican American response. HoSang, "Racial Propositions," 172–73.

23. Casstevens, *Politics, Housing, and Race Relations,* 60; Kurashige, *The Shifting Grounds of Race,* 265–66; Brilliant, "Color Lines," 253–70.

24. *California Eagle,* June 4, 1964.

25. Statement by Sal Montenegro, realtor for Fair Housing, May 1, 1964, box 5, folder 20, Max Mont Papers, Urban Archives, Cal State Northridge (hereafter MM).

26. Self, *American Babylon*, 267. On whiteness as a form of property, see George Lipsitz, *The Possessive Investment in Whiteness: How White People Profit from Identity Politics* (Philadelphia: Temple University Press, 2006); and Cheryl I. Harris, "Whiteness as Property," *Harvard Law Review* 106, no. 8 (1993): 1707.

27. A *Los Angeles Sentinel*, July 23, 1964, headline read, "UL Housing Leader Urges Total War against Prop. 14." Some individual blacks urged their community to fight the initiative. "Of course," a letter to the *California Eagle* stated, "those who would be free must strike the first blows for their own freedom. As Negroes we must take the initiative in carrying our case to the people of this state. . . . We are at a crisis time in California and we're going to have to drop some non-essentials in order to meet that crisis. Talk, the old adage goes, is cheap. We can win in the contest that lies ahead only by substituting action for talk." *California Eagle*, November 7, 1963.

28. Sides, *L.A. City Limits*, 131–69. Sides notes that the shift in the NAACP's willingness to engage in direct action and protest during the 1950s was a significant departure from its previous position of negotiation. "Eliminate Housing Discrimination in California," September 22, 1963, box 124, "NAACP" folder, Collection of Underground, Alternative and Extremist Literature, 1900–1990, UCLA Special Collections (hereafter UAEL); "Want to Help Eliminate Housing Discrimination in California," CORE/CDC flier, September 13, 1963, box 10, folder 5, California Democratic Council Records, University of Southern California Library (hereafter CDC).

29. Dear George letter, September 13, 1963, box 10, folder 5, CDC.

30. *California Eagle*, November 14, 1963. The legal appeal to prevent the initiative from reaching the ballot was organized by Loren Miller and other NAACP lawyers at the state level. The Supreme Court of California denied the appeal. California Committee for Fair Practices, November 2, 1963, box 3, folder 18, MM; *California Eagle*, January 23 and February 20, 1964. Los Angeles CORE also engaged in picketing and direct action protests against CREA throughout the spring and summer of 1964. *California Eagle*, May, 28 1964; *Los Angeles Sentinel*, May 28, 1964.

31. *Los Angeles Sentinel*, January 2 and March 5, 1964; HoSang, "Racial Propositions," 171–73. On the history of the black freedom struggle for equal housing opportunities in Los Angeles, see Sides, *L.A. City Limits*; and Kurashige, *The Shifting Grounds of Race*.

32. NAACP flier, undated, box 124, "NAACP" folder, UAEL.

33. *Los Angeles Sentinel*, September 17, September 24, and October 1, 1964.

34. *California Eagle*, February 6, 1964; *Los Angeles Sentinel*, October 8, 1964; "Want to Help Eliminate Housing Discrimination in California," CORE/CDC flier, September 13, 1963, box 10, folder 5, CDC.

35. *Los Angeles Sentinel*, June 25, July 9, and August 6, 1964; Los Angeles CORE, *Membership Bulletin*, March 31, 1964, box 14, folder 4, TCO; Dear Friend letter, UCRC, March 20, 1964, box 116, "United Civil Rights Committee 1964" folder, ACLU. There were 8,184,143 registered voters in the state of

California and 3,137,194 in Los Angeles in 1964. *Los Angeles Times*, October 2 and November 1, 1964.

36. *California Eagle*, September 10, 1964. Lawrence B. De Graaf notes that between 1961 and 1971, for example, seventeen thousand African Americans moved to the suburban city of Pomona. However, many of the migrants moved after the Watts Rebellion in 1965. Lawrence B. De Graaf, "African American Suburbanization, 1960 through 1990," in *Seeking El Dorado: African Americans in California*, ed. Lawrence B. De Graaf, Kevin Mulroy, and Quintard Taylor (Los Angeles: Autry Museum of Western Heritage, 2001), 405–10, 411–12. Andrew Wiese notes that many black suburbanites in cities across the country were of middle-class origins and able to capitalize on the fair housing laws and their economic prosperity to enhance their residential mobility. Wiese, *Places of Their Own: African American Suburbanization in the Twentieth Century* (Chicago: University of Chicago Press, 2004), 1–11, 141, 211–20, 225–26.

37. UCRC flier, undated, box 43, folder 2, 20th Century Organizational Files, University of Southern California Library (hereafter TCO); *California Eagle*, June 25, 1964.

38. James O'Toole, *Watts and Woodstock* (New York: Holt McDougal, 1973), 83.

39. Gerald Horne argues that intrablack tensions rested not only on class but also on time of arrival in California and on color distinctions between blacks; see Horne, *Fire This Time: The Watts Uprising and the 1960s* (New York: Da Capo Press, 1997), 3–43. While the black middle class had the economic resources to search for housing in areas outside the black neighborhoods along Central Avenue and Watts, housing discrimination limited their ability to purchase houses in predominantly white neighborhoods. Moreover, black suburbanization largely occurred within a structure of segregation. Indeed, suburbs could extend the lines of residential exclusion to new areas. On black suburbanization, see Wiese, *Places of Their Own*. On the class dynamics of housing discrimination, see Josh Sides and Janet L. Abu-Lughod, *New York, Chicago, Los Angeles: America's Global Cities* (Minneapolis: University of Minnesota Press, 1999).

40. *Los Angeles Sentinel*, September 3, 1964; *California Eagle*, September 3, 1964. It is likely that Lomax's reference to the old line relates to the distinction between long-time black residents of Los Angeles and those blacks who migrated in the postwar decades from the South. Josh Sides presents a good discussion of this distinction and division within Los Angeles. Sides, *L.A. City Limits*, 37–56; Josh Sides, "Rethinking Black Migration: A Perspective From the West," in *Moving Stories: Migration and the American West, 1850–2000*, ed. Scott E. Casper (Reno: University of Nevada Press, 2001), 185–211. For a similar discussion of rifts within California black communities, see Gretchen Lemke-Santangelo, *Abiding Courage: African American Migrant Women and the East Bay Community* (Chapel Hill: University of North Carolina Press, 1996); Quintard Taylor, *In Search of the Racial Frontier: African Americans in the American West, 1528–1990* (New York: W. W. Norton, 1998);

and generally Lawrence Brooks De Graaf and Quintard Taylor, eds., *Seeking El Dorado: African Americans in California* (Los Angeles: Autry Museum of Western Heritage, 2001).

41. *California Eagle,* September 24, 1964. The Afro-American Citizens Council was, according to the *California Eagle,* one of several nationalist organizations in Los Angeles: "Each has its own concentration. The council is concerned with citizenship, constitutional government, free enterprise thought and philosophy." The work of the Afro-American Citizens Council, made up largely of nationalist youth and students, in the central district is likely one reason why the NAACP was unsuccessful in mobilizing all the black voters against Proposition 14.

42. *Los Angeles Sentinel,* September 24, 1964; *Los Angeles Sentinel,* August 20, October 1, and October 8, 1964; UCRC press release, undated, box 116, "UCRC 1964" folder, ACLU; Kurashige, *The Shifting Grounds of Race,* 265.

43. Joe Saltzman and Barbara Saltzman, "Proposition 14: Appeal to Prejudice," *Frontier,* October 1964. Taylor and others effectively predicted the disillusionment in black neighborhoods that erupted in the violence of the Watts Riot in 1965.

44. O'Toole, *Watts and Woodstock,* 90.

45. UCRC press release, undated, box 116, "UCRC 1964" folder, ACLU; *Los Angeles Sentinel,* August 20, 1964; To executive board of United Civil Rights Committee, undated, box 116, "UCRC 1964" folder, ACLU.

46. *Los Angeles Times,* November 4, 1964; Becky M. Nicolaides, *My Blue Heaven: Life and Politics in the Working-Class Suburbs of Los Angeles, 1920–1965* (Chicago: University of Chicago Press, 2002), 313–15; Raymond E. Wolfinger and Fred I. Greenstein, "The Repeal of Fair Housing in California: An Analysis of Referendum Voting," *American Political Science Review* 62, no. 3 (September 1968): 753–69; Sides, *L.A. City Limits,* 168; Kurashige, *The Shifting Grounds of Race,* 264; "Report on Operation of NAACP Headquarters for No on Proposition 14," November 12, 1964, box 20, folder 21, MM. The 2,649 voters who voted in favor of Proposition 14 were likely either white residents who remained in the central district or black residents who supported the Afro-American Citizens Council and their efforts to keep middle-class blacks, businesses, and leadership in the black community rather than allowing further disinvestment and flight from segregated neighborhoods. Ethington, "Segregated Diversity," 42. When considering the voting records on Proposition 14, one must recognize that the data reflect tract- and block-level analyses of support and opposition. As a result, voting data do not necessarily illuminate the true feelings of black or Mexican American voters or community members. Moreover, voting data rely on those members of the community who were registered to vote. The historical data available for this study do not consider subtle class- and race-based analysis of voting in relation to place. A more sustained analysis of the voting returns of Proposition 14 in Los Angeles County is outside the scope of this essay and is a further avenue of research.

47. *California Eagle,* November 12, 1964, cited in Nicolaides, *My Blue Heaven,* 314.

48. *California Eagle,* November 19, 1964.

49. Horne, *Fire This Time,* 3–42; Robert Bauman, *Race and the War on Poverty: From Watts to East L.A.* (Norman: University of Oklahoma Press, 2008). Bauman argues that Watts was a manifestation of the class divide in the black community and a rejection of middle-class black leadership. See also Josh Sides, "Straight into Compton: American Dreams, Urban Nightmares, and the Metamorphosis of a Black Suburb," *American Quarterly* 56, no. 3 (2004): 591. Mark Brilliant argues that Proposition 14 was a significant turning point in the decline of racial liberalism in California. Brilliant, "Color Lines," 280–92.

50. Gonzalez argues that Mexican Americans in Los Angeles suburbs negotiated a dual identity as both homeowners and a racialized minority group, which suggests that middle-class Mexican Americans may have supported Proposition 14 as homeowners who saw the defense of property rights and individual opportunity as the means to racial progress. Gonzalez, "'A Place in the Sun.'"

51. Ibid., 132–33; *MAPA Southern Regional Newsletter,* box 9, folder 2, MRP.

52. "Dear Max Mont" letter, March 3, 1964, box 3, folder 18, MM; *Belvedere Citizen,* March 5 and March 19, 1964; "Effects of the Initiative and Fair Housing Law on the Mexican-American Community," March 19, 1964, box 57, folder 5, Ernesto Galarza Papers, M0224, Stanford Library Special Collections (hereafter EGP); statement by Sal Montenegro, realtor for Fair Housing, May 1, 1964, box 5, folder 20, MM.

53. "Effects of the Initiative and Fair Housing Law on the Mexican-American Community," March 19, 1964, box 57, folder 5, EGP; statement by Sal Montenegro, realtor for Fair Housing, May 1, 1964, box 5, folder 20, MM. On Mexican American homeownership in the suburbs, see also Anthony F. Macias, *Mexican American Mojo: Popular Music, Dance, and Urban Culture in Los Angeles, 1935–1968* (Durham, NC: Duke University Press, 2008), 214–17.

54. "Effects of the Initiative and Fair Housing Law on the Mexican-American Community," March 19, 1964, box 57, folder 5, EGP; statement by Sal Montenegro, realtor for Fair Housing, May 1, 1964, box 5, folder 20, MM.

55. Statement by Sal Montenegro, realtor for Fair Housing, May 1, 1964, box 5, folder 20, MM. Many middle-class Mexican Americans in the Southwest claimed white identity in order to gain access to white residential space and especially schools. See Neil Foley, "Becoming Hispanic: Mexican Americans and Whiteness," in *White Privilege: Essential Readings on the Other Side of Racism,* ed. Paula S. Rosenberg (New York: Worth Publishers, 2002), 49–59.

56. *Belvedere Citizen,* August 20, 1964; *Los Angeles Times,* July 5, 1964; Resolution, MAPA State Convention, box 5, folder 20, MM.

57. Resolution, MAPA State Convention, box 5, folder 20, MM.

58. *California Eagle,* July 2, 1964; MAPA newsletter, 1964, box 9, folder 2, MRP.

59. *California Eagle,* July 2, 1964. MAPA would maintain a strong anti–

Proposition 14 stance within Los Angeles. MAPA newsletter, 1964, box 9, folder 2, MRP.

60. *Carta Editorial,* August 20, 1964, box 54, folder 8, EGP; *Belvedere Citizen,* August 20, 1964; *Los Angeles Times,* August 15, 1964; *California Eagle,* August 20, 1964.

61. *California Eagle,* August 20, 1964; *Los Angeles Times,* August 15, 1964.

62. *California Eagle,* August 20, 1964.

63. *Los Angeles Times,* August 14, 1964.

64. *Belvedere Citizen,* August 20, 1964; *Eastside Sun,* August 10, 1964; *Los Angeles Sentinel,* August 20, 1964; Gonzalez, "'A Place in the Sun,'" 133–35. Members who thought that a yes stand was acceptable stated that they felt Proposition 14 was not a political issue for the Mexican American community but a socioeconomic issue. In addition, the current president of the chamber, Eugene Guterac, stated that he initially hoped the decision to support Proposition 14 would be kept private. See clippings file, box 223.5, series III, ER.

65. *Los Angeles Times,* August 20, 1964; *Belvedere Citizen,* August 27, 1964; *Carta Editorial,* September 8, 1964; box 54, folder 8, EGP. Heather Rose Parker discusses the greater level of political mobilization and participation in liberal coalitions in the Los Angeles black community in comparison to the Mexican American during Thomas Bradley's electoral campaigns. Parker, "African-American and Chicano Political Organization and Interaction in Los Angeles, 1960–1973," PhD dissertation, University of California, Los Angeles, 1996.

66. "Mexican Americans against Proposition 14," August 22, 1964, box 5, folder 20, MM; *Los Angeles Times,* September 4, 1964; "News No on 14," press release, September 2, 1964, and CDC newsletter, September 3, 1964, both in box 29, folder 1, CDC; MACAP release, September 22, 1964, box 5, folder 20, MM. It should be noted, however, that much of the funding for the campaigns was highly interrelated. The UCRC received support from the ACLU of Southern California for its voter registration drive, and the NAACP received campaign materials from the CAP 14 office in Los Angeles. On the UCRC and the ACLU, see ACLU memo, August 31, 1964, box 115, "CAP 14" folder, ACLU; on the NAACP, see "Report on Operation of NAACP Headquarters for No on Proposition 14," November, 12, 1964, box 20, folder 21, MM. As the evidence above implies, the MACAP was nominally affiliated with the official CAP 14 organization. However, members of the Mexican American community did not fully support CAP 14. They felt slighted in the campaign against Proposition 14 and felt that help in organizing the Mexican American community was somewhat of an afterthought. *Carta Editorial,* August 20, 1964, box 54, folder 8, EGP.

67. "It's YOUR Fight, Too" flier, box 5, folder 7, MM; "Vote No en La 14" flier, box 9, folder 20, Eduardo Quevedo Papers, M0349, Department of Special Collections, Stanford University Library.

68. *Belvedere Citizen,* September 3, 1964; *Los Angeles Sentinel,* September 3, 1964.

69. "News No on 14," press release, September 17, 1964, box 29, folder

1, CDC; *Belvedere Citizen*, September 24, 1964; *Eastside Sun*, September 24, 1964; Sal Montenegro, statement, undated, box 29, folder 1, CDC.

70. *Belvedere Citizen*, September 24, October 1, and October 15, 1964. I cannot comment on how widespread Mexican middle-class support was. However, it is likely that many Mexican American residents sided with Vargas, as voting results show that Mexican Americans were not as opposed to Proposition 14 as, for example, the black community was. On the dual identity of Mexican American suburbanites, see Gonzalez, "'A Place in the Sun,'" 92–96, 103–42.

71. Ethington, "Segregated Diversity," map series 5A. On the suburban Mexican American vote, see Gonzalez, "'A Place in the Sun,'" 139. On whiteness and class within the Mexican American community, see Pulido, *Black, Brown, Yellow, and Left*, 112–13; and Foley, "Becoming Hispanic," 49–59.

72. Casstevens, *Politics, Housing, and Race Relations*, 81–84; HoSang, "Racial Propositions," 182–85.

73. Horne, *Fire This Time*, 223–27; Edward J. Escobar, "The Dialectics of Repression: The Los Angeles Police Department and the Chicano Movement, 1968–1971," *Journal of American History* 79, no. 4 (March 1993): 1483–514; Robert Bauman, "The Black Power and Chicano Movements in the Poverty Wars in Los Angeles," *Journal of Urban History* 33, no. 2 (January 1, 2007): 277–95.

74. Bauman, "The Black Power and Chicano Movements in the Poverty Wars in Los Angeles," 277–95. Bauman discusses how the War on Poverty became an issue of local control and community empowerment in Los Angeles for blacks and Mexican Americans. As a result, there was tension between the two communities over resources, as each hoped to gain advantages for their own neighborhoods. Bauman, *Race and the War on Poverty*.

6

The Politics of Low and Slow/
Bajito y Suavecito

Black and Chicano Lowriders in Los Angeles,
from the 1960s through the 1970s

DENISE M. SANDOVAL

As far as I am concerned, it all started here [Los Angeles].
Period. This is the lowrider capital of the world. Everybody
tries to imitate what's done here. That's always how it's
going to be. . . . LA is it.

—Ted Wells, Professionals Car Club

We had three cultures. We had our Mexican culture at home.
Our mother spoke to us all in Spanish. Then we had our
pachuco culture—we were pachucos. And we had our Black
brothers out there. We had a variety and that was good.

—Fernando Ruelas, Dukes Car Club

INTRODUCTION

Hollywood movies have often presented sensationalized and racialized
images of lowrider culture in Los Angeles that have commonly led to the
misconception that lowriders are "gangs on wheels." *Boulevard Nights*
(1979) was one the first movies that visualized lowrider culture in East
Los Angeles by connecting it not only to the culture of "gangs," or *la vida
loca,* but also to Chicano culture by capturing the lingo, music, art, and
cruising of Chicano lowriders in the late 1970s. In one scene, the protag-
onist, Raymond, takes his *ruca*/girlfriend and younger brother, Chuco,

to cruise on Whittier Boulevard on a Friday night in his royal blue 1976 Monte Carlo (with its small chain-link steering wheel and hydraulics setup) as disco music blares in the background. When Chuco sees his *cholo* friends, he gets out of his brother's car and into a 1940s lowrider that is blasting oldies. The movie shows the links between the lowrider pachuco past and the Chicano urban reality of the late 1970s, and it has been a very popular movie within many Chicano communities .

Yet, what I find significant is that it also portrays lowriding as a primarily Chicano cultural scene. Twelve years later, not only would *Boyz n the Hood* (1991) put lowriding in South Central (and Crenshaw Boulevard) on the map, but also it celebrated the popularity of gangsta rap on the West Coast. The night scene on Crenshaw has gang member Doughboy (played by Ice Cube) sitting in his champagne gold 1963 Chevy Impala convertible, discussing religion and street politics with his homies as other lowrider cars line up on the boulevard, socializing. When schoolboy Tre and his childhood friend Rick, a star athlete and Doughboy's brother, join them, there is a gang confrontation, Crips and Blood signs are flashed, and then the social scene on the Shaw is disrupted by the gunfire of an AK-47. Lowriding on Crenshaw in the early 1990s is portrayed in the film as a primarily African American activity, when in fact that era saw the community undergoing a demographic shift toward Latinos, and both Black and Chicano lowriders frequented "the Shaw."

Boyz n the Hood and *Boulevard Nights* share themes of gang violence, family connections, hypermasculinity, and brotherhood, as well as the struggle to move out of one's neighborhood for a better way of life. Yet, each movie portrays lowriding as racially/ethnically specific to the urban spaces of East Los Angeles and South Central. What is overlooked, however, is that each of these communities, Black and Chicano, has shared a similar history of struggle in Los Angeles and that at moments cultural expressions, such as lowriding, have led to interconnections and the creation of multicultural spaces. It is the passionate love affair for lowrider cars that has often bridged the gaps between East Los Angeles and South Central or South Los Angeles.

LOS ANGELES LOWRIDERS

Lowriders in Los Angeles not only reveal their owners' passion for classic cars but also speak to the importance of visualizing and communicating cultural identity and community.[1] Using their vehicles as canvases for creative expression within the urban landscape, lowrider owners document the rich and vibrant social and cultural history of *nuestra ciudad* (our city). Lowriding is an everyday cultural practice for some Chicanos, and they are often cited as one of the creators of their culture (Trillin 1978; Plascenia 1983; Lipsitz 1990; Stone 1990; Bright 1995; Mendoza 2000; Penland 2003; Sandoval 2003). More important, the history of lowriding speaks to the long history of interconnection between Chicano and Black communities in Los Angeles, reaching back to the swing and jazz scene of the 1940s and to the R&B and rock 'n' roll scene of the 1950s, 1960s, and 1970s. The West Coast sound created by single artists and groups such as Lalo Guerrero, Chuck Higgins, Etta James, Richard Berry, Brenton Wood, Thee Midniters, Tierra, and War, who explored the rhythms and beats of jazz, swing, blues, R&B, mambo, and rock music (Lipsitz 1990; Macías 2008), became the soundtrack for lowriding in Los Angeles, especially the music of Thee Midniters, Tierra, and War, who wrote songs that specifically catered to the lowrider community (Reyes and Waldman 1998; Molina 2002). The explosion of hip-hop culture in the 1980s and 1990s in Los Angeles also displayed this interconnectedness and transformed lowrider culture. Groups and artists such N.W.A., Ice-T, Cypress Hill, and Kid Frost consistently employed lowriders in their videos as part of the West Coast hip-hop culture, and this had an impact both nationally and internationally. Los Angeles history reveals moments in which Mexican Americans and African Americans have used the dominant urban landscape in order to re-create their community and their cultural identities.

In the years since the 1965 Watts Riots, Los Angeles has often been portrayed as a city full of racial tensions, and the mainstream media have focused in particular on "Black and Brown" tensions in South Central, resulting from gang violence, issues over immigration, and even interactions between Blacks and Latinos in schools. Often overlooked, though, are the many historical moments in which these communities have come together through their love of similar cultural expressions, such as fashion, music, and cars. Documenting and understanding the earlier Black and Brown cultural histories of Los Angeles through lowrider history will, I hope, help illuminate the present and offer possible insight into how cultural expressions such lowriding offer avenues for understanding the ways these two communities have historically lived, worked, played, and created a "brotherhood" by cruising together. A core theme found within the many stories of lowriding is the pride and respect lowriders feel for their cars, their car clubs, and for other lowrider participants. Other themes include the importance of family and brotherhood. "Brotherhood" is a particularly fascinating and important aspect of these communities that embrace and practice multiculturalism. In my many years of research, I often heard that the love of lowrider cars is what brings these men together, and this precedes any "race" solidarity. But, as these stories reveal, "race" is, in fact, an aspect of how intercultural connections happen in Los Angeles through the love of lowrider cars.

Lowriding is an art form and a "way of life" that continue to express vividly the intersections of race, class, and gender, along with respect and pride. These expressions are most salient in the generation of lowriders active from the 1960s through the 1970s, a period often considered the "cultural renaissance" of lowriding and an era in Los Angeles history in which lowriders often faced segregation and discrimination for their cruising activities on L.A. streets. This essay utilizes oral histories with Chicano and Black lowriders, in particular, the Ruelas brothers (Julio, Ernie, and Fernando), who founded the Dukes Car Club of Los Angeles, the oldest lowrider car club still in existence, and who are considered the "godfathers of lowriding." I also include their friendship with two African American lowriders: Terry Andersen and Ted Wells. The Ruelas family history begins in South Central Los Angeles, not the typical Chicano barrio experience of East Los Angeles, and provides an entry point for examining the sociohistorical interconnections between Chicano and Black cultural spaces in Los Angeles through the practice of lowriding. This essay grounds itself in the Chicano cultural space of lowriding in the key years of the 1960s through the 1970s, since Chicanos are the first group that organized car clubs in Los Angeles and also had the first magazine, *Lowrider,* beginning in 1977, and beyond that it examines, through the case study of the Dukes Car Club, how Chicano and Black lowriders interacted. The Chicano story of lowriding is central to L.A. history, as well as to lowrider history in general, since it has been one of the most documented and visualized aspects of that history. More important, the politics of bajito y suavecito/low and slow has been the mantra that has defined this cultural space and Chicano cultural identity.

THE POLITICS OF BAJITO Y SUAVECITO

There is a conceptual framework for understanding the transformations and continuities of Chicano cultural identity within the urban landscape based on certain cultural knowledge of barrio life—a "barri-ology."[2] In *Barrio Logos: Space and Place in Urban Chicano Literature and Culture,* Raul Villa examines how within Los Angeles, working-class struggles and cultural movements of Mexican Americans can be mapped.[3] He labels these cultural movements and struggles "barriol-ogy," which is the documentation of the tensions based in "the prac-tice of everyday life" for barrio residents of Los Angeles. Villa further explicates the importance of barrio life to cultural space and identity: "Manifesting alternative needs and interests of those of the dominant public sphere, the expressive practices of barrio social and cultural reproduction—from the mundane exercises of daily round and leisure activities to the formal articulation of community defensive goals in organizational forums and discursive media—reveal multiple possibili-ties for re-creating and re-imagining dominant urban space as commu-nity enabling place."[4]

Villa's analysis is helpful as a starting point for examining how car culture in Chicano and Black communities has involved a re-creation or a reimagining of the urban landscape of Los Angeles. As such, I would like to add to Villa's analysis of barriology the politics and prac-tice of bajito y suavecito. Bajito y suavecito is not only a "leisure activ-ity" but also a system of cultural knowledge grounded in the everyday practices of urban life. Lowriders, in choosing a particular aesthet-ics of car customizing, have created a subculture that has moved them beyond the barrios or neighborhoods of Los Angeles through the per-formance of mobility. Automobiles, especially in the 1950s and 1960s, allowed individuals or groups a means to transcend the limits of neigh-borhood. As lowriders cruised the boulevards of Los Angeles, they visualized their particular aesthetics to people outside their communi-ties, who sometimes viewed them in the same manner they viewed the zoot-suiters, as juvenile delinquents or gang members. Many of these negative representations were due to the dominant media outlets like the *Los Angeles Times* newspaper. Luis Alvarez (2008) addresses how this racialization affected Black and Brown male bodies: "Popular dis-course characterizing nonwhite youth as animal-like, hypersexual, and criminal marked their bodies as 'other' and, when coming from city officials and the press, served to help construct for the public a social meaning of African American and Mexican American youth. In these ways, the physical and discursive bodies of nonwhite youth were the sites upon which their dignity was denied."[5]

In an era in the 1940s, when ethnic minorities were expected to conform to Anglo-American styles of dress, the wearing of zoot suits enabled young Chicanos and Blacks to challenge the expectations of the dominant culture. It also meant that cultural identities were often fluid and multicultural. The pachuco/zoot-suiter, through his clothing (the suit originated in African American jazz/swing culture), language, and style, embodied resistance and cultural adaptation, just as a low-rider did in choosing to recustomize his American-manufactured automobile and drive it low to the ground.[6] In addition, both styles are visual and performative in calling on the white dominant society to see them. Unfortunately both styles were often seen in a negative light by the dominant society and even criminalized. In the 1940s, pachucos/zoot-suiters were seen by the dominant culture as juvenile delinquents, even people to be feared, as they were, for example, in the case of the Sleepy Lagoon murder in the summer of 1942, as well as in the Zoot Suit Riots of 1943.[7] Stuart Cosgrove explains the importance of the zoot suit within the American culture of the early 1940s: "The zoot suit was more than the drape-shape of the 1940s fashion, more than a colorful stage prop hanging from the shoulders of Cab Calloway, it was in the most direct and obvious ways, an emblem of ethnicity and a way of negotiating an identity. The zoot suit was a refusal: a sub-cultural gesture that refused to concede to the manners of subservience."[8]

The pachucos existed between both American and Mexican identities, creating their own space defined by the working-class roots of the barrio. To see and be seen, as a visible marker of difference, yet also of sameness by creating a community—of pachucos/zoot-suiters and eventually lowriders. Both subcultures within Mexican American communities were an expression of youth attempting to make a new identity for themselves, as well as incorporating the themes of pride, respect, brotherhood, and family. Over time, the pachuco and the lowrider became iconic symbols of a Chicano culture that is rooted in the process of adaptation through the forces of Americanization (Sánchez 1993). But the pachuco/zoot-suiter is also the beginning of a Chicano identity rooted in rebellion and resistance found in the philosophy of low and slow.

Therefore, the politics of low and slow has a long cultural legacy in Mexican American barrios in Los Angeles as a philosophy of cultural resistance and a way of life that requires *corazón*/pride, respect, *carnalismo*/brotherhood, and family or community. It is a cultural process that is both fluid and active, since at its core it is about being seen and visualizing a particular identity that is individual and collective as well as interethnic. The use of cars and boulevards is a tactic to create "community-enabling space." Lowriders become narratives or visual texts of working-class life—secondhand cars customized to be extravagant and luxurious—and of their owners' expressions of their individuality and communities. These cars establish links between consumer car culture, labor (skills), and gendered class and "race" positions. Low and slow is more than car aesthetics; it is also a cultural expression that is grounded in the urban sociohistorical experiences of Chicanos and African Americans in Los Angeles. Their cars, moving low and slow across the land of a thousand freeways, have helped to break down some of the barriers that separate the inhabitants of Los Angeles.

THE HISTORY/*LA HISTORIA*

Lowriding in Los Angeles is a direct result of the post–World War II car culture boom when automobile manufacturing resumed and the demand for new cars increased. The rise of automobile culture in the United States has been discussed at length by Tom Wolfe (1965), James Flink (1975), and Cynthia Dettleback (1979), to name but a few. After World War II, the automobile industry quickly resumed producing new cars, which resulted in a surplus of used cars that could be bought by veterans, youth, working-class people, and ethnic minorities. Los Angeles was the perfect location for the explosion of car culture, since "in the 1950's Los Angeles' automobile industry was booming, with five factories in the county, it was the country's second-largest producer of cars and tires in the United States, after Detroit."[9] This situation, along with the affordability of used cars, was capitalized on by many working-class youth in Los Angeles. As Ernie Ruelas recalled, "You would buy a car in the 50s for fifteen dollars, it was easy to put dual pipes on it, you know, lower it and if you messed that one up you go get another one."[10] For African Americans, California in particular afforded economic opportunities, as well as freedom from Jim Crow segregation in the South, though they did face discrimination out West in the form of housing covenants and other racial restrictions in public accommodations. According to Flamming, "Restrictive covenants would be undone not by legislation but by the NAACP's dogged legal efforts, which finally resulted in favorable rulings in the U.S. Supreme Court during the late 1940s and early 1950s."[11] As housing opportunities for African Americans changed after the 1930s, automobile ownership flourished for this community. For instance, a survey of 12,142 African American households in Los Angeles in the 1930s found that 42 percent owned automobiles.[12] Also important to mention is the flourishing motorcycle culture within African American communities in California; in fact the formation of motorcycle clubs in the late 1940s and 1950s (Jimenez y West 2008) preceded the establishment of the lowrider car clubs in the late 1960s and 1970s (Penland 2003).

Another important aspect of the evolution of lowriding is its connection to American car culture in general. The surge in lowriding must also be framed within the proliferation of car leisure activities after World War II, such as hot-rodding, drag races, car shows, and demolition derbies. Cars were a extension of one's identity, becoming status symbols for working-class youth. Many car customizers used their vehicles to express resistance to the culture of conformity that existed in the 1950s. Historians trace the origins of lowriding to the birth of hot rod culture in the 1930s and 1940s in Southern California, an activity that was popular among many Anglo youth. This new "rebel culture," which transformed American popular culture after World War II, was captured in some notable Hollywood movies in the 1950s, such as *The Wild One* (1954), *Blackboard Jungle* (1955), and *Rebel without a Cause* (1955). Nora Donnelly elaborates further: "Hot rod culture evolved as an antidote to the cultural conformity of the 1950s. . . . For the first time in American history, American teenagers were free to invent their own identities. How loud and fast your car roared became the external emblem of self for the postwar generation of teens. . . . Working on your car became an acceptable craft and an artistic outlet."[13]

The various structural conditions inherent in the post–World War II economy created an environment that fostered a love affair between American males and their cars. Both hot-rodding and lowriding began as inherently masculine activities and remain so to this day. As an expressive form, lowriding was an affront to the (mostly Anglo-American) hot-rodders, who raised their cars off the ground and drove them fast. Lowriders practiced the opposite tactic: their cars were lowered to the ground and meant to go slow. Each car culture created a distinct aesthetics beckoning the viewer to look at the cars and pay respect to the cars' owners. For Chicano and African American lowriders this was particularly significant in a time period when they were often degraded in Los Angeles because of their race/ethnicity, class, and gender status. The cars represented a source of pride and quickly gained popularity in Chicano and Black communities. As Ted Wells recalls, "If you go down a street when I was growing up, your lowrider was the only car you had. You drove to school, to the store, on dates. . . . Back then during the week, during the day, there were hundreds of lowriders on the streets."[14]

Lowriding had specific connections to life in the barrio for Mexican Americans, as Mexican American youth were also racially segregated within Los Angeles. Many Mexican American men had achieved recognition during World War II through their participation in the armed forces, yet their position within American society remained unchanged: Mexican Americans continued to be treated as second-class citizens. According to Acuna, "The de facto exclusion of Mexicans from public facilities, schools, trade unions, juries, and voting was common in many sections of the country."[15] In California, beginning in the early part of the twentieth century, Mexican American children were placed in schools and classrooms separate from their Anglo American peers. In 1946, this practice would be declared unconstitutional by the federal district Judge Paul J. McCormick in the *Mendez v. Westminster School District* case, a precursor to *Brown v. Board of Education* (1954). This reality was also shared by African American veterans, who also continued to face de facto and de jure segregation in public facilities and schools and also began to fight for their civil rights. In the everyday life of these working-class youth and men, automobiles then offered an avenue to transgress the limits of territory or their barrios or neighborhoods through the mobility of their cars. Michael Stone's analysis of the impact of car culture on Mexican Americans can also be applied to African Americans, since this cultural expression influenced perceptions of community and cultural identity: "Lowriding must be seen in light of changing self-perception of class and ethnic identity on part of Mexican American youth, as played against the broader context of American youth culture, the 'car culture,' the mass media, public education, military service, and the world of work."[16]

Furthermore many World War II veterans, especially among Mexican Americans and African Americans, gained mechanical skills through their work in shipyards, military motor pools, and airplane hangars. Many of these men were also part of the "52–20 club," in which the U.S. government paid them benefits of twenty dollars a month for one year after discharge for their military service. This extra income and the mechanical skills they acquired through their wartime service then made it possible for veterans to purchase and maintain a new or used car.[17] Manuel Cruz recalled how Chicanos put their skills for car modifications to good use, and in the process they created a distinct car aesthetics:

> The cars were fixed this way—a '36 Chevy club coupe would get its front fender skirts off, no spot lights or skirts on it, usually a '34 Ford would get its front fenders and back fenders taken off. The best ones were the two door convertibles. Chicanos started fixing their cars. They would put dual pipes, rubber flaps with reflectors on them that went on the back of the rear flaps or license plates, skirts for their cars, one or two spot lights, white walls. If you wanted a lowrider, the only thing you could do then was put sand bags or cement sacks in the trunk to make them heavy . . . that was before metal shocks. Those were the first lowriders in LA in the 40s.[18]

Automobiles allowed both economic and physical mobility. A car represented a middle-class American dream that was now available to working-class people; it also created a means for Chicano and Black lowriders to physically transgress the boundaries of racially segregated neighborhoods in Los Angeles.[19] Their participation in car leisure activities also formed a collectivity with other lowriders and maintained the link found in many popular cultural forms in which the individual uses popular culture to create a community with others. The cultural space that lowriders created in the 1950s initiated a community-enabling space within the barrios of Los Angeles, much as the pachucos and zoot-suiters of the 1940s did. Ruben Ortiz-Torres writes: "With the advent of lowrider culture, the individualistic American dream of driving away to escape it all has been replaced with the notion of driving together. Lowriders organize in car clubs and go cruising on the weekends on specific boulevards, updating the old Mexican practice of walking around a town plaza on Sundays in order to socialize and flirt with girls. They drive slowly, pumping their music and blocking traffic, messing with a social system that is not eager to accept them."[20]

Hydraulics marked the beginning of a new era of lowriding in Los Angeles. In 1958, Ron Aguirre, a Chicano from Los Angeles, installed the first hydraulic system in a 1957 Chevrolet Corvette. The setup allowed his car to be lowered or raised with a flip of a switch, an important innovation in the lowriding scene. The hydraulic parts, which consisted of hydro air pumps and dumps, were surplus parts from World War II fighter planes that assisted in lowering and raising the wing flaps. During the 1960s and 1970s, a large number of lowriders would purchase government surplus parts at Palley's Surplus in Vernon (a setup cost forty dollars in the 1960s) and have them installed at places such as the Ruelas's shop in South Los Angeles, Dick and Ron's in Hawthorne, Bill Hines's shop in Compton, and Al Sullivan's in Hyde Park. These surplus parts were a valuable asset to the lowriders, since they could ride as low as they wanted to on the boulevard, then return their cars to a legal ground clearance with the flip of a switch if they saw the police. Because the California vehicle code stipulated that no part of a car could be lower than the bottom portion of the wheel rim, the police often wrote tickets to owners of lowrider cars. Many lowriders felt they were targeted more than hot-rodders on L.A. streets. The official lowrider label began to be used in the 1960s, and according to *Lowrider* magazine, the term was first coined by the police after the 1965 Watts Riots. Jack Kennedy relates in *Lowrider: History, Pride, Culture,* "They [the police] were using the term 'lowrider' as a derogatory term for the young black kids that were causing all the trouble. . . . They said that they were kids who drove cars with no springs and no seats so they could ride low."[21] The term *lowrider,* which began as an insult, took on new meaning as youth and young adults redefined it as a source of cultural pride.

THE DUKES

Los Angeles is the birthplace of the oldest lowrider car club still in existence, the Dukes, which was founded by the Ruelas brothers. The Ruelas brothers are an example of the strength of the lowriding tradition based on *la familia* (brotherhood), respect, and pride. Within the Ruelas family, lowriding is a tradition that is passed on from one generation to the next, from father to son to grandson. The important legacy of the Dukes to lowrider history was celebrated in 2007 as its members welcomed their forty-fifth anniversary as a car club. The Ruelas brothers proudly call themselves pachucos and Chicanos. They are known for customizing '39 Chevys, a choice that made them stand out from the rest of the lowriders in the 1960s and 1970s, when most lowriders customized cars from the 1950s and 1960s.

The story of the Ruelas brothers reveals the cultural links between Chicanos and Blacks in Los Angeles through the practice of lowriding. During the 1950s and 1960s, the Ruelas brothers grew up in a South Los Angeles neighborhood that included pockets of Mexican American neighborhoods, like 41st Street and Alameda, but the schools they attended were in primarily African American neighborhoods. According to Flamming, by 1960 the area along Central Avenue was 95 percent black, and there was a "seven mile stretch of African American neighborhoods locked between Main Street and Alameda."[22] The high school that the Ruelas brothers attended, Jefferson, was within this Central Avenue district, and even though they were in the minority, they were respected by African Americans there. Ernie Ruelas once explained, "We were known as the 'black Mexicans.' Our black brothers respected us for having courage."[23] Two African American friends of the Ruelas brothers, Terry Anderson and Ted Wells, remember meeting the Dukes in the early 1970s, an event about which Anderson remarked, "These guys had me at their home for *quinceañeras* (celebrations of teenage girls coming of age), funerals of car club members who died, and holidays. They took me into their family."[24] The politics of low and slow in South Central Los Angeles became a way to bridge the two divergent cultures of Mexican Americans and African Americans, and in the process life-long friendships would be formed. The story of the Dukes is not unlike other histories of lowriders in Los Angeles who live in multicultural communities, yet the story of the Ruelas brothers, the OGs (which abbreviates "original gangsters" but is used to mean veterans/*veteranos*) of the lowrider scene in Los Angeles, is a fascinating chapter that visualizes the interconnectedness of Blacks and Chicanos.

The Dukes' story begins south of downtown Los Angeles on 41st and Long Beach Avenue, in a time period in L.A. history when being Mexican was a reason to be seen as "inferior" to Anglo Americans.[25] In the mid-1950s Josefina Ruelas, a single mother, immigrated from Tijuana to Los Angeles with her four boys (Julio, Oscar, Fernando, and Ernie) and settled in with Uncle Tinker and Tia Chana. These relatives had settled in South Central Los Angeles in the mid-1930s and had an automotive shop. Uncle Tinker, who became a father figure to his nephews, introduced the boys to auto mechanics in an attempt to keep them off the streets, and in the process, he taught them about taking pride in their work. The most important lesson that he imparted to them was the positive influence of la familia working together. These would be lessons the Ruelas brothers passed on to their own sons. The love affair with cars began at a young age for Julio Ruelas, who is the oldest brother: "I got interested in lowriding through my family. Already our uncles were lowriding, and I was growing up seeing them. And around the neighborhood everybody had a low car with dual pipes. So that is when I took it from there, and I followed it ever since."[26]

When each of the brothers reached age thirteen, each had a car that he began to customize, and each became a "specialist" in certain areas of car customizing. For example, one brother specialized in bodywork, one in upholstery, and another in electrical wiring. Since each one possessed different talents, they built cars as a team. Even though they were not able to drive these cars legally, the brothers still took pleasure in their customizing work. Fernando recalls:

> Well, my first car was a 1949 Chevrolet four door; it was a deluxe. I bought it in 1963. And I bought from an individual that lived in Watts as a matter of fact. I paid fifty dollars for it, actually my brother went and bought it for me, because I was only thirteen years old. I was too young, so my brother bought it for me. And fifty dollars was a lot of money back then; it was like per se thirty thousand to buy a car right now, or forty. So it was a lot of money. It was my first car, and the first thing I done on that car is I dropped it. And you know the methods back then to dropping a car if you didn't have any money, there was two, three methods to do that, so we would either heat the coils up in the front, put a lot of weight in the back. Cement rocks anything that's weighing and lowers it down. But the very early years of the lowriding, they would drop the front a little bit and leave it like in a slant like this, and they called it "Diego"—you know like baby Diego.[27]

The early style of low and slow (before hydraulics) captured the imagination of Fernando and his brothers. The process of building a car became a family effort as the brothers worked together. Family was a central tenet of life in the barrio, and one's neighborhood also became part of one's extended family. Carnalismo, or brotherhood, among men in the neighborhood produced barrio social clubs or gangs.[28] For the Ruelas brothers, having an uncle who was a mechanic afforded them the opportunity to learn about customizing firsthand at a very early age, as well keep them off the streets of South Los Angeles. One of the Ruelas brothers explained:

> He didn't want us in the street, hanging out with the guys. Very early age he would take us out to the junk yards to pick up bicycles, this was in the 50s, 1954, and we'll get the Schwinn cause that was a better looking bike . . . we done all kinds of crazy things to lowered Cadillac lights sticking out of the back with original blinkers, you know how they had back at that time. With raising the big handle bars, like they'd be sticking up like that, maybe we will be real creative. We'll even get that and make motor bikes out of them, we'll put lawn mower motors on them.[29]

Fernando learned the laborious process of "bodywork" at a young age, a process he labeled "the old-fashioned way." Early on, his uncle took the boys to scrap yards and taught them customizing skills. Fernando was just twelve years old when he started shooting his first metal flake (a method of painting a car). His brother Ernie meanwhile learned electrical wiring from Uncle Tinker by working on an old radio. Their mother also supported their activity, since it kept them off the streets and gave them something productive to do. As young boys, the Ruelas brothers were a part of the phase of lowriding in which car owners took pride in working on the cars themselves, as opposed to those in the present era, who take their cars to various shops around Los Angeles if they can afford to. The Dukes created a historic and classic lowriding standard that others have followed, and this standard also reflects the different generations of lowriders as well as the different customizing styles of each generation. Ernie Ruelas remarks,

> The early styles were historic, and you can't even find paint anymore to paint the cars that way. I believe that the ways that people install their hydraulics are also different. The old way, especially for old cars, there was only a small amount of people who knew how to do it that way. It was a professional installation, and now people do not cater to that installation so much; they just throw it in there and that's it. Before, people were very much into research—how it works right, how it rides right, and also how it changes. I think that hydraulics in our day were more for style symbol to keep your car low and to ride smooth and all that.[30]

These features also made the car stand out, especially to law enforcement. The police wrote tickets to those who violated the law that no part of a car could be lower than the bottom portion of the wheel rim, which made lowriders one of their favorite targets. Fernando Ruelas worked for thirty-five years on installing hydraulic setups, and he recalled the treatment lowriders received from police in the 1950s and 1960s.

> Back in the earlier days, per se the police department they didn't like low riders, and they just were out there just to knick pick, you see, . . . what they could find. In opposed to the Anglo they wouldn't bother them, but they would bother the Latino low rider a lot, because basically they probably figured "What is this guy doing in this nice looking car?" so there was a big feedback on the earlier years. In opposed to the late, like we are now, things have mellowed down. . . . it's still there, but it's not as exposed as it was back then.[31]

The Ruelas brothers readily admit that as boys in the late 1950s they joined the 38th Street gang out of a need for protection. The 38th Street club achieved mainstream recognition during the Sleepy Lagoon murder case of 1942, when twenty-two of their members were found guilty of crimes ranging from assault to first-degree murder through an unfair and racist trial. More important, living in South Central in the 1950s and 1960s required the Ruelas brothers to adapt to three cultures. As young members of the 38th Street, they proudly called themselves "pachucos" and had to interact with their pachuco brothers through music, language, and dress. They also had to interact with Mexican culture in their home, where their mother spoke to them in Spanish, and they were exposed to Mexican music. Then at school and in their mostly Black neighborhood, they had to interact with Black culture in order to be accepted. Brother Fernando explains this influence of three cultures on Chicanos living in South Los Angeles in this time period: "We had three cultures. We had our Mexican culture at home. Our mother spoke to us all in Spanish. Then we had our pachuco culture— we were pachucos. And we had our Black brothers out there. We had a variety and that was good."[32]

Jefferson High School historically produced many musical artists that the brothers were influenced by and some they knew personally. Artists like Etta James, Richard Berry, Arthur Lee May, and even Barry White all went to "Jeff." African American music was a cultural bridge to American culture for many Chicanos living in Los Angeles, who lived in the same neighborhoods as Blacks or in neighborhoods adjacent to Black communities, which often in turn encouraged intercultural exchanges (Lipsitz 1990; Macías 2008). Ernie Ruelas also explains the importance of that intercultural connection in shaping his identity and the car culture's lure for him: "My family went to school in South Central. We were the minority there. Nine Mexican boys and girls at Jefferson High School. Looking back at that, it made me what I am. We understood each other. We liked cars and that brought us together."[33]

The love of cars is what brought some Chicanos and Blacks together in the streets of Los Angeles in the late 1960s and early 1970s. The Ruelas brothers' reputation as good customizers earned them respect, and they were even invited into the homes of their Black neighbors and invited to cruise with the Black lowriders. As Terry Andersen explains, growing up on the West Side, he did not even know Latin lowriders, but "everyone heard about the Dukes because they came into the 'hood. They were accepted. They showed no prejudice."[34] Ernie Ruelas recalls that they would work on cars owned by African Americans, adding, "We treated them with respect." Yet there were spaces in Los Angeles where neither group was accepted or respected. For instance, Lynwood was called "Lynchwood" by Chicanos and African Americans, because if they drove into that neighborhood, they were quickly escorted out by the police. They learned early on that Lynwood was only for white people. As Ernie recalls, "Even when white people moved out, the police department maintained a 'keep it white attitude,' and a person could get hit with a flashlight by a cop."[35] Even in Huntington Park, a person could not be out on the streets after 10 P.M. These are areas that bordered the lowriders' own neighborhoods, but they learned early on the stigma of both being Black and Mexican in the streets of Los Angeles and driving the particular cars they owned. As Ernie says, "The police left the White hot-rodders alone; they did not get harassed."[36]

In 1962, the Ruelas brothers realized their passion for cars was enough to start their own car club, which also caused some tensions in their neighborhood. The Dukes car club became an alternative to gang life—or la vida loca. The car club initially was perceived as a threat to the control of the neighborhood by the 38th Street gang, and it caused some initial hard feelings between that gang and the Dukes. Yet, this tension would soon vanish as the Dukes soon brought honor and respect to their neighborhood. Fernando remembers those tensions:

> Well actually the first thing you had to do is you had to get out of the gang you were in. Because when you were in a gang and you were trying to start a club, your peers, your gang members, they didn't want a club, 'cause you got to understand when I grew up we were pachucos, and that's the hard thing there. You're going to do a club, you going to get individuals. It doesn't take one, two, three guys to start a club to begin with, and back then you had club members that per se it was a social club so it was cars. . . . So we had to hassle there with our neighborhood guys to start this. So it was a big impact here; you know, you hassle with a society out there then if you are going to do a neighborhood club, and it was pretty hard, especially the neighborhood where I grew up—38th Street over there—its family history known with the Sleepy Lagoon murder and all this. So there's history there, so it was very hard to break away the pachuco image and to turn it into a car club thing.[37]

For the brothers, car clubs as social clubs provided an alternative option to gangs by creating a social environment that was considered respectable. So eventually the 38th Street gang agreed to let the brothers start a car club, since it would bring pride and respect to the neighborhood. In the 1970s Black car clubs like the Professionals, the Compton chapter of the Majestics, and the Individuals were established. As Ted Wells recalls, "When I turned sixteen and got a driver's license, you got a car, you were either a hot-rodder or a lowrider, and I chose a lowrider."[38] Black lowriders Ted Wells and Terry Anderson cite the Ruelas brothers as early innovators, and they often visited the brothers' shop in South Los Angeles. Yet, when the streets were turned into community-enabling space for Chicanos and Blacks, cruising locales were structured along lines of race/ethnicity. Chicanos cruised Whittier Boulevard in East Los Angeles, and Blacks cruised Crenshaw Boulevard. One reason these cruising spots were "racialized" in the development and transformation of Los Angeles neighborhoods is that historically East Los Angeles was a Mexican American neighborhood, and the neighborhood around Crenshaw Boulevard was primarily African American. So, if a Mexican American cruised Crenshaw in the early days of the late 1960s and early 1970s, they had to be invited by an African American car club. And if an African American cruised Whittier Boulevard in this same time period, they also had to be invited. Many of these protocols would disappear though by the late 1970s, as lowriding and cruising grew in popularity, and lowrider car shows became more well organized. For example, the first large-scale lowrider car show at the Los Angeles Convention Center occurred in 1979, and it was sponsored by *Lowrider* magazine.

Cruising has been an important aspect of lowrider culture and a popular pastime for American youth since the 1950s. The boulevards of Los Angeles became the perfect site to showcase their custom creations, and many lowriders have seen themselves as the "Picassos of the Boulevards." Until the end of the 1970s, one of the most popular cruising venues in the United States was Whittier Boulevard in East Los Angeles. At the height of its popularity in the 1960s and 1970s, Whittier Boulevard was the ideal place for working-class Chicanos to show off their cars, pick up dates, and have fun. According to many *veteranos* of that time, Whittier Boulevard had everything a young man desired: cars, music, and girls. Many labeled it "Chicano Disneyland," a playground for barrio youth. Whittier Boulevard was alive every weekend as the top cruising spot in Los Angeles, and the Dukes were an important part of that scene. Each lowrider club had its own spot on the boulevard, and the Dukes had the prime spot in the Huggie Boy car lot. As Fernando recalls, "Nobody parked in our lot; they knew it was ours. We filled it with '39s."[39] African Americans cruised Crenshaw, and by 1965, it was a happening spot. As Ted Wells recalls, "A friend of mine took me down to one of the all-time lowrider hangouts called Stop's Hamburgers, on the corner of Imperial and Central. Stop's was a place where on Sunday nights, in every direction, there were lowriders packing both sides of the streets."[40] And when Whittier Boulevard was shut down by law enforcement in the 1979, the traffic in South Central became more multicultural.

In 1974 Fernando Ruelas became president of the club (a position he held until his passing in 2010), and he was also responsible for the changes to come on the lowriding scene in the late 1970s. The Dukes, along with the Imperials and the Groupe car clubs, played a key role in the formation of the West Coast Association of Lowriders in 1978. The purpose of the association was to get car clubs to unite and do something positive within the Chicano community. Together these clubs put on the "Christmas Toys for Kids" car show, and all the proceeds went to purchasing toys and Christmas stockings for underprivileged children. The Dukes, however, were influenced by the growing political activism in East Los Angeles during the Chicano movement of the late 1960s and 1970s, and the way they connected the clubs to political movements like this one separates them from the other car clubs. They organized car shows to benefit the broader Chicano community, from César Chávez and the United Farmworkers, to Mecha and other Chicano organizations, to even local prisons. They owned the "Dukes Bus," which they filled with club members and took to prisons to put on lowrider shows for the inmates. All of these activities reveal the importance of la familia and the community to lowriders, who do more than just cruise the streets. The Dukes believe in "giving back to the community," a motto that sustains *Chicanismo* in the barrios of Los Angeles, especially for the younger generations. As Fernando explains:

> I've done a lot of auditorium appearances back in those days, and talked to the kids. Where you had the first, second, third graders, I've got still their crayon drawings with "I love you Dukes thank you for the toys and stocking," and little cars all crooked with their kids you know. I got tons of that stuff put away, tons of it. And I would donate my time to do this with the kids, as well as you know I used to do car shows, I used to call it car night, but it was on Saturdays in the day where I would take kids from Jefferson High School, cause that's the school where I used to go, and I used to bring them there and teach them the mechanics, body work and the whole thing on lifts, hydraulics on a car. And I just got burned out, you know every Saturday. I just got burned out, we used to take a new group of people, and what I would do every month I would get a new group, and I'll do that. Hopefully some of those kids right now have cars like this.[41]

The brothers are acutely aware that lowriding is tied to the multicultural history of Los Angeles and is an avenue to build community with other lowriders. But more important, lowriding for them is something that people should take pride in. They want the customizing work that they do to have inspirational and motivational effects on the Chicano community and the broader L.A. community, especially the youth. The Ruelas brothers have applied lessons from the Chicano movement to their work as a car club. Fernando mentioned that the sole purpose in starting the club was not to get a thousand members but instead to capture the youth and give them an alternative to gangs. The brothers also share their own stories of growing up in order to motivate youth to enter into activities in their communities. When asked what lowriding teaches youth, Ernie Ruelas responds: "I think that it is real positive, because it is bringing awareness, and it is bringing Mexican people or Chicano people to work together and to let them know that it is not about doing combat with one another, but loving one another in building something that is in our blood."[42]

According to the Dukes, their lowrider club is an extension of their family, and they believe that perspective is one of the main reasons for their longevity. In this manner, the car club is more than just cars; the Dukes believe they can use their love of cars to communicate stories to the younger generation, stories that will inspire them and teach them the lessons of pride, respect, carnalismo/brotherhood, and family. The politics of low and slow on the boulevards of Los Angeles not only links the past with the present but also speaks to lowriders' shared sense of community, Black and Chicano. This is illustrated best by the story of the Dukes, who have been innovators, artists, and "godfathers" on the scene for over forty years. Their lowrider stories of the 1960s and 1970s also demonstrate what authors writing on popular music in Los Angeles have revealed: interconnections of Black and Brown communities are at the heart of L.A. cultural history.

CONCLUSION: BLACK AND CHICANO LOWRIDERS AFTER THE 1970S

The importance of family and fraternal relationships (carnalismo) among lowriders in the 1960s and 1970s is reflected in the formation of car clubs. Generally referred to by members as "second families," most clubs were originally established by small close-knit groups of custom-car enthusiasts comprising either blood relatives or individuals from the same neighborhoods. In addition to establishing a sense of solidarity among lowriders, these associations have also supported friendly competition among members who try to outdo one another in creating the "perfect" car. Furthermore, club membership provides an alternative to gang life (la vida loca) by replacing potentially dangerous or violent activities with positive and "respectable" social behaviors. In this sense, lowriding is keeping alive the carnalismo, just like the pachucos/zoot-suiters before them, as a source of community-enabling space.

There is a diversity of car club politics within the lowriding scene, but all the clubs share similar traits of family bonds, respect, and pride for their cars. In fact, their emphasis on these themes has resulted in the longevity of the car clubs. Despite the shared themes, Chicanos have added a distinct style to lowriding that is all their own. Ernie Ruelas explains:

> I think that what we have added to lowriding has been our style. You see a Chicano car fixed up and all that, you know it is a Chicano car. You see a Black person's car and all that, and you know that it is a Black person's car. Their styles are different. I think what we have started here is using older cars with sun visors, with the hydraulics on older cars, and that kind of stuff. We started that. I think also we have brought some awareness all through this country that leads from the West Coast all the way to the East Coast.[43]

The story of the Dukes is in no way the ultimate story of Black and Brown interconnectedness within the lowriding scene, but it captures a particular moment in the 1960s and 1970s in which these communities shared a history of struggle and discrimination on the streets of Los Angeles and created a brotherhood through their mutual love of lowrider cars. The politics of low and slow provided a common ground of mutual recognition for some Chicano and Black lowriders. More important, as other scholarly work has shown, the Chicanos' struggle for a community-enabling space in Los Angeles has often meant creating new cultural identities that have borrowed and added to African American popular cultural modes of expression, like music, fashion, and dance. Although the importance of Chicanos' role as innovators and generators of lowrider culture in Los Angeles has been documented and visualized in many scholarly works and mainstream museum exhibitions, their elevation as such sometimes becomes a source of tension, because Black lowriders may feel that their stories and contributions are too minimized within lowrider history. Scholarly work is still needed to document and visualize the stories of Black lowriders in Los Angeles beyond the journalistic stories in *Lowrider* magazine and the content of hip-hop videos.

Finally, the demographic changes in the areas of South Los Angeles in the late 1980s and early 1990s, wherein African American communities became "Latino-cized" through immigration from Mexico and Central America, produced racial tensions between Black and Brown in the area's communities. Whereas earlier generations of immigrants like the Ruelas brothers were accepted by their African American peers in periods of intense "Americanization" of the 1950s and 1960s, these new generations of immigrants have often been labeled "illegal aliens" and "un-American" by some in the African American community who have viewed these people as taking their jobs.[44] Though exploring the issues born of demographic changes in South Los Angeles is out of the realm of this essay, these changes do point to the complicated patterns of community and identity in Los Angeles. For instance, in the various Latino communities here, recent immigrants and those who have been here for generations all have different connections to "American" culture, Latino immigrant culture, and Black culture. How this affects the politics of low and slow and the lowrider community remains to be documented and explored as the worlds of *Boulevard Nights* and *Boyz n the Hood* become less celebratory and more aligned with the current complicated cultural/racial politics of the City of Angels—Los Angeles.

NOTES

1. *Lowrider* is used to describe a car that is customized primarily to be low to the ground, usually containing a hydraulic set-up, with a fantastic candy paint job, chrome features, and customized upholstery. Included among the categories of lowrider cars are "bombs" (American-made cars from the late 1930s to the early 1950s) and "Euros" (import cars such as Hondas and Acuras). Many lowriding purists believe that classic Chevrolets are the only cars that, once properly customized, can carry the lowrider label, yet today virtually any kind of vehicle can be transformed into a lowrider. There are now lowrider minitrucks, SUVs, motorcycles, bicycles, and even scaled-down model cars. Most important, the lowrider label is also used to describe people who participate in this car-culture phenomenon. Lowriding is a way of life for many of its participants, and its practice varies across the United States and abroad.

2. Raul Villa explains that the term was coined in "the late 1960s by the associated members of *Con Safos* magazine, an artist collective in East Los Angeles," and he paraphrases Tomas Ybarro-Frausto's definition of the term: "Barriology was a playful but serious promotion of the cultural knowledge and practices particular to the barrio." Raul Homero Villa, *Barrio Logos: Space and Place in Urban Chicano Literature and Culture* (Austin: University of Texas Press, 2000), 6–7.

3. Ibid., 6.

4. Ibid.

5. Luis Alvarez, *The Power of the Zoot: Youth Culture and Resistance during World War II* (Berkeley: University of California Press, 2008), 43.

6. Dressing in extravagantly garbed in high-waisted trousers, oversized coats, wide-brimmed hats, and long gold watch chains, the pachucos fashioned a new identity for themselves, one that made them stand out from people who were just trying to "fit in." In addition, they wore their hair a bit longer than was the style of the time, which was military crew cuts. Their defiance of the status quo was interpreted as an important act of cultural resistance and later became a source of inspiration for Chicanos during the Chicano movement, as well as for the other lowriders in the 1950s and 1960s.

7. The Zoot Suit Riots were fights between servicemen and zoot-suiters, in which the zoot-suiters were arrested and the servicemen were applauded by the media and even law enforcement. For a more detailed analysis of both the Zoot Suit Riots and the case of the Sleepy Lagoon murder, see, respectively, Mauricio Mazon, *The Zoot Suit Riots: The Psychology of Symbolic Annihilation* (Austin: University of Texas Press, 1984); and George Sanchez, *Becoming Mexican American: Ethnicity, Culture, and Identity in Chicano Los Angeles, 1900–1945* (New York: Oxford University Press, 1993).

8. Stuart Cosgrove, "The Zoot Suit and Style Warfare," *History Workshop Journal* 18 (Autumn 1984): 77.

9. Paige Penland, *Lowrider: History, Pride, Culture* (St. Paul, MN: Motorbooks International, 2003), 13.

10. Ernie Ruelas in *Low and Slow* (South Padre Island, TX: Ritual Films, 1997), 16mm documentary, 27 minutes.

11. Douglas Flamming, *Bound for Freedom: Black Los Angeles in Jim Crow Era* (Berkeley: University of California Press, 2005), 350.

12. Ibid., 306.

13. Nora Donnelly, "Freedom, Style, Sex, Power and Motion—the Cult of Cars," in *Customized: Art Inspired by Hot Rods, Lowriders and American Car Culture,* edited by Nora Donnelly, 49–67 (Boston: Institute of Contemporary Art, 2000), 49.

14. Ted Wells, interview by author, digital recording, Altadena, CA, July 10, 2007.

15. Rodolfo Acuña, *Occupied America: A History of Chicanos,* 4th ed. (New York: Addison Wesley Longman, 2000), 279.

16. Michael Stone, "Bajito y Suavecito: Lowriding and the 'Class' of Class," *Journal of Latin American Popular Culture* 9 (1990): 87–88.

17. Ibid.

18. *Lowrider* 2, no. 2 (1977): 33.

19. Winslow Felix first opened his Chevrolet dealership in 1922 and is considered the first Mexican American car dealership owner in Southern California, according to numerous sources, including the Felix Chevrolet dealership owner Darryl Holter. Winslow Felix was a friend of filmmaker Pat Sullivan, whose animation studio created the Felix the Cat character, and Winslow was given special permission to use this image for his dealership. In an early time of consumer discrimination for many minorities in Los Angeles, this dealership provided opportunities for many first-time car owners. Winslow also created

a "trial purchase plan," founded the Greater Los Angeles Motorcar Dealers, organized the annual Southern California auto shows, and staged midget-car races. The Felix the Cat image represents Los Angeles's love affair for Chevy cars. Even today, a sign of cultural authenticity is having a Felix the Cat sticker displayed in the window of a restored vintage GM vehicle. The beautiful neon sign of Felix the Car was erected in 1957 at the Felix Chevrolet dealership in Los Angeles on the corner of Jefferson and Figueroa.

20. Ruben Ortiz Torres, "Cathedral on Wheels," in *Customized*, 37.

21. Quoted in Penland, *Lowrider*, 26.

22. Flamming, *Bound for Freedom*, 378.

23. Ernie Ruelas, interview by author, digital recording, Los Angeles, CA, July 14, 2007.

24. Terry Andersen, interview by author, digital recording, Los Angeles, CA, July 14, 2007.

25. For more detailed examination of this time period for Chicanos in Los Angeles, see Acuña, *Occupied America*; and Ricardo Romo, *East Los Angeles: History of a Barrio* (Austin: University of Texas Press, 1983).

26. Julio Ruelas, interview by author, tape recording, Los Angeles, CA, June 12, 1999.

27. Interview, Lowrider Oral History Project: Youth Voices, Los Angeles, March 15, 2008, Collection of Petersen Automotive Museum, Los Angeles (hereafter LOHP).

28. In the 1920s, most areas settled by Mexican Americans in Los Angeles began to organize their neighborhoods (barrios), such as happened in Maravilla, El Hoyo, Alpine, and Dogtown. Chicano youth would create social clubs connected to their barrios. In time these clubs were seen as gangs by the dominant culture, especially during World War II, when juvenile delinquency became a social problem for Los Angeles. By the 1950s, many of these social clubs had taken on the titles of gangs. For a more detailed look at the development of Chicano gangs in Los Angeles, see Joan Moore, *Homeboys: Gangs, Drugs and Prison in the Barrios of Los Angeles* (Philadelphia: Temple University Press, 1978); and James Diego Vigil, *Barrio Gangs: Street Life and Identity in Southern California* (Austin: University of Texas Press, 1988).

29. Interview, LOHP.

30. Ernie Ruelas, interview by author, tape recording, Los Angeles, June 12, 1999.

31. Interview, LOHP.

32. Ibid.

33. Interview, LOHP.

34. Terry Andersen, interview by author, digital recording, Los Angeles, July 14, 2007.

35. Ernie Ruelas, interview by author, digital recording, Los Angeles, July 14, 2007.

36. Ibid.

37. Interview, LOHP.

38. Ted Wells, interview by author, digital recording, Altadena, CA, July 10, 2007.

39. Fernando Ruelas, interview by author, tape recording, La Habra, CA, June 10, 1999.

40. Penland, *Lowrider,* 25.

41. Interview, LOHP.

42. Ernie Ruelas, interview by author, tape recording, Los Angeles, June 12, 1999.

43. Ibid.

44. A perfect example of this is friend and admirer of the Dukes, Terry Anderson, who spoke highly of their friendship and of other Chicano lowriders to me but also was involved in activism against Mexican immigration in Los Angeles and nationally until his death in July 2010. He hosted a weekly AM radio show on KRLA and spoke as a man who saw his once African American community of South Los Angeles being "taken over by illegals" who took away jobs from his sons. I discovered this information after he had died and was therefore unable to do a follow-up interview with him for this essay.

REFERENCES

Bright, Brenda Jo. 1995. "Re-mappings: Los Angeles Low Riders." In *Looking High and Low: Art and Cultural Identity,* ed. Brenda Jo Bright and Liza Blackwell, 89–123. Tucson: University of Arizona Press.

Dettleback, Cynthia. 1979. *In the Driver's Seat: The Automobile in American Literature and Popular Culture.* Westport, CT: Greenwood Press.

DeWitt, John. 2001. *Cool Cars, High Art: The Rise of Kustom Kulture.* Jackson: University Press of Mississippi.

Flink, James J. 1975. *The Car Culture.* Cambridge, MA: MIT Press.

Ganahl, Pat. 1996. *Hot Rods and Cool Customs.* New York: Artabras.

Geneat, Robert. 1998. *Hot Rod Nights: Boulevard Cruisin' in the USA.* Osceola, WI: Motorbooks International, 1998.

Jimenez y West, Christopher, curator. 2008. *Black Chrome* exhibit catalog. California African American Museum, Los Angeles, September 25, 2008, to April 12, 2009.

Lipsitz, George. 1990. *Time Passages: Collective Memory and American Popular Culture.* Minneapolis: University of Minnesota Press.

Macías, Anthony. 2008. *Mexican American Mojo: Popular Music, Dance, and Urban Culture in Los Angeles, 1935–1968.* Durham, NC: Duke University Press.

Mendoza, Ruben G. 2000. "Cruising Art and Culture in *Aztlán*: Lowriding in the Mexican American Southwest." In *U.S. Latino Literatures and Cultures: Transnational Perspectives,* ed. Francisco Lomeli and Karin Ikas, 3–35. Heidelberg, Germany: Carl Winter-Verlag.

Molina, Ruben. 2002. *The Old Barrio Guide to Low Rider Music, 1950–1970.* La Puente, CA: Mictlan.

Penland, Paige. 2003. *Lowrider: History, Pride, Culture.* St. Paul, MN: Motorbooks International.

Plascenia, Luis. 1983. "Lowriding in the Southwest: Cultural Symbols in the

Mexican Community." In *History, Culture and Society: Chicano Studies in the 1980s*, ed. Mario Garcia, 141–75. Ypsilanti, MI: Bilingual Review Press.

Reyes, David, and Tom Waldman. 1998. *Land of a Thousand Dances: Chicano Rock 'n' Roll from Southern California*. Albuquerque: University of New Mexico Press.

Sánchez, George. 1993. *Becoming Mexican American: Ethnicity, Culture, and Identity in Chicano Los Angeles, 1900–1945*. New York: Oxford University Press.

Sandoval, Denise Michelle. 2003. "Cruising through Lowrider Culture: Chicana/o Identity in the Marketing of LowRider Magazine." In *Velvet Barrios: Popular Culture & Chicana/o Sexualities*, ed. Alicia Gaspar de Alba, 179–96. New York: Palgrave Macmillan.

Stone, Michael. 1990. "Bajito y Suavecito: Lowriding and the 'Class' of Class." *Journal of Latin American Popular Culture* 9: 87–88.

Trillin, Calvin. 1978. "Our Far-Flung Correspondents: Low and Slow, Mean and Clean." *New Yorker* 54: 70–74.

Wolfe, Tom. 1965. *The Kandy-Kolored Tangerine-Flake Streamline Baby*. New York: Noonday Press.

PART THREE

Community Life and Politics

7

Rainbow Coalition in the Golden State?

Exposing Myths, Uncovering New Realities in Latino Attitudes toward Blacks

MATT A. BARRETO, BENJAMIN F. GONZALEZ, AND
GABRIEL R. SÁNCHEZ

INTRODUCTION

During the 1970s and 1980s Blacks and Latinos appeared close to forming a "rainbow coalition" that would work for the political and social benefit of both groups. Large metropolitan cities with sizable minority populations, like New York, Denver, and Los Angeles, saw Black-Brown coalitions to elect African American and Latino mayors, and continuing cooperation seemed to be in the best interest of both groups. In Los Angeles, Latinos were brought into the Bradley coalition over time and became important partners in electing African Americans to office in California. In Colorado, Blacks alongside Hispanics were a big part of the coalition to elect Peña as mayor of Denver. However, in recent years the possibility of a rainbow coalition has come into question, largely as a result of the rapid growth in the Latino population, which has doubled from twenty million to forty million since 1980. Latinos have now surpassed Blacks as the largest minority group in the United States, and many have argued that cooperation has given way to conflict based on real and perceived competition for resources between Blacks and Latinos.

California presents an interesting test of this theory of conflict between Latinos and Blacks. Because it has the largest Latino population in the United States and the largest Black population of all the western states, the potential for competition or conflict or both between the groups there seems high. Anecdotally, some have claimed to find evidence of conflict, at least in the political arena. In 2001, Blacks uniformly voted against the Latino mayoral candidate in Los Angeles, in 1994 they backed Proposition 187, and according to Vaca (2004), some Blacks even worked against the enforcement of equal opportunity laws for Latinos in L.A. This suggests that Latinos in California may see Blacks as direct competition for political and social resources.

Some data point to intergroup conflict between Latinos and Blacks outside the Californian context. McClain et al.'s 2006 article on intergroup conflict in North Carolina found that Latinos did not trust African Americans, and political coalitions were unlikely. Kamasaki and Yzaguirre (1994–95) have argued that Latinos are chronically underrepresented at the federal, state, and local levels and that some Latinos believe that Black leaders invoke solidarity on issues of mutual concern but use their political power to advance Black interests over mutual ones. Multicity studies have also found that Latinos are politically disadvantaged in cities with Black majorities or pluralities and that increases in the Black population have a negative effect on Latino education and income and lead to higher rates of Latino poverty (McClain and Karnig 1990; McClain and Tauber 1998). In a detailed study of intergroup attitudes in Houston, Mindiola et al. (2002) found that Latinos held more negative stereotypes about Blacks than vice versa and also that they were much cooler toward the idea of interracial dating and marriage than Blacks were, suggesting that prejudice exists in the Latino community toward Blacks. However, it is not clear if these findings can be generalized to the case of California. For example, U.S. congresswoman Maxine Waters, who is African American, represents a Los Angeles district that is majority-Latino and has been reelected eleven times with overwhelming Latino support. Thus, it is unclear whether Latinos actually perceive Blacks as threats to their group position and, if they do, exactly what kind of threat they are seen to be.

In this essay we argue that findings pointing to conflict tend to misrepresent this variable and that a new measure is needed to accurately assess Black-Brown relations. To this end we have designed new measures utilizing the Latino National Survey (LNS) to standardize Latino perceptions of competition with Blacks in California. Our analysis intends to shed some light on the exact areas of perceived competition by looking at Latino perceptions across several sociopolitical arenas in California, including gaining access to jobs, education and schools, and city and state government employment and achieving political representation. By examining these individual-level factors across each specific arena, we can determine how context shapes Latino perceptions of competition with African Americans. Additionally, this study represents an improvement over past studies in that it compares the perceived competition with Blacks with the perceived level of competition Latinos have with other Latinos, which allows us to separate racially based threats from those based simply on a general sense of competition.

The LNS also provides the advantage of isolating Latino perceptions of competition with African Americans while accounting for perceptions of overall competition. We believe that this is critical. Much of the previous literature has suggested that Latinos maintain negative attitudes toward Blacks, including the perception of African Americans as economic competitors. However, we contend that it is necessary to take into account the propensity of Latinos to view *all* groups as competitors—including co-ethnics. With the ability to test this theory through the LNS, we believe we can provide some needed clarity to the coalition politics literature.

McClain et al.'s (2006) study represents an important new area of research, given the rapid growth of the Latino immigrant population, often in urban areas with large Black populations. However, that study was limited to mostly Mexican immigrants in one southern city, with the entire Latino sample involving fewer than two hundred persons. Additionally, the Latino population in McClain et al.'s study was a relatively young one, having grown by approximately 7 percent between 1990 and 2000. The dynamics of competition between Latinos and Blacks in California are likely to differ from McClain et al.'s findings because these groups have long had contact with each other and, in the case of Los Angeles, have even been political partners. Through the rich sample sizes of the LNS, we intend to provide a more complete picture of Latinos attitudes toward African Americans in California, which will include a detailed analysis of the Afro-Latino population in the United States, allowing us situate California in the wider context of national Black-Brown relations.

COMPETITION AND INTERGROUP ATTITUDES BETWEEN LATINOS AND AFRICAN AMERICANS

According to Blalock (1967), competition between minority groups occurs when they strive for the same finite objectives so that success for one reduces the probability that the other will attain its goals. This has been defined as the zero-sum game of politics. Scholars have found that Latinos and African Americans often find themselves in this competitive situation. For example, Latinos have been found to make less progress in terms of socioeconomic well-being and political power in cities with Black majorities or pluralities (McClain and Karnig 1990). Further, biracial coalitions are less likely to occur when one group maintains a class or power advantage over the other (Giles and Evans 1986; McClain and Karnig 1990; Browning et al. 1990). This situation is reinforced by conditions associated with residential concentration of Latinos and African Americans (deteriorated living conditions, lack of services, lack of viable employment, etc.), placing members of these groups in direct competition with one another for access to limited resources, jobs, and government representation (Alozie and Ramirez 1999; Kerr et al. 2000; Betancur and Gills 2000). Therefore, it seems as though the changing demographics of the last half-century have provided the background for intensified competition between Latinos and African Americans, particularly in areas like Los Angeles, with large populations of both groups.

Research in the area of racial and ethnic interactions and intragroup attitudes has been focused almost exclusively on how African Americans view Latinos (but for Pantoja and Lopez 2004). This work has been particularly interested in how these attitudes might impact coalitions between the groups, with many finding evidence that Blacks' feelings of distrust and hostility toward Latinos have prevented political alliances between the two groups (Bobo and Massagli 2001; Bobo et al. 1994; Dyer et al. 1989; Mindiola et al. 2002). Despite this prevailing view, Pastor and Marcelli (2004) find that Blacks in Los Angeles are "ambiguous" in their views toward Latino immigrants and, in fact, view Latinos more as political allies than as economic competitors.

However, an emerging literature is developing that focuses on Latinos' attitudes toward African Americans. Among this scholarship, Bobo and Hutchings (1996) find that Latinos are surpassed only by African Americans in their propensity to view other racial/ethnic groups as competitors. In addition to perceptions of competition, scholarship in this area has also suggested that Latinos tend to harbor negative stereotypes of African Americans. For instance, Johnson, Farrell, and Guinn (1997) find that a majority of Asian Americans and a large percentage of Latinos view Blacks as less intelligent and more welfare dependent than their own groups. Similarly, the McClain et al. (2006) study of Latinos in North Carolina found that Latinos' stereotypes of Blacks are more negative than their stereotypes of Whites. Specifically, nearly 57 percent of Latinos in this study felt that few or almost no Blacks could be trusted, and nearly 59 percent believed that few or almost no Blacks are hard working (McClain et al. 2006: 578). Particularly when these perceptions are contrasted with the significantly less negative perceptions of Whites in the study, Latinos (at least those in North Carolina) appear not to have strong feelings of commonality with Blacks. This supports earlier work that suggests both African Americans and Latinos feel closer to Whites than to each other (Dyer et al. 1989). In a comparative study, Pantoja and Lopez (2004) find splits between White and Black attitudes toward programs like affirmative action, but Latinos and Asians are positioned somewhere in the middle. Interestingly, a recent study by Gonzalez (2009) found that Blacks in Washington actually held some of the most liberal views regarding immigration policy, with Blacks significantly more likely than Whites to favor amnesty or a path to citizenship for undocumented immigrants. Blacks were also more likely to strongly disagree that immigration is changing the culture of the United States for the worse. The liberal views held by Blacks in Washington toward immigration policy suggest that the question of intergroup relations is a much more complicated one than it is typically portrayed as.

We expand on this research by analyzing the overall perceptions of competition and racial identification in Latino's perceptions of competition with African Americans in California, where there is a large Latino population that also has a long history of working alongside Blacks both socially and politically. With rising Latino populations throughout the country, what must be taken into consideration is not only how a newly established population such as those in McClain et al.'s (2006) study perceive competition with Blacks but also how this differs for larger, more established populations.

GROUP THREAT

Theoretically this study is based on Blumer's (1958) group position theory, which is also often referred to as group threat theory. Blumer argued that prejudice is composed of four dimensions: a feeling of superiority, a belief the subordinate group is in some way intrinsically different or alien, a sense of entitlement to certain privileges or advantages, and finally a suspicion that the subordinate group is a threat to these privileges or advantages. Blumer's model seems logical for dominant/subordinate relations, but he never addressed how his theory would function for two groups occupying similar social positions.

Hubert Blalock filled in some of the gaps that were left unaddressed in Blumer's model by specifically focusing on minority group relations (Blalock 1967). He argued that competition between minority groups occurs when they strive for the same finite objectives, so that success for one reduces the probability that the other will attain its goals.

Bobo and Hutchings (1996) further expanded on Blumer's model to make it applicable in a multiracial context and enlarge it beyond the White/non-White dichotomy. Using data from the 1992 Los Angeles County Social Survey (LACSS), Bobo and Hutchings tested self-interest, prejudice, and stratification belief models in addition to Blumer's. They argued that racial alienation plays a role in perceived threat, with those groups who feel more alienated more likely to perceive other minority groups as a threat. Because Blumer's model recognizes three of these dimensions (social stratification, prejudice, and self-interest) and could easily be expanded to include the fourth (racial alienation), it was found to be the most parsimonious theory for explaining prejudice as a result of group threat. Bobo and Hutchings tested perceived competition across four dimensions: political, housing based, job based, and economic. They found that alienation did increase perceived threat for Latinos and that in addition to social stratification beliefs, prejudice, and self-interest also had effects.[1]

Bobo built upon this earlier work with Hutchings in 1996. In this article Bobo provided evidence that greater feelings of subordination lead to greater racial alienation, which in turn leads to a greater sense of competition with other minority groups. Bobo also found that 40 percent of the Blacks and Latinos in his sample tended to see competition in zero-sum terms and that, when assessing threat, a host of variables have to be taken into account. These include the economic resources of the group, the specific social domain in question, and the prior history, overtness, and intensity of conflict between minority groups. This is largely in line with Blumer's (1958) argument that a group's sense of social standing is predicated on a number of historical factors.

BLACK-BROWN RELATIONS IN CALIFORNIA

Questions remain regarding how group threat operates for Latinos specifically in the Californian context. As mentioned earlier, perceived conflicts between Blacks and Latinos over mayoral candidates, state laws, and equal opportunities in the past can serve as a basis for perceived competition. Yet there are few studies exploring Latino feelings of intergroup competition with Blacks, with most studies focusing instead on the Black perceptions of competition or threat from Latinos. For instance, Earl Ofari Hutchinson (2007) cites a 2006 Pew study that found that Blacks are more likely to believe that a family member lost or did not get a job because an immigrant worker was hired instead. This may be a real rather than an imagined threat according to the findings of Waldinger (1997), who found evidence that employers in Los Angeles were more open to employing Latino immigrant workers than Blacks because of more negative evaluations of Blacks as a group. Erin Kaplan (2007), writing in the *Los Angeles Times*, argues that Blacks are tired of being conflated with Latinos, and there is competition between the groups, but this is largely perceived more by Blacks than by Latinos. Blacks feel they are expected to "minimize their identity and self-interest to join a new ethnic order" in which Latinos are the majority. In an earlier article for the same newspaper, Kaplan (2006) also points out that Blacks feel as if they are being pushed out of formerly African American neighborhoods by Latino immigrants, who also take jobs that were formerly filled by Blacks. However, this perception does not always square with reality. Pastor and Marcelli (2004) note that public opinion among Blacks does not necessarily view Latino immigrants as competitors and that Latino immigrants do not crowd Blacks out of service-level jobs.

Perceptions of competition between Blacks and Latinos are no doubt driven, at least in part, by the large demographic shifts in the minority population of Los Angeles that began in the 1960s with the accelerating growth of the Latino community. By the 1970 U.S. Census, Latinos had surpassed Blacks as the largest minority population in the city of Los Angeles at 19 percent, although Blacks were a close second at 17 percent. However, the growth rate of the Latino population increased substantially, and by 2000 they represented 40 percent of the population of Los Angeles. Over this same period of time, the population of Blacks in Los Angeles declined to 11 percent (Sonenshein and Pinkus 2002). The demographic increase alone suggests the possibility of increased competition between Latinos and Blacks for economic and social resources, but Sonenshein and Pinkus also note that the number of Latinos who have voted in the mayoral elections has increased from 10 percent in the 1993 election to 22 percent in the 2001 election. While the Black vote share has also increased, from 12 to 17 percent, the declining Black population of Los Angeles suggests that even potential future increases will likely be modest, while the Latino vote share is likely to grow at a much more rapid pace as more individuals within this traditionally young demographic reach voting age.

The increasing vote share of the Latino community suggests that, beyond competition for economic and social resources, there is the possibility of increased political competition between Latinos and Blacks in Los Angeles. Sonenshein and Pinkus (2002) point out that no multiracial coalition stepped in to replace the Bradley coalition of Blacks and Jews that had kept the mayor in office for twenty years with the support of the Latino community. Instead they acknowledge that Los Angeles could see a two-headed minority movement, with both Blacks and Latinos representing substantial enough voting blocks to make for attractive coalition partners both for each other and for Whites. The result is a more complicated political scene and one in which the possibility of political competition exists. However, this competition does not seem to have surfaced so far at the mayoral level, and the election in 2005 of Antonio Villaraigosa may suggest a return to coalitional politics in Los Angeles.

There is evidence that Latinos may also see Blacks as a threat in California. In a 2002 survey David Sears found that Latinos reported themselves to be in conflict with Blacks more often than with any other ethnic group. However, this was largely based on gangs and crime rather than social or political competition, with 76 percent reporting gangs and crime as the source of intergroup conflict, compared to 48 percent who saw jobs and income as a cause of conflict (Sears 2002). Crime was also found to have an effect on Latino perceptions of Blacks in a national New America Media poll that was reported by Kristin Bender in a 2007 *Inside Bay Area* article, in which 44 percent of Latinos reported being afraid of Blacks because they were believed to be responsible for most of the crime.

A forthcoming study by Mark Sawyer based on the 2007 LACSS found that Latinos were coolest toward Asians, followed by Blacks, and overwhelmingly felt the latter preferred welfare to work and were involved in drugs and crime. Furthermore, Latinos were also significantly less likely than Blacks to report political commonality between the groups, with only 27.6 percent of Latinos believing this, while 40.7 percent of Blacks believed that the two groups had political commonality. Tanya Hernandez (2007) reports that Latinos prefer to maintain a social distance from Blacks and listed them as their least desirable marriage partners, which may indicate Latino prejudice against Blacks.

Oliver and Wong (2003) found that there were differences in Latinos' perceived competition with Blacks in Los Angeles and Boston. Latinos in L.A. were much more likely to report intergroup competition with Blacks than Latinos living in Boston. Furthermore, those Latinos living in less heterogeneous neighborhoods in Los Angeles were more likely to harbor negative stereotypes of Blacks and to have perceptions of zero-sum competition with Blacks. Increases in the Latino population in California has also driven conflict with Blacks according to Betancur (2005), who notes that competitive tension is driven by different agendas regarding immigration, bilingual education, and job opportunities. Finally, Bobo and Hutchings (1996) found that both preferred social distance and racial alienation increased Latinos' perceived competition from Blacks in Los Angeles County.

All of these findings suggest that Latinos harbor some negative attitudes toward Blacks and may see them as competitors in some cases. Yet the picture is not as clear as it may seem. A 2007 report from the Leavey Center for the Study of Los Angeles at Loyola Marymount University found that Latinos listed race relations between Latinos and Blacks as a lesser threat (23 percent) than either global warming (38 percent) or traffic congestion (40 percent) (Guerra and Nuño 2007). This suggests that there may be issues of salience in regard to Black-Latino competition, at least in regard to how this is reported in surveys. If this 2007 report had asked only about Black-Latino relations, then 23 percent would seem like a relatively large proportion, but when those relations are placed in a larger context they are shown to be of less concern than everyday issues like environment problems and gridlock.

Yet, these previous studies do not compare Latinos' perceived threat from Blacks with their perceived threat from other Latinos. As is often pointed out by Latino scholars and politicians, the Latino community is far from a homogeneous one, being composed of a variety of ethnic groups as well as established Latino-American communities and communities of recent immigrants. By examining the perceived threat from Blacks alongside the perceived threat from other Latinos, we can assess whether group threat is racially based or based more generally on a sense of competition. Without the inclusion of perceived intragroup competition in California, it is difficult to asses how racially motivated intergroup competition actually is.

Scholars have also noted that competition can extend to other segments of the political environment, including political representation and the drawing of electoral districts (Meier and Stewart 1991; Gay 2001). For example, election results from 118 large multiracial school districts indicate that when Latino population increases, Blacks lose political representation (Meier and Stewart 1991). Further, Claudine Gay finds that African-American voter turnout is lowest in districts that have a majority Latino population (Gay 2001). Elsewhere, as the Latino population has increased, some majority-Black districts have turned majority-Latino, with implications for the representation of Black interests in Congress.

There is clearly political competition between Latinos and Blacks; however, we question whether this competition is salient to the general population rather than only to those most attuned to the political dynamics in these communities. We contend that concern for the relative level of political representation and for government-specific jobs may be relevant only to the segment of the Latino community most interested and concerned with politics. For example, Latinos continue to vote overwhelmingly for Black congressional candidates in California, Texas, and New York, even as the Latino population outnumbers the Black population. Rather than exhibiting all-out conflict, Latinos typically support African American candidates for office.

One recent example highlights the possibility of both conflict and cooperation in the same district. In 2006, when the Thirty-Fourth Congressional District in California held a special election, the two candidates competing over the seat were a Black woman and a Latina. The district population was split almost exactly between Blacks and Latinos. In the primary, voters supported their co-ethnic candidate in a very close and bitterly fought campaign. When the African American candidate emerged victorious, some pundits questioned whether Latinos would go on to support her in the general election and in future elections. Despite almost universal support for the Latina candidate in the primary, Latino voters quickly backed the Black candidate in the general election and in all subsequent elections.

THE IMPACT OF RELATIVE PERCEPTIONS OF COMPETITION IN LATINOS' ATTITUDES TOWARD BLACKS

The LNS provides the opportunity to account for Latinos' perceptions of competition with Blacks *relative* to perceptions of competition with other groups as well as with other Latinos. Previous work has found Latinos to have high perceptions of conflict and competition with African Americans. However, this research has not been able to control for general perceptions of conflict or competition. Research interested in the contextual determinants of racial animosity among Whites has found that individuals faced with economic adversity tend to exhibit not only a generic distrust of out-groups but also feelings of relative deprivation, anxiety, and alienation (Oliver and Mendelberg 2000). Similarly, African Americans in urban ghettos tend to have a "deep suspicion of the motives of others, a marked lack of trust in the benevolent intentions of people and institutions" (Massey and Denton 1993: 172). Gay (2004) has also found that African Americans living in low-income neighborhoods tend to believe that racism limits their individual life chances, as well as the overall socioeconomic attainment of Blacks as a group. We contend that it is likely that Latinos, primarily those who are foreign-born, have similar worldviews marked with perceptions of competition.

During the 1980s many of the nation's major cities went through rapid demographic transformations, and government cutbacks left new immigrants and older residents in poor sections of these cities directly engaged in competition for scarce resources (Jones-Correa 2001). The upward concentration of wealth in the United States in the last two decades has been coupled with declines in real wages and lack of investments in urban neighborhoods, putting the Black and Latino working class in a disadvantaged position (Jennings 2003). Not surprisingly, foreign-born Latinos have been found to perceive greater competition with African Americans than their native-born counterparts have (Bobo and Hutchings 1996; Rodrigues and Segura 2004; Jones-Correa 2001; McClain et al. 2006).[2] However, we contend that this trend does not necessarily reflect Latinos' hostility toward Blacks but possibly reflects a more general worldview that includes high perceptions of competition. Thus, Latinos in California may be just as likely (if not more likely) to perceive competition with other Latinos as with Blacks. By accounting for this important trend, we are able to isolate competitive attitudes toward African Americans from competitive perceptions more generally. Testing of the two specific hypotheses will add significantly to our working knowledge of not only coalition politics among Latinos and African Americans in California but the nature of internal competition among Latinos as well.

DATA AND METHODS

As previously noted, the data for this study are from the 2006 Latino National Survey (LNS). The LNS, a "national" telephone survey of eighty-six hundred Latino residents of the United States, seeks a broad understanding of the qualitative nature of Latino political and social life in America. In this essay, we focus primarily on the data from California, including twelve hundred interviews with Latino respondents. The universe for the survey includes only adult Latinos (eighteen years of age and older), with surveys conducted in the preferred language of the respondent (English, Spanish, or both languages).

With the ability to account for perceptions of competition across various contexts as well as the ability to analyze perceptions of competition with African Americans relative to other Latinos, the LNS is the only dataset available to address the research questions driving this analysis. To take advantage of the unique approach and rich sample sizes of the LNS, we have implemented a wide range of statistical analyses in order to provide a comprehensive investigation of Latino perception of social and political competition. The first stage of the analysis consists of a series of descriptive statistics to determine the degree to which Latinos perceive African Americans to be competitors for economic and political resources *relative* to the perceived competition with other Latinos. Because of the large overall sample size in the LNS, we are able to observe statistically significant relationships between Latinos in Los Angeles and elsewhere in California, and this serves as a starting point for the presentation of our results.

We then present results from multivariate regression models to test a host of explanatory variables on overall perceptions of Black-Brown competition in California. In particular, we are interested in whether Latinos in the city of Los Angeles are more or less likely than Latinos elsewhere in California to perceive competition with Blacks.

Variable Construction

One of the most important contributions in this essay is the construction of the dependent variables. Most studies cited above rely on a single measure or an index of Black-Brown conflict that focuses on how Latinos perceive Blacks or how Blacks perceive Latinos. However, a Latino respondent's perception of Blacks alone is meaningless without perceptions of a comparison group. In this study, we construct a measure of Black-Brown competition based on how much competition Latinos perceive with African Americans relative to how much competition they see with other Latinos. For example, if the dependent variable was social trust, and on a 0–10 scale a respondent assigned a value of 3 to trust in Blacks, then on its face that value would appear to be very low and may appear to represent an "anti-Black" attitude. However, if we asked the same respondent how much he or she trusted other Latinos, and that person once again assigned a value of 3, then the full context illustrates that the attitudes are not anti-Black; rather, the person has low levels of trust in general, for both his or her own in-group and an out-group. Almost every previous study of Black-Brown conflict has relied on a single measure of positive or negative view-points toward just one group, either toward Blacks or toward Latinos. In this project, we take advantage of two series of questions within the LNS and create a relative measure of Black-Brown competition, a sig-nificant improvement in understanding race relations.

First, respondents were asked, "Some have suggested that Latinos are in competition with African-Americans. After each of the next items, would you tell me if you believe there is strong competition, weak com-petition, or no competition at all with African-Americans? How about

1. in getting jobs?
2. in having access to education and quality schools?
3. in getting jobs with the city or state government?
4. in having Latino representatives in elected office?"

From these four questions, we created an overall index of compe-tition with African Americans, as well as four dependent variables, one for each domain of competition. However, this is only half of the story. We are interested in knowing whether the perceived competi-tion is a unique Brown versus Black phenomenon or if competition is also perceived with other Latinos. Thus, we used the exact same series of questions again later on the survey, asked with respect to compe-tition among Latinos: "Some have suggested that [insert country of ancestry][3] are in competition with other Latinos. After each of the next items, would you tell me if you believe there is strong competition, weak competition, or no competition at all with other Latinos?" and the same four items were used: jobs, education, government jobs, and elected representation. By combining the Black competition index with the Latino competition index, we are able to arrive at an overall relative measure of Black-Brown competition.

The combined index ranges from −8 to +8 (see figure 7.1), where a value of −8 represents "high competition" with Latinos and "low com-petition" with Blacks. In contrast, a value of +8 represents "high compe-tition" with Blacks and "low competition" with Latinos. Respondents who had the same value for both groups, regardless of what that value was, are scored as a zero, because they saw no difference in the amount

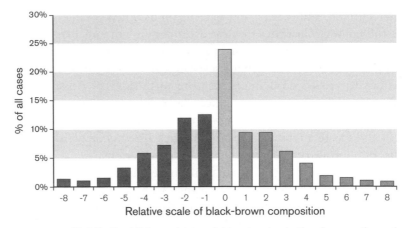

FIGURE 7.1. Distribution of dependent variable, showing Latinos' perceptions of their relative competition with other Latinos (left/dark grey) and Blacks (right/light grey).

of competition between Latinos and Blacks and Latinos and other Latinos. The basic frequencies of the full sample depicted in figure 7.1 strongly suggest that this measure provides a much clearer picture of Black-Brown competition.

We rely on a variety of well-known independent variables and some new ones in predicting Black-Brown competition. Standard demographic variables include age, education, income, gender, marital status, and homeownership. Here, we are particularly interested in class-based variables such as income, as well as an evaluation of personal financial situation and employment status. We also include many standard ethnic variables to test culture-based hypotheses, which include religion (Catholic), immigrant generation, immigrant neighborhood, Spanish usage, Latino-linked fate, importance of maintaining Latino culture, and identification as American. With respect to political variables, we include interest in politics, a political knowledge index, and party identification. (Complete coding instructions for all independent variables can be found in the appendix.)

The last grouping of variables is the least familiar yet the most interesting in this analysis. Several variables related to social interaction, contact, and association with African Americans are included to determine whether or not exposure to the Black community has a positive or negative impact on how Latinos view competition with Blacks. The first of these variables is called Black skin and is a dummy variable for whether or not the Latino respondent described himself or herself as having very dark or dark skin, a very interesting question that has rarely been included on surveys of Latinos, even as scholars promote similar research in Latin America on skin color (see Sawyer et al. 2004; Sawyer 2005). Next, two variables related to social interactions, Black friends and Black workers, are included as dummies and measure whether the respondent's friends or coworkers are mostly Black or mixed Black and Latino. In contrast to these two social interaction variables, two additional variables relate to self-reported negative experiences with African Americans, whether the respondent has been a victim of a crime or experienced discrimination by an African American. Finally, two variables measure how much Latinos feel they have in common with Blacks. The two questions related to this measure asked Latinos how much they had in common with other Latinos and with other racial groups on social and political issues. Black commonality is based just on the respondent's responses to how much he or she has in common with Blacks and ranks the relative placement of Blacks on the 1–8 scale, given how the respondent rated each other group. So if a Latino respondent had 5 out of 8 in common with Blacks but had 4 of 8 in common with Asians, 3 of 8 with Whites, and 6 of 8 with other Latinos, then Blacks would be "ranked" second in terms of commonality.

Finally, we control for the percentage of the population that is Black within the city in which the Latino respondent resides, to test whether or not population dynamics contribute to feelings of competition. For example, Latinos in cities with a very small Black population may not see much competition with Blacks, because they do not come into frequent contact, whereas Latinos residing in majority-Black cities may see Blacks as their competitors. At least, this has been the proposed theory by journalistic accounts in California. We test this through the inclusion of two population variables, percentage Black and percentage Black-squared (as of the 2006 U.S. Census Current Population Survey), the latter being included because population is unlikely to hold a simple linear relationship. In full, we employ seven variables specifically related to race.

THE RESULTS

The first set of results is a comparison of mean averages for the Black-Brown competition dependent variable. Using the relative competition variable, we compare the mean level of competition perceived by several different geographic subgroups of Latinos. A negative mean value

TABLE 7.I LATINOS' PERCEIVED BLACK-BROWN COMPETITION,
COMPARISON OF MEANS

Variable	Index of Perceived Competition
CA as a whole	–0.2949
Rest of the U.S.	–0.1648
L.A. metro area	–0.2867
Rest of CA	–0.3022
L.A. city	–0.4303
CA—foreign born	–0.4014
CA—second generation	–0.0339
CA—third generation	0.0345
CA—fourth generation	0.0571
Total LNS Sample	–0.1829

demonstrates that the group perceives more competition with other Latinos, and mean values greater than zero demonstrate that the group perceives more competition with African Americans—as depicted in figure 7.1 above. Table 7.1 reports bivariate means for Latinos across different geographies, as well as across generations. As a point of comparison, we provide the overall average score for the national LNS sample at the bottom, which registers as –0.18.

For California, the degree of Black-Brown competition is actually lower, at –0.29, suggesting Latinos in the Golden State view even less competition with Blacks than is perceived by Latinos elsewhere in the United States. Further, there is no validity to the claim that competitive tension is particularly high in Los Angeles as compared to the rest of the state. First, the L.A. metro area (the counties of L.A., Orange, Riverside, San Bernardino, and Ventura) has a mean competition level of –0.29 compared to –0.30 for the rest of California. Further, looking just at the city of Los Angeles, we find that Latinos there have an even lower degree of perceived competition with Blacks, –0.43. These results make it clear that Latinos in Los Angeles (and California) do not perceive overwhelming competition with Blacks.

Finally, while some previous research suggests immigrants are more likely to hold anti-Black attitudes (McClain et al. 2006), we find a clear linear pattern showing that the foreign born (both citizens and noncitizens) perceive the least amount of competition with Blacks, which increases slowly through the fourth generation of the U.S.-born population segment. Latino immigrants in California have an average com-

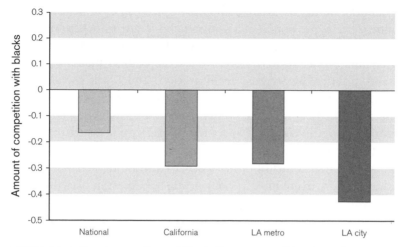

FIGURE 7.2. Latinos' perceptions of Black-Brown competition, by region.

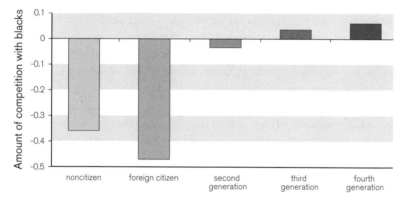

FIGURE 7.3. Latinos' perceptions of Black-Brown competition in California, by citizenship and immigrant generation.

petition score of –0.40 compared to a positive score of 0.057 by the fourth generation. The fourth-generation average is still low (recall that it varies from –8 to +8), but the positive value suggests that by the fourth generation, Latinos may, on balance, perceive Blacks as their competitors. Contrary to McClain et al. (2006), who argue that pre-existing notions of anti-Black attitudes preoccupy new arrivals from Latin America, we show that the much more exhaustive dataset from the LNS dismisses the notion that Latino immigrants perceive competition with African Americans in California.

Building on the bivariate comparison of means, we next move to a multivariate regression analysis in which we test four key hypotheses through a more rigorous set of analyses. Here, we look for statistically significant results related to resource competition (income and education), political awareness, acculturation, and Black social context. Table 7.2 contains results for two ordinary least squares regressions using the four-item index of combined Black-Brown competition. The first regression, in column 1, uses the nonrelative measure of competition, that is, only the perceived competition with Blacks, without taking the perceived competition with other Latinos into account. The second regression, in column 2, is our primary interest; it uses the relative measure of competition with other Latinos and ranges from –8 to +8. We encourage readers to compare the relative measure of competition across the two regressions and focus more heavily on the second one.

Among the resource and lifecycle variables, age demonstrates a positive and significant relationship in both models. This suggests that older Latinos are the most likely to view competition with Blacks in California and that the younger cohorts are unlikely to view competition. Again, this finding stands in contrast to the media's sensationalizing of Black-Brown conflict among young people in the schools of Los Angeles. Though our data do not include individuals under eighteen, the trend in the data does not support this claim whatsoever. If Latinos had strong feelings of competition with Blacks when in school, there is no reason to expect that this would suddenly decline when they reach eighteen. Additionally, no relationship is found with income, rejecting the hypothesis that lower-income Latinos see more competition with Blacks. Instead, we find that those who perceive their personal financial situation to be improving tend to see somewhat higher competition with Blacks in California.

Moving to the next set of cultural variables, the two regressions show different results. First, Latinos with a high sense of linked fate with other Latinos, as well as those who feel it is important to maintain a clear Latino culture, appear to perceive more competition with Blacks in column 1. However, notice that this relationship does not hold in column 2, where we provide our better-developed measure of Black-Brown competition. A strong ethnic identity, as measured by a sense of linked fate and the perceived importance of Latino culture, does not have any effect on perceptions of competition with Blacks when competition with other Latinos is also taken in to account. Further, looking at other variables such as language and Catholicism makes clear that cultural differences are not contributing to perceptions of competition

TABLE 7.2 PREDICTORS OF LATINOS' PERCEPTION OF BLACK-BROWN
COMPETITION IN CALIFORNIA

	1		2	
	Competition with Blacks		Relative Competition (Other Latinos Included)	
	Coefficient	Std. Err.	Coefficient	Std. Err.
Age	0.0134	0.0064*	0.0147	.0069*
Education	−0.0015	0.0254	−0.0156	0.0273
Income	−6.0e-06	6.3e-06	−2.7e-06	6.8e-06
Finances better	0.1948	0.1218	0.4558	0.1310***
Unemployed	0.3008	0.3097	0.4141	0.3331
Female	−0.1919	0.1777	0.0791	0.1911
Married	−0.0939	0.1829	−0.3194	0.1967
Homeowner	−0.0626	0.2099	−0.0297	0.2257
Catholicism	0.1017	0.2014	0.3272	0.2168
Generation	0.1436	0.1087	−0.0017	0.1169
Spanish language	0.0777	0.0929	−0.0934	0.0999
Spanish 'hood	0.1586	0.1006	0.0854	0.1082
Linked fate with other Latinos	0.1819	0.0933*	−0.1171	0.1005
American identity	0.2801	0.0914***	−0.1182	0.0983
Maintain culture	0.5319	0.1679***	0.0170	0.1806
Political knowledge	−0.0221	0.0915	0.0818	0.0984
Party (7 point)	0.0166	0.0525	−0.0515	0.0565
Black skin shade	−0.1187	0.2666	−0.5402	0.2868†
Black friends	−0.0747	0.4215	−0.5324	0.4533
Black coworkers	0.2337	0.5299	0.2967	0.5699
Black crime	−0.5617	0.5195	0.0552	0.5589
Black discrimination	−0.1425	0.5164	-0.3221	0.5554
Black commonality	0.1280	0.0487**	0.1023	0.0524*
City of L.A.	0.3816	0.2794	−0.2615	.3006
Black population	0.0517	0.0334	0.0794	0.0359*
Black pop.-squared	−0.0021	0.0011†	−0.0020	0.0011†
Constant	2.392	1.065	−1.454	1.146
N	952		952	
Adj. R-squared	.0378		.0169	

*=p < .05; **=p < .010; ***=p < .001; † = .10

with Blacks in California. None of these variables is statistically significant in our relative measure in column 2. And although the immigrant
generation showed significant results in the bivariate analysis reported
above in table 7.1, once additional control variables are considered,
we find no statistically significant relationship between generation and
Black-Brown competition.

Finally, we turn our attention to a series of race-related variables, which are particularly relevant to understanding Black-Brown competition. Latinos with self-reported dark skin were in fact less likely to see Blacks as their competitors, according to the negative coefficient results in column 2. This is a particularly interesting result and suggests that darker-skinned Latinos in California may be racialized by the larger White population in such a way that it causes them to view a sense of commonality and connection with African Americans. However, our results for Latinos' view of commonality with Blacks suggest the opposite. Latinos who believe they have much in common with Blacks also tend to view more competition with Blacks in California. This should give us pause in how we interpret a measure such as shared commonality, because it may imply not that these two minority groups are in a partnership or coalition but rather that they correctly observe similarity in their social circumstances, which could lead to more perceived competition.

Last, we want to focus on the findings from the Black population variables. Looking at column 2, we note that the two variables are both statistically significant, yet they have opposite effects. This is a common phenomenon with nonliner relationships when a squared term is introduced. So, on the one hand as the percentage of the Black population goes up, competition also increases. However, the negative values on the squared term indicate that at some point, an n-shaped curve will emerge, whereby a larger Black population actually decreases perceived competition. These findings illustrate that increases in the Black population do lead to increases in perceptions of competition, as is suggested by the literature, but there is a tipping point, after which further increases actually decrease the level of perceived competition. This is a fascinating finding, suggesting that although some population challenges exist, large Black and Latino populations can coexist with little competition. One potential explanation for this finding is that necessary social interactions cause an increase in the level of integration of the Latino and Black communities after the Black population reaches a particular level. Because the regression coefficients are difficult to interpret on their face, we offer a graphical presentation of the population results in figure 7.4. Again, controlling for the percentage of Black population within the different cities in California, we test how Latinos living in each city view competition with Blacks. The X-axis, at the bottom of figure 7.4, measures the Black population in a city ranging from 0 to 50 percent, while the Y-axis, on the left-hand side, measures Latino respondents' perceived degree of competition with Blacks.

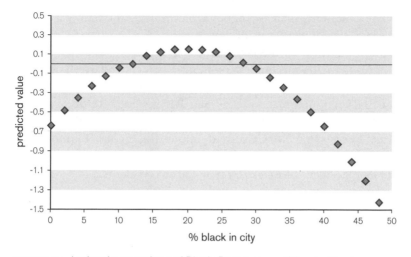

FIGURE 7.4. Latinos' perceptions of Black-Brown competition, by Black population percentage.

Values below zero indicate Latinos do not see competition with Blacks, while values above zero represent perceived competition.

Moving from left to right, as the percentage of the Black population in a city increases, we witness a slow but steady increase in Latinos' perceived competition with Blacks; however, this slope levels off in cities that are about 20 percent Black and then begins to decline much more rapidly as the Black population further increases. So in the presence of smaller African American populations—cities ranging from zero to 20 percent Black—Latinos see more competition as the population increases. However, this stands in stark contrast to the perception in cities with medium and heavy Black populations, which actually report far, far lower levels of Black-Brown competition. One possible explanation for this n-curve could be that cities that are in the 15–25 percent Black range were perhaps 45–50 percent Black ten or twenty years ago, before witnessing rapid Latino population growth. Therefore, some perceived competition exists on both sides as a result of the population replacement that has occurred, though our current data do not allow us to explicitly test this theory. In contrast, cities that maintain a large Black population have more successfully incorporated Latinos as partners, leading Latinos to view very low levels of competition, as depicted in figure 7.4.

Looking to our statewide data, we note that in cities with small

Black populations, such as Anaheim, Santa Ana, and San Jose, Latinos do in fact view lower levels of competition. At the same time, Latinos residing in cities with the largest Black population, such as Oakland, Inglewood, Richmond, and Carson, also perceive relatively low levels of competition with Blacks. In contrast, Latinos in cities with medium-sized Black populations, such as San Bernardino, Rialto, Lancaster, and Moreno Valley, tend to perceive higher rates of competition with Blacks. These same cities also had among the highest Latino population growth rates during the 1990s and 2000s, possibly creating more rapid displacement of Blacks by new Latino residents.

CONCLUSION

The 2008 presidential election highlighted the potential for conflict and also cooperation between Latinos and Blacks. At the outset of the contest, misguided observers speculated that Latinos would not vote for a Black candidate because of simmering feelings of competition between the two minority groups. Indeed the primary election results in California pointed to huge losses for Barack Obama among Latino voters. However, this sense of Black-Brown competition was both fabricated and exaggerated, as Latino voters preferred Hillary Clinton because of her high name recognition, extensive Latino outreach, and prominent endorsements from Latino officials (Barreto and Ramírez 2008; Barreto et al. 2008). Latinos were not casting ballots against Barack Obama on the basis of his race but instead for Hillary Clinton on the basis of her Latino outreach, visibility, and endorsements. Indeed, when the final votes were cast, the headlines proclaimed that Hispanic voters were a crucial component of the Obama coalition, delivering a 70 percent vote share to the Democrat, noticeably higher than for the two previous White Democrats who had run for president.

Seven years earlier Latino mayoral candidate Antonio Villaraigosa received less than 20 percent of the Black vote, and commentators were quick to point to Black-Brown competition through anecdotes and single examples. However, it is now well known that in 2005 Villaraigosa received about half of the Black vote and further increased his margin in 2009. An important rejoinder here is that we should focus on what the data tell us and not on what one or two opinionated columnists think. In this essay, we have provided a comprehensive look at Latino public opinion toward African Americans, using data from the 2006 Latino National Survey, focusing on data from the state of California.

In short, we find that only a small minority of Latinos in California view competition with Blacks and that, in comparison, California, especially Los Angeles, has even lower levels of perceived Black-Brown competition than elsewhere.

While the final election outcomes in November 2008 refuted the Latino-Black competition hypothesis with 70 percent of the Latino vote going to Obama, it drew considerable attention throughout the campaign cycle. Here, we argue that claims of mounting competition over public policy, elected office, jobs, and education is far overstated, at least from the perspective of Latinos in California. We demonstrate that traditional measures of Black-Brown competition are flawed because they lack a base of comparison. Using a relative measure of competition, we argue that Latinos actually view a higher degree of competition with fellow Latinos and that perceived competition with Blacks is not emblematic of anti-Black sentiment.

More recent research in Los Angeles has concurred with these results, finding less conflict and more cooperation between Latinos and Blacks (Guerra and Nuño 2007; Sawyer et al. 2008). While Latinos may view a moderate degree of competition with Blacks, most also view a moderate degree of competition with fellow Latinos. Thus, the perceived competition is not racially motivated but rather is based on realistic observations of their political and social environments. At the same time that Latinos view some competition with African Americans, they also view a good deal of shared commonality and even a sense of linked fate with Blacks. If anything, the Obama campaign and its successful Latino outreach highlighted the possibility of a broad minority coalition, bringing together Latinos and Blacks over their shared interests.

As the Latino population continues to grow in California, quite often alongside the existing Black population, we encourage scholars to develop new, more precise measures of intergroup relations. Whether we are measuring conflict or cooperation, we should not evaluate in-group/out-group attitudes in a vacuum but rather by using a relative methodology.

Finally, it is important to note that this essay has examined only Latinos' viewpoints of perceived competition with Blacks. As Latinos now represent the largest minority group in America, surpassing African Americans in thirty states, it may be that Blacks actually view more competition with Latinos than Latinos do with Blacks. While reliable data are an obstacle, future studies should examine both groups simultaneously to fully understand the dynamics of Black-Latino relations.

APPENDIX: VARIABLE CONSTRUCTION

TABLE 7.3 VARIABLE CONSTRUCTION FOR PREDICTING BLACK-BROWN COMPETITION

Independent Variables	Description
Age	Continuous; 18–98
Education	Categorical; 0 = none; 4.5 = less than 8th; 10.5 = some HS; 12 = HS grad; 14.5 = some college; 16 = college grad; 18 = graduate school
Income	Categorical with missing income replaced using income imputation
Finances better	Personal financial situation; 1 = worse; 2 = same; 3 = better
Unemployed	Dummy; 1 = currently unemployed
Female	Dummy; 1 = female
Married	Dummy; 1 = married
Homeowner	Dummy; 1 = homeowner
Years address	Continuous; number of years lived at current address; 0–90
Catholic	Dummy; 1 = Catholic
Generation	Categorical; 0 = foreign-born noncitizen; 1 = foreign-born citizen; 2 = second; 3 = third; 4 = fourth
Spanish (scale)	Categorical; 1 = English only; 2 = English, a little Spanish; 3 = English, adequate Spanish; 4 = fully bilingual; 5 = Spanish, adequate English; 6 = Spanish, a little English; 7 = Spanish only
Spanish 'hood	Index, see LNS question L23; 0 = no Spanish services available in community; 1 = 1 of 3 services in Spanish; 2 = 2 of 3 services in Spanish; 3 = 3 of 3 services in Spanish
Political knowledge	Index, see LNS questions J10, J11, J12; 0 = 0 of 3 correct; 1 = 1 of 3 correct; 2 = 2 of 3 correct; 3 = 3 of 3 correct
Party (7 point)	Categorical; 1 = strong Dem.; 2 = weak Dem.; 3 = lean toward Dem.; 4 = indep.; 5 = lean toward GOP; 6 = weak GOP; 7 = strong GOP
Black skin shade	Dummy; 1 = self-identify as having very dark or dark skin (see LNS question E16)
Black friends	Dummy; 1 = friends are mostly black or mix of black and Latino (see LNS question G6)
Black coworkers	Dummy; 1 = coworkers are mostly black or mix of black and Latino (see LNS question G7)
Black crime	Dummy; 1 = victim of crime committed by black (see LNS questions L18/L19)
Black discrimination	Dummy; 1 = experienced discrimination by black (see LNS questions N2/N4)

TABLE 7.3 (*continued*)

Independent Variables	Description
Black commonality	Index, see LNS questions G1A/G2A; 1 = nothing at all in common; 8 = a lot in common
Linked fate with Latinos	Categorical; 1 = none; 2 = little; 3 = some; 4 = a lot
American identity	Categorical; 1 = not at all; 2 = not strong; 3 = somewhat strong; 4 = very strong
Maintain Latino culture	Categorical; 1 = not important at all; 2 = somewhat important; 3 = very important
Black population	Continuous; % black among population in city where respondent lives
Black population-squared	Exponential; squared term of % black among population
City of L.A.	Dummy; 1 = resides in city of Los Angeles

Latino National Survey = LNS

NOTES

1. Black had the highest level of racial alienation, followed by Latinos and Asian, who differed little from one another.

2. The McClain et al. (2006) study also confirms the role of nativity in Latinos' attitudes toward African Americans, as approximately 93 percent of the sample utilized in this study is foreign-born. However, this study suggests that this trend may be a result of Latino immigrants arriving in the United States with negative stereotypes regarding Blacks that were formulated in their country of origin. In fact, a sizable literature focused on discrimination and racial stereotypes in Latin America addresses this issue (de la Cadena 2001; Dulitzky 2005; Guimaraes 2001; Hanchard 1994; Mörner 1967; Sweet 1997; Wade 1993, 1997; Winant 1992).

3. For example, the question might have read, "Some have suggested that *Puerto Ricans* are in competition with other Latinos. After each of the next items, would you tell me if you believe there is strong competition, weak competition, or no competition at all with other Latinos?"

REFERENCES

Alozie, Nicholas, and Enrique Ramirez. 1999. "A Piece of the Pie and More Competition and Hispanic Employment on Urban Police Forces." *Urban Affairs Review* 34 (3): 456–75.

Andrews, George Reid. 2004. *Afro-Latin America, 1800–2000*. New York: Oxford University Press.

Barreto, Matt, Luis Fraga, Sylvia Manzano, Valerie Martinez-Ebers, and Gary Segura. 2008. "Should They Dance with the One Who Brung 'Em? Latinos and the 2008 Presidential Election." *PS: Political Science & Politics* 41 (October).

Barreto, Matt, and Ricardo Ramírez. 2008. "The Latino Vote Is Pro-Clinton and Not Anti-Obama." Op-ed. *Los Angeles Times,* February 7.

Betancur, John J. 2005. "Framing the Discussion of African-American-Latino Relations: A Review and Analysis." In *Neither Enemies nor Friends: Latinos, Blacks, Afro-Latinos,* ed. Anani Dzidzienyo and Suzanne Oboler, 159–72. New York: Palgrave Press.

Betancur, John J., and Douglas C. Gills, eds. 2000. *The Collaborative City: Opportunities and Struggles for Blacks and Latinos in U.S. Cities.* New York: Garland Publishing.

Blalock, Hubert M. 1967. *Toward a Theory of Minority-Group Relations.* New York: Wiley.

Blumer, Herbert. 1958. "Race Prejudice as a Sense of Group Position." *Pacific Sociological Review* 1 (1): 3–7.

Bobo, Lawrence, and Vincent Hutchings. 1996. "Perceptions of Racial Group Competition: Extending Blumer's Theory of Group Position to a Multiracial Social Context." *American Sociological Review* 61 (6): 951–72.

Bobo, Lawrence D., and Michael P. Massagli. 2001. "Stereotyping and Urban Inequality." In *Urban Inequality,* ed. Alice O'Connor, Chris Tilly, and Lawrence D. Bobo, 89–162. New York: Russell Sage Foundation.

Bobo, Lawrence, C.L. Zubrinsky, James Johnson, and Melvin L. Oliver. 1994. "Public Opinion before and after a Spring of Discontent." In *The Los Angeles Riots: Lessons from the Urban Future,* ed. Mark Baldassare. Boulder, CO: Westview Press.

Borjas, George. 1999. "The Economic Analysis of Immigration." In *Handbook of Labor Economics,* vol. 3A, ed. Orley Ashenfelter and David Card, 1697–760. Amsterdam: Elsevier.

Browning, Rufus P., Dale Rodgers Marshall, and David H. Tabb. 1990. "Has Political Incorporation Been Achieved? Is It Enough?" In *Racial Politics in American Cities,* ed. Rufus Browning, Dale Rodgers Marshall, and David Tabb. New York: Longman.

de la Cadena, Marisol. 2001. "Reconstructing Race: Racism, Culture and Mestizaje in Latin America." *NACLA Report on the Americas* 34 (6): 16–23.

Denton, Nancy A., and Douglas S. Massey. 1989. "Racial Identity among Caribbean Hispanics: The Effect of Double Minority Status on Residential Segregation." *American Sociological Review* 54: 790–808.

Duchon, Deborah A., and Arthur D. Murphy. 2001. "Introduction: From *Patrones* and *Caciques* to Good Ole Boys." In *Latino Workers in the Contemporary South,* ed. Arthur D. Murphy, Colleen Blanchard, and Jennifer A. Hill, 1–9. Athens: University of Georgia Press.

Dulitzky, Ariel E. 2005. "A Region in Denial: Racial Discrimination and Racism in Latin America." In *Neither Enemies nor Friends: Latinos, Blacks, Afro-Latinos,* ed. Anani Dzidzienyo and Suzanne Oboler, 39–59. New York: Palgrave-Macmillan.

Dyer, James, Arnold Vedlitz, and Stephen Worchel. 1989. "Social Distance among Racial and Ethnic Groups." *Social Science Quarterly* 70 (3): 607–16.

Ellison, Christopher G., and Daniel A. Powers. 1994. "The Contact Hypothesis and Racial Attitudes among Black Americans." *Social Science Quarterly* 75: 385–400.

Frisbie, W. Parker, and Lisa J. Niedert. 1977. "Inequality and the Relative Size of Minority Populations: A Comparative Analysis." *American Journal of Sociology* 82 (5): 1007–30.

Gay, Claudine. 2001. "The Effect of Minority Districts and Minority Representation on Political Participation in California." Public Policy Institute of California, San Francisco.

———. 2004. "Putting Race in Context: Identifying the Environmental Determinants of Black Racial Attitudes." *American Political Science Review* 98 (4): 547–62.

———. 2005. "Your Blues Ain't Like Mine: The Effect of Economic Disparity on Black Attitudes toward Latinos." Paper presented at the annual meeting of the American Political Science Association, Washington DC.

Giles, Michael W., and Arthur S. Evans. 1986. "The Power Approach to Intergroup Hostility." *Journal of Conflict Resolution* 30 (3): 469–86.

Glaser, James. 1994. "Back to the Black Belt: Racial Environment and White Racial Hostility in the South." *Journal of Politics* 56 (1): 21–41.

Gomez, C. 2000. "The Continual Significance of Skin Color: An Explanatory Study of Latinos in the Northeast." *Hispanic Journal of Behavioral Science* 22: 94–103.

Gonzalez, Benjamin F. 2009. "How Many Is Too Many? Undocumented Immigrants, Misperceptions, and Political Attitudes." Paper presented at the annual meeting of the Pacific Northwest Political Science Association, Victoria, BC, October 17.

Guerra, Fernando J., and Stephen A. Nuño. 2007. "Political Representation and Resident Perceptions of the City of Los Angeles." *Los Angeles, State of the City Report*. Pat Brown Institute of Public Affairs, Los Angeles.

Guimaraes, Antonio Sergio. 2001. "Race, Class, and Color: Behind Brazil's 'Racial Democracy.'" *NACLA Report on the Americas* 34 (6): 38–41.

Hajnal, Zoltan, and Mark Baldassare. 2001. "Finding Common Ground: Racial and Ethnic Attitudes in California." Public Policy Institute of California, San Francisco.

Hanchard, Michael G. 1994. *Orpheus and Power: The Movimento Negro of Rio de Janeiro and São Paulo, Brazil, 1945–1988*. Princeton, NJ: Princeton University Press.

Hernández-León, Rubén. 2008. "Black, Latino, and White Competition in a Local Labor Market in the South." Paper presented at State of Black-Latino Relations conference. Los Angeles, April 18.

Hutchinson, Earl Ofari. 2007. *Latino Challenges to Black America: Towards Conversation Between African-Americans and Hispanics*. Chicago: Middle Passage Press.

Jennings, James. 2003. *Welfare Reform and the Revitalization of Inner City Neighborhoods*. East Lansing: Michigan State University Press.

Johnson, James H., Jr., Walter C. Farrell Jr., and Chandra Guinn. 1997. "Immigration Reform and the Browning of America: Tensions, Conflicts, and Community Instability in Metropolitan Los Angeles." *International Migration Review* 31 (4): 1055–95.

Jones-Correa, Michael. 2001. "Institutional and Contextual Factors in Immigrant Naturalization and Voting." *Citizenship Studies* 5 (1): 41–56.

Kamasaki, Charles, and Raul Yzaguirre. 1994–95. "Black-Hispanic Tensions: One Perspective." *Journal of Intergroup Relations* 21 (4): 17–40.

Kandel, W., and E. Parrado. 2004. "Industrial Transformation and Hispanic Migration to the American South: The Case of the Poultry Industry." In *Hispanic Spaces, Latino Places: A Geography of Regional and Cultural Diversity,* ed. Daniel D. Arreola. Austin: University of Texas Press.

Kaplan, Erin A. 2006. "Plugging Immigration's Drain on Black Employment." Op-Ed. *Los Angeles Times,* October 25.

———. 2007. "More Than Just the Latinos-Next-Door." Op-Ed. *Los Angeles Times,* March 17.

Kerr, Brinck, Will Miller, and Margeret Reid. 2000. "The Changing Face of Urban Bureaucracy: Is There Inter-Ethnic Competition for Municipal Government Jobs?" *Urban Affairs Review* 35: 770–93.

Kluegel, James R., and Eliot R. Smith. 1986. *Beliefs about Inequality: Americans' Views of What Is and What Ought to Be.* New York: Aldine de Gruyter.

Logan, John R. 2003. "How Race Counts for Hispanic Americans." A Report of the Lewis Mumford Center, the University at Albany, July 14.

Massey, Douglas S., and Nancy A. Denton. 1993. *American Apartheid.* Cambridge, MA: Harvard University Press.

McClain, Paula D., Niambi M. Carter, Victoria M. DeFrancesco Soto, Monique L. Lyle, Jeffrey D. Grynaviski, Shayla C. Nunnally, Thomas J. Scotto, J. Alan Kendrick, Gerald F. Lackey, and Kendra Davenport Cotton. 2006. "Racial Distancing in a Southern City: Latino Immigrants' Views of Black Americans." *Journal of Politics* 68 (3): 571–84.

McClain, Paula D., and Albert K. Karnig. 1990. "Black and Hispanic Socioeconomic and Political Competition." *American Political Science Review* 84 (2): 535–45.

McClain, Paula D., and Steven Tauber. 1998. "Black and Latino Socio-Economic and Political Competition: Has a Decade Made a Difference?" *American Politics Quarterly* 26 (2): 237–52.

Meier, Kenneth, Paula McClain, J.L. Polinard, and Robert D. Wrinkle. 2004. "Divided or Together? Conflict and Cooperation between African Americans and Latinos." *Political Research Quarterly* 57: 399–409.

Meier, Kenneth J., and Joseph Stewart Jr. 1991. *The Politics of Hispanic Education.* Albany: State University of New York Press.

Mindiola, Tatcho, Jr., Yolanda F. Niemann, and Nestor Rodriguez. 2002. *Black-Brown Relations and Stereotypes.* Austin: University of Texas Press.

Mörner, Magnus, ed. 1967. *Race Mixture in the History of Latin America.* Boston: Little, Brown and Company.

Nicholson, S.P., A.D. Pantoja, and G.M. Segura. 2005. "Race Matters: Latino Racial Identities and Political Beliefs." Paper presented at the annual meeting of the American Political Science Association, Washington DC, September.

Oliver, Eric, and Tali Mendelberg. 2000. "Reconsidering the Environmental Determinants of White Racial Attitudes." *American Journal of Political Science* 44 (3): 574–89.

Oliver, J. Eric, and Janelle Wong. 2003. "Inter-group Prejudice in Multiethnic Settings." *American Journal of Political Science* 47 (4): 567–82.

Pantoja, Adrian, and Linda Lopez. 2004. "Beyond Black and White: General Support for Race-Conscious Policies among African Americans, Latinos, Asian Americans, and Whites." *Political Research Quarterly* 57 (4): 633–42.

Pastor, Manuel, and E. Marcelli. 2004. "Somewhere over the Rainbow? African Americans, Unauthorized Mexican Immigration and Coalition Building." In *The Impact of Immigration on African Americans,* ed. Steven Shulman, 107–35. Piscataway, NJ: Transaction Publishers.

Peña, Yesilernis, Jim Sidanius, and Mark Sawyer. 2004. "Racial Democracy in the Americas: A Latin and U.S. Comparison." *Journal of Cross-Cultural Psychology* 35 (6): 749–62.

Perri, Giovanni. 2007. "How Immigrants Affect California Employment and Wages." *California Counts: Population Trends and Profiles* 8 (3): 1–19.

Rodrigues, Helena Alves, and Gary M. Segura. 2004. "A Place at the Lunch Counter: Latinos, African-Americans, and the Dynamics of American Race Politics." Presented at the Latino Politics: The State of the Discipline conference, Texas A&M University, College Station, April 30—May 1.

Rosenbaum, James. 1996. "Policy Uses of Research on the High School-to-Work Transition." *Sociology of Education* 69 (extra Issue): 102–22.

Sawyer, Mark. 2005. "'Race' to the Future: Racial Politics in Latin America 2015." *Perspectives on Politics* 3 (September): 561–63.

Sawyer, Mark, Yesilernis Peña, and Jim Sidanius. 2004. "Cuban Exceptionalism: Group-Based Hierarchy and the Dynamics of Patriotism in Puerto Rico, the Dominican Republic, and Cuba." *Du Bois Review* 1 (March): 93–113.

Sawyer, Mark, Janelle Wong, and Taeku Lee. 2008. "Myths and Realities: Black and Brown Politics in Los Angeles." Paper presented at State of Black-Latino Relations conference. Los Angeles. April 18.

Sears, David. 2002. "Assessment of Interracial/Interethnic Conflict in Los Angeles." UCLA Center for Study and Resolution of Interracial/Interethnic Conflict, Los Angeles.

Sigelman, Lee, and Susan Welch. 1993. "The Contact Hypothesis Revisited: Black-White Interaction and Positive Racial Attitudes." *Social Forces* 71 (3): 781–95.

Sonenshein, Raphael, and Susan Pinkus. 2002. "The Dynamics of Latino Political Incorporation: The 2001 Los Angeles Mayor Election as Seen in Los Angeles Exit Polls." *Political Science and Politics* 35 (01): 67–74.

Stokes-Brown, Atiya Kai. 2006. "Racial Identity and Latino Vote Choice." *American Politics Research* 34 (5): 627–52.

Sweet, James H. 1997. "The Iberian Roots of American Racist Thought." *William and Mary Quarterly* 54 (1): 143–66.

Taylor, Marylee C. 1998. "How White Attitudes Vary with the Racial Composition of Local Populations: Numbers Count." *American Sociological Review* 63 (4): 512–35.

Telles, Edward, and Sylvia Zamora. 2008. "Trends in Black and Latino Occupational Overlap in Metropolitan Areas." Paper presented at State of Black-Latino Relations conference. Los Angeles. April 18.

Uhlaner, Carole. 1991. "Perceived Discrimination and Prejudice and the Coalition Prospects of Blacks, Latinos, and Asian Americans." In *Racial and Ethnic Politics in California,* ed. B.o. Jackson and M.B. Preston, 339–70. Berkeley, CA: IGS Press.

Uhlaner, Carole Jean, and F. Chris Garcia. 2002. *Latino Public Opinion.* In *Understanding Public Opinion,* ed. Barbara Norrander and Clyde Wilcox. Washington DC: CQ Press.

Vaca, Nicolas C. 2004. *The Presumed Alliance: The Unspoken Conflict between Latinos and Blacks and What It Means for America.* New York: HarperCollins.

Wade, Peter. 1993. *Blackness and Race Mixture: The Dynamics of Racial Identity in Colombia.* Baltimore, MD: Johns Hopkins University Press.

———. 1997. *Race and Ethnicity in Latin America.* London: Pluto Press.

Waters, Mary C. 1994. "Ethnic and Racial Identities of Second-Generation Black Immigrants in New York City." *International Migration Review* 28 (4): 795–820.

Welch, Susan, Lee Sigelman, Timothy Bledsoe, and Michael Combs. 2001. *Race and Place: Race Relations in an American City.* New York: Cambridge University Press.

Winant, Howard. 1992. "Rethinking Race in Brazil." *Journal of Latin American Studies* 24 (1): 173–92.

Wright, Gerald. 1977. "Contextual Models of Electoral Behavior: The Southern Wallace Vote." *American Political Science Review* 71 (2): 497–508.

8

Race and the L.A. Human

Race Relations and Violence in Globalized Los Angeles

OFELIA ORTIZ CUEVAS

In the summer of 2005 I received a phone call from a friend who was being held in Men's Central Jail, of the Los Angeles County Sheriff's Department. He had already spent twenty-four hours in a four-man cell with twelve other men—all African American and Latino. There would be more as he remained there for another fifteen hours. He explained to me later that he was not afraid of dying at the hands of one of his fellow inmates, regardless of skin color. It was clear to him and everyone else in that cell that they were not one another's enemies. He told me they all knew instinctively who their adversary was—"Jesus, that fucking jail was trying to kill us all."

At the moment of what he believed to be imminent death, he was not a brother, son, or friend. Nor was he even a member of some institutional or socially constructed category—Brown, Mexican, male from Northern California—which according to most sensationalist journalistic accounts, as well as the increasing scholarship on Black and Brown relations, should make him fear his Black counterparts in the jail and prison system. It would appear that the moment my friend was arrested and processed into the Los Angeles County jail system, he became not someone whose life was of consequence but an unaccounted-for entity whose life mattered little. He became part of what radical geographer Ruth Gilmore calls the largest prison building project in the history of the world—a project that in and of itself produces a social as well as a material death through a racism defined as "the state sanctioned or extra-legal production and exploitation of group differentiated vulnerability to premature death."[1] In this project the state's capacity to eradicate life through its power to organize "various factors of production," such as land/private property and capital, is part of a what I refer to as a violent state arithmetic, in which the racial body is unified in its lack of value.[2] After all, one Brown or Black body after another forced into a cell until the number of individuals far exceeded the cell's capacity (under regulatory policy no doubt) to ensure their safety meant that the administration had lost count of the number of human beings over the course of those long three days. Or maybe that accounting had come to mean, at that moment, something altogether different. Maybe the Black and Brown men went (deliberately?) unaccounted for in that cell as if they didn't count at all. The cell had become a zero point in the cartography of L.A.'s human terrain.

Along with the other men caged in the four-man cell, my friend was no longer a countable human entity with a social and moral indentifying address that would locate him in the human terrain of Los Angeles. He became at the moment of processing: suspect, civil and civic adversary, terrorist, security threat, criminal—a twenty-first-century nonhuman. Once behind bars or, in the Althusserian sense, at the moment of being hailed by the state, he was incorporated into a global security architecture that relegated his life and those of others like him—Black and Brown alike—to outside the realm of the human. This very division—between the human and the nonhuman, the citizen and the criminal—is, I will argue, constituted in part by the contemporary discourse on race relations, a discourse enunciated in part in Los Angeles by the Los Angeles County Human Relations Commission.

And although it would seem that this incident could be an example of the way in which Black and Brown communities can align themselves as a united front—a moment of coalescence, if you will—my point is to illustrate that this group of men is formed by a moment of racial violence—a moment that is productive of a nonhumanity. It is an entity that is created, mandated, and formed by the state as criminal. It relies on an affirmation of difference that is not Black or Brown culture or identity but an existence forged from their proximity to death via punishment. They are those that presumably deserve violent punishment because they already are.

The division into human/nonhuman, citizen/criminal is itself violent. This moment of division reveals that the brothers, fathers, sons, and friends in that cell during those three long days fall under the rubric of nonhuman as they go unaccounted for—or disappear into a singular sum of a particular postracial identification that increasingly manifests in the grave statistics of legal and extralegal police shootings and custody deaths that occur all over the United States. This essay will consider how it is that this unified subject (at the moment of racial violence) comes into being in the city of Los Angeles through the production of a racially criminalized subject that is differentiated through its relation to productive citizenry and the discourses of race relations. This paper focuses specifically on race relations as those practices and engagements that identify the contacts and interactions of people with varied physical and cultural characteristics. Robert E. Park explains it as "the relations existing between peoples distinguished by marks of racial descent . . . [or] anything that intensifies race consciousness."[3] Race relations emerged as a study prior and during World War II, emphasizing the identification and delineation of groups in order to better understand the social processes that occur in organized group relations involving tensions, conflict, and resolution. For Parks, these relations are "the relations of people of diverse race and cultures who have been thrown together . . . who have not been significantly knit together."[4]

This manner of identifying divergent groups of people and studying the conflict or consciousness between groups laid the groundwork for the diversity programming and the multicultural agendas that predominated in the 1980s and 1990s. These are nowhere more hegemonic than in policy initiatives as well as in the study of race in universities across the country.[5] Cultural difference and identity classification in race relations rely on what Jodi Melamed calls a liberal racial logic that "continues to fuse technologies of racial domination with liberal freedoms to represent people who are exploited for or cut off from capitalist wealth as outsiders to liberal subjectivity for who life can be disallowed to the point of death."[6] It is there that liberal racial logic cannot, as we will discuss further, account for the violence that shapes the present-day racial subject—the L.A. nonhuman—as it exists not only outside the frame of race relations but also in part through it. The race relations cycle ultimately aspires to a transparent universalized human subject that is already a product of legible historical signifiers, what da Silva refers to as a sociohistorical logic that fails to capture racial subjection "because it (re)produces the logic of obliteration."[7]

For this essay I situate race relations and human relations in the institutions that produce them, academic, cultural, and state intellectuals alike (and more important in conjunction with each other), as part of policing and imprisonment—what I identify as a violent state arithmetic that unifies Black and Brown bodies at the point of deadly state violence. Those uncounted men were relegated to what postcolonial theorist Achille Mbembe refers to as a a sort of nonspace that belongs to those "who do not know whether they are alive or condemned." He explains that death occurs in pieces and in moments and is extracted through life in body and in time. He asks us to consider the question "But is not a death multiplied by fifteen, finally equal to a single death?"[8] This space is rendered in a critical delineation between the proper citizen subject, what I refer to as the L.A. Human, and the disavowed no-body, or the L.A. nonhuman—the criminal, the threat, the affected, the irrational. This occurs through the very institutions that work to better understand and resolve contentious relations between the "races" as they function to indentify who will or can become a productive (ac)countable citizen and take part in the cultural, economic, and social terrain of Los Angeles.

So how does this Brown/Black population that survives (if it does) and "lives" together within the confines of a place that produces the materiality of race exist not only outside the industrious discourses and practices of "race relations" but also through their very exclusion? How do these discourses and practices underlie the emerging postracial *racial* subject of criminal/nonhuman (and the work of race within that)? And critically, how have the projects of "human relations" and sociologies of "race relations" and the state and academic sponsored management of conflict and contention, as well as reconciliation and coalescence, been used to police and punish Brown and Black men, women, and children? In other words, how and why have race relations—in this instance, the study of relations between Black and Brown people—enabled divisions of difference that are ultimately between good productive legible citizens (both culturally and ethnoracially) and the transgressor or criminal. Why has it become an increasingly interesting category of study and how might these relations be connected to policing and jailing in L.A.?

To answer these questions, I will focus on two local institutions that appear to have divergent purposes—the Los Angeles County Jail and the Los Angeles Human Relations Commission. The Los Angeles County Jail is an appropriate point of departure to consider the aforementioned questions and reveal how the scholarly industry of "race relations" enables the jailing and warehousing of Black and Brown bodies and the practice of racial violence in L.A. My attempt is to reconsider and critically engage the categorization of liberal racial difference, or the idea of color lines, in relation to state violence in order to illustrate the centrality of what Dylan Rodriguez refers to as the *fatal unfreedom* of millions of men, women, and children held captive in jails and prisons across the country in a presumed postracial era.[9] Through a genealogical mapping of the Los Angeles Human Relations Commission (LAHRC), this essay considers how racial violence, via the state, forms templates of demographic and geographic rationality that elicit the conditions of possibility and the elimination of how real people live, how humans are perceived, ruled over, and subjected to the processes of state building. It shows that race relations seen in the early development of the LAHRC and its relation to the university have cultivated a population within a population along the lines of *citizen* and *criminal* versus the color/cultural lines of Black and Brown that manifest the line between human and nonhuman, or those that are off the map of L.A.'s productive human terrain.

THE GLOBAL CITY AND THE TERRAIN OF HUMAN AND RACE RELATIONS

Los Angeles, the global city, where Edward Soja (borrowing a slogan from the *L.A. Times*) so famously said, "Everything comes together," is considered the premier city of race relations in the United States.[10] It is one of the first in the United States to become a majority-minority city, the new millennial link to the Pacific Rim, and the largest city in a state that has the eighth largest economy in the world.[11] Los Angeles is a global metropolis contending with the likes of London, New York, Mumbai, and Tokyo in terms of commerce, culture, industry, and development and now has the third largest economic center in the world.[12] Teaming up with A.T. Kearny Global Management Consultants and the Chicago Council on Global Affairs, *Forgein Policy* magazine in 2008 measured globalization around the world, claiming Los Angeles as an up and coming global city. *Foreign Policy* explained that although national governments shape the outline of globalization, city centers are where the successes and failures play out and they are engines of growth for the countries in which they are situated.[13] The cities that command the largest economic markets are not the only examples of success; those cities that can integrate into the global sphere and forge important global links are also. If cities are ranked in a matrix of their business activity, information exchange, human capital, cultural experience, and political engagement, Los Angeles ranks as the sixth most important city in the world—with its human capital cited as its most valuable resource. Human capital here is defined as how well a city acts as a magnet for diverse people and talent, the size of the immigrant population, the number of international schools, the percentage of the residents with university degrees, and the manner in which the city incorporates those populations into its economy.[14] The city's ability to manage its diverse groups of people—its human capital as they contribute to the city's productive terrain and international status—has positioned Los Angeles as an up and coming global city.[15] This city's most pressing task to compete in the global marketplace is the effective administration of this resource through population management—a form of governmentality that works through an "ensemble of institutions, procedures analyses and reflection, the calculations and tactics, that allow . . . complex forms of power."[16] As Foucault states, "With governement it is a question not of imposing law on men but of disposing of things: that is to say, of employing tactics rather than laws."[17] The apparatuses that manage L.A.'s populations, the police and the jailing structures that are the *force* of law, create a classificatory division of people—those that are proper, productive citizens and those that are criminal, unproductive subjects. This sort of classification functions to manage and maintain sufficient stability to ensure continued economic productivity.

If L.A. is known for the diverse abundance of its human capital, it is also known for its racial strife and contentious human relations, what urban sociologists and criminologists explain as a form of cumulative social disorganization.[18] From the front-page *Los Angeles Times* images of Mexican youths and Anglo soldiers entangled in violent race riots in the early 1940s, to the Watts rebellion in 1965, and then to the L.A. uprising of 1992 and the more recent purported conflict between the Black and Brown people of the city, contention between racial groups has been as much a part of the city's identification as has its celebration of diversity.

The recent focus in Los Angeles on Black-Brown relations is driven by the demographic shifts from the 1970s through the first decade of the 2000s, which marked a decline of the African American population as well as significant structural changes in the city's economy, highlighting what Erin Aubry Kaplan describes as an anxiety about "unsettling changes" for African Americans in Los Angeles.[19] Moments of contention have been evident in the competition for jobs, neighborhoods, public school resources, and for political and municipal appointments and elected positions, such as mayor, police chief, and the head of the county sheriff's department.[20] Even the noted resentments over the immigration debate being compared to (or considered part of) the civil rights movement have marked a point of contention between Black and Brown communities.[21]

The most widely disseminated representations of Black-Brown relations in the city have been the anomalies: sensationalized media accounts of Black on Brown violence. These, though, have become the prevailing narratives of contention that race scholars, cultural producers, and media represent. As an example, the death of Cheryl Green, a young Black girl killed by alleged Latino gang members, was an incident in what law professor Tanya Hernandez has called "an increasingly common trend: Latino ethnic cleansing of African Americans from multiracial neighborhoods."[22] And there are the brief glimpses of jail interiors in stories of dramatic prison race wars in which Latino and Black inmates fight against one another and make headline news. Also there are the news stories that attempt to explain the contentions between rival gangs as examples of an already existing race war between Black and Brown communities in Los Angeles.

These two narratives—demographic change and sensational violence—have dominated the discourse on Black-Brown race relations among scholars as well as public intellectuals. Both narratives, in various ways, lean on an understanding of race relations that depends on—and produces—a notion of the socially integrated citizen who is understood as human and, at the same time, a notion of the opposite and the enemy of that citizen: the criminal, the delinquent, the noncitizen, who is located outside the locus of human subjectivity. The overall discourse of race relations seeks to engage the citizen-human and to manage the criminal-nonhuman.

The L.A. Human is thus in part a material and discursive product of the several key institutions that intersect at a historical point of relations management through discourses that establish the ideal of the human in social, economic, and civic participation. It came into being in part through the work of the Los Angeles Human Relations Commission (LAHRC), established during World War II as the main municipal institution to address the instability of race relations in the city. In a 1969 report titled *A 25 Year History 1944–1969,* the commission explained that it began in reaction to the "hysteria and racial prejudice" that had led to the "evacuation of 23,475 Japanese American citizens" as well as the migration of "scores of Mexicans and Negroes from Texas, Louisiana, Arizona, and New Mexico" seeking jobs in Los Angeles. Its goal was to address historical grievances against prejudice and discrimination, "which cast in doubt the very humanity of millions of American citizens." Acknowledging the discrimination faced by racial and ethnic minority groups, the commission's agenda was to "seek out the causes of racial tension and devise all means possible to eliminate them." In 1945, the commission sponsored a four-day institute at which over a thousand civil service employees were educated in the "techniques of integrating minority groups into life of the community" in order to "achieve understanding and improve the efficiency of county employees in dealing with people of different races, creeds and national origins." Interestingly, the commission's first move was to *erase* race from the discussion, because its members came to the conclusion that the answer to the broad range of problems that had led to group friction "was to be found in human relations and not race relations."[23]

Institutional discourses of human relations—designed to develop improved relationships between groups of differentiated peoples through programs promoting "unity," "tolerance," and "coalition-building"—emerged from a disciplinary foundation in the human and the political sciences. Anthropology, sociology, and psychology, as well as economics, law, and, later, planning, were the key scholarly disciplines used to determine group difference and to ultimately identify and categorize groups within an ecological framework in which the discursive features of natural science, which necessarily divide individuals into human and animal categories, were inscribed with political and social values.[24] Human relations work is theoretically one of management with a goal toward human productivity. In Los Angeles that productivity was threatened by the unstable or unusable human capital—the population that could and would incite unrest and instability to the emerging industry of the city.

Close ties between the social sciences and the state developed between the two world wars, resulting in the proliferation of social and administrative sciences that intersected with psychoanalysis and group organization theory.[25] Beginning in England after World War I, the Tavistock Institute (then called the Tavistock Clinic) developed a psychoanalytic model to deal with group dynamics and organize individuals for a more efficient group production. The institute's study of the effects of social relations and motivation through psychology would be used in the United States as a means to deal with the changes in labor brought on by the New Deal and the upsurge in union activity. Human relations as an instituted organizational practice became integrated into the training and management of labor that was in transition from scientific management processes to industrial training.[26] Fredrick Taylor's science of economic efficiency and labor productivity, used during the early years of automobile production, had shifted under the pressure of disgruntled workers resisting the complete automation of their labor. This was met with a strategy that would merge the principles of scientific management with the new field of human relations, which meant that the workforce would be managed through a mediating relations structure that would take into account the workers' psychological and behavioral makeup.[27]

Although the LAHRC has narrated its history as emerging to engage the crisis of the violent conflict between Mexicans and Anglos after the Zoot Suit riots, the earliest documentation of a coordinated effort to establish itself as a human relations commission was a meeting of members of the Los Angeles County Committee for Church and Community Cooperation in June 1940. Made up of individuals from church and government as well as business leaders, the committee initiated a commission that aimed to institute long-lasting stability and security in Los Angeles. This group established the Commission on Industrial Unity, which set forth a June 4, 1941, manifesto titled "Toward Industrial Peace." In the language of the time, *industrial peace* meant the absence of conflict with organized labor and, in this case, the stability of the production of the defense industry. With a declaration to cultivate amity and preclude "considerable economic waste," the imperative of the commission was to navigate "industrial controversies" as an arbitrator between labor and capital. Its principles of national unity, seen as indispensable to the "preservation of the democratic system," were predicated upon the idea that industrial warfare (i.e., walkouts and strikes) were militant and destabilizing acts against national security. Class interests—at least those of the workers—had to bow to the priorities of the state. This commission deemed the security of the nation a necessity that Los Angeles had a responsibility to ensure by "providing a mechanism of investigation, mediation, conciliation and arbitration that will assist employees and employers in the adjustment of their differences."[28] This facilitation was to be in coordination with local, county, state, and federal agencies and impartial citizens whose services would be made available for conciliation.

The plan, calling for the promotion of industrial unity in the city, claimed national defense, security, and safety the most important objectives of the American people. It stated that "dealing with an aggressor whose objective is the enslavement of the rest of the world" would require a high level of cooperation if fundamental American freedoms were to be protected. The cooperation from "the men who supply the money, the men who supply the management and the men who supply the labor" was key to the project of industrial unity in Los Angeles. If America "was to be defended and be made strong," the public (described as both labor and capital), out of necessity, had to comply with the war production program that had developed in the 1930s. *Industrial unity* of course was a code term for the suppression of class conflict, and the commission's function was to ensure the production of war capital by aiding in the management of conflict and precluding its potentially destabilizing effects.

Deciding to create a more comprehensive peace and security structure throughout the city, members of the Commission of Industrial Unity established three other commissions that same year: the Commission for Religious Unity, the Commission for Molding Public Opinion, and the Commission on Racial Unity. The last one began with an agenda outlining its major concerns and its ideals for a new vision of social justice for L.A.'s nonwhite population. In an early memo the Commission on Racial Unity described the Black community in L.A. as "greatly disadvantaged economically, politically and in the fuller enjoyment of those dividends of citizenship produced by the governments of democracy." It saw as its ideal the "complete integration of various racial groups into all significant levels and areas of all phases of citizenship life."[29]

Appointed to the head of the initial Commission on Racial Unity in 1941 was the president of the University of Southern California, Dr. Rufus B. von Klein Smid, internationally renowned for his work in governmental relations and his development of one of the earliest public administration departments on the West Coast. During his twenty-year reign USC developed a public administration program that included, along with the first PhD program in public administration and the country's second School of International Relations, one of the first police administration programs on the West Coast.[30] Several years prior to von Klein Smid's tenure at USC he published two papers, titled "The Psychology of the Personal Interview: Its Relation to Moral Development through Penal Institutions" and "Eugenics and the State," which are representative of his expertise in the practice of public administration and population management. In the latter, von Klein Smid positioned himself as a defender of eugenics and social stability. This paper did not explicitly espouse the eradication of racial groups for fear of miscegenation or contamination, as did the work of Charles Davenport and Madison Grant, but it warned of the "fecundity of the defective" and the dangerous "mass of the incapables" that weigh on society's economic progress and stability.[31]

For von Klein Smid, the best and most efficient means to establish the security of public resources and prevent economic waste—which in his words, society "owes to itself"—was to have an efficient scientific method of separating the "wise and the best" through the strength of an organized society.[32] Published a quarter of a century prior to his tenure as the head of the Commission on Racial Unity, the paper on eugenics was an intense promotion of the discipline of social science as a means of population control. However, the most critical aspect of von Klein Smid's appointment is not the irony of a proponent of eugenics becoming so concerned with "racial unity" but the powerful continuity between these two phases of his career. As a eugenicist and later as an expert in public administration and a social scientist, von Klein Smid firmly believed in human difference as a scientific truth that could be administered via scrupulous methods of accounting, documentation, and examination of populations that threatened the public good.

Housing, health, economics, and law enforcement were considered major problem areas that the Commission on Racial Unity felt it could be effective in improving. The acknowledgment of discriminatory practices such as in the application of housing covenants, the lack of access to healthcare, and racist policing were priority issues for the commission, which understood its role to be the arbitrator between the structures of discrimination and social justice, requiring it to "exert its influence into channels which would equalize most of these inequalities."[33] It was clear that for the commission the "ravages of poor health (and poverty) in minority groups reflect themselves in the general health status of the city at large." For the newly established Commission on Racial Unity, health, as well social behavior, was a reflection of a city's ability to maintain order, which was a necessary part of good governance. And the areas of Los Angeles that were "thickly populated with negroes," such as the Central Avenue district, required a greater stability and equality. Better standards of health and housing for the commission were related to the practices of law enforcement, which the commission saw as "a major keystone to racial unity; for in law and order one finds the essential to the stability of good government." Thus, disproportionate delinquency in certain areas required "a special intelligence of understanding and administration."[34] Sections of the community were regarded as unmanageable and resistant and, according to the commission, unable to "rid [themselves] of the inroads of imported anti-social conduct." The commission also made note of the "disproportionate rate of brutality incident to law enforcement," which they believed was due to a lack of racial understanding on the part of the officers of the "more profound socio-civic essentials of the problem." They saw the police department's failure to integrate "competent Negro law enforcement officers to important positions" as a barrier to stability, which required more intelligent planning and execution of law enforcement.[35] A call for a well thought-out system that would include the incorporation of Black or Brown individuals as specialized intelligence agents of population control—facilitators with a special kind of racial knowledge, the intimate and inherent understanding of cultural and behavioral attributes—was in line with the development of a more enlightened form of population management and the administration of the public body. Long before the civil rights movement and the institution of affirmative action, von Klein Smid, as head of the Commission on Racial Unity, had found that an integrated and multicultural police unit would assure more efficient policing and hence a more stabilized city.

The call for democratic unity, peace and social equality in L.A. was hence part of a larger rubric of human productivity that relied on the relationship between structures of knowledge and structures of power. The administering of the L.A. public, managing its "errant" populations in order to ensure economic stability in 1940s Los Angeles, was undertaken to ensure wartime productivity through the production of racial knowledge. This type of knowledge came as much from progressive ideas on integrating the police with locals as it did from von Klein Smid's ideas of early eugenics research. What seem to be disparate points of looking at race are what connect the idea of the human with the process of incorporation into the full extent of proper "American" citizenship—or its disavowal, the criminal.

As the economic terrain of Los Angeles shifted from wartime production, the commission continued to expand its role in the facilitation of human relations in the city. The LAHRC established itself as the arbitrator of relations between the L.A. Human, those who could be incorporated into civil life, and the L.A. nonhuman, those who could or would not.

After the Watts riots of 1969 and 1970, the commission grappled with what it referred to as a rapidly changing social climate—a moment of social and political crisis brought on by a failing imperial war and by resistance to social and political inequality that prompted movements of direct challenge, which then took the forefront in public discourse. The commission was unable to reckon with a population that had established itself in direct opposition to themes of American freedom and democracy, with which the commission attempted to subsume those critical of the United States into its agenda for racial peace. The twenty-five-year report illustrates the LAHRC's relationship with populations that were demanding social justice outside the parameters of liberal democracy: "Recently on local and national scenes we have heard the echoing cries for power; black power, brown power, yellow power and people power. As we view our society, it is our understanding that what many of these strident voices are calling for is not in its final essence, a destruction of our cherished system of government or total dissolution of society's governmental apparatus, but rather, what we hear people saying is that they want to become full participants in all aspects of American life."

The diplomatic refusal of the LAHRC to hear the voices of the power movements—or, rather, to hear them only as wanting to be incorporated into "all aspects of American life"—forced those who were demanding acknowledgment of racial subjection to the other side of the dividing line of proper citizen subject. While dealing with tensions that arose precisely from material circumstance—economic dispossession, imperial war, migration, exploitation of labor—the LAHRC was forging an ideal of the opposing civic entity, the L.A. nonhuman. In other words the individuals who resisted the model that produced these violent conditions became recategorized as criminal-nonhuman entities who, out of necessity, needed to be managed/policed. After the Watts riots a faction of Los Angeles County's Probation Department called the Group Guidance Section was assigned to the LAHRC. Its aim was to make contact with the neighborhood youth in order to obtain their help in quelling the riots. The youth were enlisted in a program and called upon to facilitate the identification of other community members who were inciting riotous behavior. At the same time they were taught leadership skills that were meant to contribute to establishing peace in their neighborhood. According to the commission this assignment was a great success. These two tasks worked to simultaneously map out and identify the transgressor—the L.A. nonhuman—and establish a rearticulated boundary between that entity and the L.A. Human. The voices of the power movement—which precisely did not accept the validity of that boundary and which did not fit the model of liberal democratic citizenry—were rendered not as dissenters seeking justice but as an unthinking, unreasonable mass that represented a threat to state legitimacy and L.A.'s image and productivity.

The LAHRC's twenty-five-year report in many ways marks a turning point in the management of L.A.'s human capital through the reorganized discursive and material practices of the city's governing structures. A restructuring of L.A.'s economic terrain from a solid infrastructure of manufacturing to a more global economy of intangible finance and reduced labor protection was met with a set of discourses that ultimately worked to fill the newest form of state industry—the twenty-first-century prison and the global security system.

In another period of crisis in the years following the turn of the millennium, the official discourse of the LAHRC would focus on the importance of tolerance and diversity in Los Angeles. The commission's current mission is, according to the LAHRC's website, "to foster harmonious and equitable intergroup relations, to empower communities and institutions to engage in non-violent conflict resolution, and to promote an informed and inclusive multicultural society." Despite this shift in focus, the commission continues to fulfill the same function it had since the 1940s, stabilizing conditions that ensure productivity. This no longer means "industrial unity" in the face of a world war for democracy, but all that falls under the rubric of "security," from hate crime to civil unrest to the ongoing "war on terror."

The LAHRC's current five-point list of "strategic priorities" begins with the broad notion of "public safety," which the commission defines in terms of preventing hate crime and discrimination and couples with a concern to "equip youth with the knowledge and skills to improve intergroup relations in a multicultural society." It also lists "capacity building"—strengthening state structures that work to ensure human productivity—and "crisis response," which the commission defines as including response to "civil unrest, war, terrorism and other critical incidents."[36] The fifth and final priority was to "strengthen internal management systems," to "ensure Commission compliance with County policies and procedures" that matched the agenda of other county structures, such as the Los Angeles County Sheriff's Department.

The overwhelming rhetorical concern of the commission in recent years has been to address racial violence through the rubric of "hate crime." In 2003, with the beginning of the Iraq War, the commission explicitly tied these concerns to the issue of "homeland security." In response to reports of violence against Arab Americans, Muslims Sikhs, South Asians, and anyone who looked Middle Eastern, the commission "brought together its community partners, law enforcement officials and religious leaders who announced a pledge to promote homeland security and freedom from hate and bigotry. A number of individuals signed the pledge on March 28, 2003, making sure that the message of tolerance and peace was shared with the many communities that compose the County of Los Angeles."[37]

The discourse (and often severe institutional consequences) of so called hate crimes later became the primary lens through which tensions between Blacks and Latinos would be viewed. The categorization of certain acts of presumed racial violence as hate crimes effectively criminalized specific interpersonal relationships and behaviors by incorporating a notion of criminally punishable racism into the legal system. This notion, though, was and is predicated on an understanding of racism as prejudice, as a sentiment felt by individuals, and precludes the possibility of understanding racism as institutionalized state violence. Categorized as racism, acts of violence committed by Blacks and Latinos against one another have become a special sort of crime, subject to sentencing enhancements and understood not as a failure of relations between individuals but as a crime against the fabric of liberal democratic society—against capitalism in its contemporary neoliberal manifestation.

In one program singled out for praise by the commission's 2003–5 annual report, the LAHRC worked with law enforcement, local government, and community groups to deal with gang violence in the Normandale Park district, an area that had experienced significant Black-Brown tensions. The commission's strategy "called for law enforcement suppression action, balanced by a comprehensive community development program, which included an empowerment strategy for the people living in the community."[38] As in Watts nearly forty years earlier, the commission pursued "suppression actions" within the context of an "empowerment strategy." Both of these tactics enabled each other within a structure of power, a single strategy for the production of knowledge and the racial violence of population management.

The LAHRC's plan, the 2003–5 annual report continues, "engaged members of the community in a survey that identified criminal behavior and quality of life issues that were causing havoc in the area. While this was taking place, hard core gang members were being incarcerated." Under the rubric of empowerment strategies that foster citizenship, community peace, and civic participation, the Black and Brown population of Los Angeles County Jail—already allegedly the largest in the world—would continue to grow.

THE ZERO POINT IN L.A.'S HUMAN TERRAIN: THE JAIL

More than one million predominately Black and Brown people are processed through the Los Angeles County Jail every year—an extraordinary number in a county of nine million people. What is perhaps more extraordinary is the invisibility of this population in the official discourse of race relations and the degree to which the jail as a site of racial coalescence is overlooked by scholars and public intellectuals who analyze such points of intersection but in a manner legible only in a liberal racial framework. It is for this reason all the more urgent that we consider the zero point, the institutional site in which the racial body through its disavowal goes unaccounted—a population of global proportions. The Los Angeles County Sheriff's Department (LASD) claims on its website that it administers the largest local jail system on the planet.[39] And it very well may. On any given day the Los Angeles County Jail holds an average of nineteen thousand men and women. Located in the center of downtown Los Angeles, the Twin Towers Correctional Facility and the Men's Central Jail alone hold over five thousand men at any given time. The Twin Towers is a medical-services facility of nearly 1.5 million square feet, and a pedestrian bridge crossing Fairbanks Street connects it to Men's Central, which houses maximum security inmates.[40] The Twin Towers' construction cost exceeded $390 million, and that facility alone employs a staff of twenty-four hundred. The county system as a whole, presided over by Sheriff Lee Baca, has a yearly budget of $2.5 billion dollars and houses inmates from an overall jurisdiction comprising forty incorporated and ninety unincorporated communities, nine community colleges, and 349 miles of Metrolink train routes. The county website claims that over four million people enjoy the protection of the sheriff and his staff of eighteen thousand deputies and officers.

The demographic makeup of the 1.6 million prisoners that the county jail processes each year is difficult to assess, as the LASD has kept race and ethnicity statistics for only the past seven years. The present population represents a racial schema that speaks clearly to the productive and violent work of the state in an time marked by the prevalent discourses of a postracial era. As of 2002, the racial and ethnic makeup of the county jail system (no data exist for Men's Central and the Twin Towers specifically) was 17 percent white, 34 percent Black, and 45 percent Hispanic. In 2009 the numbers remained relatively consistent: 14 percent white, 36 percent Black, and 47 percent Hispanic. Cumulatively, the Black and Brown inmates of the Los Angeles County Jail make up over 80 percent of the globe's largest jail population and "live" under conditions that John Irwin calls the cruelest form of punishment in the United States, with jail's primary purpose to "manage the rabble" of any given city.[41]

All in all, roughly one million Black and Brown people pass through the Los Angeles County Jail yearly and suffer in a limbo state of punishment, not yet sentenced or convicted. For more than thirty years, this jail has been under investigation for conditions considered inhumane by national and international rights organizations such as the American Civil Liberties Union and Human Rights Watch. Even before the epidemic growth in the state prison system in the 1980s and 1990s, Men's Central was under litigation for conditions deemed punitive for its extensive overcrowding and acts of physical violence by prison guards.[42] Over the last three decades, overcrowding has continued. A report by the ACLU explained that although the jail has expanded, so has its population, resulting in social and spatial density that dismally fails to meet even the American Correctional Association standards.[43] As my friend was, inmates are routinely confined twenty-three to twenty-four hours a day to cells that are windowless and without room to stand or walk. The lights, although insufficient for reading, are left on twenty-four hours a day, invoking certain sleep deprivation for months or (if time to trial is prolonged) even years on end. Under dozens of separate filings, the Los Angeles County Jail has been cited for conditions that have caused immediate and direct "bodily disintegration," such as physical deterioration from lack of required recreation time, outbreaks of staphylococcus infection due to extended periods without clean sheets or changes of clothes, subjection to forced x-rays and blood tests, and mental deterioration due to duress of humiliation, strip searches, months without exposure to natural light, forced idleness, and dangerous levels of spatial density.

Even if the interaction of Black and Brown people is seen as a barometer tracking the shifts toward a globalized and multicultural society, the study of race relations by state intellectuals nonetheless fails to note the largest contemporary shift on the political and economic terrain: the growth of a global security architecture, the existence of which requires an identifiable threat to the liberal democratic system and its protected population. Moreover, the antidotes most commonly prescribed—unity, diversity, and tolerance—function to veil the racial violence of the state and to abet that violence by assigning racial populations to the categories of the L.A. Human and nonhuman, the citizen and the criminal. In the end, this does in fact serve to unify Black and Brown people and provide them with a level playing field—the invisible point on the human terrain of Los Angeles, the crowded cellblocks of the county jail.

NOTES

1. Ruth Gilmore, *Golden Gulag: Prisons, Surplus, Crisis, and Opposition in Globalizing California* (Berkeley: University of California Press, 2006), 28.

2. Ibid.

3. Robert E. Park, "The Nature of Race Relations," in *Race Relations and the Race Problem*, ed. E. T. Thompson (Durham, N.C.: Duke University Press, 1939), 3.

4. Ibid., 5.

5. Steven Steinberg, "Race Relations: The Problem with the Wrong Name," *New Politics* 8, no. 2 (Winter 2001), http://newpol.org/node/20, accessed June 15, 2012.

6. Jodi Melamed, "The Spirit of Neoliberalism: From Racial Liberalism to Neoliberal Multiculturalism," *Social Text* 24, no. 4 89 (Winter 2006): 1–24.

7. Denise da Silva, *Towards a Global Idea of Race* (Minneapolis: University of Minnesota Press, 2007), 155.

8. Achille Mbembe, *On the Postcolony* (Berkeley: University of California Press, 2001), 198.

9. Dylan Rodríguez, *Forced Passages: Imprisoned Radical Intellectuals and the U.S. Prison System* (Minneapolis: University of Minnesota Press, 2004), 1.

10. Edward Soja, *Postmodern Geographies: The Reassertion of Space in Critical Social Theory* (New York: Verso Press, 1989).

11. The United States Census 2010 Interactive Map, http://2010.census .gov/2010census/popmap. The top minority-majority cities include San Antonio, Washington DC, and New York. Hawaii as a state has never had a white majority.

12. AT Kearney 2012 Global Cities Index and Emerging Cities Outlook, www .atkearney.com/documents/10192/dfedfc4c-8a62–4162–90e5–2a3f14foda3a.

13. "The 2008 Global Cities Index," *Foreign Policy,* October 15, 2008,

www.foreignpolicy.com/articles/2008/10/15/the_2008_global_cities_index ?page=f. See also www.atkearney.com/index.php/Publications/the-2008-global -cities-index.html.

14. Ibid.

15. Ibid.

16. Michel Foucault, "Governmentality," in *The Essential Foucault,* edited by Paul Rabinow and Nikolas Rose (New York: New Press, 2003), 241.

17. Ibid., 237.

18. Ernest Burgess and Donald J. Bogue, *Contributions to Urban Sociology* (Chicago: University of Chicago Press, 1964).

19. On the demographic changes, see William C. Matney and Dwight Johnson, "America's Black Population 1970–1982: A Statistical View," Special Publication of Department of Commerce, U.S. Bureau of the Census. On the economic changes for African Americans, see Erin Aubry Kaplan, "The Black and Brown Divide," May 24, 2006, http://articles.latimes.com/2006/may/24/ opinion/oe-kaplan24.

20. Roberto Suro, "Blacks and Latinos in the U.S.," *Carnegie Reporter* 5, no. 2 (Spring 2009), http://carnegie.org/publications/carnegiereporter/single/ view/article/item/214/.

21. Peter Schuck, "The Evolving Civil Rights Movement: Old Civil Rights and New Immigration," January 1994, http://heather.cs.ucdavis.edu/pub/ Immigration/EffOnMinorities/Schuck.html.

22. Tanya K. Hernandez, "Longtime Prejudices, Not Economic Rivalry, Fuel Tensions," *Los Angeles Times,* January 7, 2007, www.latimes.com/news/ opinion/la-op-hernandez7jan07,0,3588783,print.story?coll = la-opinion-right rail.

23. Los Angeles County Commission on Human Relations, *A 25 Year History 1944–1969 and Biennial Report 1967–1969* (Los Angeles, 1969), unpaginated.

24. Stanford M. Lyman, "The Race Relations Cycle of Robert E. Park," *Pacific Sociological Review* 11, no. 1 (Spring 1968): 16–22.

25. William J. Breen, "Social Science and State Policy in WWII: Human Relations, Pedagogy, and Industrial Training 1940–1945," *Business History Review* (Summer 2002): 233–66.

26. Ibid. The earliest history of this work was to study the trauma of British soldiers returning home from World War I. It was used to established the effects of war, resulting in the field of trauma studies in order to find a way to reinstitute soldiers suffering from war trauma. This was a relatively new practice, as prior to this work soldiers suffering from trauma were expelled from services and sometimes even shot. Soldiers who suffered from trauma were considered expendable prior to World War I.

27. Ibid.

28. Memo, Commission on Industrial Unity, June 1941, Los Angeles County Human Relations Commission.

29. Memo, Commission on Racial Unity, July 1941, Los Angeles County Human Relations Commission; Rufus von Klein Smid, "Eugenics and the State," Indiana Reformatory Printing Trade School, Jeffersonville, IN, 1913.

30. http://about.usc.edu/history/.

31. von Klein Smid, "Eugenics and the State"; Rufus von Klein Smid, "The Psychology of the Personal Interview: Its Relation to Moral Development through Penal Institutions," paper delivered at the Decennial Convention of the Religious Education Association, Cleveland, OH, March 1913.

32. von Klein Smid, "Eugenics and the State." He describes the mass of incapables as defined by the Mental Deficiency Act of 1913, then new, and as those wandering about neglected and cruelly treated; those habitual drunkards; idiots; those so deeply defective in mind as to be unable to guard themselves against common physical dangers; and moral imbeciles who display mental defect coupled with vicious or criminal propensity, on which punishment has little or no deterrent.

33. From memo, Commission on Racial Unity, July 1941.

34. Ibid.

35. Ibid.

36. http://humanrelations.co.la.ca.us/about/strategic.htm.

37. Annual Report, July 2003—June 2005, http://humanrelations.co.la.ca.us/news/activities.htm.

38. Ibid.

39. http://sheriff.lacounty.gov/wps/portal/lasd.

40. Ibid.

41. John Irwin, *The Jail: Managing the Underclass in American Society* (Berkeley: University of California Press, 1985), 53.

42. See *Rutherford v. Pitchess,* 457 F. Supp. 104 (C.D. Calif. 1978).

43. Terry A. Kupers, "Report on Mental Health Issues at Los Angeles County Jail," American Civil Liberties Report, Los Angeles, June 27, 2008.

PART FOUR

Reporting Black and Brown L.A.

A Journalist's View

More Than Just the Latinos-Next-Door; Piercing Black Silence on Immigration; and Plugging Immigration's Drain on Black Employment

ERIN AUBRY KAPLAN

MORE THAN JUST THE LATINOS-NEXT-DOOR

It's Hard to Shake the Feeling That Blacks, and Black Communities, Are Under Siege

A Latino family is moving onto my block. This is an unremarkable event and, in the predominantly African American part of town where I live, certainly not an unprecedented one. It's a natural part of the ebb and flow of all neighborhoods; turnover, like death and taxes, is certain. One of the great scenes of Americana is a van or a truck parked by the curb or driveway, ramp extended, as the rest of the block gathers on the sidewalk to watch the installment of new neighbors and their belongings. It represents social mobility and new beginnings at their most picturesque. I do feel some of that sidewalk curiosity about the trucks I see. But I also shrink from them. I am anxious about the newcomers—and I am not alone. I know, I know: To feel other than welcoming to new arrivals is to be racist, xenophobic, or, at the very least, neurotic about change. I adamantly reject the first two but reluctantly claim the third. Anxiety about change has been eating away at me for years, though not the change of black neighborhoods going Latino (fretting about that alone is xenophobic, not to mention fruitless). I'm talking about big, resonant, unsettling changes within black communities themselves, changes that have created vacuums that Latinos happen to be filling. This family moving onto my block brings me closer to that reality than I care to be. Frankly, giving voice to this anxiety makes me uncomfortable. But for too long Angelenos have been unable or unwilling to talk about this particular dimension of the black/Latino relationship, partly because that relationship has always been too narrowly defined and too politicized to get at the all-too-human emotions driving so much anxiety like mine. The usual conversation about black/brown relations centers on jobs, education, or common goals. These are all legitimate topics, but there is a bigger discussion: about feelings blacks have not just about Latinos but about all sorts of changes—from reconfigured census categories to the death of affirmative action—that reflect our sense of our declining importance. It's a deep, complex, historically cumulative feeling that doesn't have a regular outlet, and when it does come out, it can sound intolerant and accusatory. I recently sat through a meeting of black and Latino parents in South L.A. that was meant to bring them together over (you guessed it) education and common goals. But the meeting took a detour when a black father stood up to express concern about the administrative staff at his kids' school not speaking English. He said it as neutrally as possible, but a pall was immediately cast on the room as well as the conversation. The man went on to say, his voice rising, that he was a veteran, that he'd lived his whole life in his neighborhood as an American, that he'd paid his dues. Xenophobic? Maybe. But mostly I saw a man struggling to be heard, trying (and perhaps failing) to articulate his anxiety about change—at school, in his neighborhood, and in the country at large. He was just upset, and he wanted the right to be upset. Nobody black expects Latinos to solve our problems. But we are tired of implicit calls for us to be "reasonable." Given our crazy-making history, is it surprising that we are a bit paranoid, that we react less than ideally to things like demographic shifts in our communities? Especially when those communities feel like the only currency we have left? Yes, we've devalued that currency by leaving communities too eagerly over the years. Unlike the Irish or Italians or Jews of another era, we didn't naturally evolve as a group out of our ghettos. Quite the opposite. Some blacks—the relative few who could afford to do so—have fled the ghettos that remain. That fact, more than anything else, accounts for the anxiety I feel as I watch the trucks and vans pull up, and the lights go on, in that house down the street. *Ghetto* is far too strong a word to describe my neighborhood, by the way—it's much more than livable. Let's just say it has abandonment issues.

That's all I want the new arrivals to know. I'll get over my anxiety; I have no choice. I will almost certainly like my neighbors, unless they run roughshod on my lawn or play music too late at night. But it'll be fine because community is something I'm good at, something I know— or knew once—very, very well.

PIERCING BLACK SILENCE ON IMMIGRATION

A Panel Discussion Mulls Over the Effects of Illegal Immigration and Changing Demographics on African-American Communities

Washington—It was a sign. This city was uncharacteristically balmy last week, and L.A. was uncharacteristically frigid. Yet for some reason, it felt appropriate; although I had traveled almost twenty-seven hundred miles, it was for a conversation I should have been able to have in my hometown. Last year's discussion of immigration rights borrowed generously from the civil rights movement, but it had little space for a black position on immigration. (I don't count the simplistic statements of lone-ranger community "leaders" who advocated closing the borders, or the naive activists who declared black and brown folk natural allies who need to stop squabbling over trifles like immigration.) So when the Center for Immigration Studies invited me to attend a symposium called "Black Americans and the Challenge of Immigration," I accepted and looked forward to a more nuanced debate. Of course, the center itself is hardly neutral; it claims to support immigrants but not U.S. immigration policy, and says it is concerned first with the "broad national interest" that it feels is ignored by the powers that be. This sounds reasonable, especially to blacks who've had no real spokesperson to articulate their stake and to address their frustrations with unchecked immigration. But the symposium is also a potential minefield. Are our concerns being used to advance a larger agenda that ultimately doesn't serve us? Is this another invitation to join another opportunistic but ultimately unhelpful coalition? I wanted to find out. Daryl Scott, a professor of modern U.S. history at Howard University, discussed blacks and their long and tortured relationship to immigration. Blacks were always viewed more as aliens than as citizens, he said. The term "Great Migration"—the 1920s exodus of blacks from the

South to the North in search of work—reinforced the idea that blacks were immigrants in their own country, uprooted and unwanted. They were not simply immigrants, he said, but internal aliens. Black leaders in the late nineteenth and early twentieth centuries had critiques of the effect of immigration on black employment, Scott said—but many of those same leaders also supported immigration because it jibed with their beliefs in an open society for all and fair competition for blacks. Of course, U.S. employers supported immigration as well, but that was because they tended to prefer any labor pool but a black one.

The difference between then and now, Scott said, is that black leadership then wasn't in denial about this. But when it joined the New Deal coalition and the Democratic Party, which supported open immigration, its voice was compromised. Scott believes in coalition politics, but "blacks aren't senior partners in the coalition." George Borjas, a Harvard economist, made a point that was much appreciated in the room: It's not that American natives don't want the jobs that immigrants do, he said. It's that they don't want the jobs at the wages immigrants are currently paid. One participant stood up and made the million-dollar point: There's a difference between legal and illegal immigration, and illegal immigration affects black people more, especially poor blacks who have the lowest rates of employment. I nodded but didn't applaud. Not because I disagreed but because it felt a little unseemly to cheer for dividing people so strictly into legal and illegal, especially coming from citizen-aliens like us. It occurred to me that blacks hold on to the rule of law not so much because they're conservative or chauvinistic or nationalistic, but because laws are often the only thing standing between them and oblivion.

Frank Morris, of Morgan State University, and James Gimpel, of the University of Maryland, talked about the state of black political power, which is declining and not likely to reverse course, especially as Latinos remake black districts. Morris is incensed not about this remaking but about the deafening silence of blacks on so many matters vital to their survival. Blacks "have a dog in the fight" over immigration but aren't acting like it, he said. Morris is angry that the black position is so unrepresented even where black political representation still exists. I'm with Morris on this one—I live it. I applauded. Here was an interest that was entirely ours. I don't know what the center will do with its latest data. But for one day, at least, it succeeded in gathering a lot of black people in one place to talk about a subject too little talked about.

PLUGGING IMMIGRATION'S DRAIN ON BLACK EMPLOYMENT

A New Hotel Workers' Union Contract Finally Recognizes That More
Immigration Has Contributed to Fewer Jobs for African Americans

In a city pathologically resistant to its history and permanently enam-
ored of its future, Don Wilson is trying to bridge the gap. There are
many gaps in the L.A. worldview, but this one's bigger than most.
Remember the massive immigrant rights movement? One of the issues
it raised, however briefly, was the effect immigration had on black
employment and whether there was anything to be done about it. This
complicated issue was often reduced to a single question: Are they taking our jobs? This is where Wilson comes in. Wilson has been a hotel
chef for thirty-one years, twenty-seven of them at the Century Plaza
Hotel. Over those three decades, he has seen the workforce go from
substantially African American to overwhelmingly Latino. Last year,
he took a leave of absence to work on the diversity issue for his union,
Unite Here. A couple of weeks ago, the work paid off when the union
signed a new contract with the Beverly Hilton that encourages the hotel
to employ more African Americans. The ethnic-specific requirement
is believed to be a first among union contracts, and one that Wilson
and his union hope will fuel a larger effort to bring blacks back into
the hospitality business. Hotel managers "just stopped hiring us," said
Wilson, fifty, with characteristic bluntness. "We were locked out of
the industry, especially the culinary arts. They went to an immigrant
workforce that they figured had a docile mentality and that wouldn't
put up any resistance. But now we're taking a stand." Though historic, the contract doesn't go as far as setting hiring goals—say, 10 percent of the workforce, or about the same as the percentage of African
Americans in the city's population. Instead, the contract sets up a
committee made up of hotel, union, and community representatives
to monitor black outreach and recruitment efforts; it also calls for an
ombudsman. What's most significant about the clause, however, is that
it's a confirmation of what even the most progressive people have long
been loath to admit: Immigration is one of several factors that contribute to the ongoing crisis of black employment. That doesn't mean
blacks and Latinos are sworn enemies, as the media tend to conclude.
To the contrary, the fact that a Latino-dominated service-sector union
is attempting to adjust numbers that are frankly imbalanced is evidence
that it is concerned about economically challenged African Americans

in South L.A. and elsewhere. Even if the concern is purely political, it's the action that matters, particularly if it results in decent jobs for working-class blacks who have seen decent jobs in their communities evaporate over the last couple of decades. One irony among several is that Unite Here is pushing to share the bounty of its union activism—better wages, greater health coverage—with African Americans who enjoyed those benefits until an influx of immigrants allowed hotels to cut loose workers they viewed as too expensive and, well, too activist. The same thing happened around the same time when downtown building owners decided to replace a chiefly black janitorial staff with a cheaper immigrant staff, which later fought to regain the benefits enjoyed by their black predecessors. Wilson is not surprised that this issue has come full circle. "Blacks have a history of standing up for our rights," he said. "I've seen immigrants regularly do the work of two and three people. We're not going to do that. Nobody should do that. That's not being lazy, that's being tired. There's a difference." Los Angeles County Federation of Labor leader María Elena Durazo says the plan is to get the black recruitment clause in all twenty-five of Unite Here's contracts with local hotels, most of which expire at the end of next month. She says black leaders had been raising concerns about the dearth of black employees in hotel chains—in management positions, not necessarily in service jobs. "It's really important to set an example and show that immigrants are not opposed to African Americans," she said. "We all believe in nondiscrimination. Now we have to get results." Wilson agrees. After years of displacement, he says, blacks now find themselves in a painful predicament. Like any good Angeleno, though, Wilson is focused on the future. He hopes his union will someday make good on a pledge to establish a culinary institute similar to one in Las Vegas. "But that's long range," he said brusquely. "First things first."

10

Race, Real Estate, and the Mexican Mafia

A Report from the Black and Latino Killing Fields

SAM QUINONES

THE STORY OF HOW LATINO STREET GANGS BECAME
SOUTHERN CALIFORNIA'S NEW RACE-HATE CRIMINALS

On the afternoon of December 15, 2006, fourteen-year-old Cheryl Green was talking with friends on Harvard Boulevard, near 206th Street in a tiny working-class L.A. neighborhood in the Harbor Gateway.

The Harbor Gateway is the name given to a strip of Los Angeles that is a few blocks wide and several miles long. The strip is counted as the city, but really it serves only to connect Los Angeles with its port and the communities of San Pedro and Wilmington. The strip's size and the low income of its residents mean that, until that afternoon, it had been largely ignored by most of the city except a few cops.

As Green and her friends talked, two members of a Latino street gang known as 204th Street appeared. One had a gun. Without saying a word, he opened fire at Green and her friends. Bullets wounded three of them, but hit Green in the stomach. Her friends bundled her into a car and sped to a nearby hospital, where she died.

According to testimony in later court hearings, the gang members had had a run-in with a black man in a car, whom they may have threatened and who may have responded by brandishing a gun. (A few nights before, the uncle of a 204th Streeter had been shot and killed in his driveway. There were no suspects, but witnesses said they heard the shooter, who was hooded, yell, "Fuck Mexicans." They couldn't make out his race but believed he was black.)

Outraged, one gang member, Jonathan Fajardo, known as "Mono" or Monkey, ran to a stash house for a gun, then walked through the neighborhood looking for the black man. He was gone, but Fajardo, now accompanied by another gang member, Ernesto Alcarez, spotted the group of black youths, including Green. They walked up, and Fajardo opened fire at Green and her group.

The case remained a minor one until two weeks later, when a *Los Angeles Times* story recounted a history of racist intimidation and murder of black residents at the hands of 204th Street. Indeed, in the days that followed, the media would discover that this kind of thing was not new in Harbor Gateway. Several black men and youths, with no gang affiliation, had been murdered by members of 204th Street, in cases dating to 1997. The 204th Streeters shot at, beat, and insulted blacks, who dared not venture north of 206th Street. Blacks knew never to visit the neighborhood's lone store, the Del Amo Market, at Harvard and 204th.

Many black families feared leaving their apartments and scouted the streets for bald Latinos before going outside. A black contractor had his building firebombed.

In the weeks following Green's death, the media pored over this twelve-square-block, once-forgotten place, until finally, in front of that market where black residents could not shop, authorities held one of the city's largest press conferences in years. FBI director Robert Mueller and Los Angeles mayor Antonio Villaraigosa stood together in front of the Del Amo Market and promised to go after the gang. Standing with them were Charlene Lovett, Green's mother, as well as Sheriff Lee Baca, LAPD chief William Bratton, ATF and DEA agents, L.A. city councilwoman Janice Hahn, and many more. They promised to do more for the neighborhood. Recording it all was a phalanx of reporters and television cameras.

Both the media and the authorities were years late in coming to the Gateway and the larger story it had to tell. I came upon that larger story soon after coming to the *Los Angeles Times* in 2004, after a decade of living in Mexico. I'd been a crime reporter in Stockton from 1988 to 1992 and learned something of the gang situation statewide. Never, from what I'd seen, had black and Latino gangs targeted each other on the street. Now, within months of coming to Los Angeles, I found gangs, Latinos above all, not just targeting black gangs but going after anyone from the other race. I attended a trial for Azusa 13 gang members who went "hunting" blacks and shot a black woman because they couldn't find any men to shoot. I ended up interviewing prosecutors, gang detectives, probation officers, residents of these neighborhoods, and many, many gang members in prison who'd dropped out of their gangs but had years of street history behind them. The more I talked to people about this new racist gang activity, the more the link to prison culture and orders became clear. Gang members described meetings with Mexican Mafia emissaries where these orders were given. Within a few years, RICO (racketeer-influenced and corrupt organizations) indictments alleging this kind of racial harassment in gang garb were issued against gangs in Hawaiian Gardens, Azusa, and Florence-Firestone, among others.

What I learned from all this was that long before the day that Cheryl Green was killed, Latino street gangs had replaced white skinheads as the leading perpetrators of hate crime in Los Angeles County. The Los Angeles County Commission on Human Relations reported this. When they killed or shot at blacks, Latino gangs seemed "to be on a mission," said Robin Toma, director of the commission.

This, I came to learn, was not the result of some racist ideology. Instead it grew from a simple business decision made in the early and mid-1990s. Over the next decade, that decision would have consequences on many Southern California streets. Prison-gang leaders in far-off maximum-security cells were now giving orders to Latino gang members on the street, who followed those orders while never having met the inmates who gave them. This would transform the Latino street gang members into the region's foremost hate criminals. They would create crime waves and race wars and change California prisons.

Once, in areas where Latino street gangs had lived near black people, the gangs usually paid blacks no mind, preferring to focus on rival Latino gangs from other neighborhoods. Then, almost overnight, they began hunting blacks, attacking them, and spraying racist graffiti on their houses.

Over the next decade, black people with no gang affiliation were murdered, and many more were assaulted and harassed. For African Americans, Southern California became a hodge-podge of danger zones—the sign of which was bald Latino youths. By December 15, 2006, a lot of that had coalesced in tiny Harbor Gateway, where Cheryl Green died.

In 2008, Chief William Bratton and Sheriff Lee Baca had a dust-up over whether this kind of gang violence was fueled by drugs and turf battles (Bratton's contention) or by race hatred (as Baca believed). Both were right. The region was dealing with a new kind of hate crime.

Up to then, most people thought they had a clear idea of a hate criminal: He was young, white, and inspired by the writings of Adolph Hitler or some minister from the Idaho outback. The hate criminal who was also a Latino gang member was harder to understand. He often had no ideology beyond what his older homies fresh from prison told him to think. This influence approached a kind of brainwashing not seen in Southern California since the 1970s' heyday of eastern religions and cults. Rarely did that gang member have any books at home; he probably couldn't even identify a swastika. When he rolled up on a bicycle and shot a black man to death, he didn't usually accompany it with a racist insult—as some were reportedly warned not to do by their older homies. So prosecutors often couldn't charge him with a hate crime, and the killing didn't show up in annual hate-crime statistics. It looked like a gang crime, even when the victim had no gang affiliation.

Mingled in this new kind of hate killing and harassment were issues of gang-turf or drug-sale competition. Apart from Villaraigosa, I noticed that Latino politicians rarely touched the topic of Latino gang victimization of blacks. For these reasons, the new hate crime was easily overlooked. Southern California media's hate-crime coverage focused far more on racist graffiti on a synagogue, say, or on white youths who beat up a gay man than it did on the violent Latino street gang members terrorizing black residents in their midst. It took crimes like the murder of Cheryl Green to get them to notice something that had been going on for more than a decade. Even when they finally did pay attention, a lot was made of the small size of this interracial gang-homicide problem. It was true: Most gang killings by far continued to be black-on-black or Latino-on-Latino. Interracial killings were few.

But victims in these interracial killings usually had no gang affiliation and were just going about life: walking home from work, sitting at a bus stop. Yet they were targeted for death, not hit mistakenly by stray bullets. Campaigns of racist harassment and nonfatal violence in the neighborhood preceded their deaths. Plus, their murders crossed cultures and fueled suspicions that each group harbored about the other.

So there didn't need to be many for interracial homicides to cause lingering terror, change daily life, and divide communities far beyond their small numbers. Los Angeles's Harbor Gateway area, for example, averaged fewer than one killing of a black person by a Latino gang member a year between 1997 and 2006. Many more homicides were of and by the same Latino gangs—204th Street, Tortilla Flats, and East Side Torrance—who also feuded among themselves. Yet the interracial murders, and the unprovoked nonfatal shootings by newly paroled 204th Streeters, were enough to keep the neighborhood's black population cowed.

"If they drive by, they say, 'Fuck niggers. You niggers better move,'" said Derek Thomas, a Gateway resident who is young and black and who, by the time of Green's murder, hadn't visited the Del Amo Market three blocks away in a decade.

Between 2004 and 2006 in the Florence-Firestone district, north of Watts, the Latino gang Florencia 13 killed several black men—none of whom had anything to do with the local East Coast Crip sets that by then were dwindling and with whom Florencia was supposedly warring. Black residents stopped walking to the stores and riding bikes. Again, many families moved. Farther east, in Hawaiian Gardens, the Latino VHG gang members killed two black men, firebombed several black families, and shot at numerous other blacks in racist spasms during 1996–97 and in 2003–4. Again, many families moved, and black kids wouldn't even go south of Carson Boulevard, into HG territory.

Nor was this violence always consistent. Only Latino gangs in areas where blacks and Latinos lived together behaved this way. Plus, many Latino gangs' racist activity ebbed when hardcore members were arrested or when feuds with Latino rivals took priority. During those times, relations between blacks and Latinos would return to normal—which is to say not always great but almost never violent. The violence would flare again when hardened members returned to the streets and urged younger ones to "put in work" and "take care of the neighborhood."

Members of a Latino gang that had allowed the numbers of blacks to grow large in its barrio were ridiculed in Los Angeles County Jail. In jail, other gang members "would comment, 'Man, you guys don't even have your own neighborhood,'" one 204th Streeter told me in a 2007 interview. "'The blacks took over your neighborhood.' It's fucking embarrassing, because it's true." They'd hit the streets with renewed determination.

Some observers believed a lot of this had to do with economic competition among two low-income groups. There was some truth to that. But it was also true that none of this violence happened in Northern California,[1] where low-income Latinos and blacks lived together in Stockton, Sacramento, Richmond, Berkeley, Oakland, and San Francisco. Nor did towns in other states—Phoenix, for example—see this kind of interracial violence, though blacks and Latinos lived together.

The story of why all that happened in Southern California is a sweeping tale. It has to do with real estate, with economics, and with the crack epidemic of the 1980s in black enclaves such as Compton, Inglewood, and South-Central Los Angeles. Central to the tale is the influence of state prisons on street life. California's fiercest prison gang, the Mexican Mafia, in a move to profit from street drug dealing, reached beyond prison walls to extend its control over Sureños—Southern California Latino gangs.

But the story begins in the 1970s, long before those events, when Mexican immigrants began to find housing in predominately black areas.

. . .

By the time Latino immigrants began moving to largely black neighborhoods, those areas were spawning Crips and Bloods. The immigrants reported that these gangs constantly robbed them of their wages, sometimes in humiliating ways. One Latino reader wrote me of a robbery his cousins had endured, during which they were made to kneel on the street. They later joined the Florencia 13 gang for protection, he said.

"The truth is that blacks have victimized Hispanics since the beginning," said Richard Valdemar, a retired sheriff's sergeant, who spent much of his career investigating street gangs. But many Latinos were illegal, spoke little English, and didn't know who to turn to. Few reporters and cops spoke Spanish at the time, so the robberies weren't often reported and were publicized hardly at all—making immigrants even easier prey.[2] These crime were usually robberies, but they felt like what would later be called hate crimes. At the time, state law contained few hate-crime statutes. Cops weren't trained to look for hate crimes; the district attorney had no hate-crime prosecutors. There were few politicians Latino immigrants could go to for help. Otherwise, black street gangs might well have been counted as the county's greatest perpetrators of hate crime.

Years later, as Latino gangs gained dominance and began attacking blacks, a Latino reader of the *L.A. Times* e-mailed me, insisting that the violence wasn't racism but "payback." He recounted how immigrant men had to accompany their families to the store in these areas to protect them from black gangs and how they risked humiliation. Many young Mexican men, or the children of immigrants, joined the local Latino gang to protect themselves from black gangs.

Blacks "are more whiners compared to us," said Robert Ramirez, a thirty-one-year-old member of Florencia 13 I interviewed about his gang's attacks on blacks, which he denied were racially motivated. "My mom was robbed five times by blacks when I was growing up." A friend's mother was shot and wounded by black gangs, he said.

Amid all this, black and Latino gangs maintained a balance of power. In many areas, they occupied parallel universes on the same streets, focusing on rivals of their own race in other neighborhoods. "They tended to just ignore one another," said Wes McBride, an L.A. sheriff's gang investigator for many years and president of the California Gang Investigators Association. "There'd be a conflict once in a while, but it wasn't a racial thing."

Several things happened in the 1980s that began to change all that.

First, beginning in about 1983, the Crip Wars kicked off in California prisons. Southern California Latino street gang members in prisons, directed by the Mexican Mafia, warred with Crips in battles that started in Folsom prison, then spread to other facilities. Conflicts between the two sides dated to at least the 1970s, but the Crip Wars of the 1980s were especially ferocious.

One result has been to segregate California prisons in a kind of apartheid. "Zero tolerance towards blacks," is how one Latino gang member described it. Today, the Eme forbids Sureños to drink from water fountains or use telephones blacks have used, to touch blacks, or to accept drugs or cigarettes from blacks.

The Crip Wars solidified anti-black feelings among many Southern California Latino gang members. "That's exactly when [many Emeros] made their reputations," said Anthony "Droopy" Navarro, a Pacoima gang member and former Eme associate. "A lot of them got made. Back then if you picked up a knife and killed a couple or three blacks you became a Big Homie." Gang members brought those attitudes with them to the streets when they were paroled in the early and mid-1990s.

As racial attitudes were hardening inside prison, in Southern California another change was afoot. Interest rates declined from the historical highs of the Carter administration to a point where residential construction could begin again. That ignited a boom in apartment construction. Between 1984 and 1989, more than 211,000 apartment units were built in Los Angeles County alone—by far the most ever in such a short period, according to the local Construction Industry Research Board. (By comparison, some 134,000 units were built over the next seventeen years.)

Demand for housing was heated. Immigrants from the world's hot spots were arriving in Southern California: from Iran and its revolution of 1979; from civil wars in Lebanon and Central America; from Mexico and its "lost decade" of economic decline; from South Korea and its dictatorship; from postwar Southeast Asia. When the Berlin Wall fell in 1989, more migrants came from Eastern Europe.

Apartments went up in neighborhoods of every socioeconomic level in Southern California. But building was especially intense in low-income barrios controlled by gangs with deep connections to the Mexican Mafia—where houses could be bought cheaply and razed. These were entrenched barrios unused to change; families hadn't left them in generations. Many of their men had gone to prison for gang activity. They returned home, veterans of the Crip Wars.

Among the groups benefiting from the new housing were black families escaping the crack-and-gang war zones that Compton, Inglewood, and South-Central L.A. had famously become. They fled in droves. For a while they breathed easier in the new apartments in the Harbor Gateway, Glassell Park, and Highland Park areas of Los Angeles, as well as in Hawaiian Gardens, Duarte, San Bernardino, Azusa, and elsewhere.

The apartment boom ended with the recession of the early 1990s. Now landlords who had apartments in working-class barrios found they couldn't easily fill them. They rented to the tenants they could find: recipients of federal housing subsidies, commonly known as Section 8, many of whom were also black. Meanwhile, under President Bill Clinton and his Housing and Urban Development secretary Henry Cisneros, a new policy took hold at HUD: Section 8 recipients should no longer be packed into dense and notorious housing projects. The projects should be razed and their residents dispersed, allowed to find housing wherever they could.

In Los Angeles, two large housing projects—Normont Terrace and Aliso Village—were transformed into private housing. Section 8 recipients were encouraged to look for housing where they could find it. Among the places they looked were areas dominated by Latino street gangs, where apartments had just gone up in the late 1980s, whose landlords now struggled in the recession and sought any tenant they could find. Moreover, the government paid most of Section 8 recipients' rent, relieving the landlord of the risk.

So by the early 1990s, the situation was the following: Black families, some of whom were gang members, had moved into barrios where houses had just been razed and replaced with apartment buildings. At the same time, into these neighborhoods were paroling Latino gang members fresh from a prison system in which Sureños had just spent a decade warring with blacks.

In the neighborhoods where blacks and Latinos had lived together for years—Compton, Florence-Firestone, and South Central—blacks began leaving. They were replaced by Latinos, often newly arrived Mexican immigrants and their children, some of whom joined the gangs. So by the early 1990s, the balance of power was shifting in favor of Latino gangs.

Then another momentous event took place. The Mexican Mafia began organizing Latino street gangs outside prison walls. Initially, the Eme spun this as their way of calming gang violence—a truce, they said, among Latino gangs. Eme members or their representatives held meetings in parks or houses all across the region. Gang members stood at attention, as a Mafioso or his representative laid down the new laws. The first such meeting, which was filmed, was at Salvador Park in Santa Ana in 1992 and was led by veteran Eme member Peter "Sana" Ojeda. Ojeda stood on the bleachers above some two hundred gang members, many of whom were mortal enemies, and there and again in later orders, told gang members to stop feuding.

"He said, 'You got drug dealers operating in your area who are from Mexico. They didn't die for your neighborhoods, you did,'" said Richard Valdemar, who led the first investigation into the Mexican Mafia's conspiracy to control street gangs. "'You're going to go tax them. That money's yours.'

"'You got to stop the drive-by shootings, because the cops are doing major sweeps and they're disrupting activity.' They'd spread the false rumor that a kid related to a Mexican Mafia member was almost killed in a drive-by.

"Eventually they encouraged their gang members to burn out blacks that lived in their neighborhoods, rob their drug spots."

Other meetings like this one happened across Southern California, often with law enforcement watching.

Members of a younger Eme generation, forged during the Crip Wars, wanted to profit from their prison-gang membership, not content to simply control prison yards. One was a jailed Emero named Rene "Boxer" Enriquez. Taxing drug dealers was easier and more lucrative than selling drugs. The only question was how to collect, particularly from prison. Ojeda's meeting showed that the street gangs of Southern California would do it if so ordered.

"It was like an epiphany, a life-changing moment for the mob,"

Enriquez, now an Eme dropout, told me during interviews I did with him at the state prison in Lancaster. "Sana was the first one we saw put this together."

Thus, the Mafia also ordered gang members to tax neighborhood drug dealers and kick a percentage to Eme members from their areas. Any gang, or dealer, refusing to pay would be "greenlighted"—marked for death. Most gangs knuckled under. A few did not.

Gangs in the Maravilla area of East Los Angeles, for example, held out, proud to be "tax free." Their members were shot at and killed by other gang members and attacked in prison and jail. L.A. County jailers had to segregate them for their own safety.

As of this writing, youth groups from Maravilla still cannot travel to other Latino neighborhoods where the gangs are Eme affiliated. "It did change everything that we were doing here," said Rudy Rodriguez, youth director of the Maravilla Community Foundation, which had to drop the name on its youth basketball uniforms when it played games in other neighborhoods because of the Eme's greenlight. Today, Maravilla kids "are very isolated," Rodriguez told me. "They really can't travel and do as much as they would like. They just nest here. They nest where they're allowed to be."

A series of federal racketeering convictions through the late 1990s sent most of the Eme members who pioneered this system to prison for life. But by then their taxation system—harnessing street gangs as drug-tax collectors—was changing Southern California crime. Mafiosos used women, family members, and friends who came to visit to relay their orders to the streets. Using mime or code, they would pass these orders along through the glass partitions at Pelican Bay State Prison. Or they'd write coded letters to friends, sometimes to their lawyers, sending these orders to the street. Sometimes they'd send out micromessages—"kites," as they are known—hidden in the rectums of inmates paroling from Pelican Bay.

Shotcallers on the streets—known as *llaveros,* or keyholders—were charged with enforcing these orders. The gangs were charged with collecting taxes from local drug dealers—sometimes also prostitutes and street vendors—and funneling the proceeds to the Mafioso's representatives. It was a ragged system at times as a result of unclear communication and a weak chain of command occupied by drug users and criminals.

But the system did at least five things.

First, it brought local gangs under the control of Mafiosos who often hadn't walked their streets since before current members were born.

Second, it gave Eme members a business plan they could apply in order to profit from crime in Southern California Latino barrios, even as they sat in maximum-security cells in Pelican Bay, seven hundred miles away. Third, it allowed the Mafia to create havoc, sometimes crime waves, far from the cells in which they were held, via their orders to street gangs. This happened repeatedly throughout Southern California beginning in the mid-1990s. Fourth, it turned Latino street gangs into retail drug dealers for the first time. Before that, they existed to protect territory and had been heavy drug users, but most didn't sell dope. Eme edicts changed that.

And finally, it poisoned race relations in Southern California and turned Latino street gangsters into hate criminals. Blacks were the drug-dealing competition. In the 1980s, Eme members saw that black gangs seemed to grow rich selling crack, often to Latinos and to Latino gangs. "No buying or selling to blacks," was the Emeros' order to their gang members. The decision was rooted both in business and in years of interracial strife in the prisons.

"'Take care of your neighborhoods; don't let the *mayates* [blacks] move in.' That was part of the gang edicts that was handed down," said Leo Duarte, a gang investigator and Eme expert, now retired from the California Department of Corrections and Rehabilitation. "The Mexican Mafia was encouraging the youngsters to drive these people out, to buy drugs from only their own race."

One ex–Mafia associate from the San Gabriel Valley claims to have been at the prison in Chino in the early 1990s when these orders were being shaped by a group of long-time Mafiosos. (It's hard to document the ex-associate's claims; many of those whom he says were there are now dead or still active gang members. However, CDCR gang investigators at Chino prison say they knew him well. They confirm that he was a close associate of the Eme members with the most influence who passed through the prison during this time. Moreover, Chino prison is a reception center. Parolees come for a few months to serve time; others are about to be paroled. As such, it served then as an underworld communication center from prisons to the street and back.)

In 1993, the ex-gang member said, Eme members and their associates held a series of meetings on the handball court at the Palm Hall section of Chino prison. The meetings, he claims, were facilitated by Shayne Ziska. Ziska was a CDCR guard at Chino during these years and later the prison-guard union representative. (In 2004, Ziska was charged and later convicted of racketeering and conspiracy for working on behalf of the Nazi Low Riders prison gang, an Eme ally, and is now serving seventeen and a half years in prison.)

Passing through Chino prison during these years were numerous Eme members: the Grajeda twins—Tommy and Daniel; Benjamin "Topo" Peters, recognized then as the most influential Eme member; Arturo "Tudi" Estrada, from Cucamonga; Gilbert "Gibby" Cabral, from Redlands; Adrian "Vamp" Salmeron, from Pacoima; Ruben "Indio" Gonzalez, from Banning; and others. The Emeros discussed taxing drug dealers, organizing the gangs. Also "blacks were on the agenda," said the ex-associate, who remains in prison and requested anonymity.

"The order was: Go after any blacks. Everybody is to let their homeboys know that 'ya estuvo' [that's it; that's enough] with the mayates. It's like trying to get rid of a stomach virus—we're trying to get rid of all blacks. Which we can't really do, of course, but we're not thinking that."

At the meetings were Mafia associates—gang members hoping to become full-fledged Eme members. "We were like a handful of seeds that they threw to the wind," said the ex–Mafia associate. "Some of us land in Compton, some in Puente, some in Coachella." An LAPD internal memo in 1993 reported on one Eme-led gang meeting at Ebby Park, in Hollenbeck Division, and warned of an impending race war between Latinos and blacks. The ex–Mafia associate said he was later paroled and spent part of 1995 and 1996 on the street. He said he organized meetings of gang members, instructing them to name representatives to inform the younger members of the new rules about drug taxing and drive-by shootings.[3]

Among the rules: "If there's any mayates in the barrios, they got to go, because they're taking our profit. This was meant to apply to anyone selling—Crips and Bloods. It was never meant to go after the little kids. Then that changed." Meanwhile, street gang members on parole, fresh from the Crip Wars, had been talking to younger children in the barrios. "We start telling our families, 'Don't let me catch you fucking with them niggers,'" he said.

• • •

Yet as it happened, this was not the first example on the streets of Eme-ordered attacks on blacks.

That took place a few years before, in the mixed-race working-class East Side of Riverside.

Two gangs there—the Tiny Dukes and the 1200 Blocc Crips—had

gotten along for years, while feuding with rivals of their own races from other parts of Riverside.

In 1990, both gangs were feuding with cross-town rivals.

The 1200 Blocc Crips "came to us and said, 'Why don't we get together?' We said, 'Yeah, let's have a meeting,'" said Ignacio Chavez, a Tiny Dukes member.

So they did, three times, in Bordwell Park. There, they organized commando raids on rival parts of town. Fifteen of them commemorated one meeting by etching their monikers into a wet slab of concrete at the park.

Word of this alliance got back to an Eme member—Ruben "Indio" Gonzalez—then in Riverside County Jail.

"Indio told the Tiny Dukes to sever the ties with the blacks," said Leo Duarte, a CDCR gang investigator at Chino prison at the time. But no one in the Tiny Dukes' younger generation had been to prison. Few felt that a prison gang had any rights over the street. The gang's leader, Jesus "Sleepy" Espinoza overruled Indio's order.

"We figured that we were on the street and they were in prison, so how could they have any authority over us," Chavez, the Tiny Dukes gang member, told me in a telephone interview in 2005.

The night of the mission, a mixed-race car of East Siders shot at and missed a Crip from the West Side. A second mixed-race car shot and killed a Latino boy in another neighborhood.

The boy's killing sparked what is still the largest gang prosecution in Riverside County. Using that slab of concrete at Bordwell Park, police compiled a list of gang members who attended that night. Eventually, thirty-two members of the two gangs were convicted of or pleaded guilty to charges ranging from murder to conspiracy.

Meanwhile, from Riverside County Jail, "Indio" Gonzalez placed a greenlight on the Tiny Dukes.

Soon, Tiny Dukes in prison across California were being beaten and stabbed. "Our own members would send word to us that it was for real; these guys weren't playing," said Chavez. "Nobody had ever heard of a greenlight. It's common knowledge now. It wasn't then."

Riverside County jailers had to set up a separate cell block to house Tiny Dukes from other Latino gang members, who attacked them. As Tiny Dukes began to plead guilty, some insisted the agreement include tattoo removal so they couldn't be identified in prison.

Leo Duarte remembers several Tiny Dukes huddled together at the Chino prison reception center.

"They all told me the same story," Duarte said. "They said, 'We listened to the president [Espinoza]. We weren't thinking that we were going to go to prison.'"

Finally, the Eme set conditions to lift the Tiny Dukes' greenlight. One was to kill Espinoza, the gang president. Another was to rid the area of East Coast Crips, say gang members, Duarte, and Riverside police gang officers.

"We were happy to have had a condition, because supposedly there is no getting a greenlight off yourself when you get it," Chavez said.

A short time later, "Sleepy" Espinoza was found shot to death in a car near Patterson Park in Riverside.

"This is the way it works," said Duarte. "The Mexican Mafia reaches out with orders and says you kill your own leader; once you cleanse yourself, then target the blacks."

The Tiny Dukes went from a gang that allied with blacks to a gang that attacked any black man it saw, say Riverside police.

At first, their attacks were only on 1200 Blocc Crips, said Frank Assuma, a Riverside police gang sergeant, in a 2005 interview. "Then it evolved to any black gang members—1200 Blocc or not. Eventually, which is where we stand now, it was all black people, period. That's been since 1996 on."

For a while, Riverside police saw teams of Tiny Dukes on bicycles, some with two-way radios, scouting out and coordinating hits on blacks, Assuma said. In one case, they shot two black men on a bench waiting for a bus.

The gang's animosity toward blacks comes and goes. "There's always that flicker," Assuma said. "Every now and again, somebody will get out of prison and throw gasoline on it."

Tiny Dukes, like many other Latino gang members, insist they are not racist but only gunning for gang rivals who happen to be black. Chavez recorded a rap record, with one song urging his homies to hang 1200 Blocc members from trees, but said he harbored no ill will against black people.

"They may say they don't hate blacks and all that," said Assuma. "But what they do is shoot at blacks, beat up blacks, write '187 Niggers' on the wall. Actions speak a lot louder than words."

Years later, the effects of the fateful alliance between the Tiny Dukes and 1200 Blocc Crips were still being felt.

"I had no clue, when I was handling the case, of the long-term ramifications on the street," said John Davis, the deputy district attorney who prosecuted members of both gangs. "Some of them are horrific, but it's a little peek into the inner workings of the prison system and how the prison system dictates what happens on the outside."

. . .

Through the 1990s, orders like those given by Indio Gonzalez, and later the Emeros at the prison in Chino were disseminated to gangs throughout Southern California at meetings similar to those held by Ojeda in Orange County.

One by one, Latino street gangs submitted to the new regime. In 1994, two veteran Eme members—Frankie Buelna and Raymond "Huero" Shryock—held a meeting for San Gabriel gang members at Legg Lake. "They said, 'Instead of killing your own people, why don't you go kill those mayates and move them out of your neighborhood?'" said a gang member who said he attended the meeting.

One who said he helped organize that Legg Lake meeting was a gang member who goes by the moniker "Midget," from Lomas Rosemead. Midget had gone to county jail in 1990. There, he said, he was among a group of young gang members whom jailed Emeros recruited to run drugs to newly arrived Emeros coming in hooked on heroin.

County jail was then a place of criminal effervescence, made possible by lax vigilance. Selling drugs was easy then. Numerous Emeros passed through. They held discussions on how to modernize the Mafia, how to profit from their fearsome reputation.

"They were trying to figure out how they were going to get their power out to the streets," Midget told me in an interview at Avenal State Prison in 2006. "The county is producing a lot of money. Some of them were getting pulled back down from Pelican Bay to county because they wanted to make money.[4] This is showing them that all the money and power is coming from the streets."

By 1992, Midget was in Pelican Bay, on a tier with Eme lifers. "I was the only person [on the tier] who was going to parole for the next ten years," he said. "For six months before I go home, they're talking to me in front of my cell. I learned codes for names, phones, neighborhoods, brothers on the street, addresses for safe houses, wives. They wanted every neighborhood together, every gang member to get along and start thinking about money.

"At that point I was willing to hurt anybody for them. There were no limits at all. I would even have sacrificed myself. My girlfriend recognized it immediately when I came home. She said, 'You're a robot.

You don't belong to me no more.' She knew my love for her came second to them."

On the streets, numerous gang members who questioned or resisted the new rules were killed, he said. Years later, Midget remembered with amazement the power the Eme members, and he as their associate, wielded among the gangs.

Pomona's Cherryville gang had been greenlighted for several years for having killed an Eme member named Speedy. "We tell Cherryville that in order for the greenlight to come off, seven guys [in the gang] have to die. They were given a list," Barron said. "They killed who they had to kill. For some of them it took longer than for others, but they did it."

Meanwhile, Midget said, the *carnales* were issuing orders regarding blacks. "The first thing we were going to do was get rid of blacks," he said. "It was all for money. For three months it was every day, all day, something of that nature. It was said like this: 'If we're going to work as a team, then those areas that have blacks in the neighborhood, they need to be removed.' Shoot them, beat them, it didn't matter. Almost every day for three months. Some gangs were sharing territory with the blacks. They were told to disperse the blacks."

This message didn't concern Latino gangs in areas where blacks were few—for example, in East Los Angeles and in Orange, San Diego, and large parts of Ventura Counties. Indeed, it showed that this racism was due to Eme influence and not to some deeper ideology that in barrios with no blacks, gangs have no history of attacking blacks anywhere.

Rather, it took place in two general areas: barrios where blacks moved in in noticeable numbers, mostly into apartments built in the late 1980s; and neighborhoods where the two races had coexisted but where the balance of gang power was now shifting. Beginning in the mid-1990s, these Latino gangs were now given to spasms of racist attacks.

In neighborhoods where blacks and Latinos had lived together for years, Latino and black gangs suddenly faced off. In Compton, Tortilla Flats, and Fruittown Pirus, gangs that had lived in peace for twenty-five years went to war. So, too, did the Lueders Park Crips and the CV70 gang; Rancho San Pedro and Dodge City Crips, in San Pedro; and Venice 13 and Shoreline Crips, in Venice. A few years later, East Coast Crips and Florencia 13 would begin a war that lasted about a decade.

"It kind of caught us flat-footed when it started," said Wes McBride, the L.A. sheriff's gang investigator. "We were looking for some gang connection [to these killings and shootings]. Generally speaking, [black and Latino gangs] had ignored one another. So these [crimes] didn't even make sense in the gang world. They shot a guy because he was black, or Hispanic. Some of the shootings came down to it having to be a racist thing. It became obvious that it was racist."

"If you look at the history of Latino and black gangs, they got along," said Al Valdez, an investigator with the Orange County district attorney's office and author of a book on Los Angeles street gangs. "[But] we in law enforcement saw a major, well-defined polarization between groups that normally tolerated each other."

Keith Volm, an Ontario police officer, had just transferred to his department's gang unit in 1994 when the change happened. After years of existing to protect territory, Ontario gangs suddenly seemed much more interested in dealing drugs. "The territory was no longer as important as going out and making money from selling drugs," Volm said, in a telephone interview with me in 2005. "Protecting the territory didn't make you money. The money was being funneled to the big boys."

Even more startling, Volm said, was that Latino gang members now began attacking black people on the street. The first case involved two gang members from Ontario Varrio Sur who drove the streets one night looking for African Americans to shoot—eventually wounding three. "It was all at once," said Volm. "We started seeing a huge increase in Latino gang members shooting black people, generally not black gang members."

Volm and his colleagues learned through interviews with gang members that Eme associates had held a meeting at Prado Regional Park, in Chino Hills, to announce the new rules to Inland Empire gangs. Before that meeting, Volm said, "you didn't see the Hispanic gangs in Ontario having a problem with black people. They coexisted. Race was never an issue up to that time. Then race became an issue."

. . .

Latino gangs across Southern California began campaigns to rid their areas of blacks. Mark Fernandez, who is a member of the La Puente Blackwood gang and is now serving life in prison for murder, described his gang's situation in the years before the Mafia meetings: "My gang was getting along with [blacks] real good." But after the meetings, he said they "would like go hunting." "We'd go shoot up the projects in West Covina where they lived. We'd just go out there and shoot as many as we could till the cops came."

For some multigenerational gangs, Mexican Mafia orders to "clean the neighborhood" were unnecessary. The Avenues gangs in northeast Los Angeles had five members in the Eme, including one of the master-minds of taxation, Alex "Pee-Wee" Aguirre, who'd been made a member in state prison amid the Crip Wars of the 1980s. Generations of young men from the Avenues had been in and out of prison. "We didn't need anybody to tell us what to do," said Jesse Diaz, a Highland Park gang member. Diaz testified in court that his Avenue 43 clique watched as houses were razed and apartments erected during the late 1980s. Blacks moved in. Suddenly the neighborhood didn't feel theirs, Diaz said. "We didn't want them in the neighborhood making it look like South Central," he testified.

Avenues gang members spoke often about this state of affairs. They mounted campaigns of harassment that included insults, racist graf-fiti, and violence, Diaz said. "It was always, 'Those fucking niggers are moving in,'" he said. "We got to go put work in—whatever it takes: beating them up, shooting them, killing them. I yelled racial slurs all the time, whenever I'd come across them."

Eventually, U.S. prosecutors convicted four members of the Avenue 43 street gang for conspiracy to deprive African Americans in Highland Park of their civil rights. This included the murders of two men—Kenneth Wilson and Christopher Bowser. Wilson was gunned down while parking his car on Fifty-Second Street late one night in August 1999. Bowser was shot to death in December 2000.

The federal indictment alleged that the gang's campaign included robberies, beatings and pistol whippings, racial slurs, and confronta-tions. Gang members drew an outline of a human body in front of one man's home and released a German shepherd on him.

The Eme meetings were "like gasoline on the fire for us," explained a member of the Azusa 13 gang who is now incarcerated but asked not to be identified, fearing for his family. He said he had attended the Legg Lake meeting run by Buelna and Shryock but reported that Azusa 13 was "already thinking that way before" the meeting, although he added, "The meetings just made us do it more. Other San Gabriel gangs picked up the racist activity after the meetings: Pomona 12th Street, Baldwin Park, El Monte Flores, Puente. El Monte Flores wouldn't let nobody move in who was black."

The quiet suburb of Azusa (population: forty-seven thousand) had never had many hate crimes before the Eme began organizing Latino street gangs. But in the mid-1990s, Azusa 13 was amid a generational change. Veterans had been imprisoned in the early 1990s. The gang was relatively quiet for a few years. By the end of the decade, a younger generation of the gang was coming up, looking to make a name. When a couple of Eme associates were paroled from prison, hate crimes soared in the late 1990s and early in the first decade of the 2000s.

"We believe that that's the genesis" for the violence and hate crime the town had, said Sam Gonzalez, then an Azusa police captain. "Those directives make their way out to the street. People on the street want to make a name for themselves."

The gang in Azusa's twenty-square-block barrio, just north of the 210 freeway, had been around since the 1950s, consuming each generation of young men in turn. The barrio was an insular place, where families intermarried, and people didn't often leave. Many families had men who were locked up and were now paroling.

"Like the family teaches you to pray before a meal, they're teaching us to be racial," said one ex–gang member who grew up in the Azusa barrio and asked not to be identified. "They go in [to prison] with the strong dislike for black people; they come out with a strong hatred."

A few hundred blacks had moved into Azusa by the mid-1990s; some were gang members from other areas, possibly seeking a new start. Most were not. Azusa gang members had always been raised to see themselves as barrio defenders. In the late 1990s, the emerging generation of Azusa 13 began harassing, then attacking Azusa's black population. Quickly they targeted anyone black, particularly any black male.

Hate crimes spiked to seventeen in 2000 and another nine in 2001. These included three simultaneous firebombings of African American houses one night. Gejuan Salle, a twenty-four-year-old nurse at Cedar Sinai Hospital, was shot to death in Azusa while walking into an Auto Zone store—an unsolved crime that police believe was a rite of induction for new Azusa 13 members.

Then in early 2002, two Mafia associates—Gabriel "Downer" Aguilar and Robert "Thumper" Ramirez—were paroled to Azusa. They began organizing the gang to tax local drug dealers. Azusa police believe both men were acting on authority of Jacques "Jacko" Padilla, the Mexican Mafia member reputed to control Azusa gangs and drug dealing from his maximum-security cell—though Padilla denied that when I interviewed him several years later, after he had dropped out of the Mexican Mafia. For a time, Aguilar lived on a tier with Padilla at Pelican Bay State Prison, enhancing his reputation on Azusa streets, say police and prison officials.

Padilla "was a God-like figure" to Azusa 13, said the ex–gang member. "We don't really say his name. You say Big J or Big Homie."

Historically, Azusa usually had only one or two homicides a year. In 2002 it had six. In the trial of Aguilar, Ramirez, and three others, an Azusa 13 gang member named Eduardo Caballo testified that the gang would routinely go "hunting" black people. One night in September 2002, finding no black men to shoot, they shot forty-nine-year-old Nadine Nowlin in the back. Nowlin, a black woman standing outside her apartment saying good night to a friend, lost her spleen but lived to testify in the case.

Quiet little Azusa became known as the "Hate Crime Capital of the San Gabriel Valley." The city formed a hate-crime task force, then a Human Relations Commission. It began an annual "Hands across Azusa" multicultural celebration on Martin Luther King Jr.'s birthday.

Azusa police, meanwhile, opened a store called A Peace of Africa, stocked with African goods and staffed with undercover black officers, in the hopes of enticing the gang into committing a hate crime. Police staked it out around the clock but had to close it after a week. "I'm sure we'd have seen a hate crime committed," had officers been able to keep the store running longer, said Gonzalez. "But it was too labor intensive and too dangerous because of the hunting mentality" of Azusa 13.

Those few years in Azusa showed how orders or influence from prison could create crime waves and affect budgets and resources in a normally peaceful town. It took the arrest of just eight gang members in 2003 and 2004 for the violence to stop. They were sentenced to long prison terms. Today, Azusa averages its normal one homicide a year and virtually no hate crimes.

Meanwhile, in Pacoima another Eme-inspired race war was underway. Blacks and Latinos had lived together in Pacoima for many years. Then in the mid-1990s, Eme orders came down, just as black gang members from Compton were moving in to sell crack, along with many black families looking for an escape from the crack-and-gang nightmare that Compton had become.

Eme member Adrian "Vamp" Salmeron ignited a war with black gangs that quickly grew to target the general black population, said his cousin, Anthony "Droopy" Navarro, the Pacoima gang member now on death row. Navarro said he worked closely with his cousin during these years. He said Salmeron held meetings at Dexter Park, near a cemetery in Lopez Canyon. At times, more than two hundred gang members attended from Canoga Park, Pacoima, San Fernando, and elsewhere, Navarro said.

"They said, 'It's open season on all blacks.' That's when the homies went at it with the blacks in San Fernando Gardens [housing project]," Navarro told me in an interview. "A lot of homies died behind what he did, righteous homies. There were a lot of blacks we grew up with. Once that greenlight came out, it was like, forget that we grew up playing with Big Wheels together. We should have just made peace with the blacks and made money together. But Vamp wasn't having it, because Vamp was old school. I would tell Vamp, 'We got cousins that are Crips—half black, half Mexicans.' Vamp was like, 'It has to happen. It's coming down from above.'"

Rudy Puebla, a Humphrey Boyz gang member now in prison, remembers gang meetings during these years. "Big guys connected to the Big Homies [a term for Mafia members] would attend from time to time," Puebla said. "They'd say, 'Why are you going to let these Bloods walk into our neighborhood and write their neighborhood on the walls?' They told us we had to take care of business. We already knew what we had to do."

The Humphrey Boyz gang, claiming the area around Humphrey Park in Pacoima, proved especially violent. Salmeron provided the gang guns, and "they went commando," Navarro said. "At one point, innocent people were getting hurt. Old men sitting at bus stops were getting shot."

Meanwhile, Salmeron tried to establish alliances with Latino gangs from other parts of Los Angeles. Navarro said he and Salmeron met with members of the Avenues cliques to discuss "hit exchanges": each gang would do hits on blacks in the other's barrio to make the crimes harder to investigate. The gangs exchanged guns they'd each used in crimes, but that was as far as the alliance got, he said.

The war "went on for a year or so, off and on," said Navarro. "Sometimes Vamp would get the upper hand. Sometimes the blacks would. It died out after Vamp got busted."

Salmeron was killed in 1997. But black residents felt a lasting change. "Around 1994, 1995, that's when it really started getting bad," said Susan Jackson, a mother who moved to Lake View Terrace from South-Central Los Angeles in 1990 to escape gang violence, when I spoke to her in 2005. "Before that, it was mixed race, but there wasn't that many problems. Today, it's not safe. I'm terrified in my own house."

The Humphrey Boyz continued the fight well into the 1990s. The gang actually imposed a 10 P.M. curfew on African Americans in Pacoima, black residents said. "We were just open targets, anyone out after 10 o'clock," said Miecko Reilly, a resident who has moved from Pacoima because of the Eme-inspired attacks on African Americans.

In 1997, two youths, Gerard Harris and Demetrius Fears, were gunned down. Neither had any gang affiliation. Fears was shot while going into a 7–Eleven the night after his first day on a construction job. Two Humphrey Boyz gang members—Bulmaro Huerta and Rudy Puebla—were convicted of his murder.

(In an interview, Puebla said he was driving the car with some of his homies that night. They stopped in the 7–Eleven just as the store was closing. Fears was there as well. Puebla said he thought Huerta was going to buy beer. "Then I heard three shots. I ducked. I didn't even know he had a gun," Puebla said.)

The gang also faced off with black Juneteenth celebrants in Dexter Park in Sylmar that year. In 1999 at Humphrey Park in Pacoima, a cheerleading competition among black girls was run off when the Humphrey Boyz gang opened fire at the girls. "I had to pick my daughter up in the stroller and start running down the street," said Miecko Reilly. Again, Pacoima interracial homicides were few, but not many were needed to poison interracial relations. Even years after Salmeron's war, Pacoima blacks know where they cannot walk.

In San Bernardino during these years, a similar war broke out between West Side Verdugo and the Crips, largely on orders from Eme members in Pelican Bay prison. Their representative was Armando Ibarra. Ibarra, known as Chunkie, had grown up in the entrenched barrio on San Bernardino's west side, known as West Side Verdugo. "I grew up with nothing but blacks," he said. "We used to sell dope together. We used to get high together."

In the 1980s, Latino and black gangs from San Bernardino often worked together against gangs of both races moving in from Los Angeles. Once, some long-time San Bernardino Crips whom Ibarra knew even saved his life at a gas station when he was cornered by some Latino rivals from Los Angeles. But then he'd gone to Folsom prison, run a yard for the Eme there, and become fully drenched in Eme-ordered racism.

"It just gets into you," he said. "You could be sitting with two homies and they see some black guy walk by, and they say, 'You know what, fuck mayates.' You're not going to say, 'No, he's cool.' You're like, 'Yeah, fuck blacks.'"

In 1996, Ibarra said he was in Pelican Bay on the same tier as Mike Lerma, an Eme member from Pomona. Lerma and another Mafioso, Raul "Huero Sherm" Leon, schooled him for months in who their contacts were on the outside, Ibarra said, so that the neighborhoods could be organized in order to tax dealers. Ibarra said he was paroled with his rectum packed with "kites"—tiny notes—from Lerma explaining to gang members on the street that they were to take orders from Ibarra, who was now the Mafia's representative.

"They wanted me to take control of all the drug movement—all the dope and all the money to go to them and the barrios," he said. Much of the focus was on getting rid of blacks who controlled the drug dealing in the area. "They said, 'At all costs. Kill them, rob them, whatever,'" Ibarra told me in an interview at the state prison in Lancaster.

Ibarra held meetings at San Bernardino's Nunez Park one busy Sunday afternoon when it was filled with families and kids, and two hundred gang members wouldn't stand out. Gangs from Fontana, Rialto, Colton, Redlands, and San Bernardino attended, he said. He and an Eme member known as Stranger, from Rockwood, told the gang members the neighborhoods would be organized in order to tax drug dealers. "The shot callers said, 'The blacks got it all sewed up,'" Ibarra said. "I said, 'We'll see about that.'"

Over the next six months, Ibarra said, his cohorts held commando-style raids on Crip drug houses. "Our goal was to find the dope, the money, and the guns and take it," he said. "It was a business move."

The San Bernardino war, lasting six months, was typical of how drug competition, gang issues, and race mixed until motivation was impossible to sort out. As the war intensified, the restriction on hitting only black gang members dissolved, and it became a race war. One night, West Side Verdugo divided into carloads to stage an orchestrated hit on five black gangs. "At 9 P.M., anything that was black was getting shot," Ibarra said.

In March 1997, Ibarra was returned to prison on a parole violation, and the war, as well as the taxation, began to fade. At Chino prison, rumor circulated that he'd stolen eighty-seven thousand dollars from the Eme. He denied it then and does so still. But the Eme had no fact-checking department, so he was greenlighted. He dropped out soon after.

· · ·

Having recounted all this, I think it's important here to add a caveat or two. The Mexican Mafia's name conjures up visions of immense and monolithic control. Indeed, on the streets and in prison, the group inspires both shuddering fear and blind devotion that borders on brainwashing. But the group really has only one talent: it kills people—in prison and, as the 1990s wore on, on the streets as well. This, more than anything, kept what passed for order among gang members, who knew they would likely end up in prison one day.

The Mafia's strength is due to the obedience of thousands of gang members in prison and on the streets. One reason for this was Pelican Bay State Prison. The prison segregated the most predatory inmates. But because of that, street gangs never saw them. So Eme reputations on the street grew and inspired slavish devotion. Gang members wrote to them in the most obsequious language.

In reality, many Emeros were withered, hunched old men. They were pasty, from having lived without sunlight for years. Some were half crazy from the isolation. Touring Pelican Bay maximum-security tiers, the Eme resembles *The Wizard of Oz*—where a frumpy con man handles the controls behind the great and magnificent wizard.

But street gang members never saw these men and didn't know that. They killed on the orders of Mafiosos they'd never met. As years passed, neighborhood gang members who once displayed deep unity and loyalty toward one another began kill one another on Eme orders.

One famous example was the "Dead Presidents" case in West Side San Bernardino in July 2000. Gang members from two West Side cliques killed their own presidents—brothers Johnny and Gilbert Agudo—on what prosecutors believed were orders from a local Mafioso, Salvador "Toro" Hernandez.

Mark Fernandez, the gang member from La Puente Blackwood, told me he executed Richard Mechaca on orders from the gang's shot caller, whom he took to be taking orders from Frankie Buelna—known as "Frankie B"—the Mafioso who controlled the area. Fernandez said he'd met Buelna only once and that he'd been friends with Mechaca since kindergarten. Mechaca was even living with Fernandez's family after his own family had thrown him out.

It didn't matter. "Frankie B shot word to the street saying this guy's got to go," Fernandez said in an interview at Avenal State Prison. "[Mechaca] was my best friend since we were kids. But my crimey got the word and asked me if I would do it. I said 'Yeah, no problem.'

"We just took him for a ride. I wanted to do things for [the Eme]. That was always my goal—to be a Big Homie. It didn't matter what

Richard Mechaca had done. . . . Later, I heard that he was in debt, or his family was in debt, to Frankie B or somebody that worked for Frankie B."

Despite holding such fearsome power over young minds, the Eme could also be laughably inept. I sat in on the trial of three Pomona 12th Street members in 2008 that showed this. The gang members were ordered to plan and carry out the killing of Buelna, who other Emeros had come to believe was working with federal authorities.

Investigators followed the plot on cell-phone wiretaps. The gang members were often drunk, couldn't find a car, had to babysit. In a comedy of errors involving almost two hundred phone calls, three gang members, a couple Mafia associates, and an Emero couldn't figure out how to kill one man who frequently walked about Pomona alone. In one wiretap a woman is overheard calling them a bunch of clowns and joking that they should give her a gun and she'd go kill Buelna.

(Buelna, ironically, was shot to death in November 2007, a year after the gang members had been arrested and were by then awaiting trial. His death appeared to have been the result of a simple fight at a Pomona sports bar. Whatever the motive, his murder is unsolved.)

Moreover, the Eme's taxation system often generates paltry income. Gang members routinely collect fifty dollars, a ten-year-old Grand Marquis, or jewelry when they make the rounds for Mafiosos. Eme member Francisco "Puppet" Martinez ran a lucrative and well-organized operation using the gangs around MacArthur Park before he and many of them were convicted of conspiracy in 2001. But taxing operations can just as easily be low-budget affairs, run by drug addicts and connivers who live in motels and eat at McDonald's.

Plus, Pelican Bay prison restricts Eme contact with the world. Wives and girlfriends have become their go-betweens. (Some of these women have grown to have huge power on the street.) But Mafiosos also need shot callers on the streets to enforce their orders. When a shot caller goes to prison—which frequently happens, as they're also drug users and on parole—the Mafioso's control fades until another is found.

Furthermore, the Eme is not a top-down corporation. It resembles a street gang—with everyone equal and some exerting more influence than others. It is, in a strange way, a quintessentially American organization. Each Mafioso can use his membership to display his own (criminal) talents. Some Mafiosos have had great business dreams; others have had none.[5] But there is no president, no chain of command.

In fact, Mafiosos hate one another. Isolated in Pelican Bay, they plot against one another constantly. Many of them are heroin addicts, which also affects their abilities and judgment.

Street gangs haven't always been within Mafia influence, either. Some barrios have knuckled under for a while, then a Mafia representative is sent to prison again, and the gang returns to following local orders only. Often, too, street gangs are unsophisticated, undisciplined forces—particularly as the use of methamphetamine has spread.

For all these reasons, Latino gangs did not rise up as one and continually target blacks all over Southern California. The Eme's control hasn't been that monolithic. The violence has been prone to spasms; it comes and goes, then comes again.

. . .

Meanwhile, the balance of power between black and Latino gangs was shifting in areas where the two had coexisted for years.

Florence-Firestone had been a black enclave since the 1960s. Latinos began arriving in large numbers in the early 1990s as blacks sold and moved east to the Inland Empire and Las Vegas. By the late 1990s, an area that had been 80 percent black was 90 percent Latino. The area's main black gang, the East Coast Crips, declined. Once at least eight large ECC sets studded the streets east of the 110 Freeway from downtown Los Angeles to Watts. By the late 1990s, only the 89th Street set of the East Coast Crips existed.

Then a story circulated through the neighborhood: East Coast Crips had robbed a Florencia 13 drug connection of some dope, which may have belonged to a member of the Mexican Mafia. What drug was it, and in what quantity? When? Where? Did it even happen? It's hard to know. "You hear so many different variations of this crime," said Terry Burgin, a sheriff's gang detective, in an interview in 2007. "Who knows what really happened? [But] the effects are tremendous."

The story—true or not—ignited a war between East Coast and Florencia. Both gangs shot mostly people of the opposite race who had no gang involvement. The death balance appeared weighted toward Florencia, which, with two thousand members was at least five times larger than the East Coast Crips. The worst of it occurred in 2005. The unincorporated area registered forty-one homicides that year, triple the worst city homicide rate elsewhere in America. Homicides dropped to nineteen in 2006—still an enormous number for a community of sixty thousand people.

Arthur Stewart, a local pastor, said he remembers in 1999 watching in terror as Latino gang members drove by brandishing weapons and firing at blacks. "That was startling," Stewart told me. "I'd never seen it before." Within a few years, black male members of Stewart's congregation would report that bald Latino youths had threatened them, shot at them, yelled insults from cars.

By 2007, parts of Florence-Firestone were known to be off-limits for black men. This included Superior, the area's only supermarket, at Compton Boulevard and Florence Avenue, and the car wash near Florence and Maie. Yet, strangely, this war almost didn't happen. Indeed, the gangs had resisted outside pressures to go to war, says one gang member active in Florencia in the 1990s. Like many black and Latino gangs, they ignored one another during the late 1980s and early 1990s, while attacking rivals of their own race.

But during the mid 1990s, Eme orders hit the street. Florencia, in particular, had warred for years with 38th Street, a Latino gang to the north. Under the new Mafia rules, Florencia was now forced to get along with rival Latino gangs and even play a pickup football game with 38th Street, said the Florencia gang member active during those years, who requested anonymity fearing for his safety. The Eme "didn't understand how it worked," he told me in an interview. "I hate 38th Street. I didn't have no problem with the guys from East Coast because I grew up with them. It's kind of hard to say, 'Now I'm going to . . . kill this black guy just because he's black.' But that's how they wanted to do it."

In 1996, tensions erupted when members of the 6–5 Hustlers, a gang associated with East Coast Crips, killed a Florence member. After some retaliation, the gangs held a peace summit at Parmelee Elementary School one night, and that "kind of squashed everything," said the gang member. Then rumors of the fabled drug rip-off ignited it anew, not to be stopped.

In 2007, federal prosecutors indicted 102 members of Florencia 13, accusing them, among other things, of targeting blacks in the area. They alleged that the violence was due to a plan by Arturo "Tablas" Castellanos—the Eme member who controlled Florencia from his maximum-security cell in Pelican Bay State Prison—to organize Florencia and halt rampant in-fighting.

In court, prosecutors produced a letter from Castellanos as well, ordering Florencia gang members to unite. He ordered that each clique choose a president and vice president "by majority vote" and that the leaders hold weekly meetings to ensure that cliques respect the rules. Castellanos's letter said that when problems arose within the gang, the gang members should "box it out like real Florencianos."

Castellanos also ordered Florencia to tax Mexican drug dealers, as well as prostitutes and vendors of phony ID cards. Each of Florencia's cliques was to pay three hundred dollars a month, he wrote. That money was to be divided: 40 percent among the gang's tax-collecting crews; 20 percent to women in the gang to pay for post-office boxes, cell phones, and other expenses; and 40 percent for the three Mafia members from Florencia: Castellanos, his brother, Braulio, also in Pelican Bay, and Juan "Topo" Garcia, serving a life term in federal prison for racketeering. It was a remarkable display of attempted Eme control from a man who hadn't stepped foot in the neighborhood since 1980.

Enrique Villegas, a Florencia dropout who testified for the prosecution, said he was standing in his gang territory one day when another gang member approached with copies of Castellanos's rules. He was skeptical of the rules' origin but later came to believe Castellanos had written them. Villegas said he went to two meetings, including a large one at Roosevelt Park, where Florencia leaders explained the rules. Among those rules, Castellanos ordered Florencia to unite against the "Cripos"—the East Coast Crips—"to blast at them . . . to go shoot them," Villegas testified. "Take over block by block. Take them out of our neighborhood." Thus, beginning in late 2004, the area erupted in violence.

Any nuances to Castellanos's orders were lost, and the Florencia gang members eventually interpreted them to mean they should shoot any black man near East Coast Crip territory. Indeed, several black men with no gang ties were shot, including a few who died, for being in a Crip area. In one 2004 case, two Florencia gang members shot and killed Marlon Miller, a waiter from Jamaica who lived in Santa Monica and was buying cigarettes at a gas station in the area as he drove a coworker home. According to court testimony, the gang members were hiding behind a Dumpster. The older gang member prodded the younger one to shoot Miller, saying he knew Miller was a Crip and would make sure other gang members knew the younger one had not followed orders. The younger one demurred, saying he'd never seen the man before, but finally pointed the rifle and fired. In another July 2005 shooting, Florencia gang members shot at a group of African Americans who had gathered at a home after a funeral.

East Coast Crips also killed Latinos with no gang affiliation. Gabino

Lopez, fifty-two, a Latino man off work and going to a store for a beer, was shot and killed by a Crip for no reason other than he was Latino. Indeed, investigators say that most of the victims of that gang war were blacks and Latinos with no connection to gangs. But the violence was mostly the work of Florencia.

According to cell-phone calls introduced as evidence in the trial, Florencia gang members seemed to be hunting for black people to shoot. In one July 2005 cell-phone call introduced as evidence, gang member Noe "Lil Black" Gonzalez told another, "Somebody got to be a victim around [here]," as he drove the area looking for someone to shoot. The Florence-Firestone war illustrated the new state of affairs in Southern California.

Deputy District Attorney Olivia Rosales was sent to the neighborhood in 2005 to prosecute gang-war cases. "I grew up watching the results of the civil rights movement: MLK, the 1960s," she said in an interview in 2007. "When you get to hate crime, you think you're going to get Nazi Lowriders, skinheads. There is some of that. But it was less than 10 percent of the cases I came across."

Instead, as a hate-crime prosecutor, Rosales primarily handled gang cases. "What I heard from the gang members was, 'It's not a gang thing anymore. It's a racial thing,'" she said. "You have people in tight neighborhoods, and they don't like people of the other race. It's not that they fear the race. You see black and brown coexisting, getting along. But they fear the gang. The gang divides those people. Then fear of the gang melts into fear of race. They don't know who is the true enemy. So any young man of the opposite race within a certain age bracket is a potential rival."

In Florence-Firestone, those with no gang affiliations who were being harassed, shot at, and killed could be forgiven for missing the nuances and seeing only a race war. One of them was Chris Le Grande, pastor of the Great Hope Fellowship in Faith, a black church whose congregants reported being shot at for no reason. Years before, during the worst of the crack wars, innocent people were shot only accidentally, said Le Grande. But the new Latino/black tensions changed all that, he said. "Now it's deliberate," Le Grande said. "'I'm deliberately shooting you because of your color.'"

. . .

That's how things were in the neighborhood where Cheryl Green lived and died. The Harbor Gateway had once been a white and Latino working-class neighborhood of single-family homes, held together by union factory and longshoreman jobs. Then between 1984 and 1992, the apartment-building boom transformed the place.

Those years began with great promise, remembers Ken Sideris, who built many of the apartments. Sideris said he and others bought houses, offering eighty thousand dollars, more than double what owners had paid. Many owners eagerly took the deal. Sideris and other developers tore the houses down and put up four- and five-unit apartment buildings, which city zoning allowed. Most of Sideris's buildings were on 207th. One was where Cheryl Green later lived.

In the tiny neighborhood, 77 houses were replaced with apartment buildings—a total of 503 units—between 1985 and 1992. Yet the city never built a park, school, or community center. Nearby Torrance required developers to put in trees, landscaping, open space, and enclosed garages. Los Angeles required only sewer and school taxes. "L.A. city, I'm sorry, but it was the Wild West," Sideris said in an interview in 2007. "I tried to put in a tree, but—you know what?— it's economics. I couldn't compete. They didn't require trees, landscaping, enclosed parking. It was developed wrong. There was no plan, no thought."

At first, solid tenants with jobs were easy to find. But by 1990, the apartment boom was ending. Unsubsidized tenants had many places to choose from. Building owners in less-desirable neighborhoods, like Harbor Gateway, grew desperate.

In 1994, the Housing Authority of the City of Los Angeles closed the crumbling housing project called Normont Terrace, a couple miles from Harbor Gateway. Two years later, that area reopened as Harbor Village—a delightful mix of homeowners, renters, and Section 8 recipients, on thirty-seven acres. It is gated, guarded, and without graffiti. It features five parks, two swimming pools, a community center, computer center, a health club, and a day-care nursery.

By then, private development, recession, and limited city building requirements had turned the once-stable Harbor Gateway neighborhood into a cramped slum. Its population increased by 60 percent. With sixty-six people per acre now, it was now almost twice as dense as the Normont Terrace housing project had been, but with none of the amenities. Many of the new residents of Harbor Gateway were black. The black population went from 450 in 1990 to more than a thousand in 2000. Some were working families, but most were on Section 8 subsidies. More than half the new tenants were Latino immigrants, speaking only Spanish.

During these years, a younger generation of 204th Street was taking shape, wanting to make a name for itself and hearing from older guys how the neighborhood used to be. Their streets had once been 204th Streeters' kingdom. Pizza deliverymen wouldn't come to the area. Sometimes garbage trucks would stay away, too. The Del Amo Market became the gang's territory. Every Thanksgiving, the gang played its annual Turkey Bowl—a football game against the La Rana gang of Torrance—then held a party on the street in front of the market.

With little police presence, "it was kind of like a little TJ," said one gang member, who was referring to Tijuana and asked not to be identified fearing for his safety. He described what gang members encountered when they walked the streets: "People would say, 'Hey, what's up?' or offer us a beer. You got tamales. Drugs. It was a great neighborhood for gang members. But then [blacks] are writing on our walls, throwing bottles at us, and telling on us [to the police]."

Michael Blanco, a gang member with Tortilla Flats, said he told several 204th Streeters that they had to do something about the blacks in their area. A Mafia representative, a member of the infamous Grajeda family, held meetings of gangs in Harbor Gateway, which Blanco said he also attended.[6] The representative told the gangs they had to do something about blacks in the area, Blanco said.

Added to that provocation were long-time residents who, through the years, egged on 204th Streeters to get tough on newly arrived blacks. After Green was killed, police would mention that one man in particular, whom they did not name, often made racist comments and called on the younger gang members to attack blacks. Thus, beginning in 1997, 204th Street began to act. Marquis "Mark" Wilbert, eleven, was shot by a 204th Street gang member who was riding a bicycle. In all, seven black people with no gang affiliation were killed in the tiny neighborhood in the next nine years. Added to that were constant insults, nonfatal shootings, and racist graffiti.

As blacks and Latinos crowded together, the tiny neighborhood of Harbor Gateway became a microcosm for fraying race relations in a Southern California where blacks and Latinos often lived side by side. So close were they that shootings were often done on bikes or on foot.

"We see each other wake up in the morning. We know what time we go to work. We know which car is which," said one former 204th

Street gang member of the two communities living in the neighbor-hood. "In other barrios, the gang has to get a stolen car [to go do a shooting in a far-off rival neighborhood]. Out here, all it takes is a few beers." You get high, walk over, and do it, he said.

This was how things stood on the afternoon of December 15, 2006, when two 204th Streeters, apparently upset that a black man in a car had brandished a gun, went looking for him or someone who looked like him—or anyone black.

. . .

As of this writing, the Mexican Mafia edicts remain partly in effect. In jail and prison, a racial apartheid remains. So, too, does taxation of drug dealers wherever Latino street gangs dominate. But the no-drive-by rule isn't often enforced. Or better put, Mafiosos have made drive-by shootings a source of revenue. Gangs that do drive-bys are greenlighted until they pay some kind of fine—usually a few thousand dollars, some weapons, or both.

On the streets, some Latino gangs are given to spasms of violence against blacks. But this also depends a lot on which gang members are on parole. Nowadays, high schools are infected as violence between black and Latino students breaks out sporadically around Southern California.

(Other Latino gangs not mentioned here have exhibited concerted racist behavior targeting blacks with no gang affiliation. Among them: Olive Street in Pomona; Drew Street in Highland Park; HG13 in Hawaiian Gardens; the Tiny Dukes in Riverside; Orange Street Locos in Norwalk; West Side Wilmas in Wilmington; East Side Torrance in the Harbor Gateway strip; Canoga Park Alabama in the San Fernando Valley; and Colonia Chiques in Ventura County.)

Keith Volm, the Ontario police gang officer said, "The law was made back then, and it hasn't been repealed. That's pretty much how the gangs look at it." But black gangs are dwindling rapidly. Many are extinct, and those that remain may not be the threat they were per-ceived to be in the 1990s.

Meanwhile, Eme members have created the conditions of their own demise. One place to see why this may be is in the state prisons where the Eme started. The Mafia's *reglas* changed not just Southern California streets but the institutions as well. Here's what happened: As Mafiosos tried to control neighborhoods they hadn't walked in decades, many handed out greenlights like candy. Festering in their cells hundreds of miles away, the prison system's most sociopathic and conniving criminals grew intoxicated with their own power. Often they indicted gang members who had been fiercely loyal to their cause.

The organization, meanwhile, suffered defections. Ernie "Chuco" Castro, an influential Eme member, turned on his compatriots and became the star witness against them in the first Eme RICO trial. Later, several Mafiosos also dropped out: Rene "Boxer" Enriquez, David "Chino" Delgadillo, and Angel "Stump" Valencia in 2002 alone. Others followed. Azusa's "Jacko" Padilla is among the latest. The examples these guys set, along with the viciousness, lack of loyalty, or anything resembling coherent rules of prison-gang life, convinced many incarcerated gang members to drop out.

"One guy described [the Eme] to me as a tank of piranhas," said Richard Valdemar, the retired sheriff's gang sergeant. "Sometimes you'll see these piranhas go to the top of the tank. That doesn't mean they're in charge. It just means that right now they're at the top. But as soon as they turn the wrong direction, the other piranhas will attack them and kill them. You're always looking over your shoulder. Who's going to kill you? Your best friend."

A lot of this was due to the isolation of Pelican Bay State Prison, where most Eme members were incarcerated. Robert Marquez, a long-time gang investigator for the California Department of Corrections and Rehabilitation, described the transformation that has taken place in the prisons: "I saw an organization where the brotherhood was above everything. Now I see an organization that's factionalized—no less potent or deadly, but now you have blocs within that organization where you didn't use to have that. You lock those guys up and you remove them from the ability to attack their enemies. . . . Who then becomes the prey? Their own."

By 2004, gang members in prison were dropping out and entering protective custody in droves. This marked a radical change for the state prison system. Before that, the entire thirty-three-prison system had no more than a few cell blocks reserved for protective custody—for a few hundred old men, child molesters, ex-cops, and informants. Those who most resisted protective custody were Latino street gang members. Even when threatened with death, their aversion to PC was total, and some were known to stay in the general population until they were killed rather than "lock it up."[7]

Today, though, close to twenty thousand inmates are in protective custody. The largest numbers are Southern California Latino gang members, usually fleeing Eme greenlights caused by some real or imagined infraction. The Department of Corrections was forced to open entire yards—with more than a thousand inmates each—to protective custody, calling them sensitive needs yards, SNYs.

Most prisons now have SNYs; Mule Creek State Prison is entirely SNY. SNYs are headaches for prison officials. SNY inmates remain conniving and backstabbing. But SNYs are proof of how much of the black/Latino antagonism afflicting state prisons—and the streets of Southern California—is really due to prison gangs. In SNYs, whites, Sureños, Norteños, and blacks live together in relative peace—even side by side with child molesters and ex-cops. Any problems they have—and there are many—have to do with drugs, debts, and personal beefs; race doesn't often enter into it. Thus, SNYs also demonstrate how once-undisputed Eme power is ebbing, along with the fear and admiration it inspired among gang members. "They don't care who they hurt," said Mark Fernandez, the La Puente Blackwood gang member, now serving fifty-five years to life in prison for the Mafia-ordered murder of his friend, Richard Mechaca. "We're the pawns."

At times, SNYs feel like old-timers' conventions. Gang members who once aimed to kill one another shed their rivalries and talk and laugh about their glory days. In these yards is where the story of how the prisons changed Southern California streets can now be learned, from men who lived through that change and from some who helped it happen—many of whom will discuss their past in a way unheard of a few years ago.

One person whose life encompassed that change is Freddie Gonzalez, an Eme dropout. Gonzalez grew up in Pomona and joined the 12th Street gang young. In prison, at the behest of the Eme, he killed a Northern California Latino gang member. For this he received a sentence of life in prison and membership in the Eme. Soon he wearied with the constant plotting that accompanied prison-gang life. Gonzalez defected to an SNY at the prison in Lancaster, in the Los Angeles County high desert.

One day, a Crip from Pomona, also a dropout, recognized him. Gonzalez didn't remember him, but as the Crip talked, he remembered the man's mother, a Cuban woman, who sold weed to Pomona 12th Streeters. Gonzalez realized that in his younger days he had gone often to the Crip's house. The Crip spoke about all the places and memories they had in common. It was of an earlier time, in the 1980s, when black and Latino gangs paid little attention to each other. Now, years later, black and Latino stood in the protective-custody yard in Lancaster and reminisced about streets that were only three hours away but that they'd never walk again.

As he thought back, Gonzalez remembered that Crips used to actually walk by Sharkey Park, the center of the area that 12th Street claimed. No one had a problem with it then. Gonzalez realized that the Crip was talking about the time before the gangs had started warring. It was before the Mexican Mafia moved out of the prisons and changed the streets of Southern California. So much had happened since then that couldn't be spoken of now, Gonzalez thought. "We were talking about all this stuff," said Gonzalez, "but we were leaving out the middle part, the part where we started to kill each other."

EPILOGUE

In 2010, Jonathan Fajardo was sentenced to death for killing Cheryl Green. Two years later, Ernesto Alcarez received 238 years in prison. By then, though, Latino-on-black violence had begun to subside notably.

Gang investigators attributed this to a general retreat indoors by Latino gangs, following several federal RICO indictments and a slew of gang injunctions making it harder to associate in public. But tours of gang neighborhoods showed that they were just not as visible as they once had been. Across Southern California, liquor stores, parks, street corners were no longer encrusted with gang members hanging out like they owned them. San Bernardino's West Side Verdugo had virtually no graffiti present. Same with Cudahy, home to South Side 18th Street. Azusa streets were equally barren of the stuff. Certain crimes, too, were less common, such as carjackings, assaults; even gang murder was dropping fast, according to LAPD.

In some gang areas, blacks were now allowed to live. A housing project in Ramona Gardens had a black family. So did the area around Drew Street in Glassell Park, home to a notorious clique of the Avenues. Was there an order given? Or was it a natural by-product of gangs learning what'll get them significant prison time? I'm betting on the latter. Things change. So do gangs. There was a time when Latino gangs didn't target blacks. Things seemed headed that way again.

As I write this, graffiti is rare on the streets of Harbor Gateway. The Del Amo Market is no longer the domain of the 204th Street gang. The gang still exists but, like many others, is now underground, less visible. Still, there's a feeling of haunting memory about the tiny neighborhood. Maybe it's just me, though I think not.

One addition to the neighborhood is the Cheryl Green Community Center, which opened one block north of 204th Street. When I last visited, the center bustled with Latino kids. But the administrators told me they were having trouble getting black kids to walk the few blocks over from 206th Street. They had to provide the kids with shuttle service to and from home to get them to come.

NOTES

Since 1994, award-winning journalist Sam Quinones has been covering politics, crime, and culture in, and between, Mexico and the United States. His influential reporting for the *Los Angeles Times* and *LA Weekly* has included numerous stories on Latino and African-American relations in Southern California. This essay, the cumulative result of years of reporting, is being published here for the first time.

1. The reason has a lot to do with prison-gang alliances. For many years now, the Mexican Mafia and the Aryan Brotherhood have been allies in California prisons. Crips, the Black Guerrilla Family, and the Nuestra Familia have formed another alliance. The two sides have warred sporadically.

The prison gang Nuestra Familia controls Northern California Hispanic gangs inside the walls. Thus, their gangs on the street do not feud with black gangs or attack blacks in the style that became typical of Southern California Latino gangs in the 1990s.

The north-south division among Hispanic gangs in prison dates to the late 1960s and is too lengthy to go into here, though be assured it is a bizarre and violent story. It involves divisions between gangs from the city—mainly Los Angeles—and those from rural areas, like Stockton, Salinas, and elsewhere. Suffice to say, though, that the division has been one of the bloodiest rivalries in state prisons during those decades. Active Norteños and Sureños—as northerners and southerners are known, respectively—cannot be housed together.

2. Many Latino street gangs also victimized vulnerable illegal immigrants, according to cops and residents in these areas. Gang members, who spoke English and had little connection to Mexico, held a resentment, even hatred at times, for immigrants in their midst and preyed on them.

3. Richard Valdemar remembers: "Eighteenth Street actually violated the drive-by shooting so many times that they actually made a rule for Eighteenth Street. They'd say, 'What's a drive-by shooting? If we drive up and stop and shoot the guy, is that a drive-by shooting? Do we have to get out of the car?' The Mexican Mafia had a meeting and said, 'Here's the rule. You have to open the car door and put one foot on the ground.' So we had a whole series of Eighteenth Street shootings where they would drive up and put the foot on the ground."

4. It was common in county jail or Chino prison for Mafiosos facing some charge they knew they couldn't beat to go "pro per"—defend themselves. They would then subpoena other Mafia members, who would be transported down to county jail. It was all a scam to allow these "witnesses" some time to run dope and make money, all while staying out of solitary confinement and closer to home.

5. One Orange County gang member told me a story about the late Rick Chavez, an Eme member from Santa Ana. At the time, they were on the same tier at Chino prison. Chavez, the lone Eme member on the tier, insisted that Sureños turn over to him their Home Run Pies—cellophane-wrapped desserts that the prison occasionally served with dinner. This was how Chavez chose to use his Eme power—forcing Sureños to give up their Home Run Pies.

6. The Grajeda clan was notorious in Torrance and later in the San Pedro/ Wilmington area as a crime wave unto itself and one of the large gang families of Southern California. They lived first in the La Rana area of Torrance, a barrio now mostly redeveloped into an office park. The family later moved to the San Pedro/Wilmington area. "They were just a bunch of animals," said a former neighbor, who asked me not to identify him for fear of Grajeda family retribution. Eme members Tommy, Daniel, and Senon Grajeda were best known. Tommy and Daniel—identical twins, known respectively as Wino and Cuate—held sway from Chino prison and L.A. County Jail during the mid-1990s over street gangs in parts of the South Bay and Pacoima. There were many other Grajedas, some of whom led meetings on behalf of the Eme in the South Bay in the mid-1990s.

7. One gang member told me of a Cherryville Pomona gang member in prison who was green-lighted when his gang on the street killed an Eme member named Speedy. He refused protective custody. Even after beatings, insults, and ostracism, he remained in the prison's general population, tattooing on himself the words, "I'm Still Here." Eventually, the story goes, he was thrown off a tier and died.

PART FIVE

City Cultures

11

Landscapes of Black and Brown Los Angeles

A Photo Essay

PHOTOGRAPHS AND TEXT BY WENDY CHENG

We know the names: *South Central, Crenshaw, Watts, Compton*—places of fame and infamy. *Vermont, Slauson, Florence, Normandie, M. L. K. Jr.*—the boulevards and avenues crisscross the flatlands, where the smog settles over the cramped apartment buildings and single-family homes and vacant lots and buildings-for-lease in a pearlescent haze. We know the images writ large on a mythical collective consciousness, too well to rehearse again here. But there are also churches and liquor stores and *carnicerías*, barbershops and photo studios and schools, among faded murals broadcasting past struggles and the possibilities of other worlds. There is the rasp of skateboard wheels on asphalt, the syncopated vibrations of banda and hip-hop making the cars rattle as they pass, the tinkle of the *paletero*'s bell. Kids walk home from school, insouciant in their skinny jeans and school uniforms. Airplanes excrete jet fuel far overhead as they pass to and from LAX—to and from places that are not here. In the landscape we find the sedimentation of histories and economic and sociopolitical processes, the residues and raw materials of dreams. All of it matters.

"Celebrating Community" banner, Central Avenue, South Los
Angeles, 2007.

Storefront advertising school uniforms in English and Spanish,
Market Street, Inglewood, 2009.

Vennie Mac Meat/Carniceria Mart, Inglewood, 2009.

Jazz musicians mural, Central Avenue, South Los Angeles. 2009.

A storefront on Central Avenue in South Los Angeles advertising international calling cards in Spanish. 2009.

Thomas Jefferson High School, South Los Angeles, 2009. Jefferson is now a predominantly Latina/o school and has frequently been a site of sensationalized media coverage of Black-Latina/o student conflict.

A mural painted on the wall of a convenience store in South Los Angeles featuring Martin Luther King Jr., the Virgin of Guadalupe, and César Chávez, 2009. The mural was commissioned by building owner Asei Jimenez and painted by an artist named Saul (last name unknown).

Detail of the convenience store mural, depicting Martin Luther King Jr., South Los Angeles, 2009.

A Baptist church and the Iglesia Adventista del Séptimo Día (Seventh Day Adventist church) share a space in South Los Angeles, as a plane passes overhead en route to Los Angeles International Airport. 2009.

"Bring the Change Home from D.C. to South L.A.," Community Coalition, South Los Angeles, 2009. Nonprofit and social justice organizations are an essential part of South Los Angeles's landscape.

Noni Olabisi's 1995 mural *To Protect and Serve*, is painted on the wall of a building in Crenshaw that is also home to a barber shop and a hair salon. The mural (commissioned by SPARC and paid for by private funds after city funding fell through), illustrates violence and injustice against Black people in the United States, and the militant and community-serving aspects of the Black Panther Party for Self-Defense (BPP), ending with a listing of the BPP's Ten-Point Program. 2008.

"Hope," a mural by Miguel Ramirez depicts Catholic religious figures, Black civil rights leaders, and images of Central American political struggles, St. Lawrence of Brindisi Church, Watts, South Los Angeles. In recent years, Irish pastor Peter Banks, who gives services in English and Spanish, made efforts to bring together local Black and Latina/o populations, in particular those who live in the nearby Nickerson Gardens housing projects. According to the artist, the mural, completed in 2000, was intended to bring the people of Compton "hope and dreams" at the opening of the new century. 2009.

Empty lot, Market Street, Inglewood, 2009. Empty lots are scattered throughout South Los Angeles because of a lack of municipal investment.

Broadway Federal Bank, Inglewood, 2009. With several branches throughout South Los Angeles, Broadway Federal is a Black-owned bank that has served the community since 1946.

Three young teens enjoy skateboarding at Rogers Park, in Inglewood, 2009. Graffiti tags declare the presence of the MS-13 (or Mara Salvatrucha) and Avalon Crips gangs.

The Los Angeles County Jail (Twin Towers Correctional Facility) looms over pedestrians and businesses providing bail bonds in downtown Los Angeles, 2009. African Americans and Latinas/os are strikingly overrepresented in the prison system.

Street of single-family homes off Vermont Avenue, South Los Angeles, with a mix of Black and Latina/o residents, 2009.

"Apartment For Rent/Se Renta." Apartment buildings off Figueroa Street, South Los Angeles, 2009.

Japanese-style landscaping in Crenshaw serves as a visible remnant of the area's past as a predominantly African American and Japanese American neighborhood, 2006.

12

Spatial Entitlement

Race, Displacement, and Sonic Reclamation in Postwar Los Angeles

GAYE THERESA JOHNSON

If you are not prepared to be part of this greatness, if you
want Los Angeles to revert to pueblo status . . . then my best
advice to you is to prepare to resettle elsewhere.

—Norris Poulson, quoted in Joseph Eli Kovner,
  "Resettle Elsewhere"

[African Americans] discovered . . . that congregation in
a Jim Crow environment produced more space than power.
They used this space to gather their cultural bearings, to
mold the urban setting.

—Earl Lewis, *In Their Own Interests*

In 1948, the Black entrepreneur John Dolphin saw an opportunity, and
technology was on his side. An L.A. immigrant from Detroit, Dolphin
discovered that most music stores in Hollywood and downtown Los
Angeles refused to carry records by Black artists. Yet he knew it had
never been easier to record and market Black musicians: the postwar
acquisition of tape-recording technology meant that ordinary people
could now afford portable tape recorders, which meant that recording
could be done anywhere and transferred to records. In the 1940s, radio
stations had just begun to use recorded music instead of live music in
regular programming, and records soon became the staple of the music
industry, surpassing sheet music as the major source of revenue in 1952.

At about the same time, radio overtook jukeboxes as the number one hit-maker.[1] Eventually, all it took to create a record company and sell in a local, or even a regional, market was a small amount of capital, a magnetic tape recorder, some performers, and credit with pressing plants and printers.[2] Therefore, recording studios could be and often were in storefront offices.

By the middle of 1948, Dolphin had acquired all of these, plus his own record store in South Los Angeles and his own record-pressing machine. He named his business—located at Vernon and Central Avenues—Dolphin's of Hollywood, reasoning that if Blacks were unwelcome in Hollywood, he would "bring Hollywood to the Negroes."[3] He even named his first record label RIH: Recorded in Hollywood.

Dolphin became a pioneer of the independent record label, and the recording and broadcasting spaces he provided were prime factors in the emergence of R&B on the West Coast.[4] He recorded local artists whose music had been neglected by large recording companies: Joe Houston, Bobby Day, Linda Hayes, Jesse Belvin, Chuck Higgins, and Eddie Cochran were some of the first to record on Dolphin's labels (aptly named Lucky, Money, and Cash) in a studio at the rear of his store. In 1951 Dolphin bought radio airtime on KRKD and hired disc jockeys to play those records from the window at the front of his store.[5] Dick "Huggy Boy" Hugg was the first white DJ to broadcast from the storefront's studio: his signature and oft-repeated hook, "get on down here to Vernon and Central, Central and Vernon," summoned listeners along Central Avenue, from the East Side in Chicano and Jewish neighborhoods, from newly constructed suburbs, and from communities in the San Gabriel and Pomona Valleys.[6] Hugg and one of his contemporaries, Hunter Hancock (a later employee of Dolphin's), later recalled watching the "crawl of cruisers" that maintained Central Avenue as a predominately Black but thriving interracial space, even when the city mobilized against it.[7]

Conservative city planners and elected officials had many reasons to restrict Black and Brown spaces and spatial mobility. The Los Angeles they intended in the postwar era would reject the tenets of New Deal liberalism as it anticipated the emergence of the New Right, ultimately culminating in a vision at serious odds with that of aggrieved communities. Eric Ávila has shown that as freeways replaced streetcars, as new parks like Dodger Stadium eviscerated ethnic neighborhoods, and as suburbs provided sites of order and safety, Los Angeles entertained "a set of racialized fantasies" that depicted the region as a "southwestern outpost of white supremacy."[8] Anthony Macías has documented the calculated efforts of the Los Angeles Police Department and Los Angeles City Council members to curtail interracial musical events on Central Avenue, "afraid that whites, blacks, Mexicans, and Filipinos might be allowed to dance together." In 1940, Mayor Fletcher Bowron prohibited the sale of alcohol after 2 A.M. to reduce the "swarms of white visitors making the rounds" on Central Avenue.[9] In 1954, Dolphin's store was blockaded by Newton Division police, who turned white customers away with the admonition that it was "too dangerous to hang around all Black neighborhoods."[10]

For midcentury orchestrators of white spatial hegemony, the era could be cast as a historical leap into late twentieth-century mobility of commodities and currencies. But for many Black and Mexican American youth, the repression and demise of interracial coalitions, the growth of white suburbia, and Red Scare politics would more accurately characterize their experience of the same historical moment.[11]

In many instances overlooked by social historians, everyday reclamations of space, assertions of social citizenship, and infrapolitical struggles have created the conditions for future successes in organized collective movements.[12] Black and Brown collectivities in postwar Los Angeles enacted more than just translocal solidarities constituted by dispersal, estrangement, and marginalization. Moreover, these affinities were based on more than just eviction and exclusion from physical places: they were realized through new and creative uses of technology and spaces. Dolphin's use of discursive and physical spaces (airwaves and sites of interracial leisure) staged figurative access to one of the most significant social locations in the world (Hollywood), participated in the postwar economy, and perpetuated longtime community affiliations and created new ones.

This essay reveals one of the few modes of social entitlement available to Black and Brown communities in the postwar era: a *spatial entitlement*. Unable to access the assets and rights of full citizenship, disenfranchised groups claimed alternative, often discursive spaces in which important democratic and egalitarian visions were fashioned. These spatial claims were manifest in temporary locations and pronouncements that broadcast the relevance and rights of Black and Brown people in Los Angeles. This meant the transformation of the ways that people moved themselves *through* space, in which spaces they *congregated,* and *what entitlements were asserted* with the cultural currency they created. These unique engagements with the terms of social citizenship provoked severe retaliations, which can be interpreted as an important measure of the threat, both symbolic and material, of these assertions.[13]

Spatial entitlement refers to the spatial strategies and vernaculars utilized by working-class youth to resist the sharpening demarcations of race and class that emerged in the postwar era in the wake of the growth of privatized redevelopment and attacks on progressive unionism and popular front political culture. Studying space not just as a mode of subjugation by private and public interests but also as a critical tool deployed by aggrieved groups to assert social membership has enormous implications for understanding the sensibilities forged in multiracial working-class cultures of struggle, as well as the ways in which horizontal relationships of culture and community inform collective notions of entitlement. Spatial entitlements created new articulations, new sensibilities, and new visions about the place of Black, Brown, and working-class people on the local and national landscape. But these entitlements were also "diagnostic" of authority: following Lila Abu-Lughod and Robin D. G. Kelley, I suggest that spatial entitlement in postwar L.A. rendered everyday acts of resistance and survival more than mere examples of the "dignity and heroism of resisters." Instead, they were representative of the "complex interworkings of historically changing structures of power."[14] This makes the variety of strategies enacted by working-class youth to imagine and articulate new modes of social citizenship all the more significant: in the wake of such consistent repression of meaningful spaces of interracial congregation, these actions became a barometer of the power relationships between oppressed and oppressors and a theory of action that considered the futures of Black and Brown people in the same lens of possibility.

Black and Brown people in Los Angeles have shared more than histories of racism and segregation, of economic discrimination and immigrant exclusion, of brutality and inequality. Allison Varzally notes that even as new tensions and uncertainties were introduced into the lives of people of color after World War II, "their dedicated efforts to manage these conditions, to comfortably coexist in integrated spaces, became a kind of pan-ethnic politics arising from the everyday" and provided opportunities where integrated cultures of youth could imagine active and peaceful mixing.[15]

I am not suggesting that spatial entitlement resulted in utopian spaces of racial or class harmony; indeed, alongside spaces of mutual respect and enjoyment is a record of painful expressions of intragroup discrimination and competing desires for inclusion in the broader political economy. Instead, I want to suggest that the strategies deployed in the service of spatial entitlement were critical not only in the reclamation of social and symbolic space but also as the discursive fabric that created both moments and movements in which these groups unmasked power imbalances, sought recognition, and forged solidarities by embracing the strategies, cultures, and politics of each other's experiences. This was no easy task in the period under examination: in many cases, urban renewal demolished not only the assets that assure collective success but also the spaces of congregation that inspire it.

Urban renewal created many advantages for communities of color and low-income whites in Los Angeles. But it also created unprecedented disappointments and challenges. Between 1949 and 1973, scores of Black and Latino communities were destroyed to make way for the postindustrial, suburban sensibilities that would characterize the modern U.S. city.[16] Between the Housing Act of 1949 and 1967, 400,000 residential units were demolished in urban renewal areas across the nation, while only 10,760 low-rent public housing units replaced them.[17]

Los Angeles emerged as one of the most visible examples of spatial hegemony: several Black and Brown neighborhoods were eviscerated, even from maps themselves, as if no one had ever lived there.[18] Local and federal officials used "applied social science research, fiscal policy, and direct intervention" to justify the destruction of neighborhoods like Boyle Heights, which while primarily Mexican by this time, had maintained a prewar diversity that included Japanese.

By 1957, the construction of five freeways—the San Bernardino, the Santa Ana, the Long Beach, the Golden State, and the Pomona—had cut through and effectively destroyed the primarily Mexican neighborhood of Boyle Heights. Community groups waged protracted struggles against the California DOT's Division of Highways, arguing in 1953 that the building of the Golden State Freeway would destroy key community social service agencies such as schools, churches, hospitals, and convalescent homes.[19] Boyle Heights residents fought tirelessly against local and federal housing and transportation policies, but by 1957, the *Eastside Sun* editor Eli Kovner would lament the loss of community signposts: "Believe me, it is heartbreaking to see such old landmarks disappear."[20] George Sánchez has argued that local and federal officials used "applied social science research, fiscal policy, and direct intervention," to justify the evisceration of neighborhoods like Boyle Heights and, in the process, redefined postwar terms of racialization through the suppression of interracial spaces: "This is a 'melting pot' area and is literally honeycombed with diverse and subversive racial elements. It is seriously doubted whether there is a single block in the area which does not contain detrimental racial elements and there are very few districts which are not hopelessly heterogeneous."[21]

These justifications were also used to enable the abuse and denigration of "unfavorable" neighborhoods. Black residents in the Avalon section of South Central felt the effects of environmental racism as industry enjoyed postwar tax incentives for moving into "undesirable" areas: it was not uncommon to find "pockets of their neighborhood littered with industrial debris and saturated by industrial liquid runoff."[22] By 1960, Black neighborhoods in South Los Angeles had coalesced into a nearly forty-square-mile suburban ghetto with few jobs, poor mass transit, limited highway access, inadequate schools, repressive police, and little public housing.[23] It would become, five years later, a uniquely appropriate staging area from which to articulate long-standing and legitimate Black grievances.

Though both African and Mexican Americans achieved broader geographical opportunities for housing and employment in the postwar era, and though both subsequently observed a modicum of progress in integration and employment, both were also witness to pointed and devastating disregard for their communities, even when the physical space of their neighborhoods expanded. This seeming contradiction, between residential expansion and pervasive spatial denigration, raises a critical issue about spatial entitlement: meaningful space.

Philip J. Ethington reveals a dramatic expansion of the physical boundaries of segregated Black and Latino communities in L.A. during this period. As their residential spaces were being destroyed through the investment of public and private capital, the boundaries of more racially homogeneous residential spaces were actually expanding, even as public and private investments abandoned these same areas. Ethington demonstrates that despite the dramatic growth of diversity in Los Angeles County in the postwar era, whites became increasingly spatially separated from nonwhites, "barricaded behind walls of wealth in municipal spaces far away from the center of the metropolis." Further, Ethington reveals that official segregation between 1940 and 1965 preserved opportunity in the fastest growing and most desirable outlying areas (especially along the Pacific Coast) for whites only.[24]

Notably, the eligibility for white racial classification was becoming more refined in the same historical moment. Following historian Matthew Jacobson, George Sánchez's history of Jews in Boyle Heights grounds the geographic transformation of the area in "a changing ideology of race and a growing lack of tolerance for social mixing" throughout the 1930s and 1940s. As new racial ideologies were busy "creating Caucasians" (whereas before, Jacobson argues, there had been "so many Celts, Hebrews, Teutons, Mediterraneans, and Slavs"), "Jewish placement on one side or the other of the line between Caucasian and non-Caucasian was critical in defining the boundaries of this newly important division in American life." Therefore, the large departure of Jews from Boyle Heights, effected in part by the construction of the Golden State Freeway, was also about the complex transformation of the terms of racialization.[25]

The notion of meaningful space is at the center of spatial entitlement. Though the boundaries of segregated Black and Brown neighborhoods were expanding, both the social agencies and the social traditions that served and defined these areas were consistently under attack by city and federal policies in the postwar era. A community requires more than physical space to survive: spaces have meaning; they function to maintain both memories and practices that reinforce community knowledge and cohesiveness. Meaningful space was particularly vulnerable in postwar Los Angeles, as an attendant alignment of conservative politicians, corporate executives, and moral pundits gave rise to the appointment of William H. Parker as chief of police in 1950 and the election of Norris Poulson as mayor in 1953. Both Parker and Poulson were powerfully committed to segregated social and residential spaces.

Chief Parker was a World War II veteran who had trained police in Germany after the war, an experience that came to symbolize his approach to the policing and subjugation of Black L.A. "as if it were an alien community during wartime."[26] More than any of his predecessors, he crusaded against race mixing and "inner-city vice," using inflated crime statistics to support police persecution of youth who congregated in interracial venues.[27]

The socially conservative agendas of Poulson and Parker sanctioned white entitlement and its beneficiaries with tremendous power, echoing national patterns of entitlement and exclusion. For example, the racialization of federal policies such as loan and mortgage restrictions promoted the widespread prohibition of Blacks and Latinos from buying houses and obtaining fair mortgages. George Lipsitz documents the ways in which the Federal Housing Administration thwarted universal access to the provisions of the Federal Housing Act of 1934 by using racist categories in city surveys and appraisers' manuals. This channeled money away from communities of color and toward whites, who could in turn secure the assets that build transgenerational wealth. In St. Louis, Lipsitz shows, the "mostly white St. Louis County secured nearly five times as many FHA mortgages as the more racially mixed city of St. Louis. Home buyers in the county received six times as much loan money and enjoyed per capita mortgage spending 6.3 times greater than those in the city." In Los Angeles, FHA appraisers denied loans to prospective home buyers in racially mixed Boyle Heights not only to defeat prospective home buyers of color but also to repress the interracial demographic that distinguished it from other communities.[28]

In 1957, seventy-five hundred Mexican, Black, and low-income white Angeleno families were evicted from the three-hundred-acre community of Chávez Ravine. In the time between the designation of this community for the construction of housing projects in 1951 and its surrender to the Dodgers owner Walter O'Malley, Norris Poulson secured election over his incumbent Fletcher Bowron by promising to end support for "un-American" housing projects. The Chandler family, who owned the *Los Angeles Times* and backed the handover of Chavez Ravine to O'Malley, were key funders of the conservative Bowron's campaign and administration.[29] The families evicted were overwhelmingly Mexican, and it would take three generations for a fraction of them to regain a comparable economic level.[30] Understanding the difference between net worth and net financial assets allows us to suitably grasp what this means: net financial assets can produce money that is readily available for expenditures or emergencies. Assets, constituted by home equity, pension funds, savings accounts, and investments, are reflected in the control of the financial resources that provide freedom to create opportunities and the power to maintain quality of life.[31] In the case of Chávez Ravine and its inhabitants, aspects of urban renewal demolished not only the assets that assure collective success but also the spaces of congregation that inspire it.

There were several unintended consequences of these demolitions, namely, creative articulations of social membership by the displaced. In postwar Los Angeles, Black and Brown communities forged a politics of interracial solidarity, even when those coalitions were systematically—and often violently—suppressed. These new collectivities were more than just translocal solidarities constituted by dispersal, estrangement, or marginalization. They were a metaphor for spatial mobility and entitlement, representing an epistemological shift that made individual minority groups part of a more powerful majority and that revealed a cultural world of unity and division.

SONIC AND SPATIAL ENTITLEMENT

In his critical history of Blacks in theater and film, Cedric Robinson renders visible the incompatibility of racial regimes with discoverable history, noting their unrelenting hostility to exhibition. Here I consider space in similar terms: spaces, too, possess history, particularly when they are deployed in the service of white supremacy. In such cases, they are likewise and often hostile to their own visibility. Following Robinson, it is possible to see that spaces can often be "contrivances," designed and delegated by "interested cultural and social powers with the wherewithal sufficient to commission their imaginings, manufacture, and maintenance."[32] Indeed, the use of space to support racial hierarchies has a long history, one that has been commissioned to appear as a natural historical progression (not unlike the doctrine of manifest destiny): we are asked to believe, for example, that white monopolies on social, residential, and commercial spaces have had no correlation to the intent to advance privatization, market "discipline," and "law and order" policies all rooted in a history of racism.[33] John Powell reminds us that the arrangement of space has been one of the most important ways to distribute and hinder opportunity along racial lines.[34]

We might likewise understand the temporary spatial entitlements claimed by Black-Brown solidarities and infrapolitical struggles as contrivances, though in the service of empowerment at particular moments and in particular contexts. The social interactions and ideological conceptions that inspire horizontal relationships, as examined here, are more than just translocal and never only responding to oppression: they are contradictory and have uneven results. Nonetheless, and as to Los Angeles, interracial congregation in segregated environments created "more space than power." Few whites discerned that segregation vested excluded minorities with the power to redefine aspects of their own existence.[35] Using space to reconstitute individual and collective subjectivities in terms that are grounded in the histories and identities of aggrieved communities requires a critical engagement with the power of imagination, something Arjun Appadurai has termed "the imagination as social practice." Appadurai argues that understanding imagination as more than fantasy, escape, or pastime directs us to seeing the ways in which it has become "an organized field of social practices, [and] a form of work."[36] Fashioning a "voice, songs, articulations" can enact, as Houston A. Baker has argued, "the conversion of wish into politics."[37]

A common sphere of congregation, what Jürgen Habermas has referred to as the "public sphere," can be a crucial site of discourse among community members, where private interests are set aside and democracies are enacted in order to determine collective good.[38] Scholars of working-class resistance have argued that "subaltern counter publics" are sites where oppressed groups assert their humanity and refine their articulated opposition to dominant discourses about citizenship and social membership.[39] Scholarship on Black public spheres delineates "vernacular practices of street talk and new musics, radio shows and church voices, entrepreneurship and circulation" as fundamental practices contributing to space making. The public sphere enacted by Black and Brown youth in postwar Los Angeles constituted a "critical practice and a visionary politics, a challenge to the exclusionary violence of much public space in the U.S."[40]

Robin Kelley's essay on Black working-class opposition on Birmingham's streetcars and buses during World War II elucidates the ways that whites encountered public space as "a kind of 'democratic space' where people of different class backgrounds shared city theaters, public conveyances, streets, and parks." But for Black people in the same era, "white-dominated public space was vigilantly undemocratic and potentially dangerous."[41] In Los Angeles, the zoot suit violence of 1943, the eviction of whole communities from long-standing vibrant neighborhoods, the relocation of Japanese citizens during World War II, police repression of interracial spaces, and systematic segregation facilitated by federal mishandling of the Fair Housing Act were enduring reminders that public spaces were, at best, contested terrain. Though segregated Black and Latino communities in L.A. during this period were expanding, the symbolic place of these groups in postwar Los Angeles was diminishing. Therefore, claiming and enacting social space, both material and symbolic, was an important measure of the limits and possibilities of social membership.

One of the aspects most powerfully redefined by displaced communities in this period was the terms of social citizenship. Though citizenship has long been determined through legal means, local institutions and policies traditionally govern access to social membership. Denied access to basic housing, educational, and vocational rights, repressed communities relied upon alternative routes to becoming American. This was often achieved as much through horizontal relationships of culture and community as through attempted assimilation into mainstream society. Therefore, when the denigration of neighborhoods and the repression of leisure spaces could not be regained in physical space, people from disenfranchised groups claimed the kinds of spaces that were available to them and in those spaces often created important democratic and egalitarian visions. This did not translate, usually, into permanent spaces. But spatial claims could manifest in temporary locations that announced the relevance and rights of Black and Brown people on the landscape of postwar Los Angeles. These articulations could take place on Whittier Boulevard in East Los Angeles, where Chicano cruisers congregated in a neighborhood that was once theirs; at an A&W drive-in among Black, Brown, and white car club members; in El Monte and Pacoima, where music revues attracted interracial audiences outside city limits, where they were relatively free of police harassment. In all of these instances, spatial claims created a critical sonic narrative, and the development of radio technology became a key conduit for its circulation.[42]

It is important to note that Black and Mexican American youth in postwar Los Angeles experienced race differently from their counterparts in other U.S. cities. These experiences, in turn, generated unique racial sensibilities and cultural productions. Gerald Horne has argued that LA. displayed a "rainbow racism . . . not solely or predominately of the typical black-white dichotomy that obtained elsewhere."[43] In the immediate pre- and postwar era, studies revealed that in factories where Mexicans were categorized as "colored," Blacks not only worked with them but were also given positions over them. In other plants, Mexicans and whites worked together.[44] Further research indicated that white workers often accepted Blacks and objected to Mexicans; still another pattern was found showing that white workers accepted Mexicans but objected to Japanese.[45] These compounded racial encounters extended to interracial residential neighborhoods and influenced cultural productions and racial sensibilities.

The resultant interracial congregation on Central Avenue revealed the powerful symbolic threat posed by interracial cooperation; nevertheless, radio broadcasts from Dolphin's of Hollywood transmitted an invitation to a multiracial, *discursive* space of listenership as well as a physical space of interracial congregation. This summons suggests a spatial entitlement made possible by Dolphin and enacted by working-class youth. These spaces and places, physical and discursive, were mutually constitutive. In such a context, Huggy Boy's exhortation becomes much more than a radio show hook. In the struggle against racism, it was crucial for them, as it is crucial for us, to recognize the patterns of inclusion and exclusion that reproduce racial hierarchies. This is why studying the ways that entitlements of space and social membership are enacted through popular culture can be important: they reveal the history and the promise of shared cultural politics among Black and Brown communities. The circumstances of their production and reception can help us to understand how marginalized historical actors have worked under particular conditions to produce, elaborate, and defend unique modes of social existence.[46]

In his autobiography of life in East L.A. after World War II, Luis Rodríguez recounted, "For the most part, the Mexicans in and around Los Angeles were economically and culturally closest to Blacks. As soon as we understood English, it was usually the Black English we first tried to master. Later . . . Blacks used Mexican slang and the cholo style; Mexicans imitated the Southside swagger . . . although this didn't mean at times we didn't war with one another, such being the state of affairs at the bottom."[47]

Rodríguez's memoir describes the geographical proximity of Black and Mexican American neighborhoods and residents in interracial communities. But it also intimates a critical choice about how people who were geographically restricted articulated collective self-worth and social membership through popular linguistic and stylistic vernaculars.

Black and Brown people in Los Angeles have had a tremendous influence on each other's political and cultural sensibilities. Both groups are part of overlapping diasporas that have shaped significant intellectual traditions and visions of social justice, even as they have been embattled by the histories of racism and economic subjugation. Studying everyday resistance in spatial contexts offers, as Robin Kelley instructs, rich insights into how race, gender, class, space, time, and collective memory shape both domination and resistance.[48]

SONIC SPATIAL CLAIMS

In his history of echo and reverberation in popular recordings, Peter Doyle reveals how sonic manipulations that developed in 1940s popular recordings used reverb effects to set up "pictorial" spaces. Echo and reverb in blues, country, and rock-a-billy recordings made it seem as though the music was "coming from a somewhere—from inside an enclosed architectural or natural space or 'out of' a specific geographical location—and this 'somewhere' was often semiotically highly volatile." Therefore, a repertoire of "spatial" sonic production practices, musical and nonmusical, became available for rock 'n' roll and rhythm and blues artists and producers by the late 1940s and 1950s, and in theory these were easily reproducible for anyone with basic magnetic tape-recording equipment.[49]

White-owned radio stations, record distribution companies, and white radio-aired personalities in postwar L.A. built their successes on the cultural politics generated by multiracial frameworks and musical forms they encountered. Huggy Boy, Hunter Hancock, and Art Laboe were no exception. Police harassment of young people in interracial leisure spaces eventually inspired these emcees, along with promoters, to book acts outside L.A. city limits to avoid the juridical authority of Parker's policies. Art Laboe once boasted, "White kids from Beverly Hills, Black kids from Compton, and local Chicano kids used to come out to our shows every weekend."[50] These revues created lucrative interracial spaces for promoters and record industry executives.

Shows featuring tenor sax honker Big Jay McNeely brought "wild crowds of Black kids, drape-shape Pachucos and white teenagers [who] were all going nuts at Big Jay's shows at the Shrine and Olympic auditoriums," which led to a ban on McNeely's performances in most of Los Angeles County.[51] In 1953 *Ebony* magazine reported, "A young white lad got so hepped up over Big Jay's music that he jumped out of a balcony onto the main floor where he miraculously landed without hurting himself and went into a riotous dance. In Redondo Beach . . . last summer, a teen-aged white girl was sent into raging hysterics by the violent sounds of Big Jay's horn. She did not recover her balance until her boyfriend had slapped her face vigorously about a dozen times."[52] Local papers described "thousands of white kids dancing like Watusis" at the Rendezvous Ballroom, located outside L.A. city limits in Balboa.[53]

Reacting to the creative articulations of social membership enacted by multiracial congregation, local politicians and municipal arts administrators created the Bureau of Music in order to encourage patriotic citizenship, prevent juvenile delinquency, and promote acceptable music.[54] But it was too late: the Blendells, Willie G, the Soul-Jers, the Jaguars, Joe Liggins, Don Tosti, the Premiers, Johnny Otis, and many others had already created a soundtrack of spatial claims concomitant with the articulation of other forms of spatial entitlement. What resulted were new visions of social membership among working-class people, whose basic citizenship rights were relentlessly compromised by the repression of working-class coalitional politics and the growth of white suburbia.

Songs like "Pachuco Boogie," along with the Armenta Brothers and Lalo Guerrero's "Chucos Suaves" and "Marijuana Boogie," made Black musical forms such as jump blues and "honking" popular in the predominately Mexican American communities of East LA. In turn, these forms took on distinct sonic expressions when they became integrated with community vernaculars. The performance styles of artists like Guerrero and the Pachuco Boogie Boys rejected slanderous mischaracterizations of *pachuquismo*'s practitioners and reenvisioned the histories and futures of Black and Brown communities within a politics of respectability. By celebrating the sociopolitical and cultural identities that both Blacks and Chicanos identified with, the creation of pachuco soul and its performance became a means to project an alternative body of cultural and political expression that could consider the world differently from a new perspective: its emancipatory transformation.[55] This sonic legacy reverberated in Thee Midniters' "Whittier Boulevard" in the 1960s.

"Whittier Boulevard" is arguably one of the more representative songs of spatial reclamation in the postwar era. Part of the tangible Whittier Boulevard lay at the epicenter of the five-freeway evisceration of Boyle Heights. Just as the Avalon area, in South Los Angeles, suffered from the invasion of industrial businesses, Whittier Boulevard was targeted for retail development under urban renewal. Merchants were now "insiders," and Mexican Americans were "outsiders," even though the latter community had inhabited the area for generations. But because retailers had built their shops close to the road and flooded the area with light to attract after-work shoppers, they unwittingly created an ideal cruising environment.

We will recollect Doyle's assertion that sonic manipulations have an "inexhaustible ability" to remake space. Sonic spatial claims, articulated through *gritos* at the introduction of "Whittier Boulevard," announce the relevance of Mexican traditions, history, and persons on the literal boulevard and the figurative landscape of postwar L.A.[56] In the scheme of such devastating losses of wealth and space among aggrieved communities in the postwar era, sonic articulations may seem a poor substitute for fair housing, employment, and education. But Thee Midniters and many of their contemporaries offered a soundtrack of sonic entitlement that, even if fleeting, anticipated a potential emancipatory reality. Gritos *on* Whittier Boulevard after 1959 may have been wishful thinking, at least as sanctioned expression. But the gritos *in* "Whittier Boulevard" reimagined the spaces intended by city planners to be beyond the grasp of Mexican youth. And as many activists, artists, and theorists have opined, a utopian imagination can be a necessary component of social change.[57]

The sonic manipulations of "Whittier Boulevard" allowed listeners to engage and interact with spatial claims in ways that inspired the formation of new kinds of communities, an experience made infinitely more possible through the integration of radio technology and car culture.[58] Moreover, the particular sonic contours offered by Thee Midniters, in the blending of instruments and voices particular to Whittier Boulevard, reflect collective and social traditions among excluded communities. In this way, the democratization of sound endorses the democratization of society.[59]

By 1949, six million autos had car radios. In 1951 alone, five million auto-radio sets and over thirteen million radio receivers were sold; in 1954 the first all-transistor commercially produced auto-radio appeared.[60] Reebee Garofalo has shown that the mass commodification of Black popular forms was due in large part to the growth of portable radios. Cars with transistor radios had an enormous impact on where music was heard and transformed radio entertainment from a family-centered activity to a more personal and dispersed listening experience.[61] The new mobility of radios in the 1950s contributed to spatial articulations of social entitlement, in that it facilitated the transport and transmission of sounds and their attendant sensibilities to diverse spaces.

Tom Page, planning manager for new Ford vehicles in the early 1950s, was the first to place transistors into car radios. While planning the 1954 Thunderbird (a car successful in getting attention but not very successful in making money), Ford bought radios from Motorola until a Motorola salesman suggested a switch to transistor radios for their longevity. Consequently, the 1954 Ford models, including the Thunderbird, and the 1955 Lincoln and Mercury models were the first American vehicles with a one-year radio warranty, phenomenal in the industry.[62] These developments would make the car an integral part of youth culture in Los Angeles.

The Ford Company in particular took advantage of the increased spending power and technical skills of African Americans in the post-war era. Identifying Blacks as a major market, they advertised specifically to that segment of the population by promoting the fair hiring practices of an integrated Ford repair shop: "[We] maintain no job race lines," an advertisement declared, and "always point to our open door hiring policy which has helped build the business into the largest among 6,630 Ford dealers around the world."[63] Interestingly and by contrast, most of the cars visible in the barrios were second-hand Chevrolets, which were more stylish, less expensive, and easier to repair than Fords. The eradication of trolley cars, the movement of industries into outlying suburbs, and interest in the American Dream all contributed to the importance of owning an automobile in the post-war era. In the purchase of older cars bought cheaply or inherited, then customized to the owner's satisfaction, we find the roots of street-car culture, cruising, and, later, lowriding. But cruising was a radical departure from what postwar consensus-cultures intended for car owners. As Cameron recalled, "We worked for our *cars,* not for an apartment or a place to live. Mexicans, Blacks, white kids, we all would be in those places, looking up under the hoods of our cars, comparing the flames and designs we put on them."[64] Such stylish and often ostentatious pronouncements about social position and aspirations took on a spatial dimension in locations like Whittier Boulevard and at A&W and movie drive-ins, articulating physical and figurative entitlement to spaces once populated by Black and Brown peoples in what were often formerly their own communities.[65]

The success of Art Laboe, and to a greater extent Huggy Boy, came from the interracial spatial politics that characterized the Mexican American/Chicano musical experience in Los Angeles. Hugg became popular by playing Black music to Chicano audiences, starting with his first job as a theater manager on Whittier Boulevard in the early 1950s and subsequently his first radio job broadcasting from a drive-in in the same area. When British groups changed listener demands and sensibilities in the mid-'60s, Hugg all but lost his place in broadcasting, having been so closely identified with Black R&B artists from Los Angeles. It was Chicano teenagers that "saved Hugg from oblivion, or at least early retirement": Eddie Torres, manager of Thee Midniters, invited Hugg to emcee for the band's shows, and Hugg began touring with them in 1965, playing their records when he broadcast from his one remaining show, at Flash Records on Jefferson and Western. With his popularity renewed and assured by Chicano bands and audiences, Hugg "worked the East Side after 1965 as hard or harder than he worked South Central in the 1950s."[66]

The police had a similar work ethic in these areas: they also "worked" the East Side after 1965 as much as they had repressed the interracial leisure spaces of South Los Angeles in the 1950s. The LAPD maintained a steady repression of interracial congregation on Central Avenue; the Los Angeles County sheriff's office provided heavy policing to protect the merchants on Whittier Boulevard and other areas where car culture proliferated.

In light of this repression, one of Hugg's signature traditions takes on particular spatial significance. When he played Thee Midniters' "Whittier Boulevard," Hugg spoke "over the music, listing landmarks as he [took] the listener on a guided tour of the Boulevard, as only someone who knows East LA could."[67] Hugg's "tour" represented figurative geospatial reclamation by grounding landmarks within the subculture created by Chicano youth, artists, and activists. Hugg followed a form of interpellation that Keta Miranda has argued occurs for the band's Chicano fans: "As the band members shout, 'Let's take a trip down Whittier Boulevard,' [they] acknowledge the very street Mexican American youth have appropriated. . . . Immediately following, a single strident voice shrieks out, 'Arriba! Arriba!'" Miranda argues that this utterance "disidentifies" Mexicanos from their stereotyped representation in the cartoon character Speedy Gonzalez, whose signature salutation is "Arriba! Arriba!" Following José Esteban Muñoz, she emphasizes the song's "recognition of the contradictory facet . . . since disidentification negotiates strategies of resistance within the flux of discourse and power . . . transforming the raw material of identification." As a result, "felt meanings" are summoned in the song's initial announcement, and a collective self emerges in the act of listening, singing, and dance.[68]

City officials' containment of interracial congregation on Whittier Boulevard was reflected in other geospatial areas but also in representation, licensing, and radio play. Interracial sensibilities reflected in the postwar soundtrack of sonic spatial claims were a particular target of censure. The recording and performance careers of two bands in particular illustrate this repression.

In 1957, a mixed-race vocal doo-wop group named themselves the Miracles, explaining, "We were so different, it was a miracle we ever got together."[69] The group met at Fremont High School, one of the first public schools to integrate its classrooms before the landmark U.S.

Supreme Court desegregation decision in 1954. Located at Seventy-Sixth Street and San Pedro Boulevard, it was among the most integrated schools in Los Angeles at that time.[70]

Within a few months, the Miracles renamed themselves the Jaguars. Both lead vocalist Herman "Sonny" Chaney and bass Charles Middleton were African American, baritone Manuel "Manny" Chavez was Mexican American, and second tenor Valerio "Val" Poliuto was Italian American.

"[Radio disc jockeys] would ask us, 'Well, what are you singing? Are you singing pop [popular doo-wop ballad-style] or something else?' The thing about it was that Sonny, Manny, Charles, and I listened to all *kinda* music. And we just didn't sing in a category. In other words we didn't always sound like the same group. Were they white, or were they Black? That was our biggest problem."[71]

Integrated vocal groups like the Jaguars, the Mixtures, and the Crests found that while they personified the racial reality of postwar interracial neighborhoods and listenership, this same characteristic could severely limit the promotion and distribution of their music. Nonetheless, the Jaguars remained wildly popular at that time, appearing on Hunter Hancock's KCBS television show, *Rhythm and Bluesville,* with critical acclaim.[72] Though the performance was a success, it never segued into the national reputation that characterized the experiences of "single-race" doo-wop groups from Los Angeles.

> Because we were a mixed group, we didn't sound like all white and we didn't sound all soul. . . . And so consequently when we'd go to one [radio] station, they'd say, "Well, what *are* you guys?" And one guy said, when he heard the arrangement of "Thinking of You," he said, "Well, I thought you guys were all Black." No! I sang the lead. If my voice is in there with Manuel's voice . . . he's gonna have a different inflection. Putting it all together, we couldn't get played on a lot of stations simply because when we went to perform one guy would say, "Well, gee, I thought they were Black," and another guy would say, "Well, gee, I thought they were white."[73]

Radio and television enacted consensus-culture imperatives by targeting middle-class suburbs as ideal sites for consumption. They worked to attract them as audiences and to sell products to them. George Lipsitz has shown that in the postwar period, business executives waged a fight for authority not just in the factories but also for "power over the reception, uses, and effects of new forms of commercialized leisure." This process functioned as "a powerful agent for the nationalization and homogenization of U.S. culture. In this campaign, business executives interested in installment buying, community planners interested in residential segregation, and radio executives interested in the power of advertising money" rarely promoted anything that did not fit the national project of a uniform citizenry.[74]

An Oxnard band named the Mixtures encountered a similar set of restrictions in the following decade. Their members included Chicano pianist Steve Mendoza, Black saxophonist Delbert Franklin, Chicano drummer Eddie de Robles, Puerto Rican bass player Zag Soto, Black horn player Autry Johnson, white guitarist Dan Pollock, and an American Indian–West Indian percussionist named Johnny Wells.[75] The Mixtures recorded and released several 45s, including "Darling," featuring the vocal duo Phil and Harv, which sold over 250,000 copies in 1961, making them a successful Southern California band. The Mixtures also appeared on *Parade of Hits* on KCOP Channel 13 in Hollywood, sponsored by KRLA Radio and hosted by TV personality Bob Eubanks. But the fact that they and the Jaguars never achieved national prominence reveals the economics of scale that make homogeneous suburban homes the target audience for mass culture rather than groups mixed by class, race, and different kinds of neighborhoods.[76] The Jaguars maintained a high demand in the interracial spaces of leisure and entertainment under consideration, and the soundtrack of postwar spatial articulations grew stronger.

For example, before Anthony "Naff" Ortega became a musician on Central Avenue, he was a founding member of the Frantic Five, a Black and Mexican jazz ensemble formed out of the Jordan High School Swing Band. Ortega traveled uptown from his home in Watts to Maple Street on the Watts Local and Big Red streetcars to take saxophone lessons from famed jazz pedagogue Lloyd Reese. He noticed tags on buildings that read, "Manuel de la Colonia" or "Jr. del Watts." Rather than claim one neighborhood affiliation, Ortega, a Mexican American born and raised in Watts, expanded his purview—and history—to a much broader geographical area: he began tagging "Naff del World."[77] More than a teenage quip, Naff's tag was a signature reflective of the spatial politics of reclamation enacted by Black and Brown youth in the postwar era.

CONCLUSION

Together, Black and Brown communities and popular collectivities have consistently envisioned futures that include each other's memories and histories, even when this choice wasn't always conscious. As scholars of cultural exchange, resistance, and production, we know that organized social movements were not the only kinds of politics that yielded affirmative results, particularly in moments when there were few options for political expression available to aggrieved groups.

These articulations of spatial entitlement, sonic and symbolic, were often articulated in moments when the loss of space meant devastating losses of wealth for communities of color, wealth that was rarely regained. Considering the unrelenting efforts to keep Black and Brown people from recognizing their mutual stakes in a just future makes these spatial claims all the more remarkable.

Black-Brown antagonisms in present-day Los Angeles are real. Intragroup tensions among neighbors, coworkers, and students have sometimes resulted in demoralizing violence and lasting disunity. But we seem to forget that the root of these tensions are not of our own making: there are powerful forces at work with great stakes in generating discourse intended to obscure—if not negate—the persistent, often radical coalitional politics that are more consistent with our intertwined histories. Listening to official forecasts of Black-Brown relations in twenty-first-century Los Angeles can be a dispiriting exercise. Narrowly exposed only to this narrative, listeners might never come to know the radical past of mutual struggle that exists among these communities. It is a history worth remembering, rediscovering, and reinventing.

NOTES

The opening epigraphs are taken from Joseph Eli Kovner, "Resettle Elsewhere, Says Mayor, 'If You Don't Want Urban Renewal,'" *Eastside Sun,* January 8, 1959; and Earl Lewis, *In Their Own Interests: Race, Class, and Power in Twentieth-Century Norfolk, Virginia* (Berkeley: University of California Press, 1991), 91–92.

1. Reebee Garofalo, "Crossing Over," in *Split Image: African Americans in the Mass Media,* ed. William Barlow and Jeanette Dates (Washington DC: Howard University Press, 1990), 26–27.

2. Donald J. Mabry, "The Rise and Fall of Ace Records: A Case Study in the Independent Record Business," *Business History Review* 64, no. 3 (Autumn 1990): 411.

3. Anthony Macías, "Bringing Music to the People: Race, Urban Culture, and Municipal Politics in Postwar Los Angeles," *American Quarterly* 56, no. 3 (2004): 707–8.

4. Mabry, "The Rise and Fall of Ace Records," 411.

5. Dolphin preferred to pay cash on the spot for songs rather than royal-

ties, and this is the storied reason behind his murder in 1958 by a dissatisfied songwriter.

6. Jim Dawson, liner notes on *Boogie Down on Central: Los Angeles' Rhythm and Blues Revolution,* recorded 1999, Rhino Records 75872, 33-⅓. We will note that Art Laboe, Hunter Hancock, Dick Clark, and other white local jockeys made their success from Black music and its circulation, many times without adequate licensing compensation or proper credit given to the artists responsible for the sound that made these jockeys famous.

7. "According to Huggy Boy, his program attracted white listeners from the San Fernando Valley, who would travel thirty-five miles to Dolphin's to purchase R&B records. 'In those days, people who liked rhythm and blues had to go to Black neighborhoods to buy it,' said Huggy Boy." David Reyes and Tom Waldman, *Land of a Thousand Dances: Chicano Rock 'n' roll from Southern California* (Albuquerque: University of New Mexico Press, 1998), 49–50.

8. Eric Ávila, *Popular Culture in the Age of White Flight: Fear and Fantasy in Suburban Los Angeles* (Berkeley: University of California Press, 2004), 20.

9. "Leaders Protest Dance Hall Ban," California Eagle, May 30, 1940, quoted in Anthony Macias, "Bringing Music to the People: Race, Urban Culture, and Municipal Politics in Postwar Los Angeles" American Quarterly 56, no. 3 (2004): 707–8.

10. Mike Davis, *City of Quartz: Excavating the Future in Los Angeles* (New York: Vintage Books, 1992).

11. Similarly, Ávila has argued that disparate material productions and discursive practices often emerged out of the same historical formations in this region. Ávila, *Popular Culture in the Age of White Flight.*

12. Robin D.G. Kelley, *Race Rebels: Culture, Politics, and the Black Working Class* (New York: Free Press, 1994), 56.

13. Ibid., 8–9.

14. James C. Scott describes infrapolitics as circumspect struggles "waged daily by subordinate groups[, which,] like infrared rays, [are] beyond the visible end of the spectrum. That [they] should be invisible . . . is in large part by design—is a tactical choice born of a prudent awareness of the balance of power." James C. Scott, *Domination and the Arts of Resistance: Hidden Transcripts* (New Haven, CT: Yale University Press, 1990), 183. See also Lila Abu-Lughod, "The Romance of Resistance: Tracing Transformations of Power through Bedouin Women," *American Ethnologist* 17, no. 1 (1990): 55; and Kelley, *Race Rebels,* 8.

15. Allison Varzally, *Making a Non-White America* (Berkeley: University of California Press, 2008), 185, 198.

16. Mindy Thompson Fullilove, *Root Shock: How Tearing Up City Neighborhoods Hurts America, and What We Can Do about It* (New York: One World/Ballantine Books, 2004).

17. Marc Weiss, "The Origins and Legacy of Urban Renewal," in *Urban and Regional Planning in an Age of Austerity,* ed. Pierre Clavel, John Forrester, and William Goldsmith (New York: Pergamon Press, 1980), 53–79.

18. Norman M. Klein, *The History of Forgetting: Los Angeles and the Erasure of Memory* (London: Verso, 1997), 133. See also Josh Sides, *L.A. City*

Limits: African American Los Angeles from the Great Depression to the Present (Berkeley: University of California Press, 2004).

19. George Sánchez, "What's Good for Boyle Heights Is Good for the Jews: Creating Multiculturalism on the Eastside during the 1950s," *American Quarterly* 56, no. 3 (2004): 633–61.

20. Editorial, *Eastside Sun,* Fall 1957; quoted in Ávila, *Popular Culture in the Age of White Flight,* 210.

21. Sánchez, "What's Good for Boyle Heights Is Good for the Jews," 636, quoting from Home Owners Loan Corporation City Survey Files, Area D-53, Los Angeles, 1939, National Archives, Washington DC, 7. Also quoted in George Lipsitz, *Time Passages: Collective Memory and American Popular Culture* (Minneapolis: University of Minnesota Press, 1990), 137.

22. Sides, *L.A. City Limits,* 113.

23. Janet Abu-Lughod, *Race, Space, and Riots in Chicago, New York, and Los Angeles* (New York: Oxford University Press, 2007).

24. Philip J. Ethington, "Segregated Diversity: Race-Ethnicity, Space, and Political Fragmentation in Los Angeles County, 1940–1994," Final Report to the John Randolph Haynes and Dora Haynes Foundation, September 13, 2000.

25. Sánchez, "What's Good for Boyle Heights Is Good for the Jews," 657.

26. Gerald Horne, *Fire This Time: The Watts Uprising and the 1960s* (New York: Da Capo Press, 1997), 137.

27. Davis, *City of Quartz,* 294.

28. George Lipsitz, *The Possessive Investment in Whiteness: How White People Profit from Identity Politics* (Philadelphia: Temple University Press, 2006), 5–6; Sánchez, "What's Good for Boyle Heights Is Good for the Jews."

29. Ávila, *Popular Culture in the Age of White Flight.*

30. Kevin Baxter, "Orphans of the Ravine," *Los Angeles Times,* March 29, 2008.

31. Thomas Shapiro, *The Hidden Cost of Being African American: How Wealth Perpetuates Inequality* (London: Oxford University Press, 2005); Michael Hout, review of *The Hidden Cost of Being African-American* [by Thomas M. Shapiro], *Washington Post,* 2005, www.pbs.org/race/ooo_About/oo2_04-background-03–10.htm.

32. Cedric Robinson, *Forgeries of Memory and Meaning: Blacks and the Regimes of Race in American Theater and Film before World War II* (Chapel Hill: University of North Carolina Press, 2007), xii–xiii.

33. Lisa Duggan, *The Twilight of Equality? Neoliberalism, Cultural Politics, and the Attack on Democracy* (Boston: Beacon Press, 2004).

34. John A. Powell, "Structural Racism and Spatial Jim Crow," in *The Black Metropolis in the Twenty-First Century: Race, Power, and Politics of Place,* ed. Robert Bullard (New York: Rowman and Littlefield, 2007), 49.

35. Earl Lewis, *In Their Own Interests: Race, Class, and Power in Twentieth-Century Norfolk, Virginia* (Berkeley: University of California Press, 1991), 91–92.

36. Arjun Appadurai, "Disjuncture and Difference in the Global Cultural Economy," in *The Phantom Public Sphere,* ed. Bruce Robbins (Minneapolis: University of Minnesota Press, 1993), 269–95.

37. Houston A. Baker Jr., "Critical Memory and the Black Public Sphere," in *The Black Public Sphere*, ed. the Black Public Sphere Collective (Chicago: University of Chicago Press, 1995), 5–38.

38. Jürgen Habermas, *The Structural Transformation of the Public Sphere: An Inquiry into a Category of Bourgeois Society*, translated by Thomas Burger with Frederick Lawrence (Cambridge, MA: MIT Press, 1989).

39. Nancy Fraser, "Rethinking the Public Sphere: A Contribution to the Critique of Actually Existing Democracy," in *Habermas and the Public Sphere*, ed. Craig Calhoun (Cambridge, MA: MIT Press, 1997), 109–42.

40. The Black Public Sphere Collective, "Introduction," in *The Black Public Sphere*.

41. Kelley, *Race Rebels*, 56.

42. Susan J. Smith has argued, "Music [is] a medium through which those whose condition society tries its best not to see can begin to make themselves heard." Susan J. Smith, "Beyond Geography's Visible Worlds: A Cultural Politics of Music," *Progress in Human Geography* 21, no. 4 (1997): 502–29.

43. Horne, *Fire This Time*.

44. J. Max Bond, "The Negro in Los Angeles," PhD dissertation, University of Southern California, 1936, 98.

45. David Wyatt, *Five Fires: Race, Catastrophe, and the Shaping of California* (New York: Oxford University Press, 1998), 34.

46. Christopher Waterman, "Race Music: Bo Chatmon, 'Corrine Corrina,' and the Excluded Middle," in *Music and the Racial Imagination*, ed. Ronald M. Radano and Philip V. Bohlman (Chicago: University of Chicago Press, 2000).

47. Luis Rodríguez, *Always Running: La Vida Loca: Gang Days in L.A.* (New York: Touchstone, 1994), 126.

48. Kelley, *Race Rebels*, 56.

49. Peter J. Doyle, *Echo and Reverb: Fabricating Space in Popular Music Recording, 1900–1960* (Middletown, CT: Wesleyan University Press, 2005), 1–37.

50. Matt García, "'Memories of El Monte': Intercultural Dance halls in Post-WWII Greater Los Angeles," in *Generations of Youth: Youth Culture and History in Twentieth Century America*, ed. Michael Nevin Willard and Joe Austin (New York: New York University Press, 1989), 161.

51. Jonny Whiteside, "Nervous Man Nervous: Big Jay McNeely in 3-D," *LA Weekly*, February 4–10, 2000, 32.

52. "Big Jay McNeely!" *Ebony*, May 1953.

53. Whiteside, "Nervous Man Nervous."

54. Macías, "Bringing Music to the People."

55. Paul Gilroy calls this a "politics of transfiguration." Paul Gilroy, *The Black Atlantic: Modernity and Double Consciousness* (Cambridge, MA: Harvard University Press, 1995), 39.

56. Thee Midniters became one of the first rock acts to broadcast political entitlements of Chicanos with songs like "Chicano Power" and "The Ballad of César Chávez." See Reyes and Waldman, *Land of a Thousand Dances*.

57. See Buck-Morss's elucidation of Walter Benjamin's *Passagenwerk*, in

The Dialectics of Seeing (Cambridge, MA: MIT Press, 1991), 114–20; and Angela McRobbie, "The *Passagenwerk* and the Place of Walter Benjamin in Cultural Studies," in *Postmodernism and Popular Culture*, 96–120. See also Fredric Jameson, *The Political Unconscious: Narrative as a Socially Symbolic Act* (Ithaca, NY: Cornell University Press, 1981), 285.

58. Doyle, *Echo and Reverb.*

59. I thank George Lipsitz for this suggestion.

60. *Electronic Engineering Times* 978 (October 30, 1997): 131.

61. Garofalo, "Crossing Over," 26–27.

62. *Electronic Engineering Times* 978 (October 30, 1997): 131.

63. Boyd Gibbons, "Ford Repair Shop: Advertising Tells about Colored Personnel," *Ebony* 4, August 1949, 39.

64. David Reyes and Tom Waldman, *Land of a Thousand Dances: Chicano Rock 'n' roll from Southern California* (Albuquerque: University of New Mexico Press, 1998) 50.

65. Brenda Jo Bright and Liza Bakewell, eds., *Looking High and Looking Low: Art and Cultural Identity* (Tucson: University of Arizona Press, 1999); C. Ondine Chavoya, "Customized Hybrids: The Art of Ruben Ortiz Torres and Lowriding in Southern California," *New Centennial Review* 4, no. 2 (2004): 141–84; Lipsitz, *Time Passages.*

66. Reyes and Waldman, *Land of a Thousand Dances,* 50–51.

67. Marie "Keta" Miranda, "Dancing to 'Whittier Boulevard': Choreographing Social Identity," in *Dancing across Borders: Danzas y Bailes Mexicanos,* ed. Olga Nájera-Ramírez, Norma E. Cantú, and Brenda M. Romero (Urbana: University of Illinois Press, 2009), 73–74; José Esteban Muñoz, *Disidentifications: Queers of Color and the Performance of Politics* (Minneapolis: University of Minnesota Press, 1999).

68. Val Poliuto, personal interview by author, Ventura, CA, December 4, 2001.

69. Parents and students of Fremont High School had not always been open to integration. Bass recalled a mock lynching staged at the school in 1941: "The poster circulated preliminary to the mock lynching stated: 'we want no niggers in this school. This is a white man's school. Go to your own school, and leave us to ours. . . . the *Eagle* editor was on the scene during the entire demonstration, and there was no question in her mind but that the 500 students of Fremont had been encouraged in this hate campaign by their hate-mongering parents. . . . " Charlotta A. Bass, *Forty Years: Memoirs from the Pages of a Newspaper* (Los Angeles: self-published, 1960), 135–36.

70. Val Poliuto, personal interview by author, Ventura, CA, December 4, 2001.

71. Hunter Hancock, "Huntin' with Hunter: The Story of the West Coast's First R&B Disc Jockey!" August 17, 2000, www.electricearl.com/dws/hunter.html.

72. Val Poliuto, personal interview by author, Ventura, CA, December 4, 2001.

73. George Lipsitz, *A Rainbow at Midnight: Labor and Culture in the 1940s* (Urbana: University of Illinois Press, 1994), 259.

74. Dan Pollock, interview by author, Saticoy, CA, April 2, 2001.

75. Lipsitz, *A Rainbow at Midnight*.

76. Steven Isoardi, interviewer, "Anthony Ortega," in *Central Avenue Sounds*, tape 1, side 2, recorded September 10, 1994, UCLA Oral History Program.

77. This is taken from Peter Doyle's eloquent rumination about the pictorial spaces created by the sonic manipulations of echo and reverb. Doyle, *Echo and Reverb*, 234.

13

On Fallen Nature and the Two Cities

NERY GABRIEL LEMUS

Perhaps one of my earliest recollections of prejudice that I can remember happened around the age of eight. I recall boarding the RTD and having to explain to my mother what the bus driver said about the bus fair. The bus driver scornfully remarked, "Doesn't your mom speak English? We live in America." Indignation filled my small frame, and I felt like beating the crap out of that bigot. Somehow I knew there was a lack of empathy and a sense of contempt spewing from that man.

That childhood event weighs heavily on my practice as an artist. That is to say, my ongoing practice frequently explores the parallels found within cultures and questions the associations that divide people within society. My belief is not necessarily that my artistic endeavors will somehow solve the pressing issues of division and polarization in society but rather that they can generate a discursive dialogue about particular issues.

In my project, *Fallen Nature and the Two Cities,* I address the idea of "the shared practice." I do so by exploring the visual aesthetic of a haircut and the barbershop experiences of young Black and Latino males. I was particularly interested in a certain shared hairstyle, that of the lined-up fade. Regardless of the customer's hair texture or hairline, the same look was achieved. I wanted to document this shared practice in order to generate a dialogue about the existing acrimonious relationship between the two cultures in Los Angeles.

It has become difficult to ignore the current hostile divisions between

Latino and Black communities. The divisions have been visibly apparent through gang warfare and in schools, jails, and certain communities. Various educators have come up with theories relating to the onset of the polemic. Some argue that the problem stems from economic rivalry, while others believe it stems from longtime prejudices. My interest in the project, as mentioned before, is to formalize a structure within art that would not seek to find the origin of the division but rather would engage in dialogue.

I believe that by using the constructs of documentation, one can ponder the polemic by representing the two cultures participating in the same activity or exploring the "other's" implied space. For instance, in segments of the video in this body of work, *Proclamation of the Lined-Up Fade,* I show young Latino males receiving haircuts in Latino barbershops as well as young Black males receiving haircuts in Black barbershops. As the video progresses, a young Black man receives a haircut in a Latino barbershop, and a Latino male has his hair cut at a Black barbershop. Although these latter scenarios happen, they are not as common as the former. These scenes tell of cultural exchange or reveal a model for cultural exchange.

I believe what this project does is illustrate the complexity that accompanies the notion of identity. As the two cultures engage through a shared practice or through exploring the other's implied space, they absorb each other. The impetus for this work is to try to highlight the interaction—the moment of contact that serves as a reminder of an unfixed notion of identity. Through interaction we realize that despite apparent cultural differences, we acclimate to and in some instances adopt other cultures.

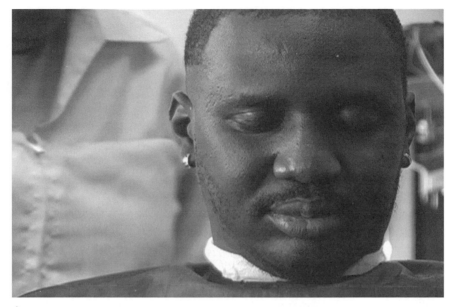

Proclamation of the Lined-Up Fade, 7 minutes, 2007, video still.

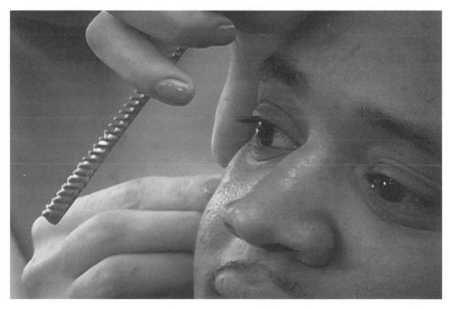

Proclamation of the Lined-Up Fade, 7 minutes, 2007, video still.

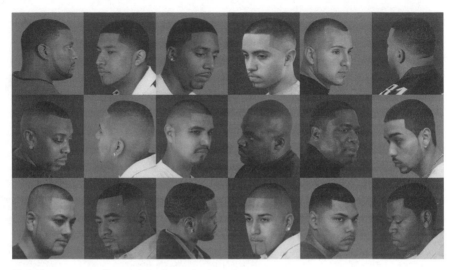

Fade Away, 2007, offset print, 28 × 42 inches.

Fade Away, 2007, installation shoot.

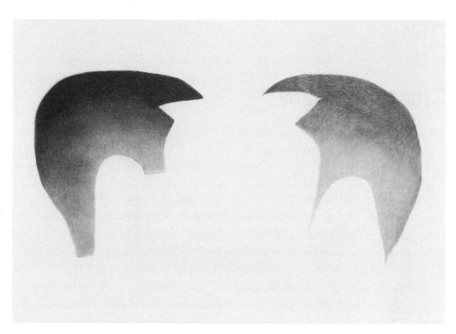

Talk to You, 2007, graphite on panel, 24 × 34 inches.

Number 2 on the Top, 2007, graphite on panel, 17 × 20 inches.

14

"Just Win, Baby!"

The Raider Nation and Second Chances for Black and Brown L.A.

PRISCILLA LEIVA

The rough-and-tumble Raiders returned to Los Angeles in style after defeating the favored Washington Redskins in the 1983 season Super Bowl. The multiday celebration commenced with two thousand fans congregating at L.A.'s airport and is still remembered twenty-five years later by journalists and witnesses alike. A Raiders rally at City Hall on January 24, 1984, drawing eight thousand fans from all over the area, followed the joyous welcome. Never before had Los Angeles won a football championship; fans reveled in the moment. Raider favorites running back Marcus Allen, a University of Southern California alumni, and coach Tom Flores exclaimed their love for their Los Angeles fans. Flores proclaimed the event was proof of a Raiders takeover of the city, and Allen surprised attendees with his own version of Randy Newman's "I Love L.A." song. The predominantly Black and Latina/o crowd outside City Hall cheered on their team, a team that rose to Super Bowl glory in the crowd's likeness—underdogs fighting for recognition and respect. The city's first African American mayor, Tom Bradley, thanked the team for bringing more to the city than its first world championship. Bradley declared the Raiders "have brought this community together as never before in the history of this city," before extending the city key to Tom Flores.[1] Upon accepting the key, the first Latino head football coach in the National Football League and his team effectively transformed Los Angeles into Raider territory,

FIGURE 14.1. Thousands gathered outside Los Angeles City Hall to celebrate the Raiders' Super Bowl victory with Mayor Tom Bradley, coach Tom Flores, and player Marcus Allen. (Photograph by James Ruebsamen, Herald Examiner Collection, Los Angeles Public Library)

a territory of overlapping landscapes embedded with the possibility of forming alliances between communities of color.[2]

The Raiders' Super Bowl victory shed light on a developing connection between the team and the city they had come to conquer only two years prior. The City Hall rally alerted the rest of the city to what communities of color already knew—African American and Latina/o fans gave the Raiders a home while the Raiders and their image provided a vehicle through which alienated communities of color could claim L.A. as their own and negotiate their relationship with each other. Celebrating the former Oakland team's win, communities of color in Los Angeles identified with the Raiders as a team that embodied the importance of second chances and the fruits of remaining loyal to your own in good times and in bad. The fans at City Hall resembled Raider fans from their former working-class home and visibly shifted the meanings and possibilities for professional sports in Los Angeles. This event marks an important moment for understanding the meanings embedded in a Raider identity before and after their arrival in Southern California and its significance to Black and Brown Los Angeles. This survey of intersections between sports fandom and ethnic Los Angeles landscapes explores the formation of the Raider Nation through media interpretations of the team and fan participation in an imagined community.[3]

THE NOTORIOUS RAIDERS ARRIVE

Before the possibility of a Raiders move from Oakland to Los Angeles materialized, Los Angeles Rams owner Carroll Rosenbloom set the stage by moving his team out of Los Angeles and disparaging the Los Angeles Memorial Coliseum's (LAMC) surrounding neighborhood. In 1978, after thirty-two years in residence at LAMC, Rosenbloom planned to relocate his team to a newly publicly funded and renovated stadium in Orange County's city of Anaheim.[4] Downplaying the enormous financial incentives awaiting him in Anaheim, Rosenbloom blamed the poor and working-class community surrounding the Coliseum for the loss of the football team. He claimed the primary reason for the move was a concern about crime and the need to protect white fans afraid of attending games in poor and predominantly Black and Brown South Central.[5]

Like other professional sports teams that define the cities in which they thrive, the Rams cast communities of color in the shadows. The Los Angeles Rams rooted a civic and sports culture in a middle- and upper-class suburban identity. Rosenbloom's comments made a distinction between Coliseum patrons and the Black and increasingly Latina/o surrounding neighborhood and rehearsed journalists' characterizations of the area. Journalists often claimed those living near LAMC posed a potential harm to stadium goers. For example, one article joked that the Coliseum needed to supply individual bodyguards to escort fans to their cars, assuming they had not been stolen.[6] These comments reinforced a racialized and economic separation between fans who entered the Coliseum and those who lived in the surrounding neighborhood. Alongside media representations, the Los Angeles Rams' relocation promoted the alienation of the nearby 20 percent Latina/o and 70 percent Black neighborhoods from the spaces they called home.[7] The Rams' departure made way for the Raiders' arrival and created an opportunity to alter a greater L.A. identity away from economic privilege. Instead, the Los Angeles Raiders and their Black and Latina/o fans contested the terms of their own representation and also altered the social and political landscape of the city's representation. A change in teams brought with it a shift in the bounds of who could claim belonging, even ownership, of the city through their team.

Eager to replace the Rams, the Los Angeles Memorial Coliseum Commission and city officials courted a few teams before the Raiders became the favored choice, after they threatened to leave what they considered a subpar Oakland stadium. Coming to Los Angeles amid lawsuits and countersuits between the Raiders and Oakland over eminent domain and between the Raiders and the National Football League concerning anti-trust laws, maverick franchise owner Al Davis managed to benefit from loans he did not have to pay back.[8] Less worried about the massive public payout, Rams fans and other suburban residents expressed concern about the respectability of the incoming team. For *Los Angeles Times* journalist Scott Ostler, the solution was to get "Oakland out of the Raiders" in order to distance idealized middle- and upper-class Los Angeles from Black working-class Oakland.[9] Steve Cotton, of Santa Monica, hoped his tax money was not being used to bring "Jack Tatum to the City of Angels."[10] Although he was released from the Raiders three years prior to the Los Angeles move, Jack "the Assassin" Tatum's reputation persisted and encompassed anxieties about the Raiders' close relationship to Oakland and players' performance as extremely aggressive football players. Beyond the preservation of L.A.'s image, residents of El Segundo, a suburban city that prided itself on maintaining a small-town intimacy and the planned site of the Raiders' practice field, were concerned about the "type" of people the Raiders brought.[11] Marking a new era for Los Angeles, the Raiders would prove to be a departure from the glitz of the city as well as from its residents who deemed themselves respectable.

Raiders critics failed to detect the role of owner Al Davis in facilitating a sinister image and the media's role in narrating a team identity through captivating descriptors such as *renegade, rambunctious,* and *terrifying.* Without a public relations department or even a point-person well into the 1980s, Al Davis and the Raiders maintained a secretive aura around the organization and reinforced an insider/outsider dynamic. Leaving sportswriters to their own devices to interpret the behavior of Davis and the team, the Raiders' unconventional approach to the media provided the fodder from which writers would take liberty to use their imagination. These journalistic inferences made for captivating pieces about the behavior of individuals as a reflection of a greater team aura. And this aura originated with Al Davis.

Davis began his career with the struggling Raiders team in 1963 as head coach and manager. Approaching the team as a package, he focused on transforming the team's image. He believed the Raiders needed to incite fear and so employed black and silver uniforms and a new logo of a pirate with an eye patch and cross-swords. Deploying preconceptions of an outlaw hypermasculinity, Davis enjoyed "the way the black made [players] look bigger than other teams."[12] Davis also assembled a team of players who would best command a fear-based respect as outlaws. He was skilled at identifying potential legends in a crowd of unwanted players and taught them to become great by any means necessary. As early as 1965, sports journalists like Edwin Shrake, of *Sports Illustrated,* identified the Raiders as a team that attracted troublemakers "who could not be controlled in other cities."[13] In accordance with the rough-and-tumble image, the Raiders maintained the highest number of penalties in the league year after year. The meaning of an outlaw shifted to denote winning and upheld the team's mottoes, "Commitment to Excellence," "Pride and Poise," and "Just Win, Baby." Over time, these mottoes provided the language through which the unconventional team and its fans could appropriate, or pirate, the traditional values of the American sport in order to emerge from the margins. Al Davis contributed to the Raider image and built a reputation as a controversial maverick and perpetual thorn in NFL Commissioner Pete Rozelle's side.[14] The Raiders reflected their leader and pushed the bounds of acceptability while demanding respect. For Oakland fans, the team represented the possibility of persevering through struggle, loosely resembling the hotbed of Black radicalism and the Black Panther Party, which originated in the same city. The Raiders franchise explicitly linked itself to the force of this movement through the shared motto "By Any Means." The Raiders' new hometown of Los Angeles readily embraced the champions and their imported Oakland-based mottoes.

The commitment to a renegade team stemmed from Davis's own life as someone who had experienced the ills of anti-Semitism and strove to embody a masculine ideal despite his lack of athleticism. Born into a Jewish American family in Brooklyn in 1929, Davis strove to replicate his father as a "tough man who grew up in a tough age." Davis's father never moved his family to more affluent neighborhoods regardless of their financial stability, opting instead to remain in a close-knit Jewish American community. The concrete of the playground was central to Davis's and other Jewish American childhoods. In Brooklyn, the playground was the youth social scene, where young, mostly Jewish

American teenagers perfected the city game.[15] Despite his skinny legs, Davis attended Syracuse University in hopes of playing basketball. He did not make the team and blamed the coach's anti-Semitism. Players said the coach employed a quota system allowing a maximum of two Jewish players on the team and ridiculed players by changing Anglo names to Jewish ones.[16] This experience drew him to football and coach Floyd "Ben" Shwartzwalder's coaching tactics, which inspired him to pursue coaching. Davis's memory of prejudice followed him into his college football (at the University of Southern California) and NFL coaching careers, in which he emphasized winning as a means of challenging racial exclusion. This commitment made him a pioneer in diversifying college and professional football. His pursuit of winning through racial diversity also encountered the broader racialized notions of Black masculinity as risky or gritty in the mainstream media.

Davis promoted a tough-guy image connected to his experience in Brooklyn's Jewish American ghetto, regardless of the material comforts he enjoyed. His friends claimed he always represented himself as a street fighter even though, as an old college teammate said, "There was a rumor that he had money, but it was hard to believe because he *acted* very often like one of these underprivileged New York kids who have to fight their way through everything" (emphasis in original).[17] Davis continued to benefit from his father's financial stability while remaining strongly connected to the tough neighborhood he had thrived in as a child.[18] He married Carol Sagal in 1954, a woman with a small family fortune, affording him financial independence from his father.[19] Despite his new wealth, Davis continued to identify with the street, extending working-class fans an opportunity to connect with the team that glorified urban surroundings familiar to them. Exclaiming, "When you grow up in the ghetto, you learn how to hustle," Davis extended this mentality to professional football and derived immense profits from Oakland and eventually Los Angeles's public investments.[20]

Davis imagined a Raiders football team reflecting the ghetto with which he identified. He openly searched for players who shared his sensibilities and who had "street in 'em."[21] The emphasis placed on the street and Davis's experience in the Jewish American ghetto also partly explains why the Raiders were more racially diverse than other professional football teams. Scholar Jonathan Kaufman contends that talk of socialism and equality permeated life in Brooklyn, "creating a world in which Blacks were objects of sympathy rather than hate, potential allies rather than foes, people who could be helped and who could make

Jews feel good for having helped them."[22] As Hasia Diner argues, Jews claimed to understand Blacks better than other groups did because of parallel histories of oppression and utilized ideas that resonated in Jewish life, including the term *ghetto*.[23] This image of being from the ghetto, coming from the bottom, or operating as the underdog was integral to the media portrayals of the Oakland Raiders as outcasts, as well as to Davis's own philosophies. While in Oakland, Al Davis and the Raiders utilized the imagery of creating champions from the ghetto to connect with the city's identity. Oakland's demographic changes were key in defining the city's mainstream identity when the Black residential population nearly doubled between 1950 and 1960, from 55,778 to 100,000, and then rose to 125,000 by 1970.[24] Furthermore, Oakland also served as a fulcrum of Black radicalism that lent itself to a rebellious Raiders identity. As national economic crises ensued in the 1970s and Black urban struggle persisted, the meanings of *ghetto* and *street* in the popular imagination were no longer affiliated with white ethnics and, instead, flattened Black subjectivities. Over time, outsiders imagined the ghetto as "a place of adventure, unbridled violence, erotic fantasy, and/or an imaginary alternative to suburban boredom."[25] While Al Davis's personal history fueled the initial diversity of the team, the racialization of Black Raider players within the context of Oakland marked a departure from Jewish American streets and facilitated the promotion of a Raiders image as organic to urban Black spaces.

FEAR OF THE RAIDERS TRAVELS FROM OAKLAND
TO LOS ANGELES

Looking to the experiences of Raiders players of the 1970s provides a window into the racialization of Black masculinities and its relationship to a Raiders image that still persists throughout California. Sports fans to this day have considered "Soul Patrol," a collection of defensive backs consisting of the African American players Jack "the Assassin" Tatum, Willie Brown, George "Butch" Atkinson," and Skip "Doctor Death" Thomas as one of the most feared units in football history. Both the historical reality and misinterpretations of Jack Tatum and George Atkinson in particular serve as important continuities between the formation of a Raiders image in Oakland and the team's easy acceptance by Black Angelenos.[26]

On opening day of 1976, tensions ran high as the Oakland Raiders confronted their most-hated rival, the Pittsburgh Steelers. Atkinson tackled the Pittsburgh wide receiver Lynn Swann fifteen yards away from the ball with his forearm at the base of Swann's helmet. Swann lost consciousness and subsequently was sidelined for the following two games. Officials did not see the play and did not call a penalty. The Raiders went on to win the game with a score of 31–28, and the game's aftermath fueled the lasting dangerous outlaw image that fixed the identities of the Soul Patrol.

Newspaper accounts suggested Atkinson's hit was akin to murderous violence. Columnists described him as "having the same behavioral failing of your unfriendly, neighborhood mugger."[27] A *Los Angeles Times* reporter argued that any time this sort of "felony" was committed, coaches should be fined and players should automatically be released from the season.[28] Another reporter went so far as to write that Atkinson was lucky that Lynn Swann's injury was not more severe, "because he could have been tried for murder."[29] Still another writer likened Lynn Swann's fall to a drop, "as if he was shot."[30] Later, the *San Jose Mercury News* published a photograph of Atkinson with a gunsight superimposed on his helmet.[31] This gunsight not only interpreted the Black body as a weapon but also suggested the gunsight was a reasonable method in achieving law and order. Lynn Swann extended attacks on Atkinson to the entire Oakland Raiders team when he stated, "If somebody dies on a football field sometime, hopefully it won't be me. It depends on how many times we play Oakland."[32] Steelers coach Chuck Noll furthered this sentiment when he assumed intent on the part of Atkinson: "You have a criminal element in all aspects of society. Apparently we have it in the National Football League too. George Atkinson's hit on Lynn Swann was with intent to maim and not with football in mind. Maybe we have a law-and-order problem."[33] Alongside journalists, Noll had a hand in linking the Raiders' reputation with brutality and criminality and suggested the Raiders had their criminal counterpart in the greater society.

Noll also indicted Jack Tatum as part of the criminal element, a charge that Tatum later refuted. When Tatum's legal hit on the Patriots player Darryl Stingley during the 1978 season left Stingley a quadriplegic, these claims resurfaced.[34] In an effort to combat totalizing stereotypes, Tatum's autobiography details Al Davis's formula of extracting better performance through job competition. In *They Call Me the Assassin*, Tatum emphasizes that players were laborers, explaining, "Because of what the owners expect of me when they give me my paycheck, I automatically reacted to the situation by going for an intimidating hit."[35] He continued, "The Raiders invested in me and I had to produce. Professional football is vicious and brutal. . . . I was being paid well for a service, and if I didn't deliver, they'd go and find someone else who would."[36]

He emphasizes that representations of himself as "the Assassin" were not his invention. Rather, the Raiders used the moniker in their first press release announcing his arrival to the team. Soon after he became a member of the Soul Patrol that could be found, as Al Davis's biographer, Mark Ribowsky claimed, in "the ghetto" of the locker room. [37] White teammates like Tom Keating also fed this image; he suggested, "Automatically, on [Tatum's] looks alone, you're gonna arrest him."[38] In addition, James Plunkett, the Mexican American quarterback who joined the Raiders in 1978, utilized this discourse in his praise of the team's camaraderie: "I've never had more fun in football than summer training camp with the Oakland Raiders. This is where I learned about the Raiders' camaraderie that holds the team together. You've got blacks and whites, crazies and straights, yet they rally together and defend one another both on and off the field. It's hard to explain; you have to live it to understand. There is a uniqueness about Raider football."[39]

For Plunkett, "Raider football" was an unordinary family united by loyalty to shared mottoes and to one another. Juxtaposing blacks to crazies and whites to straights, Plunkett marks the different ways in which the players, as racialized figures, inhabited the Raiders' outlaw image. In a sense, these players—the products of what Patricia Hill Collins refers to as the "controlling images" of Black males in America—were racialized under the guise of the Raiders' image as ghetto, deadly, and criminal.[40] These representations tended to shore up titillating stereotypes of Black bodies as inherently criminal. Similar to Plunkett's description of the Raiders, the director of player personnel Ron Wolf exalted the Raiders' identity as more important than race: "It was about being a Raider. That was far more important than any of that other stuff."[41] While this logic denied the historical realities of racism, it also suggested a hope that some held of harnessing racialized images through the Raiders before, during, and after the team was in Los Angeles. What Los Angeles skeptics of a Raiders arrival had yet to realize was that the Raiders would come to represent a different Los Angeles, one that had long operated in the shadows of economic and political dispossession.

While media and Los Angeles critics paid much attention to the Raiders' reputation, concerns like those of Steve Cotton, mentioned previously, included anxieties about rapid economic decline in urban centers with changing demographics. At the time, President Ronald Reagan's urban policies regarded the deterioration of the urban core as inevitable and argued against government intervention in poor areas. In doing so, he obfuscated the historical patterns of enforced segregation and disenfranchisement of Black and Latina/o communities through urban housing policies and underdevelopment. Similar to Oakland, uneven development in Los Angeles resulted in deindustrialization and vast unemployment in communities of color while public policy relocated government capital to the suburbs. Furthermore, the state endorsed cutbacks on expenditures for public spaces and affordable housing in Los Angeles's inner-city neighborhoods.[42] Housing segregation, economic marginalization, and a declining manufacturing economy disproportionately affected Black and Latina/o communities throughout Los Angeles County.

In conjunction with the withdrawal of industry and public services, Los Angeles's demographics changed rapidly in the 1970s and 1980s, as increasing numbers of Mexican and Central American immigrants settled throughout the city, including large concentrations in South Los Angeles. While Latinas/os continued to reside in East Los Angeles communities, an increasing number of immigrants spread into the valleys, southeast Los Angeles, and South Central. As Albert Camarillo writes, many historically Black neighborhoods became Spanish-speaking communities when some African Americans moved to nearby communities and even neighboring counties.[43] These Black and Brown communities were ready audiences for the ethnically diverse Raiders and their rambunctious reputation. The Raiders' arrival to Los Angeles both highlighted a demographically changing city and provided opportunities for communities of color scattered throughout L.A. County to negotiate a sense of belonging to a greater Los Angeles identity.

BLACK AND BROWN PIRATES INVADE LOS ANGELES

Amid the mainstream media's apprehensions, the Los Angeles Raiders played their first season at the Los Angeles Memorial Coliseum in 1982. Journalists' overreliance on stadium attendance as a gauge for fan support led them to mistakenly describe a lukewarm reception for the Raiders in their new home. Sportswriters had not yet realized those living in the shadows of glitzy L.A. would constitute the Raiders' fan base. While the franchise made efforts to court these communities, these fans were unbeknownst to the mainstream until the 1983 season Super Bowl win. The Raider Nation, consisting of Raider fans from their old and new home, gained visibility as a multiethnic community that complicated Plunkett's juxtaposition of Blacks and whites. This imagined community became a site of possibility for economically and politically marginalized people of color in Los Angeles. Al Davis's strategy of recruiting previously unwanted or misfit players continued to pay off into the 1980s and awakened hope in communities of color struggling for a better future amid difficult conditions. While Magic Johnson and the other Los Angeles Lakers served as inspiration for Black Angelenos and Fernando Valenzuela drew Mexican immigrants and Mexican Americans to Dodger Stadium in unprecedented numbers, the Raiders represented the possibility of interethnic unity through an aggressive contact sport. As a site of struggle, the Raider Nation reflects John Hoberman's warning against idealistic visions of sport as a "deracialized theatre" of interracial harmony in opposition to the racialized universe of everyday worlds.[44] More than providing Black and Latino heroes for Los Angeles, the Raider Nation represented an imagined community embedded in the experience of race and class in Los Angeles. The Raiders' pirate became the symbol of youth resistance, most notably providing an emerging late-1980s and early-1990s gangsta rap culture with its imagery. Marginalized individuals claimed belonging to a Los Angeles imaginary through the circulation of the pirate across multiple landscapes on cars, houses, sportswear, and skin. This iconography reinforced the instability of a Los Angeles identity dominated by the rolling suburbs of Anglo upper- and middle-class privilege. By claiming the Raiders from the spatial, material, and symbolic peripheries of Los Angeles, Black and Latina/o communities struggled to reimagine belonging to the heart of the city.

The legacy of gangsta rap's use of the Raiders' iconography provided a vehicle for the transmission of the Raider Nation as a resistive symbol. However, an overemphasis on rap and the Raiders has bypassed the ways in which the Raider Nation was also a multiracial vision. Al Davis courted Latinas/os as a potentially prosperous market upon arrival, especially after witnessing how the Dodgers secured a Latina/o market through Spanish broadcasting and Fernando-mania. He started by making the Raiders the first NFL team to locally broadcast their games in Spanish. The Raiders had Latino heroes in place with coach Tom Flores and starting quarterback Jim Plunkett. In addition, Mexican American marketing specialist Gil Lafferty-Hernandez became a local celebrity, handing out Raiders souvenirs at Latina/o community events in suburban working-class communities.[45] While these souvenirs provided the basis for attachment to the team, they also gave fans a means to identify with a team that created heroes from the margins.

Against a backdrop of uncertainties about the Raiders' place in "Showtime" L.A., the *Los Angeles Times* journalist Frank del Olmo drew attention to the Raiders' largely Black and Latina/o fan base.[46] Del Olmo foregrounded the working-class experience of Blacks and Latinas/os and attempted to figuratively map the Raider Nation. These fans saw players as laborers in much the same way that Tatum described. Through a racialized working class experience, del Olmo maps the Raider Nation through what he calls the "Real Los Angeles." Del Olmo's authentic city spanned from South Los Angeles to the southeastern deindustrialized suburbs and unincorporated parts of Los Angeles, including Pacoima, Boyle Heights, Pico Rivera, Huntington Park, and Wilmington.[47] In reality, the Raider Nation stretched farther into the San Gabriel and San Fernando Valleys and even into pockets of surrounding counties.

For Latinas/os in Los Angeles, coach Tom Flores was an instant hero as a quiet figure who went about his work productively against a background of rowdy Raiders.[48] Fans appreciated Flores's pioneering roles in the NFL, and they admired his unrelenting personality despite the strong team image. Following the retirement of coach John Madden, known for his strong personality, Al Davis chose assistant coach Flores as the new head coach not long before the move to Los Angeles with its large Latino demographic. Flores's first major accomplishment as coach was the recruitment of quarterback Jim Plunkett. The first Latino to earn a Heisman Trophy while at Stanford University was of primarily Mexican descent with strands of German and Irish from his great-grandfather.[49] Both Flores and Plunkett shared humble backgrounds and became inspirations for working-class Latinas/os, while media representations constructed them as proof that one could transgress class boundaries solely through hard work. Thus, they simultaneously embodied the possibility of access to institutions of privilege by the broader, marginalized working class while providing media outlets with an opportunity to downplay the role of structural inequities and barriers to success for minority populations. By the time he was five, Tom Flores was working in the San Joaquin Valley orchards, picking fruit to add to the family income. During high school and his time at Fresno City College, he worked at an ice plant for ninety cents an hour.

He put himself through the University of the Pacific and went on to play football for twelve years after taking a season off to recover from tuberculosis. He fittingly played for the Oakland Raiders after overcoming health obstacles and continued to coach the team that had once offered him the second chance for which the Raiders had become known.

Jim Plunkett's Mexican parents were blind and impoverished. In addition to financial struggles, Plunkett suffered from bone disease and a tumor in his neck. The Mexican American community celebrated his triumphs against the odds when he received the Ernie Davis Award, given to those football players who displayed Ernie Davis's "dedication to mankind, love of humanity and athletic prowess." Plunkett joined the Raiders after playing for the New England Patriots and San Francisco 49ers. After serving in a reserve capacity for two years, Flores gave Plunkett the chance to lead the Raiders. Plunkett oscillated between backup roles and leadership roles, culminating in Super Bowl victories. While media representations heralded Flores and Plunkett as proof of equal opportunity within systems of meritocracy, they also represented hope for disenfranchised communities who mirrored their struggles.

In an atmosphere of rapidly diminishing social services and the validation of self-help ideologies, Flores and Plunkett became safe role models for communities of color in the mainstream imagination. Al Davis's unofficial biographer described Flores as "*the* realization of an Al Davis head coach . . . a player and coach for Davis, an offensive-minded guy, he was a quiet company man seemingly certain to breed ideological compliance."[50] He went on to describe Flores as someone who "always knew his place—behind Al," overshadowing fan identifications with a man who simply worked hard.[51] Flores himself sought to balance ethnic pride with a need to assert himself as deserving of the job. Like Flores, Plunkett was the poster boy for the American dream, "an Alger figure in the era of Nixonian despair."[52] The media portrayed Plunkett's life story as proof that hard work and dedication could be great equalizers, regardless of racial or class background.[53]

Flores and Plunkett balanced ethnic pride with self-help ideologies in their autobiographies. Repeatedly validating his position as one gained only by hard work, Flores claimed he never made "a big deal about [his] ethnicity."[54] Flores strategically aligned himself with an idealization of Mexicans as hard workers without contesting the low numbers of Mexican Americans in football or sports. Plunkett followed suit and focused on the strength, humility, and interdependence of members within his family.[55] The emphasis each placed on personal characteristics and Mexican values stimulated ethnic pride while inadvertently drawing from and reinforcing what João Costa Vargas has identified as a "racialized matrix of thought," in which failure is correlated solely with individual deficiencies and renders structural oppressions irrelevant.[56] By emphasizing strong character traits in the pursuit of success, Flores's and Plunkett's self-described markers of success inevitably reinscribed the institutionalized practices of exclusion that allowed them to shine as exceptional.

Beyond providing a Mexican American presence in professional football, Flores and Plunkett challenged dominant representations of Latino masculinities as, at best, exotic and passionate and, at worst, volatile and violent. Alongside rowdy Raiders teammates, Flores and Plunkett operated in positions that required their skillful thinking and tactical planning. They personified the Raiders' mystique and, in doing so, provided a balance to chief image makers, like defensive linemen Lyle Alzado, notorious for his uncontrollable and steroid-enhanced behavior. Plunkett and Flores were key to maintaining a mysterious aura surrounding the Raiders, not unlike growing invisible Los Angeles communities. Praised for his "calm and clinical exterior," Flores demonstrated focus in volatile situations.[57] As the team leaders, both Flores and Plunkett countered expectations of Latino male behavior against a background of rowdiness and chaos. The journalist Frank del Olmo likened their position to that of the *real* Los Angeles, in which "citizens go about their workday lives productively but without much fanfare—the same way Tom Flores coaches the Raiders."[58] For del Olmo and others of Los Angeles's Latina/o community, Flores and Plunkett demonstrated the possibility of emerging from the shadows through quiet determination.

When Plunkett and Flores retired in 1986 and 1988, respectively, Latino journalists used their columns to thank them for their service and wish them well. However, their retirement did not mark the end of an era. Remaining an organization under the tight control of Al Davis, the Raiders sought to return the team to glory. Al Davis hired Mike Shanahan from the Denver Broncos, citing a need to bring in new ideas and inspiration and straying from his preference for promoting from within the Raiders' family.[59] However, Shanahan's instant outlawing of the Raiders' players' ritual of sitting on their helmets on the sidelines during practice suggested his fresh ideas were headed away from the Raiders' legacy.[60] Davis fired Shanahan before the end of his second season, ending his experiment of bringing non-Raiders into the organization. Guarding his team from outsiders, Davis continued hiring from

within the Raiders' organization, a move that resembled insulated survival strategies of communities of color.

Al Davis once again looked to the Raider family for a head coach
following the firing of Shanahan in 1990. Choosing former player Art
Shell as the new head coach proved to be a historic moment in Raiders,
Los Angeles, and sports history. As a former offensive tackle who tran-
sitioned into a Raiders assistant coach position upon retirement, Art
Shell represented decades of Raiders history. He had played alongside
the infamous Soul Patrol and so understood the importance of recap-
turing the silver and black, pirate and cross-swords essence. Becoming
the first African American head coach since Fritz Pollard in 1928, Hall
of Fame inductee Shell embraced the opportunity to continue a Raiders
tradition and denied claims that he was hired on the basis of his skin
color. Named the American Football Conference Coach of the Year
in 1990, Shell once again demonstrated that achievement, despite the
mainstream's doubt of his skills, was possible. It was under his leadership as coach of the Los Angeles Raiders that the Raider Nation began
to extract meanings beyond sports rivalries and championships from
the team's pirate mascot.

THE FORMATION OF RAIDER NATION

The imagined community of the Raider Nation, spanning from
Oakland to Los Angeles and beyond, provides an opportunity to
reexamine Los Angeles as an urban imaginary rooted in overlapping
territories and masculine claims to space. Rather than privilege the
areas within city limits over the peripheries, the Raider Nation traveled throughout metropolitan Los Angeles in the form of car decals,
blankets, flags, and general merchandise with the pirate logo. Akin to
Michel Foucault's notion of heterotopia as a mythic and real space, the
Raider Nation created "counter-sites, a kind of effectively enacted uto-
pia in which the real sites, all other real sites that can be found within
the culture are simultaneously represented, contested and inverted."[61]
The pirate imagery identified a team that not only built itself out of
other teams' castoffs but also created champions out of players others
assumed were destined for mediocrity. The possibility of creating greatness in the face of limited opportunity provided marginalized communities with a framework through which they could claim not just
belonging to, but also ownership of, Los Angeles.

Transforming the pirate from a team logo to a working-class, urban, and racialized symbol of identity, the Raider Nation recognized the outlaw status as the conditions for Black and Brown youth within an increasingly antagonistic metropolitan landscape. For some, Al Davis was the ultimate pirate in raiding public funds for private profit.[62] Even though these tactics furthered the economic marginalization of communities of color in Oakland and Los Angeles, fans such as rapper Ice Cube have recuperated these tactics as "gangsta." Recasting Davis's capitalist endeavors as a gangsta mentality, Ice Cube's ESPN documentary, *Straight Outta L.A.*, highlights the importance of an underdog mentality in which strategies for survival and rebellion preclude judgment. The symbolic economy of pirating complemented gangsta tactics and so gained currency among those eager to claim ownership of Los Angeles from the margins. Drawn to the pirate, members of the Raider Nation co-opted the team's imagery to navigate their everyday existence outside the franchise's control. The Raider Nation disseminated the pirate representation in football just as the neighborhoods from which fans hailed appropriated the imagery.[63]

The visibility of Black and Latina/o celebrators during and following the Raiders' win in the 1983 season Super Bowl dovetailed with the increasing anxieties about Black and Brown youth criminality. The already existing structure of media and state racial profiling of Black and Latina/o youth coupled with the image of Los Angeles Raiders fans helped facilitate the image of the Raider Nation as dangerous and illicit. As early as the season following the visibly diverse City Hall Super Bowl celebration, journalists began describing conflicts among fans as gang-related incidents. In December 1984, police arrested John Garcia, a leader of the Community Youth Gang Services Project in Pico Rivera, on suspicion of "robbery and assault with a deadly weapon in connection with a *gang assault on spectators*" (emphasis mine) at a Raiders game.[64] Newspapers reported that Garcia drove to a game with about fourteen members of the Rivera-13 gang, and a fight ensued after some "gang members" snatched a Raiders hat from another fan. Police released some of those arrested and detained others for unrelated charges. Incidents such as these facilitated the conflation of Raider fandom and unwavering assumptions that all tensions were gang-affiliated regardless of the actual circumstances surrounding conflicts.

The collapse of the Raiders' image with the marker of criminality among youth of color highlighted the extent to which the pirate became a site of overlapping meanings in struggle. What was initially a marketing strategy on the part of the Raiders soon became a symbol of resistance among youth categorized as a menace to society. In counterpart to Gil Lafferty-Hernandez's work in Latina/o communities, marketing director Michael Orenstein gave free Raiders pennants and caps to producers, radio disc jockeys, and emerging gangsta rap groups like N.W.A. and Run DMC.[65] Ice Cube's documentary *Straight Outta L.A.* describes how Raiders gear, in symbolizing struggle, subsequently became the uniform for gangsta rap. For rappers, the pirate provided the menace and determination they used in their struggle to take over Los Angeles. The mix of silver and black provided an aura of grittiness, and the dominant black remained a neutral color among youth of color hailing from potentially conflicting neighborhoods. Gangsta rappers' use of music to detail an often-ignored existence in the trenches of deindustrialized cities has led Mike Davis to argue these rappers were the next generation of Black Panthers.[66] In keeping with this suggestion, Raiders merchandise rendered forms of Black radicalism visible in the realm of popular culture. The pirate logo's circulation in gangsta rap culture popularized the detachment of the Raiders' symbol from the team and the sport and its fusion with the claim of Black and Brown ownership of the city. This pirating of the Raiders' imagery provided not only a symbol of resistance among communities of color but also a reminder that commercialization still reinforces capitalist dispossession.

The circulation of the pirate symbol demonstrated the expanse of the Raider Nation also in other realms of deindustrialized and privatized life in Los Angeles County during a moment in which the criminalization of Black and Brown bodies facilitated a growing prison industrial complex. Popular understandings soon collapsed the team's logo with the criminalized bodies that circulated it, leading to the assumption that the Raiders' logo on a person of color was proof of criminality. Sergeant Joe Holmes, a veteran gang investigator in Lynwood Station of the Los Angeles County's Sheriff's Department, alluded to that assumption: "When I'm on the street and I see certain teams, I connect it with a certain gang."[67] However, the widespread attraction of the silver and black eluded strict identification and highlighted the inaccurate presumptions of gang affiliation. While men of color gravitated to the Raiders' logo, wearing it also increased their vulnerability to police surveillance in a California context of rapidly growing and predominantly Black and Latino prisoner populations.[68]

The criminalization of the Raiders' logo pushed the franchise and journalists to create distinctions between the franchise and the youth identified with gangsta rap. Describing "a small but dangerous core of hoods, psychos and substance abusers who can ruin a good football game for everyone," journalists and the Raiders organization attempted to distinguish and disparage a criminal element as they had earlier in their focus on incidents involving Black Raiders players.[69] Arguing for stricter law enforcement, journalist Scott Ostler, who previously argued to "get Oakland out of the Raiders," jokingly advocated for even more prisons when he demanded jail cells at the Los Angeles Memorial Coliseum: "There is an alternative plan that would solve a lot of problems. Build the luxury boxes as planned but sell them to the Los Angeles Police Department and Coliseum Security, instead of to the rich and snobbish. The cops would use the luxury suites as jail cells for lawbreakers and deviates rounded up during Raider games."[70] The "round them up" mentality made men of color, who were the most vulnerable to a growing prison industrial complex, subject to surveillance within the stadium.[71] However, these racialized anxieties also hinted at perceptions of a possible takeover of public space by people of color through the Raiders.

Against increased surveillance, the merchandise continued to alter Los Angeles County's visual landscape. The criminalization of the Raiders' logo further popularized the image and fostered a profitable market, making up 20 percent of all the NFL apparel sold nationwide.[72] Police officials claimed the image attached to Raiders' apparel stemmed as much from the team's personalities as from the Los Angeles street gangs.[73] Citing the widespread use of the Raiders' logo by gangs, officials and reporters were concerned for the safety and lives of football fans who may be misidentified as gang members. Thus, while white youth were stylish or wholesome team fans because of a Raiders Starter jacket, youth of color were criminal by association with the same insignia.[74] Nonetheless, the increasing criminalization of Raiders garb also produced an opportunity for youth to signal discontent through style and to choose outlaw status over economic, social, and cultural exclusion. As Robin D. G. Kelley reminds us, media denigration of the Raiders' style as criminal, violent, and indicative of police repression enabled the popularization of style as an act of rebellion. The close association between the imagery of a team and a marginalized youth contributed to, in Tricia Rose's words, "bringing the ghetto back into public consciousness."[75] Providing an insignia for gangsta rap and appearing throughout the 'hood films emerging contemporaneously, the Raiders' pirate traveled beyond the confines of imposed boundaries. Thus, when franchise officials dramatized the Raiders' purpose by claiming the team was at war, disenfranchised youth's pirating of the pirate symbol itself demonstrated an engagement with the urgency of inequality and the struggle for alternative futures.

The visibility of the Raiders in the form of merchandising, murals, and tattoos announced a claim to ownership of Los Angeles from the margins. The Raiders' expectation of second chances resonated with shared struggles among Black and Brown working-class communities bearing the brunt of urban economic restructuring. One Latino fan remembers the Raiders being in Los Angeles at a moment when people struggled for hope: "L.A. was full of poor [people], and it was like getting a second chance too. We were supporting Al Davis, who gives second chances. Everybody's down on their luck and wants a second chance."[76] Frank del Olmo, of the *Los Angeles Times,* reiterated the promise of second chances, noting that "tough, gritty East Los Angeles" was a stronghold of Raider fandom.[77] Mario Bernal, owner of an East Los Angeles sporting goods store, testified to the popularity of the less-expensive $4.25 version of the black and silver cap in his store: "In my area, all the people of Mexican descent, the young people, they talk about the Raiders. When they're talking about the Raiders, they feel proud."[78] The popularity of Raiders' paraphernalia supported local businesses in predominantly Black and Latina/o areas while highlighting bids for an alternative Los Angeles.

The relationships among fans from different places within racially segregated Los Angeles mapped the Raider Nation as a multiracial formation. One Latino fan hailing from Huntington Park, a southeast Los Angeles city with a 35.9 percent Latina/o population in 1970, 85 percent in 1986, and 96 percent in 1990, navigated racial tensions and police repression in Los Angeles when attending a Raider game:[79]

> Around the Coliseum, there were a lot of cops and inadequate parking. So you were forced to park in someone's yard, parking lot, behind some store. You had to know where you parked and ask for insurance. Neighborhood kids would say, "You can park there, but I'll watch it for another twenty dollars." That's why we always parked toward Grand, because we felt safe. It was more Latin on the other side of the Harbor Freeway. . . . the Blacks were more on Figueroa and Vermont. We just did not park over there. We went as a group underneath the freeway and back, so we felt safe going east instead of west.[80]

While the Raider Nation provided an opportunity for multiracial connectivities, fans' experiences were still structured by L.A.'s racial geographies and the alternative economies they created. Instincts conditioned through both conflict and spatial segregation outlined the ways in which Black and Latina/o fans constructed the Raider Nation both alongside and with each other.

Opting for the familiarity of one's "home," fans often went to the Coliseum in large groups, effectively claiming sections of the stadium for their neighborhood. The same Huntington Park fan remembers:

> We always sat in the same place in every game. I think we felt safe in that section where nothing really major happened to us. . . . most of the guys where I used to go were from a gang called Florence.[81] And guys from Florence sat in Section 13. If you're from Huntington Park, South Gate, and around that area, you went to Raider games and sat in Section 13. You'd look into the crowd and see a familiar face in case you needed it—support if someone is bothering you. You could reach out and almost touch a neighbor from your town. Even if you got tickets for somewhere else you would sell them for Section 13. You knew what you were going to encounter at the Raider Stadium, so you had to sit where you felt safe and had to go with your crowd.

For some, LAMC reflected the spatial distinctions of the larger Los Angeles and reinforced the notion of security as familiarity. The notion of protection is not unlike Davis's preference for promoting from within the Raiders organization. Contrary to popular opinion, fans navigated the Coliseum in much the same way they navigated Los Angeles: they occupied familiar space in order to avoid conflict. Sitting in Section 13, members of Florencia 13 and residents from the same area made clear connections to the neighborhood from which they came. The vectors of race and class through which fans experienced Los Angeles did not stop at the Coliseum gates. Rather, the everyday experience of Los Angeles played out within the Coliseum while the Raiders were on the field.

During the Raiders era, the Los Angeles Police Department added roughly 120 officers to security detail inside LAMC because of the perceived violence and unruliness of the games' attendees. Sergeant John Byers attributed an improvement at the Coliseum to increased arrests, prohibition of beer sales after the third quarter, and a new municipal law that designated the act of throwing objects a criminal offense, regardless of whether or not it led to injury.[82] Acts of fan hostility were well publicized and accompanied increasing concerns about violence, sports, and gang members at the Coliseum. The Coliseum proved to be a site in which officers attempted to manage public space through a law and order mentality. Practicing what Mike Davis refers to as "militarization of city life," the LAPD utilized tactics used throughout

Los Angeles in the stadium and, in doing so, suggested safety in Los Angeles could be achieved by the surveillance and enclosure of people of color.[83]

While some Latina/o and Black fans may have remained distant from one another even in the Coliseum, it is important to note that the Raider Nation provided the possibility of coexistence and peace. One African American fan from Inglewood, awestruck by the power of Raiders fans in the Coliseum, commented: "The football players, instead of watching the game, they were watching the bleachers. A bunch us, Blacks and Hispanics. You could literally see them watching the bleachers. They were pointing—a couple guys watching the mayhem. It was like entertainment for them. They were spectators watching. Like reverse arena. Instead of us watching them, they were watching us."[84] This account of Black and Brown fans literally creating a spectacle from the margins serves as a reminder that social meanings are always created through struggle. Recognizing the multiracial formation of the Raider Nation allows for an understanding of the Coliseum as a site of difference filled with minoritized subjects whose experiences of race and class did not simply disappear upon entering the stadium. However, embedded in their hypervisibility was also the possibility of disruption through alliance. In fact, Raiders fandom temporarily surpassed neighborhood conflicts when the Coliseum became a site of truce on game days. Thus, while journalists and the LAPD overemphasized a gang presence in the stadium, communities of color understood the limits of this interpretation. Tailgating became more than a ritual on game days, demonstrating the heterotopic space of the Raider Nation, defined by celebration in fleeting moments. As a common cause across geographic and racial lines, the Raider Nation afforded fans the opportunity to witness excellence through aggression.

Despite the team's success in L.A., Al Davis announced intentions to return to Oakland eight years after they had arrived. Davis and the Raiders did not regard the neighborhood surrounding the Los Angeles Coliseum two years after the 1992 uprisings when he repeated the fifteen-year-old excuses of the Rams' Carrol Rosenbloom for abandoning the city. Davis complained about the low-income neighborhood, stating, "One of the [other team] owners said to me, 'I'm scared to get off the damn bus.' Howie [Long, a white Raiders star player] would always make a big issue out of it, how he wouldn't bring his wife and his kids to the game. And other guys would say, 'I'm not bringing my wife.'"[85] Contrary to Davis's hypocritical claims as the man who profited from the perpetuation and criminalization of the Raiders' image, one 1993 study showed fewer crimes were committed around the Coliseum neighborhood on game days than occurred around the Inglewood Forum, the home of the Lakers.[86] Thus, Davis capitalized on racist constructions of South Central and the loopholes in his original contract with the Coliseum Commission to escape Los Angeles all the richer.

The departure of the Raiders marked the loss of a franchise but not of a pirate mentality. Los Angeles Coliseum officials like Bill Robertson were sorry to see them leave, because the team had "appeal to middle-class people, to the working people and minorities. [Until recently] they had a Hispanic coach, Tom Flores. They had a lot of blacks. They had the right image."[87] For Robertson, the Raiders' diversity was key to Los Angeles claiming a landscape of multiracial harmony. However for fans, the Raider Nation persists through imagery in the absence of the football team in Los Angeles and throughout California. Jerseys, car decals, and other memorabilia circulate throughout Southern California as houses painted in Raiders colors and shrines in garages provide less mobile examples of Raider pride and memory.

Amid tensions emanating from the Los Angeles uprisings and other incidents delineating the racial and economic strife of the 1990s, Raiders imagery in the mainstream became synonymous with Black or Latina/o gang affiliation. California governor Pete Wilson also signed a bill in 1993 that gave school districts the right to ban certain clothing alongside crime regulation such as the "Three Strikes Law" and Proposition 187.[88] About one year later, Governor Wilson also signed a bill allowing public schools to require uniforms for students as a means of reducing gang activity and violence. Local school districts across California instantly began enforcing dress codes and outlawed what they considered "gang attire."[89] Chief among outlawed clothing was any Raiders garb. Simultaneously criminalizing and commodifying the Raiders' icon, these measures were a minor threat to the Raider Nation imagination that still claimed ownership of the physical and virtual Los Angeles landscapes.

Since the 1994 departure of the Raiders for Oakland, Los Angeles has been without a professional football team despite numerous public demands. These demands over the years have ignited conversations around the location for and the cost, and potential consequences of building a stadium in the greater Los Angeles area. After the Los Angeles City Council voted to endorse the financial agreement for a downtown NFL stadium on August 9, 2011, contentious debates reignited about the possibility of the Raiders' return. For Los Angeles members of the Raider Nation, the possible return of their team has sparked excitement. However, others who collapsed Raiders fandom and criminality oppose hosting an NFL team if it is to be the Raiders. These conflicts have only become exacerbated in the contemporary era of stadium building inspired by Al Davis, in which taxpayers fund privatized stadiums as symbols of a metropolitan identity grounded in consumption, multicultural harmony, and architectural acumen. While Al Davis's recent passing in October 2008 has highlighted the significance of the Raiders in transforming professional football, journalists have failed to recognize the perseverance of Raider fans as a continual affront to stadium efforts in regulating who belongs where. Beyond sports fans waiting for their team to return to glory, the Raider Nation continues to believe in second, third, and even more chances amid increasing economic and political insecurity.

The Raider Nation's use of the pirate as a signifier of unfettered movement in the face of surveillance and enclosure is a direct commentary on the scrutinized Black and Brown bodies that don the imagery on their clothes, cars, and skin. As an image and ethos, the Raider Nation continues to enact a zone of contact, a site of possibility in which alternative conditions and racial/ethnic affiliations in Los Angeles are imagined, facilitated, and even made possible. Providing the Raiders and their reputation a home in Los Angeles also provided Black and Latina/o communities with a common site of struggle against disenfranchisement, a heterotopia in which Raider Nation fans pirated the imagery and reputation of the team within professional sports and claimed ownership of a new Los Angeles. While the Raiders have been long gone and the possibility of their return is contentious, the "Silver and Black" persists as a vehicle through which Blacks and Latinas/os raid Los Angeles and its landscapes.

NOTES

1. Robert Lindsay, "Raiders Call Los Angeles Home at Last," *New York Times,* January, 25, 1984, B7.

2. Technically, Tom Fears was the first Mexican American football coach when he became head coach of the expansion New Orleans Saints in 1967. However, he is not officially recognized as the first Latino head coach, because the Saints did not become an NFL franchise until 1970. Fears's first season as an NFL coach was short after the Saints released him midseason.

3. In his study on nationalism, Benedict Anderson defines a nation as an imagined community, because it is not based upon direct interaction among

all members. Benedict Anderson, *Imagined Communities: Reflections on the Origin and Spread of Nationalism* (London: Verso, 1991).

4. Bill Boyarsky, "Urban Fight for Survival," *Los Angeles Times,* January 24, 1983; Melvin Durslag, "Rams Move to Anaheim Purely Act of Benevolence," *Los Angeles Times,* April 4, 1982.

5. Bob Oates, "Rams and Raiders: Animosity Hurting Both Teams," *Los Angeles Times,* May 19, 1985; Doug Krikorian, "Beleaguered L.A. Fans Would Love the Raiders," *Los Angeles Times,* January 17, 1984.

6. Scott Ostler, "Some Circus," *Los Angeles Times,* August 20, 1981.

7. Albert Camarillo, "Black and Brown in Compton: Demographic Change, Suburban Decline and Intergroup Relations in a South Central Los Angeles Community, 1950 to 2000," in *Not Just Black and White: Historical and Contemporary Perspectives on Immigration, Race, and Ethnicity in the United States,* ed. Nancy Foner and George M. Frederickson (New York: Russell Sage Foundation, 2004).

8. For more information on the deal between the Los Angeles Memorial Coliseum Commission and the Raiders, including court suits, see Charles C. Euchner, *Playing the Field: Why Sports Teams Move and Cities Try to Keep Them* (Baltimore, MD: Johns Hopkins University Press, 1993).

9. Scott Ostler, "Let's Get Oakland out of the Raiders," *Los Angeles Times,* January 6, 1983, E3.

10. "Letters: The Raiders," *Los Angeles Times,* March 15, 1980, D1.

11. Rich Connell, "El Segundo Divided," *Los Angeles Times,* August 29, 1982.

12. Mark Ribowsky, *Slick: The Silver and Black Life of Al Davis* (New York: Macmillan Publishing , 1991), 156.

13. Edwin Shrake, "Thunder out of Oakland," *Sports Illustrated* 23, no. 20, November 15, 1965, 92.

14. Ibid., 91.

15. Ribowsky, *Slick,* 17–18.

16. Ibid., 33.

17. Ibid., 32.

18. Ibid., 18.

19. Ibid., 58.

20. Dave Anderson, "Sports of the Times: Super Bowl Villain," *New York Times,* January 25, 1981, A1.

21. William F. Brown, "The Controversial Move of the Oakland Raiders' Professional Football Team from Oakland to Los Angeles," MA thesis, California State University, Long Beach, 1993, 49.

22. Jonathan Kaufman, "Blacks and Jews: The Struggle in the Cities," in *Struggles in the Promised Land: Toward a History of Black-Jewish Relations in the United States,* ed. Jack Salzman and Cornel West (Oxford: Oxford University Press, 1997), 109.

23. Hasia Diner, *In the Almost Promised Land: American Jews and Blacks, 1915–1935* (Baltimore, MD: John Hopkins University Press, 1995),113.

24. Robert Self, *American Babylon: Race and the Struggle for Postwar Oakland* (Princeton, NJ: Princeton University Press, 2003), 161.

25. Robin D.G. Kelley, "Kickin' Reality, Kickin' Ballistics: 'Gangsta Rap' and Postindustrial Los Angeles," in *Race Rebels: Culture, Politics, and the Black Working Class* (New York: Free Press, 1994), 191.

26. These players are regularly featured in numerous top ten "Most Feared" NFL lists in sports journalism. It is also important to note that the naming of the Soul Patrol creates another connection to the different ways that Black radicalism was introduced into popular culture, resonating in Oakland, Los Angeles, and beyond.

27. John Schulian, "Atkinson Seeks Mr. Nice Guy Image," *Los Angeles Times,* December 16, 1976, D3.

28. John Hall, "The Gallery," *Los Angeles Times,* September 15, 1976, D3.

29. Dave Kindred, "NFL'S Man on the Spot Denies Excess Rough Stuff," *Washington Post,* July 30, 1977.

30. William Oscar Johnson, "A Walk on the Sordid Side," *Sports Illustrated,* August 1, 1977, 15.

31. "Gunsight Scares Atkinson," *Los Angeles Times,* December 23, 1976, D1.

32. "'Criminal Element' in NFL: Noll," *Chicago Tribune,* September 14, 1976, C4; "Noll Implies Raiders Head-Hunt Criminally," *Los Angeles Times,* September 14, 1976, D1.

33. "Noll Implies Raiders Head-Hunt Criminally," *Los Angeles Times,* September 14, 1976, D1.

34. "'Criminal Element' in NFL: Noll." These accusations were not taken lightly, as Al Davis helped fund Atkinson's suit against Noll and the Steelers for slander, demanding two million in damages. A ten-day trial ensued with vicious accusations from all quarters, ending with a verdict against Atkinson.

35. Jack Tatum, *Final Confessions of NFL Assassin Jack Tatum,* with Bill Kushner (Coal Valley, IL: Quality Sports Publications, 1996), 28, 136, 272.

36. Ibid., 28.

37. Ribowsky, *Slick,* 241.

38. Ibid., 242.

39. Jim Plunkett and Dave Newhouse, *The Jim Plunkett Story: The Saga of a Man Who Came Back* (New York: Dell Publishing, 1982), 184.

40. In her discussion of intersecting oppressions of race, gender, and sexuality upon African American women, Patricia Hill Collins refers to "controlling images" as stereotypical images that take on special meaning. When these images permeate social structures and become hegemonic, the consequences of racial, sexual, and other forms injustice appear inevitable. Patricia Hill Collins, *Black Feminist Thought: Knowledge Consciousness and the Politics of Empowerment,* 2nd ed. (New York: Routledge, 2000).

41. NFL Films, *Raiders: The Complete History* (Mt. Laurel, NJ: NFL Films, 2004).

42. Kelley, "Kickin' Reality, Kickin' Ballistics," 192.

43. Camarillo, "Black and Brown in Compton," 366.

44. John Hoberman, *Darwin's Athletes: How Sport Has Damaged Black America and Preserved the Myth of Race* (New York: Houghton Mifflin Harcourt, 1997), xxiv.

45. Frank del Olmo, "Is It Adios from the Silver and Black?" *Los Angeles Times*, August 24, 1989.

46. Showtime L.A. refers to an era in Lakers history mostly defined by Earvin "Magic" Johnson.

47. Frank del Olmo, "Rah Rah Raiders: A Lot of Hearts Beat for You in Real Los Angeles," *Los Angeles Times*, January 19, 1984.

48. Ibid.

49. Roy Damer, "Fortune Falls Heavily on Plunkett," *Chicago Tribune*, July 4, 1971, B-3.

50. Ribowsky, *Slick*, 273.

51. Ribowsky, *Slick*, photo caption.

52. Michael Silver, "Painful Reminders," *Sports Illustrated*, July 11, 2005.

53. David Flores, "Flores Also Made NFL History for Minorities," *Conexión* (San Antonio), February 1, 2007, 12A.

54. Tom Flores and Frank Cooney, *Fire in the Iceman: Autobiography of Tom Flores* (Chicago: Bonus Books, 1992), 3.

55. Jim Plunkett and Dave Newhouse, *The Jim Plunkett Story: The Saga of a Man Who Came Back* (New York: Arbor House, 1981), 20–28.

56. João H. Costa Vargas, *Catching Hell in the City of Angels: Life and Meanings of Blackness in South Central Los Angeles* (Minneapolis: University of Minnesota Press, 2006), 208.

57. Dave Anderson, "A Clinical Flores and a Personal Gibbs," *New York Times*, January 22, 1984, A1.

58. del Olmo, "Rah Rah Raiders."

59. Mark Heisler, "Directional Problem for Raiders On and Off the Field," *Los Angeles Times*, September 5, 1989, 1.

60. Scott Ostler, "L.A. Sports Teams Seeking Quick Fix, Look No Further," *Los Angeles Times*, January 5, 1989, 3.

61. Michel Foucault, "Of Other Spaces," *Diacritics* 16 (Spring 1986): 24.

62. Euchner, *Playing the Field*, 100.

63. These meanings overlap with notions of piracy and its policing as the outcome of capitalist abandonment. Historians Peter Linebaugh and Marcus Rediker define piracy as a slow, uneven process initially serving the needs of the maritime state and merchant community in England. However, piracy drifted downward, and exploited laborers organized a "social world apart from the dictates of mercantile and imperial authority" and attacked merchant property. Shortly thereafter, military and penal measures ensued to eradicate piracy. Peter Linebaugh and Marcus Rediker, *The Many-Headed Hydra: Sailors, Slaves, Commoners, and the Hidden History of the Revolutionary Atlantic* (Boston: Beacon Press, 2000), 156. For Linebaugh and Rediker, the ship served as both an engine of capitalism and a space of resistance in which "practices of revolutionaries defeated and repressed by Cromwell and then by King Charles escaped, re-formulated, circulated and persisted" (145).

64. Pico Rivera is a predominantly Latina/o working-class city on the borders of southeast Los Angeles along the 5 and 605 freeways.

65. Marc Lacey, "No Sporting Chance: Danger Lurks for Fans as Gang Adopt Pro Attire," *Los Angeles Times*, March 20, 1991.

66. Mike Davis, *City of Quartz: Excavating the Future in Los Angeles* (New York: Vintage Books, 1992), 300.

67. The prisoner population grew nearly 500 percent between 1982 and 2000, although crime rates actually decreased after their peak in 1980. Ruth Wilson Gilmore, *Golden Gulag: Prisons, Surplus, Crisis and Opposition in Globalizing California* (Berkeley: University of California Press, 2006), 107.

68. Ibid.

69. Scott Ostler, "Has Commitment to Excellence Come to Such a Sad End?" *Los Angeles Times,* September 2, 1986.

70. Ibid.

71. See Gilmore, *Golden Gulag.*

72. Tim Golden, "Raiders Chic: A Style and Sinister Overtones," *New York Times,* February 4, 1991.

73. Ibid.

74. "Opinion: Killing Clothes?" *Sentinel* (Los Angeles), November 18, 1990.

75. Tricia Rose, *"Black Noise: Rap Music and Black Culture in Contemporary America,* (Middletown, CT: Wesleyan University Press, 1994), 11.

76. Interview with author, February 22, 2009.

77. del Olmo, "Rah Rah Raiders."

78. David Ferrell, "Renegades Won Loyal Fans in Inner City," *Los Angeles Times,* March 13, 1990, 1.

79. Raymond Rocco, "Latino Los Angeles: Reframing Boundaries/Borders," in *The City: Los Angeles and Urban Theory at the End of the Twentieth Century,* ed. Allen J. Scott and Edward W. Soja (Berkeley: University of California Press, 1998), 401.

80. Interview with author, February 22, 2009.

81. Florence is a reference to Florencia 13, one of the largest Latino gangs in Los Angeles.

82. Ostler, "Has Commitment to Excellence Come to Such a Sad End?"

83. Davis, *City of Quartz,* 224.

84. Interview with author, September 7, 2008.

85. Bill Boyarsky, "It's about Time to Quit Bashing the Coliseum's Neighborhood," *Los Angeles Times,* September 6, 1996, 1.

86. Ibid.

87. Ferrell, "Renegades Won Loyal Fans in Inner City."

88. California Proposition 184, also known as the Three Strikes Initiative, passed on November 8, 1994, and mandated a twenty-five to life sentence for third-time felony offenders. Eight days later, 59 percent of California voters passed Proposition 187. This law banned undocumented immigrants, whom nativists referred to as "illegal aliens," from receiving public health, education, and social services. These policies aimed to undo the ethnic transformation of Los Angeles and contributed to the creation of an antagonistic environment for people of color.

89. David L. Brunsma, *The School Uniform Movement and What It Tells Us about American Education: A Symbolic Crusade* (Lanham, MD: Scarecrow Education, 2004), 19.

What Is an MC If He Can't Rap to Banda?

Making Music in Nuevo L.A.

JOSH KUN

I LOVE MEXICANS

In the weeks before the 2003 California recall election wrapped production on a hot new political farce starring Arnold Schwarzenegger, the governor-to-be hit the campaign trail. He wanted to make it clear that even though he opposes his gardeners and nannies having driver's licenses and even though he supported Proposition 187, he actually likes Mexicans. Or at least that's what he told a crowd at the Inner City Games softball tournament in Santa Fe Springs, where he was forced to appear after he was disinvited from a Mexican Independence Day parade in East L.A.

"I love Mexico," he said. "I've done four movies down there."

For Schwarzenegger, Mexicans in California do not exist. There is only "Mexico," not actual Mexico, but virtual Hollywood Mexico: a distant "down there," a Mexico that is used but never actually seen. This is not just an Arnold problem of course: Mexicans in California have long existed at the surreal junction between cinematic imagination and brutal political reality. By going "down there" to understand Mexicans in California, Schwarzenegger was eliding their very presence, ignoring the multiple ways in which Mexican immigration continues to transform the state he recently governed and reducing Mexicans "here" to a country "down there."

This rhetorical deportation of California Mexicans was, to say the least, a bold move, considering just how obvious a cover-up it was in a state that in 2000 became the first U.S. state to become a "majority minority," with whites occupying a minority position for the first time since the nineteenth century. And as Mike Davis and many other critics have argued, the prime impetus for this demographic shift has been the "Mexicanization" of then Governor Schwarzenegger's very own backyard: Southern California.[1] In the 1990 U.S. Census, Los Angeles County was 37.8 percent Latino, with Mexicans constituting almost 30 percent of the total (during the 1980s, the Latino population of Los Angeles and Orange Counties grew by 1.5 million). In the city of Los Angeles alone, one out of every three residents was Mexican.[2]

MEXICAN RADIO

While Schwarzenegger was busy pretending that the Mexicanization of "up here" hadn't happened, Mexican Los Angeles was doing its own publicity. He could have just turned on the radio to hear it: the biggest urban hit of summer 2003, Akwid's "No hay manera." Alongside MTV favorites like the music of Lumidee, Wayne Wonder, Beyoncé, and Sean Paul, it was the summer's most radical song—radical because of the cultural realities it fused and performed, radical because of where you could hear it and what that told you about the changing profile of Mexican Los Angeles. "No hay manera" got airtime on both KPWR 105.9, one of L.A.'s leading hip-hop and R&B stations ("urban," in industry parlance), and on La Que Buena (KBUE), one of the city's top regional Mexican music stations (home to traditional styles like the accordion-driven trio and quartet sounds of norteño and grupero from the north of Mexico and the larger-scale brass marches of banda music from the northwest).

Where KPWR's target audience is generally thought to be primarily black and Latino (when in fact the station notes that its prime marketing target is L.A. Latinos), Que Buena's is predominantly immigrant Mexican. Never before had a song been in rotation cycles on both stations and in both markets—U.S. "urban" and Mexican "regional"— at once, but there it was, a song that immediately shot to number 7 on Billboard's specialty market Latin chart while also reaching the Top 20 on Billboard's overall, cross-market Heatseekers charts. In its first three months on the shelves, Akwid's debut album, *Proyecto Akwid,* went platinum, a significant sales achievement in both the Latino hip-hop and Mexican regional markets.

"No hay manera," a song rapped in Spanish over samples of Mexican banda music, was played first on La Que Buena, where the song's update of traditional banda styles found an immediate home with the station's listeners.[3] Hearing banda—albeit cloaked in hip-hop—on KPWR was the bigger coup, but one that still makes sense, as the Mexicanization of Southern California has led to a dramatic transformation in the demographics of the region's radio markets. Where in the '80s, Mexican and Latino radio audiences were considered specialty or niche markets better left to Mexican stations, Latinos in Southern California are now a primary and coveted piece of the city's overall market share. This is especially true for stations like KPWR, where *urban* increasingly signifies *Latino* as much it does *black*. According to KPWR's senior vice-president, Val Maki, "We target Latinos, young Latinos. In Southern California, they are the new mainstream. Hip hop is the global youth culture and the most popular music among young Latinos."[4]

Hip-hop may indeed be "the global youth culture," but its singular globality depends upon multiple localities—its creation, production, and reception within local and translocal sites like Los Angeles. Hip-hop is not just popular *among* Latinos; hip-hop is a music *of* and *by* young Latinos, music they make as well as consume, music they customize and reinvent according to their own rules and styles. Akwid's "No hay manera," with its U.S. West Coast rhymes and its northwest coast Mexican tubas and trumpets, represents the relocalization of global hip-hop culture and its recontexualization in twenty-first-century Mexican Los Angeles. The popularity of *Proyecto Akwid* spawned an instant market-driven movement: the urban regional movement, a catch-all term for artists who blend regional Mexican music with hip-hop sensibilities. In the year after Akwid's debut, Los Angeles was flooded with "urban regional" releases from artists such as Jae-P, David Rolas, Mexiclan, and Flakiss (all signed to the Univision Music Group), and numerous Mexican regional artists—Adán Sánchez, Yolanda "La Potranquita" Pérez—began incorporating hip-hop elements into their more traditional banda and norteño repertoires.[5] "We all grew up listening to Mexican music at home and listening to hip-hop with our friends," Akwid's Sergio Gómez has explained. "Our music is the inevitable outcome of this fusion between these two different cultures."[6]

As the pioneering anthem of urban regional music in Mexican Los Angeles, "No hay manera" is the perfect place to unpack the abstractions of "fusion" by focusing instead on what Theodor Adorno called the "congealed history" of the song—its historical layers, its union of disparate elements and epochs into a singular musical space.[7] What congeals in "No hay manera" is three issues I wish to highlight in the following pages: the ongoing Mexicanization of South Los Angeles in the context of economic globalization and deindustrialization and the subsequent centrality of Mexican migrant identity to the social structures and economic circuits of contemporary Los Angeles; the ongoing transformation of Mexican migrant cultural expressions from banda and norteño forms to new urban hybrids based in genre mixing, bilingualism, and generational reinvention; and the extent to which the creation of local musical forms in Los Angeles is both the *product* of the global flows of commercial popular culture and the *producer* of them. That is, Akwid's music responds to circuits of global culture, but as a local form it also changes what that global culture looks and sounds like.

Akwid's music and the urban regional movement that has sprung up around it offer a new stage in the creation of the kind of flexible ethnic identities that, as George Sánchez has argued, have long characterized Mexican American identity in L.A. In his study of Chicano identity between 1900 and 1945, Sánchez argues that ethnicity "was not a fixed set of customs growing from life in Mexico, but rather a collective identity that emerged from daily experience in the U.S."[8] Akwid's music at the other end of the twentieth century supports this notion, I believe, but also expands on it. As a music born of migration and globalization, it performs an ethnic identity that is indeed based on a daily experience in the United States, but one that remains influenced and informed by a new set of customs produced within U.S.-Mexico migration—customs based not only on life in Mexico but also on life between Mexico and the United States. Instead of being heard solely within the critical context of Chicano identity formation, then, Akwid's music forces us to listen as well for migrant identity formation—a kind of "becoming Mexican *in* America"—how ethnicity is further transformed by the experience of urban migration.

The new migrant L.A. ethnicity that Akwid performs requires a surrendering of older models of nationalism and national identity as static entities permanently tied to fixed places on fixed maps. In her recent critique of postcolonialism within the diasporic circuits of economic globalization, Gayatri Chakravorty Spivak urges us to think of nationalism as "a moving base . . . of differences, as dangerous as it is powerful, always ahead or deferred by definitions, pro or contra, upon which it relies."[9] The Mexicanization of South Los Angeles is one local effect of what Spivak calls "the financialization of the globe, or globalization." Though Spivak's critique deals with labor—specifically that of migrant women workers—and not culture, her analysis of nationalism's transformation within economic globalization is equally valuable when looking at cultural workers like Akwid. She sees women workers as "victims below but . . . agents above, resisting the consequences of globalization as well as redressing the cultural vicissitudes of migrancy." One result is a new relationship with the country of origin, so that "home" is no longer simply "a repository of cultural nostalgia" but a part of "the geopolitical present."[10]

What I am suggesting here is that "No hay manera" in particular and Akwid's music and the music of the urban regional movement more generally enact this very shift—from passive repository to active producer—even as they participate, via the recording industry, in the "financialization of the globe." Mexico is not a repository of nostalgia here but a generative, living source of knowledge and history. Which is not, in any way, to write off the importance of nostalgia as a potential mode of progressive thinking. Akwid's treatment of the Mexican past through music is more akin to what Svetlana Boym has called "reflective nostalgia," individually based nostalgia that *reflects on* national or collective pasts instead of attempting to restore and monumentalize them in the present. Reflective musical nostalgia, then, is not about memorializing a collective past but is an individual musician's way of using the past, through performance, to structure the present as it "cherishes shattered fragments of memory and temporalizes space" without pretending to rebuild a mythical home.[11]

Where previous models of nation and home might see the migrant experience as simply adding new ingredients to the American cultural mix via paradigms such as the melting pot, Akwid's music points us elsewhere. Their music may be located and produced within the geopolitical boundaries of the United States, but the transnational movements through space and time that it contains and performs beg a reevaluation of cultural production in Los Angeles. Their music should not be heard solely as producing a "new" U.S. multicultural or postethnic national identity and therefore enabling the typically reactionary state and federal "investments" in cultural diversity that so often result.[12] Indeed, instead of adding "No hay manera" to discussions of U.S. national identity, we might better hear the song through the ear of the new transnational cartography that Michael Dear and Gustavo

LeClerc have recently dubbed "Bajalta California," the transfrontier "global metropolis" that joins Southern California to northern Mexico, "a single, integrated system of global significance." Following Dear and LeClerc, the Mexicanization of South L.A. that Akwid is a part of is a prime factor in the emergence of this region of transnational culture, economics, and identity.[13] By placing Akwid's South Los Angeles on the map of Bajalta California, the region's cultural products begin to be heard within new geopolitical contexts, with "No hay manera" as the soundtrack not to the formation of new national identities but to the formation of new transnational, mobile ones.

I also want to offer Akwid's music as a way of understanding the transformation of Los Angeles's racial communities that does not necessarily replicate the apocalyptic tendencies of some recent L.A. urban theory that has developed in the noirish wake of Mike Davis's groundbreaking revision of California sunshine, *City of Quartz : Excavating the Future of Los Angeles*.[14] Deepak Narang Sawhney's recent anthology, for example, *Unmasking L.A.: Third World and the City,* portrays Los Angeles as "an epic tale of racial disharmony, territorial conquest, and the attempted extermination of original peoples."[15] Sawhney rightly calls our attention to histories of economic apartheid, racial segregation, spatial incarceration, militaristic neighborhood policing, and reckless environmental destruction. But Akwid's "No hay manera"— a song produced at the juncture of Mexican immigrant and African American life in South Central L.A.—asks us to think about what cultural practices emerge within these systems of exploitation and abuse, within these histories of disharmony.

As one of *Unmasking*'s own contributors, Roger Keil points out, accepting Los Angeles as one big metaphor for global urban distress turns the lived city into "a place without people." He asks, "Where is the Los Angeles filled with human interaction, a place where incredibly complex social relationships . . . are reproduced daily?"[16] Indeed, what relationships are heard and performed in popular music? "No hay manera" is a reminder that for all of L.A.'s "global urban distress," the city is not simply a metaphor. It is a place where people respond to this distress using global and local languages, where people make culture happen by reinventing their identities in response to urban transformation and to the limits (and opportunities) of economic change within globalization. Indeed, while Akwid's music points to cross-racial dialogue and migrant cultural production, the social reality of urban racialization and discrimination never goes away. Just weeks after the release of *Proyecto Akwid,* the Gómez brothers were denied entrance to the Saddle Ranch restaurant on Los Angeles's Universal City Walk and roughed up by the club's bouncers because of "how they looked." The civil suit against the restaurant got under way just as their single began climbing the charts.

Akwid's music also urges us to reconsider another key theme in recent Los Angeles studies: the city as a site of collective amnesia, where ethnic and racial pasts are continually buried and erased in the drive to construct new urban presents. Norman Klein has rightly argued that L.A. is a city that has historically based its presence on its desire to erase itself. For Klein, L.A. history can be read as a "history of forgetting," in which urban development and demographic displacement create "social imaginaries" of erasure and absence, "built environments" that "contain an evacuation."[17] Yet, I think it would be a mistake to accept these erasures and evacuations—for all of their urgent political and social import—as decidedly final. Indeed, popular culture and popular media within Los Angeles have historically served as a countereffect to these drives for urban amnesia. In the case of Mexican migrants, the preservation of memory in the face of erasure is a central facet of their cultural production. As I will argue below, "No hay manera" is a song that excavates buried memories and puts them into play within the present. The deindustrialized zone of South Central in which the song is produced may contain evacuation, but "No hay manera" is a good example of how expressive culture can fill those voids back up, reinserting memories of the past and even the immediate present into a social and economic landscape determined to forget them. The song demonstrates Iain Chambers's point about the role of popular music—what he calls a "journey in sound"—in maintaining memory and culture within the geopolitical and economic dispersals of globalization. The languages of popular music, he argues, "speak of the powers and potential of a specific cultural place where the inscription of memory and the prescriptions of the past come to be recited and resited."[18]

STRAIGHT OUTTA MICHOACÁN

The place of Akwid is a double place, a translocal site sustained in the movement between Mexico and the United States, Akwid's Sergio and Francisco Gómez were born in the southern Mexican state of Michoacán and migrated in the 1980s to South Central Los Angeles, where they were raised. On the cover of *Proyecto Akwid*, they sport shaved heads and football jerseys and sit on the hood of a convertible Porsche between the two worlds they straddle: the tubas, beer, cacti, and Mexican flags of Michoacán, and the palm trees and office buildings of downtown Los Angeles. "We identify with this mix," Sergio Gómez has said. "We were brought from Mexico at a very young age and raised in L.A. and we spoke Spanish at home. But at school it was all English. [This mix] was something that always existed in the communities."[19] The Gómez brothers left Michoacán when they were nine, and their music carries this transnational migrant route with it— L.A. hip-hop done Mexican migrant style, or what one song proclaims, "tipo Hollywooood." They pile clapping g-funk beats and Spanish-language rhymes on top of the brassy horns of traditional Mexican regional music, especially the marching oom-pah of *banda sinaloense*. The album's opening skit dramatizes both the transnational migrant circuitry at work and their avowed merger of traditional (a Mexican *banda de viento*) and contemporary (hip-hop MCs) musical modes. Before we even hear any music, we hear the Gómezes preparing a banda de viento for their new style of banda hip-hop. The tubas, trumpets, and snare drums get in tune as the Gómezes warn the musicians that what they are about to play is like nothing they have ever played before.

The Gómez brothers have not always been this committed to translating traditional Mexican regional music into new hip-hop vocabularies. Before they were Akwid, they were Juvenile Style, rapping in English over stock '90s West Coast beats and samples. In numerous press interviews, the duo has spoken openly about previously not wanting to, or knowing how to, mix their Mexican regional affiliations with the DJ Quik and N.W.A. records they grew up hearing in South Central. They had listened to the rough *narcocorridos* of Chalino Sánchez at home, but on the street, they belonged to the South Central L.A. hip-hop scene of the 1990s and were cautious about overidentifying themselves with their Mexican migrant roots. In the band's press release, Sergio Gómez explains it this way, "When you're young and you're growing up in an environment that is totally different than your culture, you find yourself being forced to adapt and assimilate, only to later evolve and reunite with your own roots."[20]

"No hay manera" tracks that evolution and that return. I focus on this one song not only because of its cross-market popularity in 2003 and its profound impact on the birth of other "urban regional" musical projects but also because of what the song itself contains. It is built in three separate musical layers, each of which tells its own story about Mexican migration to Los Angeles and the formation of identities in Mexican Los Angeles. The first layer consists of the lyrics themselves, a series of fairly typical hip-hop boasts, in which Akwid brags about the inventiveness of their style, bridging the traditional with the new. "Como un corrido," they rap, "Akwid ha regresado con un nuevo sonido." Their rapping owes as much to the vocal styles of veteran L.A. African American MCs like Snoop Dogg, DJ Quik, and Ice Cube as it does to the Spanish and Spanglish wordplay of the '90s Chicano hip-hop scene (groups like Delinquent Habits, Proper Dos, Frost).

The song's second layer is the sample of Banda El Recodo's "Te lo pido por favor," which structures the melodies and rhythms of Akwid's verses and the lyrics and melodies of the chorus itself (Akwid's chorus comes directly from Recodo's). The group Banda El Recodo is made up of perhaps commercial banda music's most recognizable, familiar, and endurable stars. Named for El Recodo, a small Sinaloan village near Mazatlán, Banda El Recodo was founded in 1954 by Don Cruz Lizárraga and is currently still run by his son Germán. Originally a typical banda de viento, Lizárraga soon transformed Recodo into what would become the blueprint for a commercial *banda orquesta,* complete with music stands, suits and ties, musicians organized into rows—a hybrid of U.S. big bands and Mexican orchestras. From 1954 to the present, Recodo has evolved along with the banda genre: from viento to orquesta to the more current "tecnobanda" style developed in Guadalajara that incorporates synthesizers, electric guitars, electric basses, and drum sets.[21]

Banda El Recodo was a perfect choice for Akwid to sample—a banda that signifies the transformation of banda music from a music of small-town Mexico to a transnational, commercial music fused with pop and rock elements that has become the soundtrack to Mexican migration to California. Recodo remains one of the most popular banda ensembles among Mexican immigrants in Los Angeles, which became, in the '90s, banda's capital outside Mexico. Fueled by radio stations like KLAX (the top-rated station in L.A. in 1992), banda music spoke directly to the rising number of Mexican migrants who began arriving in South Los Angeles in the 1980s as a result of the Mexican economic crisis. This economic push only intensified in the '90s when the passing of the North American Free Trade agreement provided even more of an impetus to leave Mexico for higher-paying jobs in the United States. George Lipsitz has rightly called banda a register of "the dislocation of low-wage labor" and a signal of "a new cultural moment, one that challenges traditional categories of citizenship and culture on both sides of the border."[22] But he is careful not to lose the singularity of banda in Mexican Los Angeles by calling it a new form of Mexican American or even American music. As it grew in the '90s, banda became more and more the music of Mexicans *in* the United States, a music that has refused to choose between assimilation and ethnic isolation and instead has celebrated what Lipsitz calls "a re-combinant Mexican identity inside the U.S."[23]

The third layer of Akwid's "No hay manera" makes this point even clearer. Akwid does indeed choose a Banda El Recodo song to sample and rap over, but the song it chooses has a history of its own— "Te lo pido por favor" was originally written and recorded by veteran Mexican pop and mariachi star Juan Gabriel in 1986. Gabriel, a revered Mexican national icon, was, like Akwid, born in Michoacán and was also a product of the musical flows of the U.S.-Mexico border, having begun his career as a singer in the night clubs of Ciudad Juárez (across the line from El Paso, Texas).[24] Yet Gabriel's enormous popularity (and his ability to traverse the worlds of radio pop balladry and traditional mariachi) has led him to become synonymous with Mexican national music, which makes Recodo's cover of him and Akwid's indirect sampling of him all the more relevant for Mexican migrants in Los Angeles—a "transborder population," in Rubén Martínez's words— who want to sustain a transnational balance between the United States and Mexico, blending patrimonies and preserving allegiances while creating new ones.[25]

When Gabriel recorded the song in the '80s, the South Central neighborhood where the Gómez brothers were raised was a key hub in the emergence of postindustrial L.A., an area that was then in the midst of a demographic transformation that had begun during the early stages of the deindustrialization of South Los Angeles in the 1960s and '70s.[26] The accompanying white flight and displacement of manufacturing jobs opened up "rustbelt" communities like South Gate, Bell, Maywood, and Compton to new waves of Mexican immigrants taking advantage of the more relaxed immigration restrictions of the 1965 Hart Cellar Immigration Act.[27] As a result, through the 1970s and '80s, the notion of East L.A. as the exclusive capital of Mexican life in Los Angeles had been displaced by a constellation of Southeast and South Central communities that Victor Valle and Rodolfo Torres have dubbed "the Greater East Side." The suburban, deindustrialized

Greater East Side that the Gómez brothers migrated to and grew up in would also become known, especially in music circles, as "Nuevo L.A.," the part of the L.A. map (comprising over a million people) most familiar to promoters and performers of Mexican regional music where Latinos make up roughly 90 percent of the population.[28]

The migrant audiences and migrant experiences that Akwid's music grows out of can be traced back to the key role that Southeast and South Central Los Angeles played in attracting more Mexican and Latino immigrants in the 1960s and '70s, the very period when changes in national immigration policy helped secure the United States' dominance in the global economic system. As Saskia Sassen has argued of this period, "The central military, political, and economic role the US played in the emergence of a global economic order contributed . . . both to the creation of conditions that mobilized people into migration, whether local or international, and to the formation of links between the US and other countries that subsequently were to serve as bridges for international migration."[29] The rise of Mexican immigration that began in the late '60s has led to what Mike Davis has called "the browning of LA's industrial working-class" in several communities once populated by blue-collar whites and African Americans. Davis uses South Central and Southeast L.A., "Latino L.A.," as lead examples of how Latino immigration is transforming U.S. cities in terms of economics, culture, and politics. In these areas in L.A. alone, he notes, Latinos have replaced blue-collar whites and African Americans in various communities throughout Nuevo L.A. In a dramatic and highly symbolic example, Central Avenue, the former main street of black Los Angeles, is now 75 percent Latino.[30]

Akwid's arrival in Los Angeles in the '80s was part of not only a larger wave of general Mexican immigration but also one that was dominated specifically by migrants from their home state of Michoacán, a prolific "sender" state matched only by Jalisco in the '70s and early '80s.[31] Akwid's music, then, can also be heard as a product of the specific Michoacán sector of Mexican migration that has led to over three million Michoacanos now living and working in the United States and sending home over five billion dollars a year. In his study of migrants from Michoacán—specifically Purépecha Indians from the pueblo of Cherán—Rubén Martínez characterizes the Mexican migrant trail not as a one-way route of departure and arrival, typical of classic twentieth-century models of European immigration, but also as a mobile loop in both space and time. "The movement is circular," Martínez has argued. "You meet the future by moving out, render tribute to the past by coming back home to visit and spend your hard-earned American dollars."[32] Roger Rouse, in his study of migration between Alguililla, Michoacán, and Redwood City, California, has called this Michoacán-California loop a "transnational migrant circuit" that leads to an "alternative cartography of social space."[33]

This migration back and forth from Michoacán produces new formations of community, identity, and culture within a "network of settlements" organized according to movements across transnational U.S.-Mexican spaces. The result is that now to be Michoacano, to be Purépecha, is to be part of this loop of traveling ideas and circulating culture. Martínez, for example, meets Chaco, who boasts of being 100 percent Purépecha while listening to house and banda and identifying with East L.A. To be Purépecha in the age of economic globalization and transnational immigration, Martínez argues, is to be a Tupac fan, wear an NBA jersey, and watch satellite TV in your village home.

Akwid's Gómez brothers are not Purépecha Indians and are not direct participants in the transnational migrant loops that Martínez examines. But their experience as Michoacán immigrants in South Central Los Angeles, the way their music is born from these circulations of ideas and culture and these negotiations between past and future, is part of a new paradigm of Mexican migrant identity in which the local and global, the regional and the urban, the traditional and the modern are not strictly opposed. Instead, they are mutually enabling, nearly complementary, nodes within a migrant, cross-border continuum both forced and enabled by the hand of economic globalization. What Martínez writes of the migrants he meets also applies to Akwid on the northern side of the borderline: "They can participate in—indeed, be protagonists of—transnational or 'global' culture even as they nurture the vestiges of their roots. In this context, the regional is global and vice-versa."[34] In songs like "No hay manera," the new loop of social space produced by this regional-global nexus is not just audible but also retheorized and reimagined at the level of music within the song's three layers of migrant sound.

The historical layers that congeal in "No hay manera," however, do more than tell us about the resiting of identity in transnational movement. The song's sampled and covered layers—its congealing of Gabriel, Recodo, and Akwid—also involve passages in time, from recent pasts to immediate presents. The song participates in what Andreas Huyssen has explored as "the current transformation of the temporal imaginary" within "the globalization of memory." The sample of Recodo covering Gabriel contains two of Huyssen's "present pasts" at once, two pasts kept alive within the present time of South Central. Akwid use musical sampling, then, as a technology of migrant memory, a digital aide-memoire that does not just preserve memory within cultures of migration, displacement, and exile but also reanimates it by putting it into living dialogues with newly generated forms, creating "the memories needed to construct differential local futures in a global world."[35]

NI DE AQUÍ NI DE ALLÁ

The spatial and temporal movements of Akwid's music are typical of those of most of the artists who align themselves with the urban regional banner. In different ways, these artists all perform themselves as moving between spatial sites and, in a temporal move of counter-assimilation, between Mexican pasts in Mexico and Mexican futures in the United States. The first artist to follow Akwid in this genre, the South Central rapper Jae-P, began his 2003 *Ni de aquí ni de allá* album with another "present past," as Pancho Huerta sings what at first sounds like a traditional acoustic Mexican corrido but then becomes a warning to listeners not to pirate what they are about to hear. The song is followed by the album's title track, which details an illegal border crossing into the United States from Mexico and highlights his dual spatial belonging. That Jae-P chooses to rap from the point of view of an undocumented migrant when he himself was actually born in South Central only further highlights the centrality of migrant experience to the formation of identity in Nuevo L.A.

Jae-P dedicates his norteño-tinged hip-hop—"corridos just like rappin'"—to portraying a Mexican American urban experience that vacillates between the 'hood and the campo. On the CD's cover, his own image is superimposed on a collage of a Mexican flag on a hillside and a strip of downtown L.A., and inside there's a shot of him squatting in an underground tunnel that runs from the Tijuana border checkpoint directly to the L.A. City Hall. He boasts that he listens to La Qué Buena and to KPWR (where "they freak the beat") and warns, "No desprecies mi sonido cuz it's born in L.A." Where Akwid concentrates on the regional Mexican music the Gómezes sample, language is the material Jae-P uses to build his one tunnel–two countries identity. He may make it in the United States, but he'll do it with "dos accentos en la lengua." He tells us that while he has learned to speak English (he also used to rap in it), he has no interest in assimilating. "I'm from Califas," he boasts, "pura sangre azteca." When he throws a "West Coast party," he does it "al estilo Mexicano."

Switching between Spanish and English is Jae-P's way of performing his temporal and spatial doubleness. His Spanglish fluency is not a mark of being lost between languages but precisely the opposite, of being a master of both, knowing the right moment when to choose one or the other. Echoing the regional-global loop of Martínez's migrants, Jae-P wants to be able to embrace hip-hip without sacrificing corridos, without assimilating into whitewashed, English-only Americanism, without having to stop being a Mexicano in Los Angeles. "You want me to change my culture," he says, "fuck that."

Other urban regional artists follow similar formulas, combining elements of hip-hop (sampled beats, rapping) with elements of Mexican regional music. David Rolas's *Nuestra vida* starts with Cecilia Brizuela hyping Rolas in a traditional *ranchera grito* style that ends with her breaking into English and issuing a common hip-hop warning: "Don't hate the playah, hate the game." Yolanda Pérez's debut album of otherwise straightforward Mexican regional songs also begins with a nod to hip-hop: a bilingual argument with her father (played by La Que Buena DJ Don Cheto) about her independence carried out over hip-hop beats and done in the style of a rap duet. Cheto raps in a heavily accented Spanish; Pérez switches between Spanish and English: "Y voy a tener novia, and I don't care if you get mad!" Later in the album, Pérez delivers a romantic banda song in English, Barbara Lynn's "You'll Lose a Good Thing," an R&B ballad as done by a Mexican banda.

All of these mergers of regional Mexico and regional Mexican L.A., of hip-hop with bandas and corridos, of two accents on one tongue and two flags in one heart, could have come out of Nuevo L.A. only at the turn of the twenty-first century, a time when both hip-hop and Mexican regional music are the dueling dominant forces in urban L.A. popular culture. In 2002, regional Mexican star Pepe Aguilar became the first artist in any genre to play a series of sold-out concerts at the prestigious Kodak Theater, in Hollywood. The year 2001 saw the debut of Mex 2 the Max, a Mexican regional music video show, on KJLA-LATV, reaching over three million homes throughout Southern California. Concerts by leading regional acts like Los Tigres del Norte and Lupillo Rivera regularly sell out multiple nights, and groups like Oxnard's Los Razos sell twenty thousand copies of an album in one week with virtually no mainstream publicity from their label.

What began in Los Angeles as largely the music of swap meets, homegrown indie labels, and car trunks is now very big business central to the growing corporatization of Mexican media in the United States. The label that Akwid's music was released through, Univision Music, was then part of the Univision empire that included the USA network, Telefutura TV network, Univision Music group, Venevision, Galavision, and the Hispanic Broadcasting Company, the largest Spanish-language radio broadcast company in the United States.

This is all happening, of course while hip-hop remains the dominant commercial force of American popular music and a major soundtrack to life in Los Angeles. From the high school cheerleaders who appear in Akwid's videos and stage shows to their football jerseys, from the live banda ensemble the duo often performs with to their samples and their beats, Akwid gives us a fully integrated merger of hip-hop identities and Mexican regional identities, a new hybrid that does not ask them to choose one world over the other but allows them to flow between both. Where Jae-P declares that he is "ni de aquí, ni de allá," from neither here nor there, Akwid says that they are *de aquí,* it's just that their *aquí* carries *allá* with it. In "No hay manera," there is no *aquí* without *allá,* no corridos without hip-hop, no hip-hop without banda, no L.A. without Michoacán.

The merger of Mexican regional music and L.A. hip-hop in urban regional music does not, of course, emerge from a historical vacuum and in fact speaks directly to two related histories of migrant cultural production in Mexican and African American neighborhoods in Los Angeles. First, as the journalist Sam Quinones has pointed out, with the success of Mexican corrido singer Chalino Sánchez in Los Angeles in the late 1980s, the early '90s saw a sudden rise in young L.A. Mexicanos who, otherwise immersed in the popular styles of urban culture, now wanted to play Mexican regional music. What they once considered the corny and uncool music of their parents was now cool and rebellious, thanks to the underground popularity of Sánchez's raw tales of cross-border narco life. When Sánchez was killed in 1992, his popularity escalated even further. As one L.A. Mexicano noted, "When we were small, we always wanted to fit in, so we'd listen to rap. The other kids were all listening to rap, so I guess we felt that if we listened to Spanish music we'd be beaners or something. But after Chalino died, everybody started listening to corridos. People wanted to feel more Mexican."[36]

So kids who were hip-hop fans now also wanted to play corridos and banda, leading to the rise of the "chalinazo"—young L.A. Mexicans who fused their love for Sánchez's immigrant outlaw stance as a narco badboy with the gangsta poses of N.W.A. into "narcotraficante chic." What Quinones dubs the post-Chalino "Sinaloaization of L.A." led to the rise of gangsta regional/gangsta Mexicano hybridizations by Lupillo and Jenni Rivera, son and daughter of corrido singer and label owner Pedro Rivera—Long Beach twenty-somethings who started putting Stetson hats on the gangsta lean of Ice-T and fusing the iconography and attitudes of "the 'hood" with the iconography and attitudes of a rancho that they had never lived on. But the Riveras never actually made hip-hop records. They stuck to corridos, rancheras, and banda, albeit with Lexuses on their album covers. The shift marked by Akwid and the rest of the regional urbanites is that they actually do both—they bring corridos and banda into the hip-hop form.

IT WOULDN'T BE L.A. WITHOUT MEXICANS

There is a final "congealed history" contained in Akwid's "No hay manera," that of Mexican and African American musical dialogue in L.A. More specifically, Akwid's regionalization of hip-hop is a reminder that South Central and Southeast Los Angeles have long been vital spaces of exchange and coalition between black and Mexican communities. These populations have often engaged in common struggles against legislative power, white supremacy, and urban renewal—even as these very forces conspire to keep them separated, divided, and, more important, at war with each other. The South Central neighborhoods that Akwid's Gómez brothers grew up in, neighborhoods that are now predominantly Latino, were once overwhelmingly African American, and the world they grew up in was based on the styles and sensibilities of African American hip-hop culture.

"It wouldn't be L.A. without Mexicans," Tupac Shakur rapped in 1996, "black love brown pride and the sets again, Pete Wilson tryin to see us all broke, on some bullshit, out for everything they owed." The line is from Shakur's "To Live and Die in L.A.," a song that seems to be simply a rendering of black Los Angeles, specifically South Central Los Angeles, as "the city of angels in constant danger." Tupac's L.A. is a city divided by its neighborhoods, policed by "ghetto bird helicopters," and torn apart by the crack economy's war for drugs that turned into Darryl Gates and Nancy Reagan's war on drugs.

His L.A. may be the home of "niggas gettin three strikes tossed in jail," but it's also Nuevo L.A., Latino L.A., the L.A. of the Greater East Side. South Central L.A. may be cemented in the public imagination as a black community by the media coverage of the 1992 uprisings (as the black home of a black riot), but it is now well over half Latino. Tupac reminds us that African American cultural activism and struggle must be in chorus with Chicano resistance to nativist legislation like Proposition 187, precisely because Pete Wilson is trying to "see them *all* broke." Blacks and Mexicans in South Central L.A. may use some different instruments, may occasionally sing in different languages, but they hear the same song.

Just to prove Tupac right, Delinquent Habits—a hip-hop trio of a *"guero loco,"* a Chicano, and a "Blaxican," best known for their use of Herb Alpert, mariachi, and tango records as samples—returned the favor by recognizing Tupac's acknowledgment of Mexican L.A. They built their song "This Is L.A." on a sampled loop of Tupac's verse. The exchange that these two songs represent—in George Lipsitz's formulation, "the families of resemblance" they speak to—are of course also part of a "bloc of opposition," a pop musical conversation that rehearses and enacts a political coalition built on shared resistance to shared systems of oppression within Los Angeles.[37] "We might fight each other," Tupac sings, "but we'll burn this bitch down if you get us pissed." Part Los Illegals' "El Lay" (in which the LAPD hunts undocumented Mexicans) and part N.W.A.'s "Fuck Tha Police" (in which the LAPD hunts blacks in Compton), Tupac's burning city is still fresh from the uprisings and intimate with the National Guard, a Los Angeles ready to go up in flames, be torn down and built anew, always at war.

This black and Mexican back-and-forth is perhaps best summed up by Ozomatli, a band of multiracial urban fusionists, self-professed anarchists, and red diaper babies, many hailing from across the Greater East Side of Nuevo L.A. In 1998, in the middle of a beat-juiced Mexican ranchera hoedown they call "La misma canción," the same old song, they asked, "What is a DJ if he can't scratch to a ranchera?" When you are a band of Chicanos and Basques and Jews and Creoles and blacks and whites and browns, a band synonymous with post–urban uprising Los Angeles, the answer to that question is simple. The DJ who's been schooled on funk breakbeats or jazz bridges or Roland 808 kick patterns who can scratch to the Watts funk of Charles Wright or the South Central electro of World Class Wreckin Crew but who can't scratch to the accordions and rural romance of a Mexican ranchera is a DJ who will become obsolete. The DJ of Nuevo L.A. is no DJ if a ranchera can't be turned out under a stylus scratch so you can still get your groove on at a *quinceañera*. The same goes for any musician who can't reshape banda around a rhyme or any hip-hop crew who can't cut tubas from Banda El Recodo into a looped beat.

After all, the question they pose isn't even theirs. They're sampling too. It was first asked in the early '80s by pioneering African American rap and electro artist Egyptian Lover. But when he asked it, it was just "What is a DJ if he can't scratch?"—one of L.A. hip-hop's first DJ dares. Ozomatli's addition to it ups the ante on the DJ's skill: it's no longer purely about just technical ability (can you scratch?); it's about creative selection (what can you scratch to?). For Ozomatli, the DJ can't know just hip-hop, can't just scratch over a James Brown "Funky Drummer" break, but must also know what to do with the acoustic guitars, accordions, and simple snare steps of a ranchera or the tubas and snare rolls of a Banda El Recodo cover of Juan Gabriel. The ability of the DJ working in an African American art form to scratch over Mexican music is the ability to be a cultural crossfader, a DJ who can cut between the cultures he or she lives in, a DJ who understands cultural exchange and cultural collision well enough to make music out of it. After all, part of the point of the scratch is to transform (there is even a specific kind of scratch that has been labeled "the transformer scratch"), to take one musical unit, change its shape, blur its message, reduce it to skeletal percussive noise, then allow it to gather itself and re-form and rediscover its code, changed and different, a new sound with new tones.

So when Akwid samples Banda El Recodo covering Juan Gabriel, the duo ups Ozomatli's ante and ask, "What is an MC if he can't rap to banda?" The question is actually a challenge, a challenge to contemporary Los Angeles to listen to itself, to turn on the radio and hear through the static of disharmony and urban unrest, to hear—in beats, in tubas, in rhymes, and in samples—the sound of its communities, the sound of its dialogues, the new sound of Nuevo L.A.

NOTES

1. Mike Davis, *Magical Urbanism: Latinos Reinvent the U.S. City* (London: Verso, 2000), 2.

2. Rodolfo F. Acuña, *Anything but Mexican: Chicanos in Contemporary Los Angeles* (London: Verso, 1996), 3.

3. Brass bands in northwestern Mexico have been performing "banda" music—literally, "band music"—for more than a century. Born and developed in the state of Sinaloa under the influence of military marching bands, banda was initially an instrumental music limited to village brass bands playing trumpets, tubas, trombones, and drums, with no guitars and no vocalists. Over the last century, traditional banda ensembles like *bandas de viento* (wind bands) and *bandas de orquesta* (orchestra bands) gave way in the '90s to the birth of "tecnobanda," a modernized banda style that adds electric guitars, bass, and synthesizer to the traditional mix. The development of banda is chronicled in detail by Helena Simonett in *Banda: Mexican Musical Life across Borders* (Middletown, CT: Wesleyan University Press, 2001).

4. Nicole Taylor, "Top Radio Stations: Ranked by Audience Share, Summer 2002," *Los Angeles Business Journal*, November 25, 2002.

5. Yolanda Pérez, *Dejenme llorar* (Fonovisa); David Rolas, *Nuestra vida* (Fonovisa); Jae-P, *Ni de aquí, ni de allá* (Univision Music Group); Mexiclan, *Mexiclan* (Univision Music Group).

6. Sergio Gómez, "Urban Legends: The Rise of Urban Regional," *Urban Latino Magazine*, November/December 2003.

7. Robert Witkin, *Adorno on Music* (New York: Routledge, 1998).

8. George Sánchez, *Becoming Mexican-American: Ethnicity, Culture and Identity in Chicano Los Angeles, 1900–1945* (New York: Oxford University Press, 1993), 11.

9. Gayatri Chakravorty Spivak, *A Critique of Postcolonial Reason: Toward a History of the Vanishing Present* (Cambridge, MA: Harvard University Press, 1999), 363.

10. Ibid., 360.

11. Svetlana Boym, *The Future of Nostalgia* (New York: Basic Books, 2001), 49–50.

12. I realize that Spivak would no doubt disapprove of my insertion of popular culture into her analysis of agency and nationalism within globalization. She critiques the cultural studies tendency to culturalize transnationalism, arguing, "To recode a change in the determination of capital as a cultural change is a scary symptom of cultural studies, especially feminist cultural studies. Everything is being made 'cultural'" (Spivak, *A Critique of Postcolonial Reason*, 412). My aim here is not to use Akwid to culturalize economic globalization as a means of diluting the political and financial urgencies of labor inequities and social injustices within processes of immigration and diaspora. Yet, I do want to make a case for the enduring importance of understanding culture's role in the forging of new identities and the performance of new communities, especially as modes of translocal articulation and social survival within globalization. Likewise, I think discussions and critiques of globalization must continue to consider culture's relationship to economic structures of displacement and labor migration.

13. Michael Dear and Gustavo LeClerc, "The Postborder Condition: Art and Urbanism in Bajalta California," in *Postborder City: Cultural Spaces of Bajalta California,* ed. Michael Dear and Gustavo LeClerc (New York: Routledge, 2003), 2.

14. Mike Davis, *City of Quartz: Excavating the Future of Los Angeles* (New York: Vintage, 1992); see also Mike Davis, *The Ecology of Fear: Los Angeles and the Imagination of Disaster* (New York: Vintage, 1999).

15. Deepak Narang Sawhney, "Journey beyond the Stars: Los Angeles and Third Worlds," in *Unmasking L.A.: Third World and the City,* ed. Deepak Narang Sawhney (New York: Palgrave, 2002), 2.

16. Roger Keil, "Los Angeles as Metaphor," in *Unmasking L.A.*, 202.

17. Norman M. Klein, *The History of Forgetting: Los Angeles and the Erasure of Memory* (London: Verso, 1997), 10.

18. Iain Chambers, "Citizenship, Language, and Modernity," *PMLA: Mobile Citizens, Media States* 117, no. 1 (January 2002): 29.

19. Ramiro Burr, "New, Traditional Music Enjoying Broad Appeal," *Houston Chronicle,* January 14, 2004.

20. Official press release, *Akwid: Proyecto Akwid,* CD, Unision Music Group, 2003.

21. Simonett, *Banda,* 169.

22. George Lipsitz, "Home Is Where the Hatred Is: Work, Music, and the Transnational Economy," in *Home, Exile, Homeland: Film, Media, and the Politics of Place,* ed. Hamid Naficy (New York: Routledge, 1999), 195.

23. Ibid., 210.

24. Banda El Recodo, "Te lo pido por favor," included on the compilation, *Pa' que te enamores,* ProTel, Universal, 2000; Juan Gabriel, "Te lo pido por favor," *Pensamientos,* RCA, 1986.

25. Simonett, *Banda,* 85.

26. For one look at L.A. as a case study in postindustrialization and the flows of global capital, see Richard P. Appelbaum, "Multiculturalism and Flexibility: Some New Directions in Global Capitalism," in *Mapping Multiculturalism,* ed. Avery F. Gordon and Christopher Newfield (Minneapolis: University of Minnesota, 1996).

27. Victor Viesca, "Straight Out the Barrio: Ozomatli and the Importance of Place in the Formation of Chicano/a Popular Culture in Los Angeles," *Cultural Values* 4, no. 4 (October 2000).

28. Victor Valle and Rodolfo Torres, *Latino Metropolis* (Minneapolis: University of Minnesota Press, 2000); Victor Valle and Rodolfo Torres, "Latinos in a Post-Industrial Order," *Socialist Review* 93, no. 4 (1994): 1–28; and for "Nuevo L.A.," see Simonett, *Banda.*

29. Saskia Sassen, "U.S. Immigration Policy toward Mexico in a Global Economy," in *Between Two Worlds: Mexican Immigrants in the United States,* ed. David G. Gutiérrez (Wilmington, DE: Scholarly Resources, 1996), 214.

30. Davis, *City of Quartz,* 39.

31. Dolores Acevedo and Thomas J. Espenshade, "Implications of the North American Free Trade Agreement for Mexican Migration into the United States," in *Between Two Worlds,* 233.

32. Rubén Martínez, *Crossing Over: A Mexican Family on the Migrant Trail* (New York: Picador, 2002), 25.

33. Roger Rouse, "Mexican Migration and the Social Space of Postmodernism," in *Between Two Worlds,* 257.

34. Martínez, *Crossing Over,* 132.

35. Andreas Huyssen, "Present Pasts: Media, Politics, Amnesia," in *Globalization,* ed. Arjun Appadurai (Durham, NC: Duke University Press, 2001), 74–76.

36. Sam Quinones, *True Tales from Another Mexico: The Lynch Mob, the Popsicle Kings, Chalino, and the Bronx* (Albuquerque: University of New Mexico Press, 2001), 24.

37. George Lipsitz, *Time Passages: Collective Memory and American Popular Culture* (Minneapolis: University of Minnesota Press, 1990), 158.

Contributors

MATT A. BARRETO is Associate Professor of Political Science and Adjunct Professor of Law at the University of Washington. His research examines public opinion and political participation of Latinos in the United States, and he is cofounder of the research and polling firm Latino Decisions.

WENDY CHENG is Assistant Professor of Asian Pacific American Studies and Justice and Social Inquiry, in the School of Social Transformation at Arizona State University. She is coauthor, with Laura Pulido and Laura Barraclough, of *A People's Guide to Los Angeles* and author of *The Changs Next Door to the Diazes: Remapping Race in Suburban California* (2013).

OFELIA ORTIZ CUEVAS is a Visiting Scholar at the Center for Social Theory and Comparative History at University of California, Los Angeles, and a recent UC President's Postdoctoral Fellow. Her work examines the processes through which racial violence in the interest of capital and state building in the United States is normalized, which she explores in her forthcoming book, *Mortifications of the Flesh: Racial Discipline in a Time of Crisis.*

MAX FELKER-KANTOR is a PhD candidate in the Department of History at the University of Southern California. His research focuses on post–World War II urban history and social movements. He is currently working on a dissertation examining social control and community empowerment in Los Angeles between 1965 and 1992.

LORRIE FRASURE-YOKLEY is Assistant Professor of Political Science at the University of California, Los Angeles. Her research interests include racial/ethnic politics, political behavior, and state and local governance. Some of her recent work appears in *Urban Affairs Review* and *National Political Science Review*. She is also Co-Principal Investigator of the Collaborative Multi-Racial Post-Election Survey (CMPS 2008 and 2012), a national, multiracial, multilingual postelection study of racial and political preferences and behavior among registered voters in the United States.

BENJAMIN F. GONZALEZ is a PhD candidate at the University of Washington. His research interests include immigration policy, public opinion, and political psychology. His dissertation examines the criminalization of undocumented immigration in policy and elite rhetoric. Benjamin's favorite animal is the aye-aye.

STACEY GREENE is a PhD candidate in Political Science at the University of California, Los Angeles. Her work focuses on American political behavior, with an emphasis on race/ethnic politics, and political psychology.

GAYE THERESA JOHNSON is Associate Professor of Black Studies at the University of California, Santa Barbara. She is the author of *Spaces of Conflict, Sounds of Solidarity: Music, Race, and Spatial Entitlement in Los Angeles.*

ERIN AUBRY KAPLAN is a journalist and writer and has been an op-ed columnist for the *Los Angeles Times* and a staff writer for the *LA Weekly*. She has contributed to many publications, including *Essence, Ms. Magazine,* and the *Oxford-American. A* collection of her essays and reportage, *Black Talk, Blue Thoughts and Walking the Color Line: Dispatches from a Black Journalista,* was published in 2011.

JOSH KUN is Associate Professor in the Annenberg School for Communication and Journalism at the University of Southern California, where he directs the Popular Music Project of the Norman Lear Center. His most recent book is *Songs in the Key of Los Angeles* (2013), a collaboration with the Library Foundation of Angeles and the Los Angeles Public Library.

PRISCILLA LEIVA is a PhD candidate in the Department of American Studies and Ethnicity at the University of Southern California. Her research examines the relationship between stadiums and civic identity in majority-minority cities during the postwar era.

NERY GABRIEL LEMUS is a contemporary artist who has exhibited nationally and internationally. His most recent solo exhibition, *A Hero Ain't Nothin' but a Sandwich,* was held at the Charlie James Gallery in Chinatown, Los Angeles. He is currently a recipient of a Rema Hort Mann Foundation award and a COLA award.

DANIEL MARTINEZ HOSANG is Associate Professor of Political Science and Ethnic Studies at the University of Oregon. He is the author of *Racial Propositions: Ballot Initiatives and the Making of Postwar California* (UC Press, 2010) and coeditor (with Laura Pulido and Oneka LaBennett) of *Racial Formation in the Twenty-First Century* (UC Press, 2012).

MANUEL PASTOR is Professor of Sociology and American Studies and Ethnicity at the University of Southern California, where he also directs the Program for Environmental and Regional Equity and codirects the Center for the Study of Immigrant Integration. His most recent books are *Just Growth: Inclusion and Prosperity in America's Metropolitan Regions* (with Chris Benner) (2012) and *Uncommon Common Ground: Race and America's Future* (with Angela Glover Blackwell and Stewart Kwoh) (2010).

LAURA PULIDO is Professor of American Studies and Ethnicity at the University of Southern California, where she teaches courses on race, political activism, and Los Angeles. Her recent books include *A People's Guide to Los Angeles.* (with Laura Barraclough and Wendy Cheng) and *Black, Brown, Yellow, and Left: Radical Activism in Los Angeles.*

SAM QUINONES is a journalist and author of two books of narrative nonfiction stories about Mexico and Mexican immigration. He currently works at the *Los Angeles Times.* Contact him at www.samquinones.com.

ABIGAIL ROSAS is a postdoctoral fellow at the Center for the Study of Women, Gender, and Sexuality at Rice University. She received her PhD from the Department of American Studies and Ethnicity at the University of Southern California and her BA in Comparative Studies in Race and Ethnicity and Sociology from Stanford University. She is working on a book manuscript that examines the generative relational community formation of Latina/o and African American residents in South Central Los Angeles in the post–World War II period.

GABRIEL R. SÁNCHEZ is Associate Professor of Political Science at the University of New Mexico. His fields of interest are racial and ethnic politics with a focus on Latino political behavior. His articles have been published in *Political Research Quarterly, Social Science Quarterly, Urban Affairs Review, PS: Political Science and Politics,* and *American Politics Research,* among other peer-reviewed journals.

DENISE M. SANDOVAL, PhD, is Professor of Chicana and Chicano Studies at California State University, Northridge. She teaches classes on Chicana/o History and Culture, as well as Multicultural U.S. History; and her research interests include community histories and popular culture/the arts. She has curated two museum exhibitions on lowrider culture at the Petersen Automotive Museum in Los Angeles and has written numerous essays on lowrider culture.

Index